A General Introduction to Psychoanalysis

SCHWIND, *The Dream of the Prisoner*

See page 109 for analysis

A General Introduction to Psychoanalysis

BY

PROF. SIGMUND FREUD, LL.D.

Authorized Translation
With a Preface

BY

G. STANLEY HALL
President, Clark University

HORACE LIVERIGHT
PUBLISHER   NEW YORK

Published, 1920, by
HORACE LIVERIGHT, INC.

PREFACE

Few, especially in this country, realize that while Freudian themes have rarely found a place on the programs of the American Psychological Association, they have attracted great and growing attention and found frequent elaboration by students of literature, history, biography, sociology, morals and aesthetics, anthropology, education, and religion. They have given the world a new conception of both infancy and adolescence, and shed much new light upon characterology; given us a new and clearer view of sleep, dreams, reveries, and revealed hitherto unknown mental mechanisms common to normal and pathological states and processes, showing that the law of causation extends to the most incoherent acts and even verbigerations in insanity; gone far to clear up the *terra incognita* of hysteria; taught us to recognize morbid symptoms, often neurotic and psychotic in their germ; revealed the operations of the primitive mind so overlaid and repressed that we had almost lost sight of them; fashioned and used the key of symbolism to unlock many mysticisms of the past; and in addition to all this, affected thousands of cures, established a new prophylaxis, and suggested new tests for character, disposition, and ability, in all combining the practical and theoretic to a degree salutary as it is rare.

These twenty-eight lectures to laymen are elementary and almost conversational. Freud sets forth with a frankness almost startling the difficulties and limitations of psychoanalysis, and also describes its main methods and results as only a master and originator of a new school of thought can do. These discourses are at the same time simple and almost confidential, and they trace and sum up the results of thirty years of devoted and painstaking research. While they are not at all controversial, we incidentally see in a clearer light the distinctions between the master and some of his distinguished pupils. A text like this is the most opportune and will naturally more or less supersede all other introductions to the general subject of psychoanalysis. It presents the author in a new light, as an effective and successful

v

popularizer, and is certain to be welcomed not only by the large and growing number of students of psychoanalysis in this country but by the yet larger number of those who wish to begin its study here and elsewhere.

The impartial student of Sigmund Freud need not agree with all his conclusions, and indeed, like the present writer, may be unable to make sex so all-dominating a factor in the psychic life of the past and present as Freud deems it to be, to recognize the fact that he is the most original and creative mind in psychology of our generation. Despite the frightful handicap of the *odium sexicum*, far more formidable today than the *odium theologicum*, involving as it has done for him lack of academic recognition and even more or less social ostracism, his views have attracted and inspired a brilliant group of minds not only in psychiatry but in many other fields, who have altogether given the world of culture more new and pregnant *appercus* than those which have come from any other source within the wide domain of humanism.

A former student and disciple of Wundt, who recognizes to the full his inestimable services to our science, cannot avoid making certain comparisons. Wundt has had for decades the prestige of a most advantageous academic chair. He founded the first laboratory for experimental psychology, which attracted many of the most gifted and mature students from all lands. By his development of the doctrine of apperception he took psychology forever beyond the old associationism which had ceased to be fruitful. He also established the independence of psychology from physiology, and by his encyclopedic and always thronged lectures, to say nothing of his more or less esoteric seminary, he materially advanced every branch of mental science and extended its influence over the whole wide domain of folklore, mores, language, and primitive religion. His best texts will long constitute a thesaurus which every psychologist must know.

Again, like Freud, he inspired students who went beyond him (the Wurzburgers and introspectionists) whose method and results he could not follow. His limitations have grown more and more manifest. He has little use for the unconscious or the abnormal, and for the most part he has lived and wrought in a preevolutionary age and always and everywhere underestimated the genetic standpoint. He never transcends the conventional 'imits in dealing, as he so rarely does, with sex. Nor does he contribute much likely to be of permanent value in any part of the wide domain of affectivity. We cannot forbear to express the hope that Freud will not repeat Wundt's error in making too abrupt a break with his more advanced pupils like Adler or the Zurich group. It is rather precisely just the topics that Wundt neglects that Freud makes his chief corner-stones, viz., the unconscious, the abnormal, sex, and affectivity generally, with many genetic, especially ontogenetic, but also phylogenetic factors. The Wundtian influence has been great in the past, while Freud has a great present and a yet greater future.

In one thing Freud agrees with the introspectionists, viz., in deliberately neglecting the "physiological factor" and building on purely psychological foundations, although for Freud psychology is mainly unconscious, while for the introspectionists it is pure consciousness. Neither he nor his disciples have yet recognized the aid proffered them by students of the autonomic system or by the distinctions between the epicritic and protopathic functions and organs of the cerebrum, although these will doubtless come to have their due place as we know more of the nature and processes of the unconscious mind.

If psychologists of the normal have hitherto been too little disposed to recognize the precious contributions to psychology made by the cruel experiments of Nature in mental diseases, we think that the psychoanalysts, who work predominantly in this field, have been somewhat too ready to apply their findings to the operations of the normal mind; but we are optomistic enough to believe that in the end both these errors will vanish and that in the great synthesis of the future that now seems to impend our science will be made vastly richer and deeper on the theoretical side and also far more practical than it has ever been before.

G. STANLEY HALL.

Clark University,
April, 1920.

CONTENTS

PART ONE

The Psychology of Errors

                                                                              PAGE
PREFACE G. Stanley Hall   v

LECTURE

    I. INTRODUCTION   1
   II. THE PSYCHOLOGY OF ERRORS 10
  III. THE PSYCHOLOGY OF ERRORS —(Continued) 23
  IV. THE PSYCHOLOGY OF ERRORS —(Conclusion) 41

PART TWO

The Dream

   V. DIFFICULTIES AND PRELIMINARY APPROACH 63
  VI. HYPOTHESIS AND TECHNIQUE OF INTERPRETATION 78
 VII. MANIFEST DREAM CONTENT AND LATENT DREAM THOUGHT 90
VIII. DREAMS OF CHILDHOOD 101
  IX. THE DREAM CENSOR 110
   X. SYMBOLISM IN THE DREAM 122
  XI. THE DREAM-WORK 141
 XII. ANALYSES OF SAMPLE DREAMS 153
XIII. ARCHAIC REMNANTS AND INFANTILISM IN THE DREAM . . 167
 XIV. WISH FULFILLMENT 180
  XV. DOUBTFUL POINTS AND CRITICISM 194

PART THREE

General Theory of the Neuroses

 XVI. PSYCHOANALYSIS AND PSYCHIATRY 209
XVII. THE MEANING OF THE SYMPTOMS 221
XVIII. TRAUMATIC FIXATION—THE UNCONSCIOUS 236
 XIX. RESISTANCE AND SUPRESSION 248
  XX. THE SEXUAL LIFE OF MAN 262
 XXI. DEVELOPMENT OF THE LIBIDO AND SEXUAL ORGANIZATIONS 277
XXII. THEORIES OF DEVELOPMENT AND REGRESSION—ETIOLOGY . 294
XXIII. THE DEVELOPMENT OF THE SYMPTOMS 311

x   Contents.

LECTURE   PAGE
   XXIV. ORDINARY NERVOUSNESS 328
    XXV. FEAR AND ANXIETY 340
   XXVI. THE LIBIDO THEORY AND NARCISM 356
  XXVII. TRANSFERENCE 372
 XXVIII. ANALYTICAL THERAPY 388
INDEX 403

PART I
THE PSYCHOLOGY OF ERRORS

FIRST LECTURE

INTRODUCTION

I DO not know how familiar some of you may be, either from your reading or from hearsay, with psychoanalysis. But, in keeping with the title of these lectures — *A General Introduction to Psychoanalysis* — I am obliged to proceed as though you knew nothing about this subject, and stood in need of preliminary instruction.

To be sure, this much I may presume that you do know, namely, that psychoanalysis is a method of treating nervous patients medically. And just at this point I can give you an example to illustrate how the procedure in this field is precisely the reverse of that which is the rule in medicine. Usually when we introduce a patient to a medical technique which is strange to him, we minimize its difficulties and give him confident promises concerning the result of the treatment. When, however, we undertake psychoanalytic treatment with a neurotic patient we proceed differently. We hold before him the difficulties of the method, its length, the exertions and the sacrifices which it will cost him; and, as to the result, we tell him that we make no definite promises, that the result depends on his conduct, on his understanding, on his adaptability, on his perseverance. We have, of course, excellent motives for conduct which seems so perverse, and into which you will perhaps gain insight at a later point in these lectures.

Do not be offended, therefore, if, for the present, I treat you as I treat these neurotic patients. Frankly, I shall dissuade you from coming to hear me a second time. With this intention I shall show what imperfections are necessarily involved in the teaching of psychoanalysis and what difficulties stand in the way of gaining a personal judgment. I shall show you how the whole trend of your previous training and all your accustomed mental habits must unavoidably have made you opponents of psychoanalysis, and how much you must overcome :

1

selves in order to master this instinctive opposition. Of course I cannot predict how much psychoanalytic understanding you will gain from my lectures, but I can promise this, that by listening to them you will not learn how to undertake a psychoanalytic treatment or how to carry one to completion. Furthermore, should I find anyone among you who does not feel satisfied with a cursory acquaintance with psychoanalysis, but who would like to enter into a more enduring relationship with it, I shall not only dissuade him, but I shall actually warn him against it. As things now stand, a person would, by such a choice of profession, ruin his every chance of success at a university, and if he goes out into the world as a practicing physician, he will find himself in a society which does not understand his aims, which regards him with suspicion and hostility, and which turns loose upon him all the malicious spirits which lurk within it.

However, there are always enough individuals who are interested in anything which may be added to the sum total of knowledge, despite such inconveniences. Should there be any of this type among you, and should they ignore my dissuasion and return to the next of these lectures, they will be welcome. But all of you have the right to know what these difficulties of psychoanalysis are to which I have alluded.

First of all, we encounter the difficulties inherent in the teaching and exposition of psychoanalysis. In your medical instruction you have been accustomed to visual demonstration. You see the anatomical specimen, the precipitate in the chemical reaction, the contraction of the muscle as the result of the stimulation of its nerves. Later the patient is presented to your senses; the symptoms of his malady, the products of the pathological processes, in many cases even the cause of the disease is shown in isolated state. In the surgical department you are made to witness the steps by which one brings relief to the patient, and are permitted to attempt to practice them. Even in psychiatry, the demonstration affords you, by the patient's changed facial play, his manner of speech and his behavior, a wealth of observations which leave far-reaching impressions. Thus the medical teacher preponderantly plays the role of a guide and instructor who accompanies you through a museum in which you contract an immediate relationship to the exhibits, and in which you believe yourself to have been convinced through your own observation of the existence of the new things you see.

Unfortunately, everything is different in psychoanalysis. In psychoanalysis nothing occurs but the interchange of words between the patient and the physician. The patient talks, tells of his past experiences and present impressions, complains, confesses his wishes and emotions. The physician listens, tries to direct the thought processes of the patient, reminds him of things, forces his attention into certain channels, gives him explanations and observes the reactions of understanding or denial which he calls forth in the patient. The uneducated relatives of our patients—persons who are impressed only by the visible and tangible, preferably by such procedure as one sees in the moving picture theatres—never miss an opportunity of voicing their scepticism as to how one can "do anything for the malady through mere talk." Such thinking, of course, is as short-sighted as it is inconsistent. For these are the very persons who know with such certainty that the patients "merely imagine" their symptoms. Words were originally magic, and the word retains much of its old magical power even to-day. With words one man can make another blessed, or drive him to despair; by words the teacher transfers his knowledge to the pupil; by words the speaker sweeps his audience with him and determines its judgments and decisions. Words call forth effects and are the universal means of influencing human beings. Therefore let us not underestimate the use of words in psychotherapy, and let us be satisfied if we may be auditors of the words which are exchanged between the analyst and his patient.

But even that is impossible. The conversation of which the psychoanalytic treatment consists brooks no auditor, it cannot be demonstrated. One can, of course, present a neurasthenic or hysteric to the students in a psychiatric lecture. He tells of his complaints and symptoms, but of nothing else. The communications which are necessary for the analysis are made only under the conditions of a special affective relationship to the physician; the patient would become dumb as soon as he became aware of a single impartial witness. For these communications concern the most intimate part of his psychic life, everything which as a socially independent person he must conceal from others; these communications deal with everything which, as a harmonious personality, he will not admit even to himself.

You cannot, therefore, "listen in" on a psychoanalytic treatment. You can only hear of it. You will get to know psychoanalysis, in the strictest sense of the word, only by hearsay.
Such instruction even at second hand, will place you in quite
an unusual position for forming a judgment. For it is obvious
that everything depends on the faith you are able to put in the
instructor.

Imagine that you are not attending a psychiatric, but an
historical lecture, and that the lecturer is telling you about the
life and martial deeds of Alexander the Great. What would
be your reasons for believing in the authenticity of his statements? At first sight, the condition of affairs seems even more
unfavorable than in the case of psychoanalysis, for the history
professor was as little a participant in Alexander's campaigns
as you were; the psychoanalyst at least tells you of things in
connection with which he himself has played some role. But
then the question turns on this—what set of facts can the historian marshal in support of his position? He can refer you
to the accounts of ancient authors, who were either contemporaries themselves, or who were at least closer to the events in
question; that is, he will refer you to the books of Diodor,
Plutarch, Arrian, etc. He can place before you pictures of the
preserved coins and statues of the king and can pass down your
rows a photograph of the Pompeiian mosaics of the battle of
Issos. Yet, strictly speaking, all these documents prove only
that previous generations already believed in Alexander's existence and in the reality of his deeds, and your criticism might
begin anew at this point. You will then find that not everything
recounted of Alexander is credible, or capable of proof in
detail; yet even then I cannot believe that you will leave the
lecture hall a disbeliever in the reality of Alexander the Great.
Your decision will be determined chiefly by two considerations;
firstly, that the lecturer has no conceivable motive for presenting as truth something which he does not himself believe to be
true, and secondly, that all available histories present the events
in approximately the same manner. If you then proceed to the
verification of the older sources, you will consider the same data,
the possible motives of the writers and the consistency of the
various parts of the evidence. The result of the examination
will surely be convincing in the case of Alexander. It will

probably turn out differently when applied to individuals like Moses and Nimrod. But what doubts you might raise against the credibility of the psychoanalytic reporter you will see plainly enough upon a later occasion.

At this point you have a right to raise the question, "If there is no such thing as objective verification of psychoanalysis, and no possibility of demonstrating it, how can one possibly learn psychoanalysis and convince himself of the truth of its claims?" The fact is, the study is not easy and there are not many persons who have learned psychoanalysis thoroughly; but nevertheless, there is a feasible way. Psychoanalysis is learned, first of all, from a study of one's self, through the study of one's own personality. This is not quite what is ordinarily called self-observation, but, at a pinch, one can sum it up thus. There is a whole series of very common and universally known psychic phenomena, which, after some instruction in the technique of psychoanalysis, one can make the subject matter of analysis in one's self. By so doing one obtains the desired conviction of the reality of the occurrences which psychoanalysis describes and of the correctness of its fundamental conception. To be sure, there are definite limits imposed on progress by this method. One gets much further if one allows himself to be analyzed by a competent analyst, observes the effect of the analysis on his own ego, and at the same time makes use of the opportunity to become familiar with the finer details of the technique of procedure. This excellent method is, of course, only practicable for one person, never for an entire class.

There is a second difficulty in your relation to psychoanalysis for which I cannot hold the science itself responsible, but for which I must ask you to take the responsibility upon yourselves, ladies and gentlemen, at least in so far as you have hitherto pursued medical studies. Your previous training has given your mental activity a definite bent which leads you far away from psychoanalysis. You have been trained to reduce the functions of an organism and its disorders anatomically, to explain them in terms of chemistry and physics and to conceive them biologically, but no portion of your interest has been directed to the psychic life, in which, after all, the activity of this wonderfully complex organism culminates. For this reason psychological thinking has remained strange to you and you have accustomed yourselves to regard it with suspicion, to deny it the character of the scientific, to leave it to the laymen, poets, natural philosophers and mystics. Such a delimitation is surely harmful to your medical activity, for the patient will, as is usual in all human relationships, confront you first of all with his psychic facade; and I am afraid your penalty will be this, that you will be forced to relinquish a portion of the therapeutic influence to which you aspire, to those lay physicians, nature-cure fakers and mystics whom you despise.

I am not overlooking the excuse, whose existence one must admit, for this deficiency in your previous training. There is no philosophical science of therapy which could be made practicable for your medical purpose. Neither speculative philosophy nor descriptive psychology nor that so-called experimental psychology which allies itself with the physiology of the sense organs as it is taught in the schools, is in a position to teach you anything useful concerning the relation between the physical and the psychical or to put into your hand the key to the understanding of a possible disorder of the psychic functions. Within the field of medicine, psychiatry does, it is true, occupy itself with the description of the observed psychic disorders and with their grouping into clinical symptom-pictures; but in their better hours the psychiatrists themselves doubt whether their purely descriptive account deserves the name of a science. The symptoms which constitute these clinical pictures are known neither in their origin, in their mechanism, nor in their mutual relationship. There are either no discoverable corresponding changes of the anatomical organ of the soul, or else the changes are of such a nature as to yield no enlightenment. Such psychic disturbances are open to therapeutic influence only when they can be identified as secondary phenomena of an otherwise organic affection.

Here is the gap which psychoanalysis aims to fill. It prepares to give psychiatry the omitted psychological foundation, it hopes to reveal the common basis from which, as a starting point, constant correlation of bodily and psychic disturbances becomes comprehensible. To this end, it must divorce itself from every anatomical, chemical or physiological supposition which is alien to it. It must work throughout with purely psychological therapeutic concepts, and just for that reason I fear that it will at first seem strange to you.

I will not make you, your previous training, or your mental bias share the guilt of the next difficulty. With two of its assertions, psychoanalysis offends the whole world and draws aversion upon itself. One of these assertions offends an intellectual prejudice, the other an aesthetic-moral one. Let us not think too lightly of these prejudices; they are powerful things, remnants of useful, even necessary, developments of mankind. They are retained through powerful affects, and the battle against them is a hard one.

The first of these displeasing assertions of psychoanalysis is this, that the psychic processes are in themselves unconscious, and that those which are conscious are merely isolated acts and parts of the total psychic life. Recollect that we are, on the contrary, accustomed to identify the psychic with the conscious. Consciousness actually means for us the distinguishing characteristic of the psychic life, and psychology is the science of the content of consciousness. Indeed, so obvious does this identification seem to us that we consider its slightest contradiction obvious nonsense, and yet psychoanalysis cannot avoid raising this contradiction; it cannot accept the identity of the conscious with the psychic. Its definition of the psychic affirms that they are processes of the nature of feeling, thinking, willing; and it must assert that there is such a thing as unconscious thinking and unconscious willing. But with this assertion psychoanalysis has alienated, to start with, the sympathy of all friends of sober science, and has laid itself open to the suspicion of being a fantastic mystery study which would build in darkness and fish in murky waters. You, however, ladies and gentlemen, naturally cannot as yet understand what justification I have for stigmatizing as a prejudice so abstract a phrase as this one, that "the psychic is consciousness." You cannot know what evaluation can have led to the denial of the unconscious, if such a thing really exists, and what advantage may have resulted from this denial. It sounds like a mere argument over words whether one shall say that the psychic coincides with the conscious or whether one shall extend it beyond that, and yet I can assure you that by the acceptance of unconscious processes you have paved the way for a decisively new orientation in the world and in scie- -

Just as little can you guess how intimate a connection this initial boldness of psychoanalysis has with the one which follows. The next assertion which psychoanalysis proclaims as one of its discoveries, affirms that those instinctive impulses which one can only call sexual in the narrower as well as in the wider sense, play an uncommonly large role in the causation of nervous and mental diseases, and that those impulses are a causation which has never been adequately appreciated. Nay, indeed, psychoanalysis claims that these same sexual impulses have made contributions whose value cannot be overestimated to the highest cultural, artistic and social achievements of the human mind.

According to my experience, the aversion to this conclusion of psychoanalysis is the most significant source of the opposition which it encounters. Would you like to know how we explain this fact? We believe that civilization was forged by the driving force of vital necessity, at the cost of instinct-satisfaction, and that the process is to a large extent constantly repeated anew, since each individual who newly enters the human community repeats the sacrifices of his instinct-satisfaction for the sake of the common good. Among the instinctive forces thus utilized, the sexual impulses play a significant role. They are thereby sublimated, i.e., they are diverted from their sexual goals and directed to ends socially higher and no longer sexual. But this result is unstable. The sexual instincts are poorly tamed. Each individual who wishes to ally himself with the achievements of civilization is exposed to the danger of having his sexual instincts rebel against this sublimation. Society can conceive of no more serious menace to its civilization than would arise through the satisfying of the sexual instincts by their redirection toward their original goals. Society, therefore, does not relish being reminded of this ticklish spot in its origin; it has no interest in having the strength of the sexual instincts recognized and the meaning of the sexual life to the individual clearly delineated. On the contrary, society has taken the course of diverting attention from this whole field. This is the reason why society will not tolerate the above-mentioned results of psychoanalytic research, and would prefer to brand it as aesthetically offensive and morally objectionable or dangerous. Since, however, one cannot attack an ostensibly objective result of scientific inquiry with such objections, the criticism must be translated to an intellectual level if it is to be voiced. But it is a predisposition of human nature to consider an unpleasant idea untrue, and then it is easy to find arguments against it. Society thus brands what is unpleasant as untrue, denying the conclusions of psychoanalysis with logical and pertinent arguments. These arguments originate from affective sources, however, and society holds to these prejudices against all attempts at refutation.

However, we may claim, ladies and gentlemen, that we have followed no bias of any sort in making any of these contested statements. We merely wished to state facts which we believe to have been discovered by toilsome labor. And we now claim the right unconditionally to reject the interference in scientific research of any such practical considerations, even before we have investigated whether the apprehension which these considerations are meant to instil are justified or not.

These, therefore, are but a few of the difficulties which stand in the way of your occupation with psychoanalysis. They are perhaps more than enough for a beginning. If you can overcome their deterrent impression, we shall continue.

SECOND LECTURE

WE begin with an investigation, not with hypotheses. To this end we choose certain phenomena which are very frequent, very familiar and very little heeded, and which have nothing to do with the pathological, inasmuch as they can be observed in every normal person. I refer to the errors which an individual commits—as for example, errors of speech in which he wishes to say something and uses the wrong word; or those which happen to him in writing, and which he may or may not notice; or the case of misreading, in which one reads in the print or writing something different from what is actually there. A similar phenomenon occurs in those cases of mishearing what is said to one, where there is no question of an organic disturbance of the auditory function. Another series of such occurrences is based on forgetfulness—but on a forgetfulness which is not permanent, but temporary, as for instance when one cannot think of a name which one knows and always recognizes; or when one forgets to carry out a project at the proper time but which one remembers again later, and therefore has only forgotten for a certain interval. In a third class this characteristic of transience is lacking, as for example in mislaying things so that they cannot be found again, or in the analogous case of losing things. Here we are dealing with a kind of forgetfulness to which one reacts differently from the other cases, a forgetfulness at which one is surprised and annoyed, instead of considering it comprehensible. Allied with these phenomena is that of erroneous ideas—in which the element of transience is again prominent, inasmuch as for a while one believes something which, before and after that time, one knows to be untrue—and a number of similar phenomena of different designations.

These are all occurrences whose inner connection is expressed

in the use of the same prefix of designation.[1] They are almost
all unimportant, generally temporary and without much significance in the life of the individual. It is only rarely that one of
them, such as the phenomenon of losing things, attains to a certain practical importance. For that reason also they do not
attract much attention, they arouse only weak affects.

It is, therefore, to these phenomena that I would now direct
your attention. But you will object, with annoyance: "There
are so many sublime riddles in the external world, just as there
are in the narrower world of the psychic life, and so many
wonders in the field of psychic disturbances which demand and
deserve elucidation, that it really seems frivolous to waste labor
and interest on such trifles. If you can explain to us how an
individual with sound eyes and ears can, in broad daylight, see
and hear things that do not exist, or why another individual
suddenly believes himself persecuted by those whom up to that
time he loved best, or defend, with the most ingenious arguments,
delusions which must seem nonsense to any child, then we will
be willing to consider psychoanalysis seriously. But if psychoanalysis can do nothing better than to occupy us with the question of why a speaker used the wrong word, or why a housekeeper
mislaid her keys, or such trifles, then we know something better
to do with our time and interest."

My reply is: "Patience, ladies and gentlemen. I think your
criticism is not on the right track. It is true that psychoanalysis
cannot boast that it has never occupied itself with trifles. On
the contrary, the objects of its observations are generally those
simple occurrences which the other sciences have thrown aside
as much too insignificant, the waste products of the phenomenal
world. But are you not confounding, in your criticism, the
sublimity of the problems with the conspicuousness of their
manifestations? Are there not very important things which
under certain circumstances, and at certain times, can betray
themselves only by very faint signs? I could easily cite a great
many instances of this kind. From what vague signs, for instance, do the young gentlemen of this audience conclude that
they have won the favor of a lady? Do you await an explicit
declaration, an ardent embrace, or does not a glance, scarcely
perceptible to others, a fleeting gesture, the prolonging of a

[1] "Fehl-leistungen."

hand-shake by one second, suffice? And if you are a criminal lawyer, and engaged in the investigation of a murder, do you actually expect the murderer to leave his photograph and address on the scene of the crime, or would you, of necessity, content yourself with fainter and less certain traces of that individual? Therefore, let us not undervalue small signs; perhaps by means of them we will succeed in getting on the track of greater things. I agree with you that the larger problems of the world and of science have the first claim on our interest. But it is generally of little avail to form the definite resolution to devote oneself to the investigation of this or that problem. Often one does not know in which direction to take the next step. In scientific research it is more fruitful to attempt what happens to be before one at the moment and for whose investigation there is a discoverable method. If one does that thoroughly without prejudice or predisposition, one may, with good fortune, and by virtue of the connection which links each thing to every other (hence also the small to the great) discover even from such modest research a point of approach to the study of the big problems."

Thus would I answer, in order to secure your attention for the consideration of these apparently insignificant errors made by normal people. At this point, we will question a stranger to psychoanalysis and ask him how he explains these occurrences.

His first answer is sure to be, "Oh, they are not worth an explanation; they are merely slight accidents." What does he mean by this? Does he mean to assert that there are any occurrences so insignificant that they fall out of the causal sequence of things, or that they might just as well be something different from what they are? If any one thus denies the determination of natural phenomena at one such point, he has vitiated the entire scientific viewpoint. One can then point out to him how much more consistent is the religious point of view, when it explicitly asserts that "No sparrow falls from the roof without God's special wish." I imagine our friend will not be willing to follow his first answer to its logical conclusion; he will interrupt and say that if he were to study these things he would probably find an explanation for them. He will say that this is a case of slight functional disturbance, of an inaccurate psychic act whose causal factors can be outlined. A man who otherwise speaks correctly may make a slip of the tongue—

when he is slightly ill or fatigued; when he is excited; when his attention is concentrated on something else. It is easy to prove these statements. Slips of the tongue do really occur with special frequency when one is tired, when one has a headache or when one is indisposed. Forgetting proper names is a very frequent occurrence under these circumstances. Many persons even recognize the imminence of an indisposition by the inability to recall proper names. Often also one mixes up words or objects during excitement, one picks up the wrong things; and the forgetting of projects, as well as the doing of any number of other unintentional acts, becomes conspicuous when one is distracted; in other words, when one's attention is concentrated on other things. A familiar instance of such distraction is the professor in *Fliegende Blätter*, who takes the wrong hat because he is thinking of the problems which he wishes to treat in his next book. Each of us knows from experience some examples of how one can forget projects which one has planned and promises which one has made, because an experience has intervened which has preoccupied one deeply.

This seems both comprehensible and irrefutable. It is perhaps not very interesting, not as we expected it to be. But let us consider this explanation of errors. The conditions which have been cited as necessary for the occurrence of these phenomena are not all identical. Illness and disorders of circulation afford a physiological basis. Excitement, fatigue and distraction are conditions of a different sort, which one could designate as psycho-physiological. About these latter it is easy to theorize. Fatigue, as well as distraction, and perhaps also general excitement, cause a scattering of the attention which can result in the act in progress not receiving sufficient attention. This act can then be more easily interrupted than usual, and may be inexactly carried out. A slight illness, or a change in the distribution of blood in the central organ of the nervous system, can have the same effect, inasmuch as it influences the determining factor, the distribution of attention, in a similar way. In all cases, therefore, it is a question of the effects of a distraction of the attention, caused either by organic or psychic factors.

But this does not seem to yield much of interest for our psychoanalytic investigation. We might even feel tempted to give up the subject. To be sure, when we look more closely we find that not everything squares with this attention theory of psychological errors, or that at any rate not everything can be directly deduced from it. We find that such errors and such forgetting occur even when people are not fatigued, distracted or excited, but are in every way in their normal state; unless, in consequence of these errors, one were to attribute to them an excitement which they themselves do not acknowledge. Nor is the mechanism so simple that the success of an act is assured by an intensification of the attention bestowed upon it, and endangered by its diminution. There are many acts which one performs in a purely automatic way and with very little attention, but which are yet carried out quite successfully. The pedestrian who scarcely knows where he is going, nevertheless keeps to the right road and stops at his destination without having gone astray. At least, this is the rule. The practiced pianist touches the right keys without thinking of them. He may, of course, also make an occasional mistake, but if automatic playing increased the likelihood of errors, it would be just the virtuoso whose playing has, through practice, become most automatic, who would be the most exposed to this danger. Yet we see, on the contrary, that many acts are most successfully carried out when they are not the objects of particularly concentrated attention, and that the mistakes occur just at the point where one is most anxious to be accurate—where a distraction of the necessary attention is therefore surely least permissible. One could then say that this is the effect of the "excitement," but we do not understand why the excitement does not intensify the concentration of attention on the goal that is so much desired. If in an important speech or discussion anyone says the opposite of what he means, then that can hardly be explained according to the psycho-physiological or the attention theories.

There are also many other small phenomena accompanying these errors, which are not understood and which have not been rendered comprehensible to us by these explanations. For instance, when one has temporarily forgotten a name, one is annoyed, one is determined to recall it and is unable to give up the attempt. Why is it that despite his annoyance the individual cannot succeed, as he wishes, in directing his attention to the word which is "on the tip of his tongue," and which he instantly recognizes when it is pronounced to him? Or, to take another example, there are cases in which the errors multiply, link themselves together, substitute for each other. The first time one forgets an appointment; the next time, after having made a special resolution not to forget it, one discovers that one has made a mistake in the day or hour. Or one tries by devious means to remember a forgotten word, and in the course of so doing loses track of a second name which would have been of use in finding the first. If one then pursues this second name, a third gets lost, and so on. It is notorious that the same thing can happen in the case of misprints, which are of ocurse to be considered as errors of the typesetter. A stubborn error of this sort is said to have crept into a Social-Democratic paper, where, in the account of a certain festivity was printed, "Among those present was His Highness, the Clown Prince." The next day a correction was attempted. The paper apologized and said, "The sentence should, of course, have read 'The Clown Prince.'" One likes to attribute these occurrences to the printer's devil, to the goblin of the typesetting machine, and the like — figurative expressions which at least go beyond a psycho-physiological theory of the misprint.

I do not know if you are acquainted with the fact that one can provoke slips of the tongue, can call them forth by suggestion, as it were. An anecdote will serve to illustrate this. Once when a novice on the stage was entrusted with the important role in *The Maid of Orleans* of announcing to the King, "Connétable sheathes his sword," the star played the joke of repeating to the frightened beginner during the rehearsal, instead of the text, the following, "Comfortable sends back his steed,"[2] and he attained his end. In the performance the unfortunate actor actually made his début with this distorted announcement; even after he had been amply warned against so doing, or perhaps just for that reason.

These little characteristics of errors are not exactly illuminated by the theory of diverted attention. But that does not necessarily prove the whole theory wrong. There is perhaps something missing, a complement by the addition of which the theory

[2] In the German, the correct announcement is, "Connetable schickt sein Schwert zurück." The novice, as a result of the suggestion, announced instead that "Komfortabel schickt sein Pferd zurück."

would be made completely satisfactory. But many of the errors themselves can be regarded from another aspect.

Let us select slips of the tongue, as best suited to our purposes. We might equally well choose slips of the pen or of reading. But at this point, we must make clear to ourselves the fact that so far we have inquired only as to when and under what conditions one's tongue slips, and have received an answer on this point only. One can, however, direct one's interest elsewhere and ask why one makes just this particular slip and no other; one can consider what the slip results in. You must realize that as long as one does not answer this question—does not explain the effect produced by the slip—the phenomenon in its psychological aspect remains an accident, even if its physiological explanation has been found. When it happens that I commit a slip of the tongue, I could obviously make any one of an infinite number of slips, and in place of the one right word say any one of a thousand others, make innumerable distortions of the right word. Now, is there anything which forces upon me in a specific instance just this one special slip out of all those which are possible, or does that remain accidental and arbitrary, and can nothing rational be found in answer to this question?

Two authors, Meringer and Mayer (a philologist and a psychiatrist) did indeed in 1895 make the attempt to approach the problem of slips of the tongue from this side. They collected examples and first treated them from a purely descriptive standpoint. That, of course, does not yet furnish any explanation, but may open the way to one. They differentiated the distortions which the intended phrase suffered through the slip, into: interchanges of positions of words, interchanges of parts of words, perseverations, compoundings and substitutions. I will give you examples of these authors' main categories. It is a case of interchange of the first sort if someone says "the Milo of Venus" instead of "the Venus of Milo." An example of the second type of interchange, "I had a blush of rood to the head" instead of "rush of blood"; a perseveration would be the familiar misplaced toast, "I ask you to join me in hiccoughing the health of our chief."[3] These three forms of slips are not very frequent. You will find those cases much more frequent in which the slip results from a drawing together or compounding of syllables;

[3] "Aufstossen" instead of "anstossen."

for example, a gentleman on the street addresses a lady with the words, "If you will allow me, madame, I should be very glad to *inscort* you."[4] In the compounded word there is obviously besides the word "escort," also the word "insult" (and parenthetically we may remark that the young man will not find much favor with the lady). As an example of the substitution, Meringer and Mayer cite the following: "A man says, 'I put the specimens in the letterbox,' instead of 'in the hot-bed,' and the like."[5]

The explanation which the two authors attempt to formulate on the basis of this collection of examples is peculiarly inadequate. They hold that the sounds and syllables of words have different values, and that the production and perception of more highly valued syllables can interfere with those of lower values. They obviously base this conclusion on the cases of fore-sounding and perseveration which are not at all frequent; in other cases of slips of the tongue the question of such sound priorities, if any exist, does not enter at all. The most frequent cases of slips of the tongue are those in which instead of a certain word one says another which resembles it; and one may consider this resemblance sufficient explanation. For example, a professor says in his initial lecture, "I am not *inclined* to evaluate the merits of my predecessor."[6] Or another professor says, "In the case of the female genital, despite many *temptations* . . . I mean many attempts . . . etc."[7]

The most common, and also the most conspicuous form of slips of the tongue, however, is that of saying the exact opposite of what one meant to say. In such cases, one goes far afield from the problem of sound relations and resemblance effects, and can cite, instead of these, the fact that opposites have an obviously close relationship to each other, and have particularly close relations in the psychology of association. There are historical examples of this sort. A president of our House of Representatives once opened the assembly with the words, "Gentlemen, I declare a quorum present, and herewith declare the assembly *closed*."

[4] "Begleit-digen" compounded of "begleiten" and "beleidigen."
[5] "Briefkasten" instead of "Brütkasten."
[6] "Geneigt" instead of "geeignet."
[7] "Versuchungen" instead of "Versuche."

Similar, in its trickiness, to the relation of opposites is the effect of any other facile association which may under certain circumstances arise most inopportunely. Thus, for instance, there is the story which relates that on the occasion of a festivity in honor of the marriage of a child of H. Helmholtz with a child of the well-known discoverer and captain of industry, W. Siemon, the famous physiologist Dubois-Reymond was asked to speak. He concluded his undoubtedly sparkling toast with the words, "Success to the new firm—Siemens and—Halski!" That, of course, was the name of the well-known old firm. The association of the two names must have been about as easy for a native of Berlin as "Weber and Fields" to an American.

Thus we must add to the sound relations and word resemblances the influence of word associations. But that is not all. In a series of cases, an explanation of the observed slip is unsuccessful unless we take into account what phrase had been said or even thought previously. This again makes it a case of perseveration of the sort stressed by Meringer, but of a longer duration. I must admit, I am on the whole of the impression that we are further than ever from an explanation of slips of the tongue!

However, I hope I am not wrong when I say that during the above investigation of these examples of slips of the tongue, we have all obtained a new impression on which it will be of value to dwell. We sought the general conditions under which slips of the tongue occur, and then the influences which determine the kind of distortion resulting from the slip, but we have in no way yet considered the effect of the slip of the tongue in itself, without regard to its origin. And if we should decide to do so we must finally have the courage to assert, "In some of the examples cited, the product of the slip also makes sense." What do we mean by "it makes sense"? It means, I think, that the product of the slip has itself a right to be considered as a valid psychic act which also has its purpose, as a manifestation having content and meaning. Hitherto we have always spoken of errors, but now it seems as if sometimes the error itself were quite a normal act, except that it has thrust itself into the place of some other expected or intended act.

In isolated cases this valid meaning seems obvious and unmistakable. When the president with his opening words closes the session of the House of Representatives, instead of opening it, we are inclined to consider this error meaningful by reason of our knowledge of the circumstances under which the slip occurred. He expects no good of the assembly, and would be glad if he could terminate it immediately. The pointing out of this meaning, the interpretation of this error, gives us no difficulty. Or a lady, pretending to admire, says to another, "I am sure you must have messed up this charming hat yourself."* No scientific quibbles in the world can keep us from discovering in this slip the idea "this hat is a mess." Or a lady who is known for her energetic disposition, relates, "My husband asked the doctor to what diet he should keep. But the doctor said he didn't need any diet, he should eat and drink whatever *I* want." This slip of tongue is quite an unmistakable expression of a consistent purpose.

Ladies and gentlemen, if it should turn out that not only a few cases of slips of the tongue and of errors in general, but the larger part of them, have a meaning, then this meaning of errors of which we have hitherto made no mention, will unavoidably become of the greatest interest to us and will, with justice, force all other points of view into the background. We could then ignore all physiological and psycho-physiological conditions and devote ourselves to the purely psychological investigations of the sense, that is, the meaning, the purpose of these errors. To this end therefore we will not fail, shortly, to study a more extensive compilation of material.

But before we undertake this task, I should like to invite you to follow another line of thought with me. It has repeatedly happened that a poet has made use of slips of the tongue or some other error as a means of poetic presentation. This fact in itself must prove to us that he considers the error, the slip of the tongue for instance, as meaningful; for he creates it on purpose, and it is not a case of the poet committing an accidental slip of the pen and then letting his pen-slip stand as a tongue-slip of his character. He wants to make something clear to us by this slip of the tongue, and we may examine what it is, whether he wishes to indicate by this that the person in question is distracted or fatigued. Of course, we do not wish to exaggerate the importance of the fact that the poet did make use of

*" Aufgepatzt " instead of " aufgeputzt."

a slip to express his meaning. It could nevertheless really be a psychic accident, or meaningful only in very rare cases, and the poet would still retain the right to infuse it with meaning through his setting. As to their poetic use, however, it would not be surprising if we should glean more information concerning slips of the tongue from the poet than from the philologist or the psychiatrist.

Such an example of a slip of the tongue occurs in *Wallenstein* (*Piccolomini*, Act 1, Scene 5). In the previous scene, Max Piccolomini has most passionately sided with the Herzog, and dilated ardently on the blessings of peace which disclosed themselves to him during the trip on which he accompanied Wallenstein's daughter to the camp. He leaves his father and the courtier, Questenberg, plunged in deepest consternation. And then the fifth scene continues:

Q.

Alas! Alas! and stands it so?
What friend! and do we let him go away
In this delusion—let him go away?
Not call him back immediately, not open
His eyes upon the spot?

OCTAVIO.

(*Recovering himself out of a deep study*)
He has now opened mine,
And I see more than pleases me.

Q.

What is it?

OCTAVIO.

A curse on this journey!

Q.

But why so? What is it?

OCTAVIO.

Come, come along, friend! I must follow up
The ominous track immediately. Mine eyes
Are opened now, and I must use them. Come!
(*Draws Q. on with him.*)

Q.

What now? Where go you then?

OCTAVIO.

    (*Hastily.*)   To *her* herself

Q.

                      To—

OCTAVIO.

    (*Interrupting him and correcting himself.*)
    To the duke. Come, let us go—.

Octavio meant to say, "To him, to the lord," but his tongue slips and through his words *"to her"* he betrays to us, at least, the fact that he had quite clearly recognized the influence which makes the young war hero dream of peace.

A still more impressive example was found by O. Rank in Shakespeare. It occurs in the *Merchant of Venice,* in the famous scene in which the fortunate suitor makes his choice among the three caskets; and perhaps I can do no better than to read to you here Rank's short account of the incident:

"A slip of the tongue which occurs in Shakespeare's *Merchant of Venice,* Act III, Scene II, is exceedingly delicate in its poetic motivation and technically brilliant in its handling. Like the slip in *Wallenstein* quoted by Freud (*Psychopathology of Everyday Life,* 2d ed., p. 48), it shows that the poets well know the meaning of these errors and assume their comprehensibility to the audience. Portia, who by her father's wish has been bound to the choice of a husband by lot, has so far escaped all her unfavored suitors through the fortunes of chance. Since she has finally found in Bassanio the suitor to whom she is attached, she fears that he, too, will choose the wrong casket. She would like to tell him that even in that event he may rest assured of her love, but is prevented from so doing by her oath. In this inner conflict the poet makes her say to the welcome suitor:

PORTIA:

    I pray you tarry; pause a day or two,
    Before you hazard; for, in choosing wrong
    I lose your company; therefore, forbear a while:
    There's something tells me, (but it is not love)
    I would not lose you: * * *
    * * * I could teach you
    How to choose right, but then I am forsworn,

> So will I never be: so may you miss me;
> But if you do, you'll make me wish a sin
> That I had been forsworn. Beshrew your eyes.
> They have o'erlook'd me, and divided me;
> One half of me is yours, the other half *yours*,
> *Mine own*, I would say: but if mine, then yours,
> And so all yours.

Just that, therefore, which she meant merely to indicate faintly to him or really to conceal from him entirely, namely that even before the choice of the lot she was his and loved him, this the poet—with admirable psychological delicacy of feeling—makes apparent by her slip; and is able, by this artistic device, to quiet the unbearable uncertainty of the lover, as well as the equal suspense of the audience as to the issue of the choice."

Notice, at the end, how subtly Portia reconciles the two declarations which are contained in the slip, how she resolves the contradiction between them and finally still manages to keep her promise:

> "* * * but if mine, then yours,
> And so all yours."

Another thinker, alien to the field of medicine, accidentally disclosed the meaning of errors by an observation which has anticipated our attempts at explanation. You all know the clever satires of Lichtenberg (1742-1749), of which Goethe said, "Where he jokes, there lurks a problem concealed." Not infrequently the joke also brings to light the solution of the problem. Lichtenberg mentions in his jokes and satiric comments the remark that he always read "Agamemnon" for "angenomen,"* so intently had he read Homer. Herein is really contained the whole theory of misreadings.

At the next session we will see whether we can agree with the poets in their conception of the meaning of psychological errors.

*"Angenomen" is a verb, meaning "to accept."

THIRD LECTURE

A T the last session we conceived the idea of considering the error, not in its relation to the intended act which it distorted, but by itself alone, and we received the impression that in isolated instances it seems to betray a meaning of its own. We declared that if this fact could be established on a larger scale, then the meaning of the error itself would soon come to interest us more than an investigation of the circumstances under which the error occurs.

Let us agree once more on what we understand by the "meaning" of a psychic process. A psychic process is nothing more than the purpose which it serves and the position which it holds in a psychic sequence. We can also substitute the word "purpose" or "intention" for "meaning" in most of our investigations. Was it then only a deceptive appearance or a poetic exaggeration of the importance of an error which made us believe that we recognized a purpose in it?

Let us adhere faithfully to the illustrative example of slips of the tongue and let us examine a larger number of such observations. We then find whole categories of cases in which the intention, the meaning of the slip itself, is clearly manifest. This is the case above all in those examples in which one says the opposite of what one intended. The president said, in his opening address, "I declare the meeting closed." His intention is certainly not ambiguous. The meaning and purpose of his slip is that he wants to terminate the meeting. One might point the conclusion with the remark "he said so himself." We have only taken him at his word. Do not interrupt me at this point by remarking that this is not possible, that we know he did not want to terminate the meeting but to open it, and that he himself, whom we have just recognized as the best judge of his intention, will affirm that he meant to open it. In so doing you forget that we have agreed to consider the error entirely by itself. Its

tion to the intention which it distorts is to be discussed later. Otherwise you convict yourself of an error in logic by which you smoothly conjure away the problem under discussion; or "beg the question," as it is called in English.

In other cases in which the speaker has not said the exact opposite of what he intended, the slip may nevertheless express an antithetical meaning. "I am not *inclined* to appreciate the merits of my predecessor." *"Inclined"* is not the opposite of *"in a position to,"* but it is an open betrayal of intent in sharpest contradiction to the attempt to cope gracefully with the situation which the speaker is supposed to meet.

In still other cases the slip simply adds a second meaning to the one intended. The sentence then sounds like a contradiction, an abbreviation, a condensation of several sentences. Thus the lady of energetic disposition, "He may eat and drink whatever *I* please." The real meaning of this abbreviation is as though the lady had said, "He may eat and drink whatever he pleases. But what does it matter what *he* pleases! It is *I* who do the pleasing." Slips of the tongue often give the impression of such an abbreviation. For example, the anatomy professor, after his lecture on the human nostril, asks whether the class has thoroughly understood, and after a unanimous answer in the affirmative, goes on to say: "I can hardly believe that is so, since the people who understand the human nostril can, even in a city of millions, be counted on *one finger*—I mean, on the fingers of one hand." The abbreviated sentence here also has its meaning: it expresses the idea that there is only one person who thoroughly understands the subject.

In contrast to these groups of cases are those in which the error does not itself express its meaning, in which the slip of the tongue does not in itself convey anything intelligible; cases, therefore, which are in sharpest opposition to our expectations. If anyone, through a slip of the tongue, distorts a proper name, or puts together an unusual combination of syllables, then this very common occurrence seems already to have decided in the negative the question of whether all errors contain a meaning. Yet closer inspection of these examples discloses the fact that an understanding of such a distortion is easily possible, indeed, that the difference between these unintelligible cases and the previous comprehensible ones is not so very great.

A man who was asked how his horse was, answered, "Oh, it may *stake*—it may take another month." When asked what he really meant to say, he explained that he had been thinking that it was a *sorry* business and the coming together of *"take"* and *"sorry"* gave rise to *"stake."* (Meringer and Mayer.)

Another man was telling of some incidents to which he had objected, and went on, "and then certain facts were *re-filed."* Upon being questioned, he explained that he meant to stigmatize these facts as *"filthy." "Revealed"* and *"filthy"* together produced the peculiar *"re-filled."* (Meringer and Mayer.)

You will recall the case of the young man who wished to *"inscort"* an unknown lady. We took the liberty of resolving this word construction into the two words *"escort"* and *"insult,"* and felt convinced of this interpretation without demanding proof of it. You see from these examples that even slips can be explained through the concurrence, the interference, of two speeches of different intentions. The difference arises only from the fact that in the one type of slip the intended speech completely crowds out the other, as happens in those slips where the opposite is said, while in the other type the intended speech must rest content with so distorting or modifying the other as to result in mixtures which seem more or less intelligible in themselves.

We believe that we have now grasped the secret of a large number of slips of the tongue. If we keep this explanation in mind we will be able to understand still other hitherto mysterious groups. In the case of the distortion of names, for instance, we cannot assume that it is always an instance of competition between two similar, yet different names. Still, the second intention is not difficult to guess. The distorting of names occurs frequently enough not as a slip of the tongue, but as an attempt to give the name an ill-sounding or debasing character. It is a familiar device or trick of insult, which persons of culture early learned to do without, though they do not give it up readily. They often clothe it in the form of a joke, though, to be sure, the joke is of a very low order. Just to cite a gross and ugly example of such a distortion of a name, I mention the fact that the name of the President of the French Republic, *Poincaré*, has been at times, lately, transformed into *"Schweinskarré."* It is therefore easy to assume that the also such an intention to insult in the case of other slips of the tongue which result in the distortion of a name. In consequence of our adherence to this conception, similar explanations force themselves upon us, in the case of slips of the tongue whose effect is comical or absurd. "I call upon you to *hiccough* the health of our chief."[1] Here the solemn atmosphere is unexpectedly disturbed by the introduction of a word that awakens an unpleasant image; and from the prototype of certain expressions of insult and offense we cannot but suppose that there is an intention striving for expression which is in sharp contrast to the ostensible respect, and which could be expressed about as follows, "You needn't believe this. I'm not really in earnest. I don't give a whoop for the fellow—etc." A similar trick which passes for a slip of the tongue is that which transforms a harmless word into one which is indecent and obscene.[2]

We know that many persons have this tendency of intentionally making harmless words obscene for the sake of a certain lascivious pleasure it gives them. It passes as wit, and we always have to ask about a person of whom we hear such a thing, whether he intended it as a joke or whether it occurred as a slip of the tongue.

Well, here we have solved the riddle of errors with relatively little trouble! They are not accidents, but valid psychic acts. They have their meaning; they arise through the collaboration—or better, the mutual interference—of two different intentions. I can well understand that at this point you want to swamp me with a deluge of questions and doubts to be answered and resolved before we can rejoice over this first result of our labors. I truly do not wish to push you to premature conclusions. Let us dispassionately weigh each thing in turn, one after the other.

What would you like to say? Whether I think this explanation is valid for all cases of slips of the tongue or only for a certain number? Whether one can extend this same conception to all the many other errors—to mis-reading, slips of the pen, forgetting, picking up the wrong object, mislaying things, etc? In the face of the psychic nature of errors, what meaning is left to the factors of fatigue, excitement, absent-mindedness and

[1] The young man here said "aufzustossen" instead of "anzustossen."
[2] Prof. Freud here gives the two examples, quite untranslatable, of " apopos " instead of " apropos," and " eischeissweibchen " instead of " eiweissscheibchen."

distraction of attention? Moreover, it is easy to see that of the two competing meanings in an error, one is always public, but the other not always. But what does one do in order to guess the latter? And when one believes one has guessed it, how does one go about proving that it is not merely a probable meaning, but that it is the only correct meaning? Is there anything else you wish to ask? If not, then I will continue. I would remind you of the fact that we really are not much concerned with the errors themselves, but we wanted only to learn something of value to psychoanalysis from their study. Therefore, I put the question: What are these purposes or tendencies which can thus interfere with others, and what relation is there between the interfering tendencies and those interfered with? Thus our labor really begins anew, after the explanation of the problem.

Now, is this the explanation of all tongue slips? I am very much inclined to think so and for this reason, that as often as one investigates a case of a slip of the tongue, it reduces itself to this type of explanation. But on the other hand, one cannot prove that a slip of the tongue cannot occur without this mechanism. It may be so; for our purposes it is a matter of theoretical indifference, since the conclusions which we wish to draw by way of an introduction to psychoanalysis remain untouched, even if only a minority of the cases of tongue slips come within our conception, which is surely not the case. I shall anticipate the next question, of whether or not we may extend to other types of errors what we have gleaned from slips of the tongue, and answer it in the affirmative. You will convince yourselves of that conclusion when we turn our attention to the investigation of examples of pen slips, picking up wrong objects, etc. I would advise you, however, for technical reasons, to postpone this task until we shall have investigated the tongue slip itself more thoroughly.

The question of what meaning those factors which have been placed in the foreground by some authors,—namely, the factors of circulatory disturbances, fatigue, excitement, absent-mindedness, the theory of the distraction of attention—the question of what meaning those factors can now have for us if we accept above described psychic mechanism of tongue slips, deser᷄ more detailed answer. You will note that we do not deny factors. In fact, it is not very often that psychoanalysis denies anything which is asserted on the other side. As a rule psychoanalysis merely adds something to such assertions and occasionally it does happen that what had hitherto been overlooked, and was newly added by psychoanalysis, is just the essential thing. The influence on the occurrence of tongue slips of such physiological predispositions as result from slight illness, circulatory disturbances and conditions of fatigue, should be acknowledged without more ado. Daily personal experience can convince you of that. But how little is explained by such an admission! Above all, they are not necessary conditions of the errors. Slips of the tongue are just as possible when one is in perfect health and normal condition. Bodily factors, therefore, have only the value of acting by way of facilitation and encouragement to the peculiar psychic mechanism of a slip of the tongue.

To illustrate this relationship, I once used a simile which I will now repeat because I know of no better one as substitute. Let us suppose that some dark night I go past a lonely spot and am there assaulted by a rascal who takes my watch and purse; and then, since I did not see the face of the robber clearly, I make my complaint at the nearest police station in the following words: "Loneliness and darkness have just robbed me of my valuables." The police commissioner could then say to me: "You seem to hold an unjustifiably extreme mechanistic conception. Let us rather state the case as follows: Under cover of darkness, and favored by the loneliness, an unknown robber seized your valuables. The essential task in your case seems to me to be to discover the robber. Perhaps we can then take his booty from him again."

Such psycho-physiological moments as excitement, absentmindedness and distracted attention, are obviously of small assistance to us for the purpose of explanation. They are mere phrases, screens behind which we will not be deterred from looking. The question is rather what in such cases has caused the excitement, the particular diversion of attention. The influence of syllable sounds, word resemblances and the customary associations which words arouse should also be recognized as having significance. They facilitate the tongue slip by pointing the path which it can take. But if I have a path before

me, does that fact as a matter of course determine that I will
follow it? After all, I must have a stimulus to make me decide
for it, and, in addition, a force which carries me forward on
this path. These sound and word relationships therefore serve
also only to facilitate the tongue slip, just as the bodily dispositions facilitate them; they cannot give the explanation for
the word itself. Just consider, for example, the fact that in an
enormously large number of cases, my lecturing is not disturbed
by the fact that the words which I use recall others by their
sound resemblance, that they are intimately associated with their
opposites, or arouse common associations. We might add here
the observation of the philosopher Wundt, that slips of the
tongue occur when, in consequence of bodily fatigue, the tendency to association gains the upper hand over the intended
speech. This would sound very plausible if it were not contradicted by experiences which proved that from one series of
cases of tongue-slips bodily stimuli were absent, and from
another, the association stimuli were absent.

However, your next question is one of particular interest to
me, namely: in what way can one establish the existence of the
two mutually antagonistic tendencies? You probably do not
suspect how significant this question is. It is true, is it not, that
one of the two tendencies, the tendency which suffers the interference, is always unmistakable? The person who commits the
error is aware of it and acknowledges it. It is the other tendency, what we call the interfering tendency, which causes
doubt and hesitation. Now we have already learned, and you
have surely not forgotten, that these tendencies are, in a series
of cases, equally plain. That is indicated by the effect of the
slip, if only we have the courage to let this effect be valid in
itself. The president who said the opposite of what he meant
to say made it clear that he wanted to open the meeting, but
equally clear that he would also have liked to terminate it.
Here the meaning is so plain that there is nothing left to be
interpreted. But the other cases in which the interfering tendency merely distorts the original, without bringing itself to
full expression—how can one guess the interfering meaning
from the distortion?

By a very sure and simple method, in the first series of cases,
namely, by the same method by which one establis'

existence of the meaning interfered with. The latter is immediately supplied by the speaker, who instantly adds the originally intended expression. "It may *stake*—no, it may *take* another month." Now we likewise ask him to express the interfering meaning; we ask him: "Now, why did you first say *stake*?" He answers, "I meant to say—'This is a *sorry* business.' " And in the other case of the tongue slip—*re-filed*—the subject also affirms that he meant to say "It is a *fil-thy* business," but then moderated his expression and turned it into something else. Thus the discovery of the interfering meaning was here as successful as the discovery of the one interfered with. Nor did I unintentionally select as examples cases which were neither related nor explained by me or by a supporter of my theories. Yet a certain investigation was necessary in both cases in order to obtain the solution. One had to ask the speaker why he made this slip, what he had to say about it. Otherwise he might perhaps have passed it by without seeking to explain it. When questioned, however, he furnished the explanation by means of the first thing that came to his mind. And now you see, ladies and gentlemen, that this slight investigation and its consequence are already a psychoanalysis, and the prototype of every psychoanalytic investigation which we shall conduct more extensively at a later time.

Now, am I unduly suspicious if I suspect that at the same moment in which psychoanalysis emerges before you, your resistence to psychoanalysis also raises its head? Are you not anxious to raise the objection that the information given by the subject we questioned, and who committed the slip, is not proof sufficient? He naturally has the desire, you say, to meet the challenge, to explain the slip, and hence he says the first thing he can think of if it seems relevant. But that, you say, is no proof that this is really the way the slip happened. It might be so, but it might just as well be otherwise, you say. Something else might have occurred to him which might have fitted the case just as well and better.

It is remarkable how little respect, at bottom, you have for a psychic fact! Imagine that someone has decided to undertake the chemical analysis of a certain substance, and has secured a sample of the substance, of a certain weight—so and so many milligrams. From this weighed sample certain definite conclusions can be drawn. Do you think it would ever occur to a chemist to discredit these conclusions by the argument that the isolated substance might have had some other weight? Everyone yields to the fact that it was just this weight and no other, and confidently builds his further conclusions upon that fact. But when you are confronted by the psychic fact that the subject, when questioned, had a certain idea, you will not accept that as valid, but say some other idea might just as easily have occurred to him! The trouble is that you believe in the illusion of psychic freedom and will not give it up. I regret that on this point I find myself in complete opposition to your views.

Now you will relinquish this point only to take up your resistance at another place. You will continue, "We understand that it is the peculiar technique of psychoanalysis that the solution of its problems is discovered by the analyzed subject himself. Let us take another example, that in which the speaker calls upon the assembly 'to *hiccough* the health of their chief.' The interfering idea in this case, you say, is the insult. It is that which is the antagonist of the expression of conferring an honor. But that is mere interpretation on your part, based on observations extraneous to the slip. If in this case you question the originator of the slip, he will not affirm that he intended an insult, on the contrary, he will deny it energetically. Why do you not give up your unverifiable interpretation in the face of this plain objection?"

Yes, this time you struck a hard problem. I can imagine the unknown speaker. He is probably an assistant to the guest of honor, perhaps already a minor official, a young man with the brightest prospects. I will press him as to whether he did not after all feel conscious of something which may have worked in opposition to the demand that he do honor to the chief. What a fine success I'll have! He becomes impatient and suddenly bursts out on me, "Look here, you'd better stop this cross-examination, or I'll get unpleasant. Why, you'll spoil my whole career with your suspicions. I simply said '*auf*-gestossen' instead of '*an*-gestossen,' because I'd already said '*auf*' twice in the same sentence. It's the thing that Meringer calls a perservation, and there's no other meaning that you can twist out of it. Do you understand me? That's all." H'm, this is ⌐

surprising reaction, a really energetic denial. I see that there is nothing more to be obtained from the young man, but I also remark to myself that he betrays a strong personal interest in having his slip mean nothing. Perhaps you, too, agree that it is not right for him immediately to become so rude over a purely theoretical investigation, but, you will conclude, he really must know what he did and did not mean to say.

Really? Perhaps that's open to question nevertheless.

But now you think you have me. "So that is your technique," I hear you say. "When the person who has committed a slip gives an explanation which fits your theory, then you declare him the final authority on the subject. 'He says so himself!' But if what he says does not fit into your scheme, then you suddenly assert that what he says does not count, that one need not believe him."

Yet that is certainly true. I can give you a similar case in which the procedure is apparently just as monstrous. When a defendant confesses to a deed, the judge believes his confession. But if he denies it, the judge does not believe him. Were it otherwise, there would be no way to administer the law, and despite occasional miscarriages you must acknowledge the value of this system.

Well, are you then the judge, and is the person who committed the slip a defendant before you? Is a slip of the tongue a crime?

Perhaps we need not even decline this comparison. But just see to what far-reaching differences we have come by penetrating somewhat into the seemingly harmless problems of the psychology of errors, differences which at this stage we do not at all know how to reconcile. I offer you a preliminary compromise on the basis of the analogy of the judge and the defendant. You will grant me that the meaning of an error admits of no doubt when the subject under analysis acknowledges it himself. I in turn will admit that a direct proof for the suspected meaning cannot be obtained if the subject denies us the information; and, of course, that is also the case when the subject is not present to give us the information. We are, then, as in the case of the legal procedure, dependent on circumstances which make a decision at one time seem more, and at another time, less probable to us. At law, one has to declare a defendant guilty on circumstantial evidence for practical reasons. We see no such necessity; but neither are we forced to forego the use of these circumstances. It would be a mistake to believe that a science consists of nothing but conclusively proved theorems, and any such demand would be unjust. Only a person with a mania for authority, a person who must replace his religious catechism with some other, even though it be scientific, would make such a demand. Science has but few apodeictic precepts in its catechism; it consists chiefly of assertions which it has developed to certain degrees of probability. It is actually a symptom of scientific thinking if one is content with these approximations of certainty and is able to carry on constructive work despite the lack of the final confirmation.

But where do we get the facts for our interpretations, the circumstances for our proof, when the further remarks of the subject under analysis do not themselves elucidate the meaning of the error? From many sources. First of all, from the analogy with phenomena extraneous to the psychology of errors; as, for example, when we assert that the distortion of a name as a slip of the tongue has the same insulting significance as an intentional name distortion. We get them also from the psychic situation in which the error occurred, from our knowledge of the character of the person who committed the error, from the impressions which that person received before making the error, and to which he may possibly have reacted with this error. As a rule, what happens is that we find the meaning of the error according to general principles. It is then only a conjecture, a suggestion as to what the meaning may be, and we then obtain our proof from examination of the psychic situation. Sometimes, too, it happens that we have to wait for subsequent developments, which have announced themselves, as it were, through the error, in order to find our conjecture verified .

I cannot easily give you proof of this if I have to limit myself to the field of tongue slips, although even here there are a few good examples. The young man who wished to *"inscort"* the lady is certainly shy; the lady whose husband may eat and drink whatever *she* wants I know to be one of those energetic women who know how to rule in the home. Or take the following case: At a general meeting of the Concordia Club, a young memb‑ delivers a vehement speech in opposition, in the course of wh' he addresses the officers of the society as: "Fellow commit lenders." We will conjecture that some conflicting idea militated in him against his opposition, an idea which was in some way based on a connection with money lending. As a matter of fact, we learn from our informant that the speaker was in constant money difficulties, and had attempted to raise a loan. As a conflicting idea, therefore, we may safely interpolate the idea, "Be more moderate in your opposition, these are the same people who are to grant you the loan."

But I can give you a wide selection of such circumstantial proof if I delve into the wide field of other kinds of error.

If anyone forgets an otherwise familiar proper name, or has difficulty in retaining it in his memory despite all efforts, then the conclusion lies close at hand, that he has something against the bearer of this name and does not like to think of him. Consider in this connection the following revelation of the psychic situation in which this error occurs:

"A Mr. Y. fell in love, without reciprocation, with a lady who soon after married a Mr. X. In spite of the fact that Mr. Y. has known Mr. X. a long time, and even has business relations with him, he forgets his name over and over again, so that he found it necessary on several occasions to ask other people the man's name when he wanted to write to Mr. X."[3]

Mr. Y. obviously does not want to have his fortunate rival in mind under any condition. "Let him never be thought of."

Another example: A lady makes inquiries at her doctor's concerning a mutual acquaintance, but speaks of her by her maiden name. She has forgotten her married name. She admits that she was much displeased by the marriage, and could not stand this friend's husband.[4]

Later we shall have much to say in other relations about the matter of forgetting names. At present we are predominantly interested in the psychic situation in which the lapse of memory occurs.

The forgetting of projects can quite commonly be traced to an antagonistic current which does not wish to carry out the project. We psychoanalysts are not alone in holding this view, but this is the general conception to which all persons subscribe the daily affairs, and which they first deny in theory.

---

[3] From C. G. Jung.
[4] From A. A. Brill.

The patron who makes apologies to his protegé, saying that he has forgotten his requests, has not squared himself with his protegé. The protegé immediately thinks: "There's nothing to that; he did promise but he really doesn't want to do it." Hence, daily life also proscribes forgetting, in certain connections, and the difference between the popular and the psychoanalytic conception of these errors appears to be removed. Imagine a housekeeper who receives her guest with the words: "What, you come to-day? Why, I had totally forgotten that I had invited you for to-day"; or the young man who might tell his sweetheart that he had forgotten to keep the rendezvous which they planned. He is sure not to admit it, it were better for him to invent the most improbable excuses on the spur of the moment, hindrances which prevented him from coming at that time, and which made it impossible for him to communicate the situation to her. We all know that in military matters the excuse of having forgotten something is useless, that it protects one from no punishment; and we must consider this attitude justified. Here we suddenly find everyone agreed that a certain error is significant, and everyone agrees what its meaning is. Why are they not consistent enough to extend this insight to the other errors, and fully to acknowledge them? Of course, there is also an answer to this.

If the meaning of this forgetting of projects leaves room for so little doubt among laymen, you will be less surprised to find that poets make use of these errors in the same sense. Those of you who have seen or read Shaw's *Caesar and Cleopatra* will recall that Caesar, when departing in the last scene, is pursued by the idea that there was something more he intended to do, but that he had forgotten it. Finally he discovers what it is: to take leave of Cleopatra. This small device of the author is meant to ascribe to the great Caesar a superiority which he did not possess, and to which he did not at all aspire. You can learn from historical sources that Caesar had Cleopatra follow him to Rome, and that she was staying there with her little Caesarion when Caesar was murdered, whereupon she fled the city.

The cases of forgetting projects are as a rule so clear that they are of little use for our purpose, i.e., discovering in the psychic situation circumstantial evidence of the meaning the error. Let us, therefore, turn to a particularly ambiguous and untransparent error, that of losing and mislaying objects. That we ourselves should have a purpose in losing an object, an accident frequently so painful, will certainly seem incredible to you. But there are many instances similar to the following: A young man loses the pencil which he had liked very much. The day before he had received a letter from his brother-in-law, which concluded with the words, "For the present I have neither the inclination nor the time to be a party to your frivolity and your idleness."³ It so happened that the pencil had been a present from this brother-in-law. Without this coincidence we could not, of course, assert that the loss involved any intention to get rid of the gift. Similar cases are numerous. Persons lose objects when they have fallen out with the donors, and no longer wish to be reminded of them. Or again, objects may be lost if one no longer likes the things themselves, and wants to supply oneself with a pretext for substituting other and better things in their stead. Letting a thing fall and break naturally shows the same intention toward that object. Can one consider it accidental when a school child just before his birthday loses, ruins or breaks his belongings, for example his school bag or his watch?

He who has frequently experienced the annoyance of not being able to find something which he has himself put away, will also be unwilling to believe there was any intent behind the loss. And yet the examples are not at all rare in which the attendant circumstances of the mislaying point to a tendency temporarily or permanently to get rid of the object. Perhaps the most beautiful example of this sort is the following: A young man tells me: "A few years ago a misunderstanding arose in my married life. I felt my wife was too cool and even though I willingly acknowledged her excellent qualities, we lived without any tenderness between us. One day she brought me a book which she had thought might interest me. I thanked her for this attention, promised to read the book, put it in a handy place, and couldn't find it again. Several months passed thus, during which I occasionally remembered this mislaid book and tried in vain to find it. About half a year later my beloved mother, who lived at a distance from us, fell ill. My wife left

From B. Dattner.

the house in order to nurse her mother-in-law. The condition of the patient became serious, and gave my wife an opportunity of showing her best side. One evening I came home filled with enthusiasm and gratitude toward my wife. I approached my writing desk, opened a certain drawer with no definite intention but as if with somnambulistic certainty, and the first thing I found is the book so long mislaid."

With the cessation of the motive, the inability to find the mislaid object also came to an end.

Ladies and gentlemen, I could increase this collection of examples indefinitely. But I do not wish to do so here. In my *Psychopathology of Everyday Life* (first published in 1901), you will find only too many instances for the study of errors.[a]

All these examples demonstrate the same thing repeatedly: namely, they make it seem probable that errors have a meaning, and show how one may guess or establish that meaning from the attendant circumstances. I limit myself to-day because we have confined ourselves to the purpose of profiting in the preparation for psychoanalysis from the study of these phenomena. I must, however, still go into two additional groups of observations, into the accumulated and combined errors and into the confirmation of our interpretations by means of subsequent developments.

The accumulated and combined errors are surely the fine flower of their species. If we were interested only in proving that errors may have a meaning, we would limit ourselves to the accumulated and combined errors in the first place, for here the meaning is unmistakable, even to the dullest intelligence, and can force conviction upon the most critical judgment. The accumulation of manifestations betrays a stubbornness such as could never come about by accident, but which fits closely the idea of design. Finally, the interchange of certain kinds of error with each other shows us what is the important and essential element of the error, not its form or the means of which it avails itself, but the purpose which it serves and which is to be achieved by the most various paths. Thus I will give you a case of repeated forgetting. Jones recounts that he once allowed a letter to lie on his writing desk several days for reasons quite

[a] So also in the writings of A. Maeder (French), A. A. Brill (Eng—) J. Stärke (Dutch) and others.

unknown. Finally he made up his mind to mail it; but it was returned from the dead letter office, for he had forgotten to address it. After he had addressed it he took it to the post office, but this time without a stamp. At this point he finally had to admit to himself his aversion against sending the letter at all.

In another case a mistake is combined with mislaying an object. A lady is traveling to Rome with her brother-in-law, a famous artist. The visitor is much fêted by the Germans living in Rome, and receives as a gift, among other things, a gold medal of ancient origin. The lady is vexed by the fact that her brother-in-law does not sufficiently appreciate the beautiful object. After she leaves her sister and reaches her home, she discovers when unpacking that she has brought with her—how, she does not know—the medal. She immediately informs her brother-in-law of this fact by letter, and gives him notice that she will send the medal back to Rome the next day. But on the following day, the medal has been so cleverly mislaid that it can neither be found nor sent, and at this point it begins to dawn upon the lady that her "absent-mindedness" means, namely, that she wants to keep the object for herself.'

I have already given you an example of a combination of forgetfulness and error in which someone first forgot a rendezvous and then, with the firm intention of not forgetting it a second time, appeared at the wrong hour. A quite analogous case was told me from his own experience, by a friend who pursues literary interests in addition to his scientific ones. He said: "A few years ago I accepted the election to the board of a certain literary society, because I hoped that the society could at some time be of use to me in helping obtain the production of my drama, and, despite my lack of interest, I took part in the meetings every Friday. A few months ago I received the assurance of a production in the theatre in F., and since that time it happens regularly that I forget the meetings of that society. When I read your article on these things, I was ashamed of my forgetfulness, reproached myself with the meanness of staying away now that I no longer need these people and determined to be sure not to forget next Friday. I kept reminding myself of this resolution until I carried it out and

'From R. Reitler.

stood before the door of the meeting room. To my astonishment, it was closed, the meeting was already over; for I had mistaken the day. It was already Saturday."

It would be tempting enough to collect similar observations, but I will go no further; I will let you glance instead upon those cases in which our interpretation has to wait for its proof upon future developments.

The chief condition of these cases is conceivably that the existing psychic situation is unknown to us or inaccessible to our inquiries. At that time our interpretation has only the value of a conjecture to which we ourselves do not wish to grant too much weight. Later, however, something happens which shows us how justified was our interpretation even at that time. I was once the guest of a young married couple and heard the young wife laughingly tell of a recent experience, of how on the day after her return from her honeymoon she had hunted up her unmarried sister again in order to go shopping with her, as in former times, while her husband went to his business. Suddenly she noticed a gentleman on the other side of the street, and she nudged her sister, saying, "Why look, there goes Mr. K." She had forgotten that this gentleman was her husband of some weeks' standing. I shuddered at this tale but did not dare to draw the inference. The little anecdote did not occur to me again until a year later, after this marriage had come to a most unhappy end.

A. Maeder tells of a lady who, the day before her wedding, forgot to try on her wedding dress and to the despair of the dressmaker only remembered it later in the evening. He adds in connection with this forgetfulness the fact that she divorced her husband soon after. I know a lady now divorced from her husband, who, in managing her fortune, frequently signed documents with her maiden name, and this many years before she really resumed it. I know of other women who lost their wedding rings on their honeymoon and also know that the course of the marriage gave a meaning to this accident. And now one more striking example with a better termination. It is said that the marriage of a famous German chemist did not take place because he forgot the hour of the wedding, and instead of going to the church went to the laboratory. He was wise enough to rest satisfied with this one attempt, and died unmarried at a ripe old age.

Perhaps the idea has also come to you that in these cases mistakes have taken the place of the *Omina* or omens of the ancients. Some of the *Omina* really were nothing more than mistakes; for example, when a person stumbled or fell down. Others, to be sure, bore the characteristics of objective occurrences rather than that of subjective acts. But you would not believe how difficult it sometimes is to decide in a specific instance whether the act belongs to the one or the other group. It so frequently knows how to masquerade as a passive experience.

Everyone of us who can look back over a longer or shorter life experience will probably say that he might have spared himself many disappointments and painful surprises if he had found the courage and decision to interpret as omens the little mistakes which he made in his intercourse with people, and to consider them as indications of the intentions which were still being kept secret. As a rule, one does not dare do this. One would feel as though he were again becoming superstitious via a detour through science. But not all omens come true, and you will understand from our theories that they need not all come true.

FOURTH LECTURE

THE PSYCHOLOGY OF ERRORS—(*Conclusion*)

WE may certainly put it down as the conclusion of our labors up to this point that errors have a meaning, and we may make this conclusion the basis of our further investigations. Let me stress the fact once more that we do not assert—and for our purposes need not assert—that every single mistake which occurs is meaningful, although I consider that probable. It will suffice us if we prove the presence of such a meaning with relative frequency in the various forms of errors. These various forms, by the way, behave differently in this respect. In the cases of tongue slips, pen slips, etc., the occurrences may take place on a purely physiological basis. In the group based on forgetfulness (forgetting names or projects, mislaying objects, etc.) I cannot believe in such a basis. There does very probably exist a type of case in which the loss of objects should be recognized as unintentional. Of the mistakes which occur in daily life, only a certain portion can in any way be brought within our conception. You must keep this limitation in mind when we start henceforth from the assumption that mistakes are psychic acts and arise through the mutual interference of two intentions.

Herein we have the first result of psychoanalysis. Psychology hitherto knew nothing of the occurrence of such interferences and the possibility that they might have such manifestations as a consequence. We have widened the province of the world of psychic phenomena quite considerably, and have brought into the province of psychology phenomena which formerly were not attributed to it.

Let us tarry a moment longer over the assertion that errors are psychic acts. Does such an assertion contain more than the former declaration that they have a meaning? I do not believe so. On the contrary, it is rather more indefinite and open to greater misunderstanding. Everything which can be

observed about the psychic life will on occasion be designated
as a psychic phenomenon. But it will depend on whether the
specific psychic manifestations resulted directly from bodily,
organic, material influences, in which case their investigation
will not fall within the province of psychology, or whether it was
more immediately the result of other psychic occurrences back
of which, somewhere, the series of organic influences then begins.
We have the latter condition of affairs before us when we designate a phenomenon as a psychic manifestation, and for that
reason it is more expedient to put our assertion in this form:
the phenomena are meaningful; they have a meaning. By
"meaning" we understand significance, purpose, tendency and
position in a sequence of psychic relations.

There are a number of other occurrences which are very
closely related to errors, but which this particular name no
longer fits. We call them *accidental and symptomatic* acts.
They also have the appearance of being unmotivated, the appearance of insignificance and unimportance, but in addition, and
more plainly, of superfluity. They are differentiated from errors
by the absence of another intention with which they collide and
by which they are disturbed. On the other side they pass over
without a definite boundary line into the gestures and movements which we count among expressions of the emotions.
Among these accidental acts belong all those apparently playful,
apparently purposeless performances in connection with our
clothing, parts of our body, objects within reach, as well as the
omission of such performances, and the melodies which we hum
to ourselves. I venture the assertion that all these phenomena
are meaningful and capable of interpretation in the same way
as are the errors, that they are small manifestations of other
more important psychic processes, valid psychic acts. But I do
not intend to linger over this new enlargement of the province of
psychic phenomena, but rather to return to the topic of errors,
in the consideration of which the important psychoanalytic inquiries can be worked out with far greater clarity.

The most interesting questions which we formulated while
considering errors, and which we have not yet answered, are,
I presume, the following: We said that the errors are the result
of the mutual interference of two different intentions, of which
the one can be called the intention interfered with, and the

other the interfering intention. The intentions interfered with give rise to no further questions, but concerning the others we want to know, firstly, what kind of intentions are these which arise as disturbers of others, and secondly, in what proportions are the interfering related to the interfered?

Will you permit me again to take the slip of the tongue as representative of the whole species and allow me to answer the second question before the first?

The interfering intention in the tongue slip may stand in a significant relation to the intention interfered with, and then the former contains a contradiction of the latter, correcting or supplementing it. Or, to take a less intelligible and more interesting case, the interfering intention has nothing to do with the intention interfered with.

Proofs for the first of the two relations we can find without trouble in the examples which we already know and in others similar to those. In almost all cases of tongue slips where one says the contrary of what he intended, where the interfering intention expresses the antithesis of the intention interfered with, the error is the presentation of the conflict between two irreconcilable strivings. "I declare the meeting opened, but would rather have it closed," is the meaning of the president's slip. A political paper which has been accused of corruptibility, defends itself in an article meant to reach a climax in the words: "Our readers will testify that we have always interceded for the good of all in the most *disinterested* manner." But the editor who had been entrusted with the composition of the defence, wrote, "in the most *interested* manner." That is, he thinks "To be sure, I have to write this way, but I know better." A representative of the people who urges that the Kaiser should be told the truth *"rückhaltlos,"* hears an inner voice which is frightened by his boldness, and which through a slip changes the *"rückhaltlos"* into *"rückgratlos."*[1]

In the examples familiar to you, which give the impression of contraction and abbreviation, it is a question of a correction, an addition or continuation by which the second tendency manifests itself together with the first. "Things were revealed, but better say it right out, they were *filthy,* therefore, things were

[1] In the German Reichstag, November, 1908. " Rückhaltos " means " unreservedly." " Rückgratlos " means " without backbone."

refiled."[2] "The people who understand this topic can be counted on the *fingers of one hand,* but no, there is really only *one* who understands it; therefore, counted *on one finger.*" Or, "My husband may eat and drink whatever *he* wants. But you know very well that *I* don't permit him to want anything; therefore he may eat and drink whatever *I want.*" In all these cases, therefore, the slip arises from the content of the intention itself, or is connected with it.

The other type of relationship between the two interfering intentions seems strange. If the interfering intention has nothing to do with the content of the one interfered with, where then does it come from and how does it happen to make itself manifest as interference just at that point? The observation which alone can furnish an answer here, recognizes the fact that the interference originates in a thought process which has just previously occupied the person in question and which then has that after-effect, irrespective of whether it has already found expression in speech or not. It is therefore really to be designated as perseveration, but not necessarily as the perseveration of spoken words. Here also there is no lack of an associative connection between the interfering and the interfered with, yet it is not given in the content, but artificially restored, often by means of forced connecting links.

Here is a simple example of this, which I myself observed. In our beautiful Dolomites, I meet two Viennese ladies who are gotten up as tourists. I accompany them a short distance and we discuss the pleasures, but also the difficulties of the tourist's mode of life. One lady admits this way of spending the day entails much discomfort. "It is true," she says, "that it is not at all pleasant, when one has tramped all day in the sun, and waist and shirt are soaked through." At this point in this sentence she suddenly has to overcome a slight hesitancy. Then she continues: "But then, when one gets *nach Hose,* and can change . . ."[3] We did not analyze this slip, but I am sure

---

[2] "Zum Vorschein bringen," means to bring to light. "Schweinereien" means filthiness or obscurity. The telescoping of the two ideas, resulting in the word "Vorschwein," plainly reveals the speaker's opinion of the affair.

[3] The lady meant to say "Nach Hause," "to reach home." The word "Hose" means "drawers." The preservating content of her hesitancy is hereby revealed.

you can easily understand it. The lady wanted to make the enumeration more complete and to say, "Waist, shirt and drawers." From motives of propriety, the mention of the drawers (Hose) was suppressed, but in the next sentence of quite independent content the unuttered word came to light as a distortion of the similar word, house (Hause).

Now we can turn at last to the long delayed main question, namely, what kind of intentions are these which get themselves expressed in an unusual way as interferences of others, intentions within whose great variety we wish nevertheless to find what is common to them all? If we examine a series of them to this end, we will soon find that they divide themselves into three groups. In the first group belong the cases in which the interfering tendency is known to the speaker, and which, moreover, was felt by him before the slip. Thus, in the case of the slip *"refilled,"* the speaker not only admits that he agreed with the judgment *"filthy,"* on the incidents in question, but also that he had the intention (which he later abandoned) of giving it verbal expression. A second group is made up of those cases in which the interfering tendency is immediately recognized by the subject as his own, but in which he is ignorant of the fact that the interfering tendency was active in him just before the slip. He therefore accepts our interpretation, yet remains to a certain extent surprised by it. Examples of this situation can perhaps more easily be found among errors other than slips of the tongue. In a third group the interpretation of the interfering intention is energetically denied by the speaker. He not only denies that the interfering tendency was active in him before the slip, but he wants to assert that it was at all times completely alien to him. Will you recall the example of "hiccough," and the absolutely impolite disavowal which I received at the hands of this speaker by my disclosure of the interfering intention. You know that so far we have no unity in our conception of these cases. I pay no attention to the toastmaster's disavowal and hold fast to my interpretation; while you, I am sure, are yet under the influence of his repudiation and are considering whether one ought not to forego the interpretation of such slips, and let them pass as purely physiological acts, incapable of further analysis. I can imagine what it is that frightens you off. My interpretation draws the conclusion that intentions of which he himself knows nothing may manifest themselves in a speaker, and that I can deduce them from the circumstances. You hesitate before so novel a conclusion and one so full of consequences. I understand that, and sympathize with you to that extent. But let us make one thing clear: if you want consistently to carry through the conception of errors which you have derived from so many examples, you must decide to accept the above conclusion, even though it be unpleasant. If you cannot do so, you must give up that understanding of errors which you have so recently won.

Let us tarry a while over the point which unites the three groups, which is common to the three mechanisms of tongue slips. Fortunately, that is unmistakable. In the first two groups the interfering tendency is recognized by the speaker; in the first there is the additional fact that it showed itself immediately before the slip. In both cases, however, *it was suppressed. The speaker had made up his mind not to convert the interfering tendency into speech and then the slip of the tongue occurred; that is to say, the suppressed tendency obtains expression against the speaker's will, in that it changes the expression of the intention which he permits, mixes itself with it or actually puts itself in its place.* This is, then the mechanism of the tongue slip.

From my point of view, I can also best harmonize the processes of the third group with the mechanism here described. I need only assume that these three groups are differentiated by the different degrees of effectiveness attending the suppression of an intention. In the first group, the intention is present and makes itself perceptible before the utterance of the speaker; not until then does it suffer the suppression for which it indemnifies itself in the slip. In the second group the suppression extends farther. The intention is no longer perceptible before the subject speaks. It is remarkable that the interfering intention is in no way deterred by this from taking part in the causation of the slip. Through this fact, however, the explanation of the procedure in the third group is simplified for us. I shall be so bold as to assume that in the error a tendency can manifest itself which has been suppressed for even a longer time, perhaps a very long time, which does not become perceptible and which, therefore, cannot be directly denied by the speaker. But leave the problem of the third group; from the observation of the other cases, you must draw the conclusion that *the suppression of the existing intention to say something is the indispensable condition of the occurrence of a slip.*

We may now claim that we have made further progress in understanding errors. We know not only that they are psychic acts, in which we can recognize meaning and purpose, and that they arise through the mutual interference of two different intentions, but, in addition, we know that one of these intentions must have undergone a certain suppression in order to be able to manifest itself through interference with the other. The interfering intention must itself first be interfered with before it can become interfering. Naturally, a complete explanation of the phenomena which we call errors is not attained to by this. We immediately see further questions arising, and suspect in general that there will be more occasions for new questions as we progress further. We might, for example, ask why the matter does not proceed much more simply. If there is an existing purpose to suppress a certain tendency instead of giving it expression, then this suppression should be so successful that nothing at all of the latter comes to light; or it could even fail, so that the suppressed tendency attains to full expression. But errors are compromise formations. They mean some success and some failure for each of the two purposes. The endangered intention is neither completely suppressed nor does it, without regard to individual cases, come through wholly intact. We can imagine that special conditions must be existent for the occurrence of such interference or compromise formations, but then we cannot even conjecture what sort they may be. Nor do I believe that we can uncover these unknown circumstances through further penetration into the study of errors. Rather will it be necessary thoroughly to examine other obscure fields of psychic life. Only the analogies which we there encounter can give us the courage to draw those assumptions which are requisite to a more fundamental elucidation of errors. And one thing more. Even working with small signs, as we have constantly been in the habit of doing in this province, brings its dangers with it. There is a mental disease, combined paranoia, in which the utilization of such small signs is practiced without restriction, and I naturally would not wish to give it as my opinion that these conclusions, built up on this basis, are correct throughout. We can be protected from such dangers only by the broad basis of our observations, by the repetition of similar impressions from the most varied fields of psychic life.

We will therefore leave the analysis of errors here. But may I remind you of one thing more: keep in mind, as a prototype, the manner in which we have treated these phenomena. You can see from these examples what the purposes of our psychology are. We do not wish merely to describe the phenomena and to classify them, but to comprehend them as signs of a play of forces in the psychic, as expressions of tendencies striving to an end, tendencies which work together or against one another. We seek a dynamic conception of psychic phenomena. The perceived phenomena must, in our conception, give way to those strivings whose existence is only assumed.

Hence we will not go deeper into the problem of errors, but we can still undertake an expedition through the length of this field, in which we will reëncounter things familiar to us, and will come upon the tracks of some that are new. In so doing we will keep to the division which we made in the beginning of our study, of the three groups of tongue slips, with the related forms of pen slips, misreadings, mishearings, forgetfulness with its subdivisions according to the forgotten object (proper names, foreign words, projects, impressions), and the other faults of mistaking, mislaying and losing objects. Errors, in so far as they come into our consideration, are grouped in part with forgetfulness, in part with mistakes.

We have already spoken in such detail of tongue slips, and yet there are still several points to be added. Linked with tongue slips are smaller effective phenomena which are not entirely without interest. No one likes to make a slip of the tongue; often one fails to hear his own slip, though never that of another. Tongue slips are in a certain sense infectious; it is not at all easy to discuss tongue slips without falling into slips of the tongue oneself. The most trifling forms of tongue slips are just the ones which have no particular illumination to throw on the hidden psychic processes, but are nevertheless not difficult to penetrate in their motivation. If, for example, anyone pronounces a long vowel as a short, in consequence of an interference no matter how motivated, he will for that reason soon after lengthen a short vowel and commit a new slip in compensation for the earlier one. The same thing occurs when one has pronounced a double vowel unclearly and hastily; for example, an "eu" or an "oi" as "ei." The speaker tries to correct it by changing a subsequent "ei" or "eu" to "oi." In this conduct the determining factor seems to be a certain consideration for the hearer, who is not to think that it is immaterial to the speaker how he treats his mother tongue. The second, compensating distortion actually has the purpose of making the hearer conscious of the first, and of assuring him that it also did not escape the speaker. The most frequent and most trifling cases of slips consist in the contractions and foresoundings which show themselves in inconspicuous parts of speech. One's tongue slips in a longer speech to such an extent that the last word of the intended speech is said too soon. That gives the impression of a certain impatience to be finished with the sentence and gives proof in general of a certain resistance to communicating this sentence or speech as a whole. Thus we come to borderline cases in which the differences between the psychoanalytic and the common physiological conception of tongue slips are blended. We assume that in these cases there is a tendency which interferes with the intention of the speech. But it can only announce that it is present, and not what its own intention is. The interference which it occasions then follows some sound influences or associative relationship, and may be considered as a distraction of attention from the intended speech. But neither this disturbance of attention nor the associative tendency which has been activated, strikes the essence of the process. This hints, however, at the existence of an intention which interferes with the purposed speech, an intention whose nature cannot (as is possible in all the more pronounced cases of tongue slips) this time be guessed from its effects.

Slips of the pen, to which I now turn, are in agreement with those of the tongue to the extent that we need expect to gain no new points of view from them. Perhaps we will be content with a small gleaning. Those very common little slips of the pen—contractions, anticipations of later words, particularly of the last words—again point to a general distaste for writing, and to an impatience to be done; the pronounced effects of pen slips permit the nature and purpose of the interfering tendency to be recognized. One knows in general that if one finds a slip of the pen in a letter everything was not as usual with the writer. What was the matter one cannot always establish. The pen slip is frequently as little noticed by the person who makes it as the tongue slip. The following observation is striking: There are some persons who have the habit of always rereading a letter they have written before sending it. Others do not do so. But if the latter make an exception and reread the letter, they always have the opportunity of finding and correcting a conspicuous pen slip. How can that be explained? This looks as if these persons knew that they had made a slip of the pen while writing the letter. Shall we really believe that such is the case?

There is an interesting problem linked with the practical significance of the pen slip. You may recall the case of the murderer H., who made a practice of obtaining cultures of the most dangerous disease germs from scientific institutions, by pretending to be a bacteriologist, and who used these cultures to get his close relatives out of the way in this most modern fashion. This man once complained to the authorities of such an institution about the ineffectiveness of the culture which had been sent to him, but committed a pen slip and instead of the words, "in my attempts on mice and guinea pigs," was plainly written, "in my attempts on people."[1] This slip even attracted the attention of the doctors at the institution, but so far as I know, they drew no conclusion from it. Now what do you think? Might not the doctors better have accepted the slip as a confession and instituted an investigation through which the murderer's handiwork would have been blocked in time? In this case was not ignorance of our conception of errors to blame for an omission of practical importance? Well, I am inclined to think that such a slip would surely seem very suspicious to me, but a fact of great importance stands in the way of its utilization as a confession. The thing is not so simple. The pen slip is surely an indication, but by itself it would not have been sufficient to instigate an investigation. That the man is preoccupied with the thought of infecting human beings, the slip certainly does betray, but it does not make it possible to decide whether this thought has the value of a clear plan of

[1] The German reads, " bei meinen Versuchen an Mausen," which, through the slip of the pen, resulted in " bei meinen Versuchen an Menschen."

injury or merely of a phantasy having no practical consequence. It is even possible that the person who made such a slip will deny this phantasy with the best subjective justification and will reject it as something entirely alien to him. Later, when we give our attention to the difference between psychic and material reality, you will understand these possibilities even better. Yet this is again a case in which an error later attained unsuspected significance.

In misreading, we encounter a psychic situation which is clearly differentiated from that of the tongue slips or pen slips. The one of the two rival tendencies is here replaced by a sensory stimulus and perhaps for that reason is less resistant. What one is reading is not a production of one's own psychic activity, as is something which one intends to write. In a large majority of cases, therefore, the misreading consists in a complete substitution. One substitutes another word for the word to be read, and there need be no connection in meaning between the text and the product of the misreading. In general, the slip is based upon a word resemblance. Lichtenberg's example of reading "*Agamemnon*" for "*angenommen*"[1] is the best of this group. If one wishes to discover the interfering tendency which causes the misreading, one may completely ignore the misread text and can begin the analytic investigation with the two questions: What is the first idea that occurs in free association to the product of the misreading, and, in what situation did the misreading occur? Now and then a knowledge of the latter suffices by itself to explain the misreading. Take, for example, the individual who, distressed by certain needs, wanders about in a strange city and reads the word "*Closethaus*" on a large sign on the first floor of a house. He has just time to be surprised at the fact that the sign has been nailed so high up when he discovers that, accurately observed, the sign reads "*Corsethaus*." In other cases the misreadings which are independent of the text require a penetrating analysis which cannot be accomplished without practice and confidence in the psychoanalytic technique. But generally it is not a matter of much difficulty to obtain the elucidation of a misreading. The substituted word, as in the example, "*Agamemnon*," betrays without more ado the thought sequence from which the interference results. In

[1] "Angenommen" is a verb, meaning "to accept."

war times, for instance, it is very common for one to read into everything which contains a similar word structure, the names of the cities, generals and military expressions which are constantly buzzing around us. In this way, whatever interests and preoccupies one puts itself in the place of that which is foreign or uninteresting. The after-effects of thoughts blur the new perceptions.

There are other types of misreadings, in which the text itself arouses the disturbing tendency, by means of which it is then most often changed into its opposite. One reads something which is undesired; analysis then convinces one that an intensive wish to reject what has been read should be made responsible for the alteration.

In the first mentioned and more frequent cases of misreading, two factors are neglected to which we gave an important role in the mechanism of errors: the conflict of two tendencies and the suppression of one which then indemnifies itself by producing the error. Not that anything like the opposite occurs in misreading, but the importunity of the idea content which leads to misreading is nevertheless much more conspicuous than the suppression to which the latter may previously have been subjected. Just these two factors are most tangibly apparent in the various situations of errors of forgetfulness.

Forgetting plans is actually uniform in meaning; its interpretation is, as we have heard, not denied even by the layman. The tendency interfering with the plan is always an antithetical intention, an unwillingness concerning which we need only discover why it does not come to expression in a different and less disguised manner. But the existence of this unwillingness is not to be doubted. Sometimes it is possible even to guess something of the motives which make it necessary for this unwillingness to disguise itself, and it always achieves its purpose by the error resulting from the concealment, while its rejection would be certain were it to present itself as open contradiction. If an important change in the psychic situation occurs between the formulation of the plan and its execution, in consequence of which the execution of the plan does not come into question, then the fact that the plan was forgotten is no longer in the class of errors. One is no longer surprised at it, and one understands that it would have been superfluous to have remembered

the plan; it was then permanently or temporarily effaced. Forgetting a plan can be called an error only when we have no
reason to believe there was such an interruption.

The cases of forgetting plans are in general so uniform and
transparent that they do not interest us in our investigation.
There are two points, however, from which we can learn something new. We have said that forgetting, that is, the non-
execution of a plan, points to an antipathy toward it. This
certainly holds, but, according to the results of our investigations, the antipathy may be of two sorts, direct and indirect.
What is meant by the latter can best be explained by one or
two examples. If a patron forgets to say a good word for his
protegé to a third person, it may be because the patron is not
really very much interested in the protegé, therefore, has no
great inclination to commend him. It is, at any rate, in this
sense that the protegé will construe his patron's forgetfulness.
But the matter may be more complicated. The patron's antipathy
to the execution of the plan may originate in another quarter
and fasten upon quite a different point. It need not have anything to do with the protegé, but may be directed toward the
third person to whom the good word was to have been said.
Thus, you see what doubts here confront the practical application of our interpretation. The protegé, despite a correct interpretation of the forgetfulness, stands in danger of becoming too
suspicious, and of doing his patron a grave injustice. Or, if an
individual forgets a rendezvous which he has made, and which
he had resolved to keep, the most frequent basis will certainly
be the direct aversion to encountering this person. But analysis
might here supply the information that the interfering intention
was not directed against that person, but against the place in
which they were to have met, and which was avoided because of
a painful memory associated with it. Or, if one forgets to mail
a letter, the counter-intention may be directed against the content of that letter, yet this does not in any way exclude the possibility that the letter is harmless in itself, and only subject to
the counter-intention because something about it reminds the
writer of another letter written previously, which, in fact, did
afford a basis for the antipathy. One can say in such a case that
the antipathy has here transferred itself from that former letter
where it was justified to the present one in which it really has

no meaning. Thus you see that one must always exercise restraint and caution in the application of interpretations, even though the interpretations are justified. That which is psychologically equivalent may nevertheless in practice be very ambiguous.

Phenomena such as these will seem very unusual to you. Perhaps you are inclined to assume that the "indirect" antipathy is enough to characterize the incident as pathological. Yet I can assure you that it also occurs in a normal and healthy setting. I am in no way willing to admit the unreliability of our analytic interpretation. After all, the above-discussed ambiguity of plan-forgetting exists only so long as we have not attempted an analysis of the case, and are interpreting it only on the basis of our general suppositions. When we analyze the person in question, we discover with sufficient certainty in each case whether or not it is a direct antipathy, or what its origin is otherwise.

A second point is the following: when we find in a large majority of cases that the forgetting of a plan goes back to an antipathy, we gain courage to extend this solution to another series of cases in which the analyzed person does not confirm, but denies, the antipathy which we inferred. Take as an example the exceedingly frequent incidents of forgetting to return books which one has borrowed, or forgetting to pay one's bills or debts. We will be so bold as to accuse the individual in question of intending to keep the books and not to pay the debts, while he will deny such an intention but will not be in a position to give us any other explanation of his conduct. Thereupon we insist that he has the intention, only he knows nothing about it; all we need for our inference is to have the intention betray itself through the effect of the forgetfulness. The subject may then repeat that he had merely forgotten it. You now recognize the situation as one in which we once before found ourselves. If we wish to be consistent in our interpretation, an interpretation which has been proved as manifold as it is justified, we will be unavoidably forced to the conclusion that there are tendencies in a human being which can become effective without his being conscious of them. By so doing, however, we place ourselves in opposition to all the views which prevail in daily life and in psychology.

Forgetting proper names and foreign names as well as foreign words can be traced in the same manner to a counter-intention which aims either directly or indirectly at the name in question. I have already given you an example of such direct antipathy. The indirect causation, however, is particularly frequent and generally necessitates careful analysis for its determination. Thus, for example, in war times which force us to sacrifice so many of our former inclinations, the ability to recall proper names also suffers severely in consequence of the most peculiar connections. A short time ago it happened that I could not reproduce the name of that harmless Moravian city of Bisenz, and analysis showed that no direct dislike was to blame, but rather the sound resemblance to the name of the Bisenzi palace in Orrieto, in which I used to wish I might live. As a motive for the antagonism to remembering the name, we here encounter for the first time a principle which will later disclose to us its whole tremendous significance in the causation of neurotic symptoms, viz., the aversion on the part of the memory to remembering anything which is connected with unpleasant experience and which would revive this unpleasantness by a reproduction. This intention of avoiding unpleasantness in recollections of other psychic acts, the psychic flight from unpleasantness, we may recognize as the ultimate effective motive not only for the forgetting of names, but also for many other errors, such as omissions of action, etc.

Forgetting names does, however, seem to be especially facilitated psycho-physiologically and therefore also occurs in cases in which the interference of an unpleasantness-motive cannot be established. If anyone once has a tendency to forget names, you can establish by analytical investigation that he not only loses names because he himself does not like them, or because they remind him of something he does not like, but also because the same name in his mind belongs to another chain of associations, with which he has more intimate relations. The name is anchored there, as it were, and denied to the other associations activated at the moment. If you will recall the tricks of mnemonic technique you will ascertain with some surprise that one forgets names in consequence of the same associations which one otherwise purposely forms in order to save them from being forgotten. The most conspicuous example of this is afforded by proper names of persons, which conceivably enough must have very different psychic values for different people. For example, take a first name, such as Theodore. To one of you it will mean nothing special, to another it means the name of his father, brother, friend, or his own name. Analytic experience will then show you that the first person is not in danger of forgetting that a certain stranger bears this name, while the latter will be constantly inclined to withhold from the stranger this name which seems reserved for intimate relationships. Let us now assume that this associative inhibition can come into contact with the operation of the unpleasantness-principle, and in addition with an indirect mechanism, and you will be in a position to form a correct picture of the complexity of causation of this temporary name-forgetting. An adequate analysis that does justice to the facts, however, will completely disclose these complications.

Forgetting impressions and experiences shows the working of the tendency to keep unpleasantness from recollection much more clearly and conclusively than does the forgetting of names. It does not, of course, belong in its entirety to the category of errors, but only in so far as it seems to us conspicuous and unjustified, measured by the measuring stick of our accustomed conception—thus, for example, where the forgetfulness strikes fresh or important impressions or impressions whose loss tears a hole in the otherwise well-remembered sequence. Why and how it is in general that we forget, particularly why and how we forget experiences which have surely left the deepest impressions, such as the incidents of our first years of childhood, is quite a different problem, in which the defense against unpleasant associations plays a certain role but is far from explaining everything. That unpleasant impressions are easily forgotten is an indubitable fact. Various psychologists have observed it, and the great Darwin was so struck by it that he made the "golden rule" for himself of writing down with particular care observations which seemed unfavorable to his theory, since he had convinced himself that they were just the ones which would not stick in his memory.

Those who hear for the first time of this principle of defense against unpleasant recollections by means of forgetting, seldom fail to raise the objection that they, on the contrary, have had the experience that just the painful is hard to forget, inasmuch

as it always comes back to mind to torture the person against
his will—as, for example, the recollection of an insult or humiliation. This fact is also correct, but the objection is not valid.
It is important that one begin betimes to reckon with the fact
that the psychic life is the arena of the struggles and exercises
of antagonistic tendencies, or, to express it in non-dynamic terminology, that it consists of contradictions and paired antag-
onisms. Information concerning one specific tendency is of no
avail for the exclusion of its opposite; there is room for both of
them. It depends only on how the opposites react upon each
other, what effects will proceed from the one and what from the
other.

Losing and mislaying objects is of especial interest to us
because of the ambiguity and the multiplicity of tendencies in
whose services the errors may act. The common element in all
cases is this, that one wished to lose something. The reasons
and purposes thereof vary. One loses an object when it has
become damaged, when one intends to replace it with a better
one, when one has ceased to like it, when it came from a person
whose relations to one have become strained, or when it was
obtained under circumstances of which one no longer wishes to
think. The same purpose may be served by letting the object
fall, be damaged or broken. In the life of society it is said to
have been found that unwelcome and illegitimate children are
much more often frail than those born in wedlock. To reach
this result we do not need the coarse technique of the so-called
angel-maker. A certain remissness in the care of the child is
said to suffice amply. In the preservation of objects, the case
might easily be the same as with the children.

But things may be singled out for loss without their having
forfeited any of their value, namely, when there exists the intention to sacrifice something to fate in order to ward off some
other dreaded loss. Such exorcisings of fate are, according to
the findings of analysis, still very frequent among us; therefore,
the loss of things is often a voluntary sacrifice. In the same
way losing may serve the purposes of obstinacy or self-punish-
ment. In short, the more distant motivation of the tendency to
get rid of a thing oneself by means of losing it is not overlooked.

Mistakes, like other errors, are often used to fulfill wishes
which one ought to deny oneself. The purpose is thus masked

as fortunate accident; for instance, one of our friends once took the train to make a call in the suburbs, despite the clearest antipathy to so doing, and then, in changing cars, made the mistake of getting into the train which took him back to the city. Or, if on a trip one absolutely wants to make a longer stay at a half-way station, one is apt to overlook or miss certain connections, so that he is forced to make the desired interruption to the trip. Or, as once happened to a patient of mine whom I had forbidden to call up his fiancée on the telephone, "by mistake" and "absent-mindedly" he asked for a wrong number when he wanted to telephone to me, so that he was suddenly connected with the lady. A pretty example and one of practical significance in making a direct mistake is the observation of an engineer at a preliminary hearing in a damage suit:

"Some time ago I worked with several colleagues in the laboratory of a high school on a series of complicated elasticity experiments, a piece of work which we had undertaken voluntarily but which began to take more time than we had expected. One day as I went into the laboratory with my colleague F., the latter remarked how unpleasant it was to him to lose so much time that day, since he had so much to do at home. I could not help agreeing with him, and remarked half jokingly, alluding to an incident of the previous week: 'Let's hope that the machine gives out again so that we can stop work and go home early.'

"In the division of labor it happened that F. was given the regulation of the valve of the press, that is to say, he was, by means of a cautious opening of the valve, to let the liquid pressure from the accumulator flow slowly into the cylinder of the hydraulic press. The man who was directing the job stood by the manometer (pressure gauge) and when the right pressure had been reached called out in a loud voice: 'Stop.' At this command F. seized the valve and turned with all his might— to the left! (All valves, without exception, close to the right.) Thereby the whole pressure of the accumulator suddenly became effective in the press, a strain for which the connecting pipes are not designed, so that a connecting pipe immediately burst— quite a harmless defect, but one which nevertheless forced us to drop work for the day and go home.

"It is characteristic, by the way, that some time afterward when we were discussing this occurrence, my friend F. had no recollection whatever of my remark, which I could recall with certainty."

From this point you may reach the conjecture that it is not harmless accident which makes the hands of your domestics such dangerous enemies to your household property. But you can also raise the question whether it is always an accident when one damages himself and exposes his own person to danger. There are interests the value of which you will presently be able to test by means of the analysis of observations.

Ladies and gentlemen, this is far from being all that might be said about errors. There is indeed much left to investigate and to discuss. But I am satisfied if, from our investigations to date, your previous views are somewhat shaken and if you have acquired a certain degree of liberality in the acceptance of new ones. For the rest, I must content myself with leaving you face to face with an unclear condition of affairs. We cannot prove all our axioms by the study of errors and, indeed, are by no means solely dependent on this material. The great value of errors for our purpose lies in the fact that they are very frequent phenomena that can easily be observed on oneself and the occurrence of which do not require a pathological condition. I should like to mention just one more of your unanswered questions before concluding: "If, as we have seen in many examples, people come so close to understanding errors and so often act as though they penetrated their meaning, how is it possible that they can so generally consider them accidental, senseless and meaningless, and can so energetically oppose their psychoanalytic elucidation?"

You are right; that is conspicuous and demands an explanation. I shall not give this explanation to you, however, but shall guide you slowly to the connecting links from which the explanation will force itself upon you without any aid from me.

II

THE DREAM

FIFTH LECTURE

THE DREAM

ulties and Preliminary Approach

the discovery was made that the disease symp-
f certain nervous patients have a meaning.[1]
pon the psychoanalytic method of therapy was
d. In this treatment it happened that the
esented dreams in place of their symptoms.
ated the conjecture that these dreams also have

however, pursue this historical path, but enter
site one. We wish to discover the meaning of
paration for the study of the neuroses. This
stified, for the study of dreams is not only the
n for that of the neuroses, but the dream itself
tic symptom, and in fact one which possesses for
lable advantage of occurring in all normals. In-
man beings were well and would dream, we could
r dreams almost all the insight to which the study
s has led.

nat the dream becomes the object of psychoanalytic
in an ordinary, little-considered phenomenon, ap-
o practical value, like the errors with which, indeed,
character of occurring in normals. But otherwise
s are rather less favorable for our work. Errors
lected only by science, which had paid little atten-
; but at least it was no disgrace to occupy one's self
People said there are indeed more important things,
something may come of it. Preoccupation with the
ever, is not merely impractical and superfluous, but
ominious; it carries the odium of the unscientific,
suspicion of a personal leaning towards mysticism.
a physician busying himself with dreams when even
thology and psychiatry there are matters so much

uer, in the years 1880–1882. Cf. also my lectures on psycho-
vered in the United States in 1909.

63

more serious — tumors the size of apples which incapacitate the organ of the psyche, hemorrhages, and chronic inflammations in which one can demonstrate changes in the tissues under the microscope! No, the dream is much too trifling an object, and unworthy of Science.

And besides, it is a condition which in itself defies all the requirements of exact research—in dream investigation one is not even sure of one's object. A delusion, for example, presents itself in clear and definite outlines. "I am the Emperor of China," says the patient aloud. But the dream? It generally cannot be related at all. If anyone relates a dream, has he any guarantee that he has told it correctly, and not changed it during the telling, or invented an addition which was forced by the indefiniteness of his recollection? Most dreams cannot be remembered at all, are forgotten except for small fragments. And upon the interpretation of such material shall a scientific psychology or method of treatment for patients be based?

A certain excess in judgment may make us suspicious. The objections to the dream as an object of research obviously go too far. The question of insignificance we have already had to deal with in discussing errors. We said to ourselves that important matters may manifest themselves through small signs. As concerns the indefiniteness of the dream, it is after all a characteristic like any other. One cannot prescribe the characteristics of an object. Moreover, there are clear and definite dreams. And there are other objects of psychiatric research which suffer from the same trait of indefiniteness, e.g., many compulsion ideas, with which even respectable and esteemed psychiatrists have occupied themselves. I might recall the last case which occurred in my practice. The patient introduced himself to me with the words, "I have a certain feeling as though I had harmed or had wished to harm some living thing—a child? —no, more probably a dog—perhaps pushed it off a bridge—or something else." We can overcome to some degree the difficulty of uncertain recollection in the dream if we determine that exactly what the dreamer tells us is to be taken as his dream, without regard to anything which he has forgotten or may have changed in recollection. And finally, one cannot make so general an assertion as that the dream is an unimportant thing. We know from our own experience that the mood in which one wakes up after a dream may continue throughout the whole day. Cases have been observed by physicians in which a psychosis begins with a dream and holds to a delusion which originated in it. It is related of historical personages that they drew their inspiration for important deeds from dreams. So we may ask whence comes the contempt of scientific circles for the dream?

I think it is the reaction to their over-estimation in former times. Reconstruction of the past is notoriously difficult, but this much we may assume with certainty—if you will permit me the jest—that our ancestors of 3000 years ago and more, dreamed much in the way we do. As far as we know, all ancient peoples attached great importance to dreams and considered them of practical value. They drew omens for the future from dreams, sought premonitions in them. In those days, to the Greeks and all Orientals, a campaign without dream interpreters must have been as impossible as a campaign without an aviation scout to-day. When Alexander the Great undertook his campaign of conquests, the most famous dream interpreters were in attendance. The city of Tyrus, which was then still situated on an island, put up so fierce a resistance that Alexander considered the idea of raising the siege. Then he dreamed one night of a satyr dancing as if in triumph; and when he laid his dream before his interpreters he received the information that the victory over the city had been announced to him. He ordered the attack and took Tyrus. Among the Etruscans and the Romans other methods of discovering the future were in use, but the interpretation of dreams was practical and esteemed during the entire Hellenic-Roman period. Of the literature dealing with the topic at least the chief work has been preserved to us, namely, the book of Artemidoros of Daldis, who is supposed to have lived during the lifetime of the Emperor Hadrian. How it happened subsequently that the art of dream interpretation was lost and the dream fell into discredit, I cannot tell you. Enlightenment cannot have had much part in it, for the Dark Ages faithfully perserved things far more absurd than the ancient dream interpretation. The fact is, the interest in dreams gradually deteriorated into superstition, and could assert itself only among the ignorant. The latest misuse of dream interpretation in our day still tries to discover in dreams the numbers which are going to be drawn in the small lottery. On the other hand, the exact science of to-day has repeatedly dealt with dreams, but always only with the purpose of applying its physiological theories to the dream. By physicians, of course, the dream was considered as a non-psychic act, as the manifestation of somatic irritations in the psychic life. Binz (1876) pronounced the dream "a bodily process, in all cases useless, in many actually pathological, above which the world-soul and immortality are raised as high as the blue ether over the weed-grown sands of the lowest plain." Maury compared it with the irregular twitchings of St. Vitus' Dance in contrast to the co-ordinated movements of the normal person. An old comparison makes the content of the dream analogous to the tones which the "ten fingers of a musically illiterate person would bring forth if they ran over the keys of the instrument."

Interpretation means finding a hidden meaning. There can be no question of interpretation in such an estimation of the dream process. Look up the description of the dream in Wundt, Jodl and other newer philosophers. You will find an enumeration of the deviations of dream life from waking thought, in a sense disparaging to the dream. The description points out the disintegration of association, the suspension of the critical faculty, the elimination of all knowledge, and other signs of diminished activity. The only valuable contribution to the knowledge of the dream which we owe to exact science pertains to the influence of bodily stimuli, operative during sleep, on the content of the dream. There are two thick volumes of experimental researches on dreams by the recently deceased Norwegian author, J. Mourly Vold, (translated into German in 1910 and 1912), which deal almost solely with the consequences of changes in the position of the limbs. They are recommended as the prototype of exact dream research. Now can you imagine what exact science would say if it discovered that we wish to attempt to find the meaning of dreams? It may be it has already said it, but we will not allow ourselves to be frightened off. If errors can have a meaning, the dream can, too, and errors in many cases have a meaning which has escaped exact science. Let us confess to sharing the prejudice of the ancients and the common people, and let us follow in the footsteps of the ancient dream interpreters.

First of all, we must orient ourselves in our task, and take a bird's eye view of our field. What is a dream? It is difficult to say in one sentence. But we do not want to attempt any definition where a reference to the material with which everyone is familiar suffices. Yet we ought to select the essential element of the dream. How can that be found? There are such monstrous differences within the boundary which encloses our province, differences in every direction. The essential thing will very probably be that which we can show to be common to all dreams.

Well, the first thing which is common to all dreams is that we are asleep during their occurrence. The dream is apparently the psychic life during sleep, which has certain resemblances to that of the waking condition, and on the other hand is distinguished from it by important differences. That was noted even in Aristotle's definition. Perhaps there are other connections obtaining between the dream and sleep. One can be awakened by a dream, one frequently has a dream when he wakes spontaneously or is forcibly awakened from sleep. The dream then seems to be an intermediate condition between sleeping and waking. Thus we are referred to the problem of sleep. What, then, is sleep?

That is a physiological or biological problem concerning which there is still much controversy. We can form no decision on the point, but I think we may attempt a psychological characterization of sleep. Sleep is a condition in which I wish to have nothing to do with the external world, and have withdrawn my interest from it. I put myself to sleep by withdrawing myself from the external world and by holding off its stimuli. I also go to sleep when I am fatigued by the external world. Thus, by going to sleep, I say to the external world, "Leave me in peace, for I wish to sleep." Conversely, the child says, "I won't go to bed yet, I am not tired, I want to have some more fun." The biological intention of sleep thus seems to be recuperation; its psychological character, the suspension of interest in the external world. Our relation to the world into which we came so unwillingly, seems to include the fact that we cannot endure it without interruption. For this reason we revert from time to time to the pre-natal existence, that is, to the intra-uterine existence. At least we create for ourselves conditions quite similar to those obtaining at that time—warmth, darkness and the

absence of stimuli. Some of us even roll ourselves into tight
packages and assume in sleep a posture very similar to the intra-
uterine posture. It seems as if the world did not wholly possess
us adults, it has only two-thirds of our life, we are still one-third
unborn. Each awakening in the morning is then like a new
birth. We also speak of the condition after sleep with the words,
"I feel as though I had been born anew," by which we probably
form a very erroneous idea of the general feeling of the newly
born. It may be assumed that the latter, on the contrary, feel
very uncomfortable. We also speak of birth as "seeing the light
of day." If that be sleep, then the dream is not on its program
at all, rather it seems an unwelcome addition. We think, too,
that dreamless sleep is the best and only normal sleep. There
should be no psychic activity in sleep; if the psyche stirs, then
just to that extent have we failed to reduplicate the foetal condition; remainders of psychic activity could not be completely
avoided. These remainders are the dream. Then it really does
seem that the dream need have no meaning. It was different in
the case of errors; they were activities of the waking state. But
when I am asleep, have quite suspended psychic activity and
have suppressed all but certain of its remainders, then it is by
no means inevitable that these remainders have a meaning. In
fact, I cannot make use of this meaning, in view of the fact that
the rest of my psyche is asleep. This must, of course, be a
question only of twitching, like spasmodic reactions, a question
only of psychic phenomena such as follow directly upon somatic
stimulation. The dream, therefore, appears to be the sleep-disturbing remnant of the psychic activity of waking life, and we
may make the resolution promptly to abandon a theme which is
so ill-adapted to psychoanalysis.

However, even if the dream is superfluous, it exists nevertheless and we may try to give an account of its existence.
Why does not the psyche go to sleep? Probably because there
is something which gives it no rest. Stimuli act upon the psyche,
and it must react to them. The dream, therefore, is the way
in which the psyche reacts to the stimuli acting upon it in the
sleeping condition. We note here a point of approach to the
understanding of the dream. We can now search through different dreams to discover what are the stimuli which seek to
disturb the sleep and which are reacted to with dreams. Thus
we might be said to have discovered the first common element.

Are there other common elements? Yes, it is undeniable that there are, but they are much more difficult to grasp and describe. The psychic processes of sleep, for example, have a very different character from those of waking. One experiences many things in the dream, and believes in them, while one really has experienced nothing but perhaps the one disturbing stimulus. One experiences them predominantly in visual images; feelings may also be interspersed in the dream as well as thoughts; the other senses may also have experiences, but after all the dream experiences are predominantly pictures. A part of the difficulty of dream telling comes from the fact that we have to transpose these pictures into words. "I could draw it," the dreamer says frequently, "but I don't know how to say it." That is not really a case of diminished psychic activity, like that of the feeble-minded in comparison with the highly gifted; it is something qualitatively different, but it is difficult to say wherein the difference lies. G. T. Fechner once hazarded the conjecture that the scene in which dreams are played is a different one from that of the waking perceptual life. To be sure, we do not understand this, do not know what we are to think of it, but the impression of strangeness which most dreams make upon us does really bear this out. The comparison of the dream activity with the effects of a hand untrained in music also fails at this point. The piano, at least, will surely answer with the same tones, even if not with melodies, as soon as by accident one brushes its keys. Let us keep this second common element of all dreams carefully in mind, even though it be not understood.

Are there still further traits in common? I find none, and see only differences everywhere, differences indeed in the apparent length as well as the definiteness of the activities, participation of effects, durability, etc. All this really is not what we might expect of a compulsion-driven, irresistible, convulsive defense against a stimulus. As concerns the dimensions of dreams, there are very short ones which contain only one picture or a few, one thought—yes, even one word only—, others which are uncommonly rich in content, seem to dramatize whole novels and to last very long. There are dreams which are as plain as an experience itself, so plain that we do not recognize them as dreams for a long time after waking; others which are indescribably weak, shadowy and vague; indeed in one and the same dream, the overemphasized and the scarcely comprehensible, indefinite parts may alternate with each other. Dreams may be quite meaningful or at least coherent, yes, even witty, fantastically beautiful. Others, again, are confused, as if feeble-minded, absurd, often actually mad. There are dreams which leave us quite cold, others in which all the effects come to expression—pain deep enough for tears, fear strong enough to waken us, astonishment, delight, etc. Dreams are generally quickly forgotten upon waking, or they may hold over a day to such an extent as to be faintly and incompletely remembered in the evening. Others, for example, the dreams of childhood, are so well preserved that they stay in the memory thirty years later, like fresh experiences. Dreams, like individuals, may appear a single time, and never again, or they may repeat themselves unchanged in the same person, or with small variations. In short, this nightly psychic activity can avail itself of an enormous repertoire, can indeed compass everything which the psychic accomplishes by day, but yet the two are not the same.

One might try to give an account of this many-sidedness of the dream by assuming that it corresponds to different intermediate stages between sleeping and waking, different degrees of incomplete sleep. Yes, but in that case as the psyche nears the waking state, the conviction that it is a dream ought to increase along with the value, content and distinctiveness of the dream product, and it would not happen that immediately beside a distinct and sensible dream fragment a senseless and indistinct one would occur, to be followed again by a goodly piece of work. Surely the psyche could not change its degree of somnolence so quickly. This explanation thus avails us nothing; at any rate, it cannot be accepted offhand.

Let us, for the present, give up the idea of finding the meaning of the dream and try instead to clear a path to a better understanding of the dream by means of the elements common to all dreams. From the relation of dreams to the sleeping condition, we concluded that the dream is the reaction to a sleep-disturbing stimulus. As we have heard, this is the only point upon which exact experimental psychology can come to our assistance; it gives us the information that stimuli applied during sleep appear in the dream. There have been many such investigations carried out, including that of the above mentioned

Mourly Vold. Indeed, each of us must at some time have been
in a position to confirm this conclusion by means of occasional
personal observations. I shall choose certain older experiments
for presentation. Maury had such experiments made on his own
person. He was allowed to smell cologne while dreaming. He
dreamed that he was in Cairo in the shop of Johann Marina
Farina, and therewith were linked further extravagant adventures. Or, he was slightly pinched in the nape of the neck;
he dreamed of having a mustard plaster applied, and of a doctor
who had treated him in childhood. Or, a drop of water was
poured on his forehead. He was then in Italy, perspired pro-
fusely, and drank the white wine of Orvieto.

What strikes us about these experimentally induced dreams
we may perhaps be able to comprehend still more clearly in
another series of stimulated dreams. Three dreams have been
recounted by a witty observer, Hildebrand, all of them reactions
to the sound of the alarm clock:

"I go walking one spring morning and saunter through the
green fields to a neighboring village. There I see the inhabitants
in gala attire, their hymn books under their arms, going church-
ward in great numbers. To be sure, this is Sunday, and the
early morning service will soon begin. I decide to attend, but
since I am somewhat overheated, decide to cool off in the cemetery
surrounding the church. While I am there reading several inscriptions, I hear the bell ringer ascend the tower, and now see
the little village church bell which is to give the signal for the
beginning of the service. The bell hangs a good bit longer, then
it begins to swing, and suddenly its strokes sound clear and
penetrating, so clear and penetrating that they make an end of
—my sleep. The bell-strokes, however, come from my alarm
clock.

"A second combination. It is a clear winter day. The streets
are piled high with snow. I agree to go on a sleighing party,
but must wait a long time before the announcement comes that
the sleigh is at the door. Then follow the preparations for
getting in—the fur coat is put on, the footwarmer dragged
forth—and finally I am seated in my place. But the departure
is still delayed until the reins give the waiting horses the tangible
signal. Now they pull; the vigorously shaken bells begin their
familiar Janizary music so powerfully that instantly the spider

web of the dream is torn. Again it is nothing but the shrill tone of the alarm clock.

"And still a third example. I see a kitchen maid walking along the corridor to the dining room with some dozens of plates piled high. The pillar of porcelain in her arms seems to me in danger of losing its balance. 'Take care!' I warn her. 'The whole load will fall to the ground.' Naturally, the inevitable retort follows: one is used to that, etc., and I still continue to follow the passing figure with apprehensive glances. Sure enough, at the threshold she stumbles—the brittle dishes fall and rattle and crash over the floor in a thousand pieces. But—the endless racket is not, as I soon notice, a real rattling, but really a ringing and with this ringing, as the awakened subject now realizes, the alarm has performed its duty."

These dreams are very pretty, quite meaningful, not at all incoherent, as dreams usually are. We will not object to them on that score. That which is common to them all is that the situation terminates each time in a noise, which one recognizes upon waking up as the sound of the alarm. Thus we see here how a dream originates, but also discover something else. The dream does not recognize the alarm—indeed the alarm does not appear in the dream—the dream replaces the alarm sound with another, it interprets the stimulus which interrupts the sleep, but interprets it each time in a different way. Why? There is no answer to this question, it seems to be something arbitrary. But to understand the dream means to be able to say why it has chosen just this sound and no other for the interpretation of the alarm-clock stimulus. In quite analogous fashion, we must raise the objection to the Maury experiment that we see well enough that the stimulus appears in the dream, but that we do not discover why it appears in just this form; and that the form taken by the dream does not seem to follow from the nature of the sleep-disturbing stimulus. Moreover, in the Maury experiments a mass of other dream material links itself to the direct stimulus product; as, for example, the extravagant adventures in the cologne dream, for which one can give no account.

Now I shall ask you to consider the fact that the waking dreams offer by far the best chances for determining the influence of external sleep-disturbing stimuli. In most of the other cases it will be more difficult. One does not wake up in all

dreams, and in the morning, when one remembers the dream of
the night, how can one discover the disturbing stimulus which
was perhaps in operation at night? I did succeed once in subsequently establishing such a sound stimulus, though naturally
only in consequence of special circumstances. I woke up one
morning in a place in the Tyrolese Mountains, with the certainty
that I had dreamt the Pope had died. I could not explain the
dream, but then my wife asked me: "Did you hear the terrible
bell ringing that broke out early this morning from all the
churches and chapels?" No, I had heard nothing, my sleep is
a sound one, but thanks to this information I understood my
dream. How often may such stimuli incite the sleeper to dream
without his knowing of them afterward? Perhaps often, perhaps
infrequently; when the stimulus can no longer be traced, one
cannot be convinced of its existence. Even without this fact we
have given up evaluating the sleep disturbing stimuli, since we
know that they can explain only a little bit of the dream, and
not the whole dream reaction.

But we need not give up this whole theory for that reason.
In fact, it can be extended. It is clearly immaterial through
what cause the sleep was disturbed and the psyche incited to
dream. If the sensory stimulus is not always externally induced,
it may be instead a stimulus proceeding from the internal organs,
a so-called somatic stimulus. This conjecture is obvious, and it
corresponds to the most popular conception of the origin of
dreams. Dreams come from the stomach, one often hears it
said. Unfortunately it may be assumed here again that the cases
are frequent in which the somatic stimulus which operated during the night can no longer be traced after waking, and has
thus become unverifiable. But let us not overlook the fact that
many recognized experiences testify to the derivation of dreams
from the somatic stimulus. It is in general indubitable that the
condition of the internal organs can influence the dream. The
relation of many a dream content to a distention of the bladder
or to an excited condition of the genital organs, is so clear that
it cannot be mistaken. From these transparent cases one can
proceed to others in which, from the content of the dream, at
least a justifiable conjecture may be made that such somatic
stimuli have been operative, inasmuch as there is something in
this content which may be conceived as elaboration, representa-

tion, interpretation of the stimuli. The dream investigator Schirmer (1861) insisted with particular emphasis on the derivation of the dream from organic stimuli, and cited several splendid examples in proof. For example, in a dream he sees "two rows of beautiful boys with blonde hair and delicate complexions stand opposite each other in preparation for a fight, fall upon each other, seize each other, take up the old position again, and repeat the whole performance; here the interpretation of these rows of boys as teeth is plausible in itself, and it seems to become convincing when after this scene the dreamer "pulls a long tooth out of his jaws." The interpretation of "long, narrow, winding corridors" as intestinal stimuli, seems sound and confirms Schirmer's assertion that the dream above all seeks to represent the stimulus-producing organ by means of objects resembling it.

Thus we must be prepared to admit that the internal stimuli may play the same role in the dream as the external. Unfortunately, their evaluation is subject to the same difficulties as those we have already encountered. In a large number of cases the interpretation of the stimuli as somatic remains uncertain and undemonstrable. Not all dreams, but only a certain portion of them, arouse the suspicion that an internal organic stimulus was concerned in their causation. And finally, the internal stimuli will be as little able as the external sensory stimuli to explain any more of the dream than pertains to the direct reaction to the stimuli. The origin, therefore, of the rest of the dream remains obscure.

Let us, however, notice a peculiarity of dream life which becomes apparent in the study of these effects of stimuli. The dream does not simply reproduce the stimulus, but it elaborates it, it plays upon it, places it in a sequence of relationships, replaces it with something else. That is a side of dream activity which must interest us because it may lead us closer to the nature of the dream. If one does something under stimulation, then this stimulation need not exhaust the act. Shakespeare's *Macbeth*, for example, is a drama created on the occasion of the coronation of the King who for the first time wore upon his head the crown symbolizing the union of three countries. But does this historical occasion cover the content of the drama, does it explain its greatness and its riddle? Perhaps the external and

internal stimuli, acting upon the sleeper, are only the incitors of
the dream, of whose nature nothing is betrayed to us from our
knowledge of that fact

The other element common to dreams, their psychic peculiarity, is on the one hand hard to comprehend, and on the other
hand offers no point for further investigation. In dreams we
perceive a thing for the most part in visual forms. Can the
stimuli furnish a solution for this fact? Is it actually the stimulus which we experience? Why, then, is the experience visual
when optic stimulation incited the dream only in the rarest
cases? Or can it be proved, when we dream speeches, that
during sleep a conversation or sounds resembling it reached our
ear? This possibility I venture decisively to reject.

If, from the common elements of dreams, we get no further,
then let us see what we can do with their differences. Dreams
are often senseless, blurred, absurd; but there are some that are
meaningful, sober, sensible. Let us see if the latter, the sensible
dreams, can give some information concerning the senseless ones.
I will give you the most recent sensible dream which was told
me, the dream of a young man: "I was promenading in Kärtner
Street, met Mr. X. there, whom I accompanied for a bit, and
then I went to a restaurant. Two ladies and a gentleman seated
themselves at my table. I was annoyed at this at first, and
would not look at them. Then I did look, and found that they
were quite pretty." The dreamer adds that the evening before
the dream he had really been in Kärtner Street, which is his
usual route, and that he had met Mr. X. there. The other portion of the dream is no direct reminiscence, but bears a certain
resemblance to a previous experience. Or another meaningful
dream, that of a lady. "Her husband asks, 'Doesn't the piano
need tuning?' She: 'It is not worth while; it has to be newly
lined.'" This dream reproduces without much alteration a
conversation which took place the day before between herself and
her husband. What can we learn from these two sober dreams?
Nothing but that you find them to be reproductions of daily life
or ideas connected therewith. This would at least be something
if it could be stated of all dreams. There is no question, however,
that this applies to only a minority of dreams. In most dreams
there is no sign of any connection with the previous day, and
no light is thereby cast on the senseless and absurd dream. We

know only that we have struck a new problem. We wish to know not only what it is that the dream says, but when, as in our examples, the dream speaks plainly, we also wish to know why and wherefore this recent experience is repeated in the dream.

I believe you are as tired as I am of continuing attempts like these. We see, after all, that the greatest interest in a problem is inadequate if one does not know a path which will lead to a solution. Up to this point we have not found this path. Experimental psychology gave us nothing but a few very valuable pieces of information concerning the meaning of stimuli as dream incitors. We need expect nothing from philosophy except that lately it has taken haughtily to pointing out to us the intellectual inferiority of our object. Let us not apply to the occult sciences for help. History and popular tradition tell us that the dream is meaningful and significant; it sees into the future. Yet that is hard to accept and surely not demonstrable. Thus our first efforts end in entire helplessness.

Unexpectedly we get a hint from a quarter toward which we have not yet looked. Colloquial usage—which after all is not an accidental thing but the remnant of ancient knowledge, though it should not be made use of without caution—our speech, that is to say, recognizes something which curiously enough it calls "day dreaming." Day dreams are phantasies. They are very common phenomena, again observable in the normal as well as in the sick, and access to their study is open to everyone in his own person. The most conspicuous feature about these phantastic productions is that they have received the name "day dreams," for they share neither of the two common elements of dreams. Their name contradicts the relation to the sleeping condition, and as regards the second common element, one does not experience or hallucinate anything, one only imagines it. One knows that it is a phantasy, that one is not seeing but thinking the thing. These day dreams appear in the period before puberty, often as early as the last years of childhood, continue into the years of maturity, are then either given up or retained through life. The content of these phantasies is dominated by very transparent motives. They are scenes and events in which the egoistic, ambitious and power-seeking desires of the individual find satisfaction. With young men the ambition phantasies generally prevail; in women, the erotic, since they have banked their ambition on success in love. But often enough the erotic desire appears in the background with men too; all the heroic deeds and incidents are after all meant only to win the admiration and favor of women. Otherwise these day dreams are very manifold and undergo changing fates. They are either, each in turn, abandoned after a short time and replaced by a new one, or they are retained, spun out into long stories, and adapted to changes in daily circumstances. They move with the time, so to speak, and receive from it a "time mark" which testifies to the influence of the new situation. They are the raw material of poetic production, for out of his day dreams the poet, with certain transformations, disguises and omissions, makes the situations which he puts into his novels, romances and dramas. The hero of the day dreams, however, is always the individual himself, either directly or by means of a transparent identification with another.

Perhaps day dreams bear this name because of the similarity of their relation to reality, in order to indicate that their content is as little to be taken for real as that of dreams. Perhaps, however, this identity of names does nevertheless rest on a characteristic of the dream which is still unknown to us, perhaps even one of those characteristics which we are seeking. It is possible, on the other hand, that we are wrong in trying to read a meaning into this similarity of designation. Yet that can only be cleared up later.

SIXTH LECTURE

THE DREAM

Hypothesis and Technique of Interpretation

WE must find a new path, a new method, in order to proceed with the investigation of the dream. I shall now make an obvious suggestion. Let us assume as a hypothesis for everything which follows, that *the dream is not a somatic but a psychic phenomenon*. You appreciate the significance of that statement, but what justification have we for making it? None; but that alone need not deter us from making it. The matter stands thus: If the dream is a somatic phenomenon, it does not concern us. It can be of interest to us only on the supposition that it is a *psychic* phenomenon. Let us therefore work upon that assumption in order to see what comes of it. The result of our labor will determine whether we are to hold to this assumption and whether we may, in fact, consider it in turn a result. What is it that we really wish to achieve, to what end are we working? It is what one usually seeks to attain in the sciences, an understanding of phenomena, the creation of relationships between them, and ultimately, if possible, the extension of our control over them.

Let us then proceed with the work on the assumption that the dream is a psychic phenomenon. This makes it an achievement and expression of the dreamer, but one that tells us nothing, one that we do not understand. What do you do when I make a statement you do not understand? You ask for an explanation, do you not? Why may we not do the same thing here, *ask the dreamer to give us the meaning of his dream?*

If you will remember, we were in this same situation once before. It was when we were investigating errors, a case of a slip of the tongue. Someone said: *"Da sind dinge zum vorschwein gekommen,"* whereupon we asked—no, luckily, not

78

we, but others, persons in no way associated with psychoanalysis
—these persons asked him what he meant by this unintelligible
talk. He immediately answered that he had intended to say
"Das waren schweinereien," but that he had suppressed this
intention, in favor of the other, more gentle *"Da sind dinge
zum vorschein gekommen."*[1] I explained to you at the time that
this inquiry was typical of every psychoanalytical investigation,
and now you understand that psychoanalysis follows the technique, as far as possible, of having the subjects themselves discover the solutions of their riddles. The dreamer himself, then,
is to tell us the meaning of his dream.

It is common knowledge, however, that this is not such an
easy matter with dreams. In the case of slips, our method
worked in a number of cases, but we encountered some where
the subject did not wish to say anything—in fact, indignantly
rejected the answer that we suggested. Instances of the first
method are entirely lacking in the case of dreams; the dreamer
always says he knows nothing. He cannot deny our interpretation, for we have none. Shall we then give up the attempt?
Since he knows nothing and we know nothing and a third person
surely knows nothing, it looks as though there were no possibility
of discovering anything. If you wish, discontinue the investigation. But if you are of another mind, you can accompany me
on the way. For I assure you, it is very possible, in fact,
probable, that the dreamer does know what his dream means,
but does *not know that he knows, and therefore believes he does
not know.*

You will point out to me that I am again making an assumption, the second in this short discourse, and that I am greatly
reducing the credibility of my claim. On the assumption that
the dream is a psychic phenomenon, on the further assumption
that there are unconscious things in man which he knows without
knowing that he knows, etc.—we need only realize clearly the
intrinsic improbability of each of these two assumptions, and
we shall calmly turn our attention from the conclusions to be
derived from such premises.

Yet, ladies and gentlemen, I have not invited you here to
delude you or to conceal anything from you. I did, indeed,
announce a *General Introduction to Psychoanalysis,* but I

---

[1] The reader will recall the example: " things were re-filled."

did not intend the title to convey that I was an oracle, who would show you a finished product with all the difficulties carefully concealed, all the gaps filled in and all the doubts glossed over, so that you might peacefully believe you had learned something new. No, precisely because you are beginners, I wanted to show you our science as it is, with all its hills and pitfalls, demands and considerations. For I know that it is the same in all sciences, and must be so in their beginnings particularly. I know, too, that teaching as a rule endeavors to hide these difficulties and these incompletely developed phases from the student. But that will not do in psychoanalysis. I have, as a matter of fact, made two assumptions, one within the other, and he who finds the whole too troublesome and too uncertain or is accustomed to greater security or more elegant derivations, need go no further with us. What I mean is, he should leave psychological problems entirely alone, for it must be apprehended that he will not find the sure and safe way he is prepared to go, traversable. Then, too, it is superfluous for a science that has something to offer to plead for auditors and adherents. Its results must create its atmosphere, and it must then bide its time until these have attracted attention to themselves.

I would warn those of you, however, who care to continue, that my two assumptions are not of equal worth. The first, that the dream is a psychic phenomenon, is the assumption we wish to prove by the results of our work. The other has already been proved in another field, and I take the liberty only of transferring it from that field to our problem.

Where, in what field of observation shall we seek the proof that there is in man a knowledge of which he is not conscious, as we here wish to assume in the case of the dreamer? That would be a remarkable, a surprising fact, one which would change our understanding of the psychic life, and which would have no need to hide itself. To name it would be to destroy it, and yet it pretends to be something real, a contradiction in terms. Nor does it hide itself. It is no result of the fact itself that we are ignorant of its existence and have not troubled sufficiently about it. That is just as little our fault as the fact that all these psychological problems are condemned by persons who have kept away from all observations and experiments which are decisive in this respect.

The proof appeared in the field of hypnotic phenomena. When, in the year 1889, I was a witness to the extraordinarily enlightening demonstrations of Siebault and Bernheim in Nancy, I witnessed also the following experiment: If one placed a man in the somnambulistic state, allowed him to have all manner of hallucinatory experience, and then woke him up, it appeared in the first instance that he knew nothing about what had happened during his hypnotic sleep. Bernheim then directly invited him to relate what had happened to him during the hypnosis. He maintained he was unable to recall anything. But Bernheim insisted, he persisted, he assured him he did know, that he must recall, and, incredible though it may seem, the man wavered, began to rack his memory, recalled in a shadowy way first one of the suggested experiences, then another; the recollection became more and more complete and finally was brought forth without a gap. The fact that he had this knowledge finally, and that he had had no experiences from any other source in the meantime, permits the conclusion that he knew of these recollections in the beginning. They were merely inaccessible, he did not know that he knew them; he believed he did not know them. This is exactly what we suspect in the dreamer.

I trust you are taken by surprise by the establishment of this fact, and that you will ask me why I did not refer to this proof before in the case of the slips, where we credited the man who made a mistake in speech with intentions he knew nothing about and which he denied. "If a person believes he knows nothing concerning experiences, the memory of which, however, he retains," you might say, "it is no longer so improbable that there are also other psychic experiences within him of whose existence he is ignorant. This argument would have impressed us and advanced us in the understanding of errors." To be sure, I might then have referred to this but I reserved it for another place, where it was more necessary. Errors have in a measure explained themselves, have, in part, furnished us with the warning that we must assume the existence of psychic processes of which we know nothing, for the sake of the connection of the phenomena. In dreams we are compelled to look to other sources for explanations; and besides, I count on the fact that you will permit the inference I draw from hypnotism more readily in this instance. The condition in which we r

mistakes must seem to you to be the normal one. It has no
similarity to the hypnotic. On the other hand, there is a clear
relationship between the hypnotic state and sleep, which is the
essential condition of dreams. Hypnotism is known as artificial
sleep; we say to the person whom we hypnotize, "Sleep," and
the suggestions which we throw out are comparable to the dreams
of natural sleep. The psychical conditions are in both cases
really analogous. In natural sleep we withdraw our attention
from the entire outside world; in the hypnotic, on the other
hand, from the whole world with the exception of the one person
who has hypnotized us, with whom we remain in touch. Furthermore, the so-called nurse's sleep in which the nurse remains in
touch with the child, and can be waked only by him, is a normal
counterpart of hypnotism. The transference of one of the conditions of hypnotism to natural sleep does not appear to be such
a daring proceeding. The inferential assumption that there is
also present in the case of the dreamer a knowledge of his dream,
a knowledge which is so inaccessible that he does not believe it
himself, does not seem to be made out of whole cloth. Let us
note that at this point there appears a third approach to the
study of the dream; from the sleep-disturbing stimuli, from the
day-dreams, and now in addition, from the suggested dreams of
the hypnotic state.

Now we return, perhaps with increased faith, to our problem.
Apparently it is very probable that the dreamer knows of his
dream; the question is, how to make it possible for him to
discover this knowledge, and to impart it to us? We do not
demand that he give us the meaning of his dream at once, but
he will be able to discover its origin, the thought and sphere of
interest from which it springs. In the case of the errors, you
will remember, the man was asked how he happened to use the
wrong word, "*vorschwein*," and his next idea gave us the explanation. Our dream technique is very simple, an imitation of
this example. We again ask how the subject happened to have
the dream, and his next statement is again to be taken as an
explanation. We disregard the distinction whether the dreamer
believes or does not believe he knows, and treat both cases in the
same way.

This technique is very simple indeed, but I am afraid it will
arouse your sharpest opposition. You will say, "a new assump-

tion. The third! And the most improbable of all! If I ask the dreamer what he considers the explanation of his dream to be, his very next association is to be the desired explanation! But it may be he thinks of nothing at all, or his next thought may be anything at all. We cannot understand upon what we can base such anticipation. This, really, is putting too much faith in a situation where a slightly more critical attitude would be more suitable. Furthermore, a dream is not an isolated error, but consists of many elements. To which idea should we pin our faith?"

You are right in all the non-essentials. A dream must indeed be distinguished from a word slip, even in the number of its elements. The technique is compelled to consider this very carefully. Let me suggest that we separate the dream into its elements, and carry on the investigation of each element separately; then the analogy to the word-slip is again set up. You are also correct when you say that in answer to the separate dream elements no association may occur to the dreamer. There are cases in which we accept this answer, and later you will hear what those cases are. They are, oddly enough, cases in which we ourselves may have certain associations. But in general we shall contradict the dreamer when he maintains he has no associations. We shall insist that he must have some association and—we shall be justified. He will bring forth some association, any one, it makes no difference to us. He will be especially facile with certain information which might be designated as historical. He will say, "that is something that happened yesterday" (as in the two "prosaic" dreams with which we are acquainted); or, "that reminds me of something that happened recently," and in this manner we shall notice that the act of associating the dreams with recent impressions is much more frequent than we had at first supposed. Finally, the dreamer will remember occurrences more remote from the dream, and ultimately even events in the far past.

But in the essential matters you are mistaken. If you believe that we assume arbitrarily that the dreamer's next association will disclose just what we are seeking, or must lead to it, that on the contrary the association is just as likely to be entirely inconsequential, and without any connection with what we are seeking, and that it is an example of my unbounded optimism to expect anything else, then you are greatly mistaken. I have already taken the liberty of pointing out that in each one of you there is a deep-rooted belief in psychic freedom and volition, a belief which is absolutely unscientific, and which must capitulate before the claims of a determinism that controls even the psychic life. I beg of you to accept it as a fact that only this one association will occur to the person questioned. But I do not put one belief in opposition to another. It can be proved that the association, which the subject produces, is not voluntary, is not indeterminable, not unconnected with what we seek. Indeed, I discovered long ago—without, however, laying too much stress on the discovery—that even experimental psychology has brought forth this evidence.

I ask you to give your particular attention to the significance of this subject. If I invite a person to tell me what occurs to him in relation to some certain element of his dream I am asking him to abandon himself to free association, *controlled by a given premise*. This demands a special delimitation of the attention, quite different from cogitation, in fact, exclusive of cogitation. Many persons put themselves into such a state easily; others show an extraordinarily high degree of clumsiness. There is a higher level of free association again, where I omit this original premise and designate only the manner of the association, e.g., rule that the subject freely give a proper name or a number. Such an association would be more voluntary, more indeterminable, than the one called forth by our technique. But it can be shown that it is strongly determined each time by an important inner mental set which, at the moment at which it is active, is unknown to us, just as unknown as the disturbing tendencies in the case of errors and the provocative tendencies in the case of accidental occurrences.

I, and many others after me, have again and again instigated such investigations for names and numbers which occur to the subject without any restraint, and have published some results. The method is the following: Proceeding from the disclosed names, we awaken continuous associations which then are no longer entirely free, but rather are limited as are the associations to the dream elements, and this is true until the impulse is exhausted. By that time, however, the motivation and significance of the free name associations is explained. The investigations always yield the same results, the information often covers a wealth of material and necessitates lengthy elaboration. The associations to freely appearing numbers are perhaps the most significant. They follow one another so quickly and approach a hidden goal with such inconceivable certainty, that it is really startling. I want to give you an example of such a name analysis, one that, happily, involves very little material.

In the course of my treatment of a young man, I referred to this subject and mentioned the fact that despite the apparent volition it is impossible to have a name occur which does not appear to be limited by the immediate conditions, the peculiarities of the subject, and the momentary situation. He was doubtful, and I proposed that he make such an attempt immediately. I know he has especially numerous relations of every sort with women and girls, and so am of the opinion that he will have an unusually wide choice if he happens to think of a woman's name. He agrees. To my astonishment, and perhaps even more to his, no avalanche of women's names descends upon my head, but he is silent for a time, and then admits that a single name has occurred to him—and no other: *Albino*. How extraordinary, but what associations have you with this name? How many albinoes do you know? Strangely enough, he knew no albinoes, and there were no further associations with the name. One might conclude the analysis had proved a failure; but no—it was already complete; no further association was necessary. The man himself had unusually light coloring. In our talks during the cure I had frequently called him an albino in fun. We were at the time occupied in determining the feminine characteristics of his nature. He himself was the Albino, who at that moment was to him the most interesting feminine person.

In like manner, melodies, which come for no reason, show themselves conditioned by and associated with a train of thought which has a right to occupy one, yet of whose activity one is unconscious. It is easily demonstrable that the attraction to the melody is associated with the text, or its origin. But I must take the precaution not to include in this assertion really musical people, with whom, as it happens, I have had no experience. In their cases the musical meaning of the melody may have occasioned its occurrence. More often the first reason holds. I

know of a young man who for a time was actually haunted by
the really charming melody of the song of Paris, from *The
Beautiful Helen,* until the analysis brought to his attention the
fact that at that time his interest was divided between an Ida
and a Helen.

If then the entirely unrestrained associations are conditioned
in such a manner and are arranged in a distinct order, we are
justified in concluding that associations with a single condition,
that of an original premise, or starting point, may be conditioned
to no less degree. The investigation does in fact show that aside
from the conditioning which we have established by the premise,
a second farther dependence is recognizable upon powerful
affective thoughts, upon cycles of interest and complexes of whose
influence we are ignorant, therefore unconscious at the time.

Associations of this character have been the subject matter
of very enlightening experimental investigations, which have
played a noteworthy role in the history of psychoanalysis. The
Wundt school proposed the so-called association-experiment,
wherein the subject is given the task of answering in the quickest
possible time, with any desired reaction, to a given stimulus-
word. It is then possible to study the interval of time that
elapses between the stimulus and the reaction, the nature of the
answer given as reaction, the possible mistake in a subsequent
repetition of the same attempt, and similar matters. The Zurich
School under the leadership of Bleuler and Jung, gave the
explanation of the reactions following the association-experiment, by asking the subject to explain a given reaction by means
of further associations, in the cases where there was anything
extraordinary in the reaction. It then became apparent that
these extraordinary reactions were most sharply determined
by the complexes of the subject. In this matter Bleuler and
Jung built the first bridge from experimental psychology to
psychoanalysis.

Thus instructed, you will be able to say, "We recognize now
that free associations are predetermined, not voluntary, as we
had believed. We admit this also as regards the associations
connected with the elements of the dream, but that is not what
we are concerned with. You maintain that the associations to the
dream element are determined by the unknown psychic background of this very element. We do not think that this is a

proven fact. We expect, to be sure, that the association to the dream element will clearly show itself through one of the complexes of the dreamer, but what good is that to us! That does not lead us to understand the dream, but rather, as in the case of the association-experiment, to a knowledge of the so-called complexes. What have these to do with the dream!"

You are right, but you overlook one point, in fact, the very point because of which I did not choose the association-experiment as the starting point for this exposition. In this experiment the one determinate of the reaction, viz., the stimulus word, is voluntarily chosen. The reaction is then an intermediary between this stimulus word and the recently aroused complex of the subject. In the dream the stimulus word is replaced by something that itself has its origin in the psychic life of the dreamer, in sources unknown to him, hence very likely itself a product of the complex. It is not an altogether fantastic hypothesis, then, that the more remote associations, even those that are connected with the dream element, are determined by no other complex than the one which determines the dream element itself, and will lead to the disclosure of the complex.

Let me show you by another case that the situation is really as we expect it to be. Forgetting proper names is really a splendid example for the case of dream analysis; only here there is present in one person what in the dream interpretation is divided between two persons. Though I have forgotten a name temporarily I still retain the certainty that I know the name; that certainty which we could acquire for the dreamer only by way of the Bernheim experiment. The forgotten name, however, is not accessible. Cogitation, no matter how strenuous, does not help. Experience soon tells me that. But I am able each time to find one or more substitute names for the forgotten name. If such a substitute name occurs to me spontaneously then the correspondence between this situation and that of the dream analysis first becomes evident. Nor is the dream element the real thing, but only a substitute for something else, for what particular thing I do not know, but am to discover by means of the dream anaylsis. The difference lies only in this, that in forgetting a name I recognize the substitute automatically as unsuitable, while in the dream element we must acquire this interpretation with great labor. When a name is forgotten too, there is a way to go from the substitute to the unknown reality, to arrive at the forgotten name. If I centre my attention on the substitute name and allow further associations to accumulate, I arrive in a more or less roundabout way at the forgotten name, and discover that the spontaneous substitute names, together with those called up by me, have a certain connection with the forgotten name, were conditioned by it.

I want to show you an analysis of this type. One day I noticed that I could not recall the name of the little country in the Riviera of which Monte Carlo is the capital. It is very annoying, but it is true. I steep myself in all my knowledge about this country, think of Prince Albert, of the house of Lusignan, of his marriages, his preference for deep-sea study, and anything else I can think of, but to no avail. So I give up the thinking, and in place of the lost name allow substitute names to suggest themselves. They come quickly—Monte Carlo itself, then Piedmont, Albania, Montevideo, Colico. Albania is the first to attract my attention, it is replaced by Montenegro, probably because of the contrast between black and white. Then I see that four of these substitutes contain the same syllable *mon*. I suddenly have the forgotten word, and cry aloud, *"Monaco."* The substitutes really originated in the forgotten word, the four first from the first syllable, the last brings back the sequence of syllables and the entire final syllable. In addition, I am also able easily to discover what it was that took the name from my memory for a time. Monaco is also the Italian name of Munich; this latter town exerted the inhibiting influence.

The example is pretty enough, but too simple. In other cases we must add to the first substitute names a long line of associations, and then the analogy to the dream interpretation becomes clearer. I have also had such experiences. Once when a stranger invited me to drink Italian wine with him, it so happened in the hostelry that he forgot the name of the wine he had intended to order just because he had retained a most pleasant memory of it. Out of a profusion of dissimilar substitute associations which came to him in the place of the forgotten name, I was able to conclude that the memory of some one named Hedwig had deprived him of the name of the wine, and he actually confirmed not only that he had first tasted this wine in the company of a Hedwig, but he also, as a result of this declaration, recollected the name again. He was at the time happily married, and this Hedwig belonged to former times, not now recalled with pleasure.

What is possible in forgetting names must work also in dream interpretation, viz., making the withheld actuality accessible by means of substitutions and through connecting associations. As exemplified by name-forgetting, we may conclude that in the case of the associations to the dream element they will be determined as well by the dream element as by its unknown essential. Accordingly, we have advanced a few steps in the formulation of our dream technique.

Manifest Dream Content and Latent Dream Thought

WE have not studied the problem of errors in vain. Thanks to our efforts in this field, under the conditions known to you, we have evolved two different things, a conception of the elements of the dream and a technique for dream interpretation. The conception of the dream element goes to show something unreal, a substitute for something else, unknown to the dreamer, similar to the tendency of errors, a substitute for something the dreamer knows but cannot approach. We hope to transfer the same conception to the whole dream, which consists of just such elements. Our method consists of calling up, by means of free associations, other substitute formations in addition to these elements, from which we divine what is hidden.

Let me ask you to permit a slight change in our nomenclature which will greatly increase the flexibility of our vocabulary. Instead of hidden, unapproachable, unreal, let us give a truer description and say inaccessible or unknown to the consciousness of the dreamer. By this we mean only what the connection with the lost word or with the interfering intention of the error can suggest to you, namely, unconscious *for the time being*. Naturally in contrast to this we may term *conscious* the elements of the dream itself and the substitute formations just gained by association. As yet there is absolutely no theoretical construction implied in this nomenclature. The use of the word unconscious as a suitable and intelligible descriptive epithet is above criticism.

If we transfer our conception from a single element to the entire dream, we find that the dream as a whole is a distorted substitute for something else, something unconscious. To discover this unconscious thing is the task of dream interpretation. From this, three important rules, which we must observe in the work of dream interpretation, are straightway derived:

1. What the dream seems to say, whether it be sensible or absurd, clear or confused is not our concern, since it can under no condition be that unconscious content we are seeking. Later we shall have to observe an obvious limitation of this rule. 2. The awakening of substitute formations for each element shall be the sole object of our work. We shall not reflect on these, test their suitability or trouble how far they lead away from the element of the dream. 3. We shall wait until the hidden unconscious we are seeking appears of itself, as the missing word *Monaco* in the experiment which we have described.

Now we can understand, too, how unimportant it is how much, how little, above all, how accurately or how indifferently the dream is remembered. For the dream which is remembered is not the real one, but a distorted substitute, which is to help us approach the real dream by awakening other substitute formations and by making the unconscious in the dream conscious. Therefore if our recollection of the dream was faulty, it has simply brought about a further distortion of this substitute, a distortion which cannot, however, be unmotivated.

One can interpret one's own dreams as well as those of others. One learns even more from these, for the process yields more proof. If we try this, we observe that something impedes the work. Haphazard ideas arise, but we do not let them have their way. Tendencies to test and to choose make themselves felt. As an idea occurs, we say to ourselves "No, that does not fit, that does not belong here"; of a second "that is too senseless"; of a third, "this is entirely beside the point"; and one can easily observe how the ideas are stifled and suppressed by these objections, even before they have become entirely clear. On the one hand, therefore, too much importance is attached to the dream elements themselves; on the other, the result of free association is vitiated by the process of selection. If you are not interpreting the dream alone, if you allow someone else to interpret it for you, you will soon discover another motive which induces you to make this forbidden choice. At times you say to yourself, "No, this idea is too unpleasant, I either will not or cannot divulge this."

Clearly these objections are a menace to the success of our work. We must guard against them, in our own case by the firm resolve not to give way to them; and in the interpretation of the dreams of others by making the hard and fast rule for them, never to omit any idea from their account, even if one of the following four objections should arise: that is, if it should seem too unimportant, absurd, too irrelevant or too embarrassing to relate. The dreamer promises to obey this rule, but it is annoying to see how poorly he keeps his promise at times. At first we account for this by supposing that in spite of the authoritative assurance which has been given to the dreamer, he is not impressed with the importance of free association, and plan perhaps to win his theoretic approval by giving him papers to read or by sending him to lectures which are to make him a disciple of our views concerning free association. But we are deterred from such blunders by the observation that, in one's own case, where convictions may certainly be trusted, the same critical objections arise against certain ideas, and can only be suppressed subsequently, upon second thought, as it were.

Instead of becoming vexed at the disobedience of the dreamer, these experiences can be turned to account in teaching something new, something which is the more important the less we are prepared for it. We understand that the task of interpreting dreams is carried on against a certain *resistance* which manifests itself by these critical objections. This resistance is independent of the theoretical conviction of the dreamer. Even more is apparent. We discover that such a critical objection is never justified. On the contrary, those ideas which we are so anxious to suppress, prove *without exception* to be the most important, the most decisive, in the search for the unconscious. It is even a mark of distinction if an idea is accompanied by such an objection.

This resistance is something entirely new, a phenomenon which we have found as a result of our hypotheses although it was not originally included in them. We are not too pleasantly surprised by this new factor in our problem. We suspect that it will not make our work any easier. It might even tempt us to abandon our entire work in connection with the dream. Such an unimportant thing as the dream and in addition such difficulties instead of a smooth technique! But from another point of view, these same difficulties may prove fascinating, and suggest that the work is worth the trouble. Whenever we try to penetrate to the hidden unconscious, starting out from the substitute which the dream element represents, we meet with resistance. Hence, we are justified in supposing that something of weight must be hidden behind the substitute. What other reason could there be for the difficulties which are maintained for purposes of concealment? If a child does not want to open his clenched fist, he is certainly hiding something he ought not to have.

Just as soon as we bring the dynamic representation of resistance into our consideration of the case, we must realize that this factor is something quantitatively variable. There may be greater or lesser resistances and we are prepared to see these differences in the course of our work. We may perhaps connect this with another experience found in the work of dream interpretation. For sometimes only one or two ideas serve to carry us from the dream element to its unconscious aspect, while at other times long chains of associations and the suppression of many critical objections are necessary. We shall note that these variations are connected with the variable force of resistance. This observation is probably correct. If resistance is slight, then the substitute is not far removed from the unconscious, but strong resistance carries with it a great distortion of the unconscious and in addition a long journey back to it.

Perhaps the time has come to take a dream and try out our method to see if our faith in it shall be confirmed. But which dream shall we choose? You cannot imagine how hard it is for me to decide, and at this point I cannot explain the source of the difficulty. Of course, there must be dreams which, as a whole, have suffered slight distortion, and it would be best to start with one of these. But which dreams are the least distorted? Those which are sensible and not confused, of which I have already given you two examples? This would be a gross misunderstanding. Testing shows that these dreams have suffered by distortion to an exceptionally high degree. But if I take the first best dream, regardless of certain necessary conditions, you would probably be very much disappointed. Perhaps we should have to note such an abundance of ideas in connection with single elements of dream that it would be absolutely impossible to review the work in perspective. If we write the dream out and confront it with the written account of all the ideas which arise in connection with it, these may easily amount to a reiteration of the text of the dream. It would therefore seem most practical to choose for analysis several short dreams of which each one can at least reveal or confirm something. This is what we shall decide upon, provided experience should not point out where we shall really find slightly distorted dreams.

But I know of another way to simplify matters, one which, moreover, lies in our path. Instead of attempting the interpretation of entire dreams, we shall limit ourselves to single dream elements and by observing a series of examples we shall see how these are explained by the application of our method.

1. A lady relates that as a child she often dreamt *"that God had a pointed paper hat on his head."* How do you expect to understand that without the help of the dreamer? Why, it sounds quite absurd. It is no longer absurd when the lady testifies that as a child she was frequently made to wear such a hat at the table, because she could not help stealing glances at the plates of her brothers and sisters to see if one of them had gotten more than she. The hat was therefore supposed to act as a sort of blinder. This explanation was moreover historic, and given without the least difficulty. The meaning of this fragment and of the whole brief dream, is clear with the help of a further idea of the dreamer. "Since I had heard that God was all-knowing and all-seeing," she said, "the dream can only mean that I know everything and see everything just as God does, even when they try to prevent me." This example is perhaps too simple.

2. A sceptical patient has a longer dream, in which certain people happen to tell her about my book concerning laughter and praise it highly. Then something is mentioned about a certain *" 'canal,' perhaps another book in which 'canal' occurs, or something else with the word 'canal'* . . . *she doesn't know* . . . *it is all confused."*

Now you will be inclined to think that the element "canal" will evade interpretation because it is so vague. You are right as to the supposed difficulty, but it is not difficult because it is vague, but rather it is vague for a different reason, the same reason which also makes the interpretation difficult. The dreamer can think of nothing concerning the word canal, I naturally can think of nothing. A little while later, as a matter of fact on the next day, she tells me that something occurred to her that *may perhaps* be related to it, a joke that she has heard. On a ship between Dover and Calais a well-known author is conversing with an Englishman, who quoted the following proverb in a certain connection: *"Du sublime au ridicule, il n'y a qu'un pas."*[1] The author answers, *"Oui, le pas de Calais,"*[2] with which he wishes to say that he finds France sublime and England ridiculous. But the *"Pas de Calais"* is really a canal, namely, the English Channel. Do I think that this idea has anything to do with the dream? Certainly, I believe that it really gives the solution to the puzzling dream fragments. Or can you doubt that this joke was already present in the dream, as the unconscious factor of the element, "canal." Can you take it for granted that it was subsequently added to it? The idea testifies to the scepticism which is concealed behind her obtrusive admiration, and the resistance is probably the common reason for both phenomena, for the fact that the idea came so hesitatingly and that the decisive element of the dream turned out to be so vague. Kindly observe at this point the relation of the dream element to its unconscious factor. It is like a small part of the unconscious, like an allusion to it; through its isolation it became quite unintelligible.

3. A patient dreams, in the course of a longer dream: *"Around a table of peculiar shape several members of his family are sitting, etc."* In connection with this table, it occurs to him that he saw such a piece of furniture during a visit to a certain family. Then his thoughts continue: In this family a peculiar relation had existed between father and son, and soon he adds to this that as a matter of fact the same relation exists between himself and his father. The table is therefore taken up into the dream to designate this parallel.

This dreamer had for a long time been familiar with the claims of dream interpretation. Otherwise he might have taken exception to the fact that so trivial a detail as the shape of a table

---

[1] From the sublime to the ridiculous is but a narrow passage.
[2] Yes, the passage from Calais.

should be taken as the basis of the investigation. As a matter
of fact we judge nothing in the dream as accidental or indifferent, and we expect to reach our conclusion by the explanation of just such trivial and unmotivated details. Perhaps you
will be surprised that the dream work should arouse the thought
"we are in exactly the same position as they are," just by the
choice of the table. But even this becomes clear when you
learn that the name of the family in question is *Tischler*. By
permitting his own family to sit at such a table, he intends to
express that they too are *Tischler*. Please note how, in
relating such a dream interpretation, one must of necessity
become indiscreet. Here you have arrived at one of the difficulties in the choice of examples that I indicated before. I
could easily have substituted another example for this one, but
would probably have avoided this indiscretion at the cost of
committing another one in its place.

The time has come to introduce two new terms, which we
could have used long ago. We shall call that which the dream
relates, the manifest content of the dream; that which is hidden,
which we can only reach by the analysis of ideas we shall call
latent dream thoughts. We may now consider the connection
between the manifest dream content and the latent dream
thoughts as they are revealed in these examples. Many different
connections can exist. In examples 1 and 2 the manifest content is also a constituent part of the latent thought, but only
a very small part of it. A small piece of a great composite
psychic structure in the unconscious dream thought has penetrated into the manifest dream, like a fragment of it, or in
other cases, like an allusion to it, like a catchword or an
abbreviation in the telegraphic code. The interpretation must
mould this fragment, or indication, into a whole, as was done
most successfully in example 2. One sort of distortion of which
the dream mechanism consists is therefore substitution by means
of a fragment or an allusion. In the third, moreover, we must
recognize another relation which we shall see more clearly and
distinctly expressed in the following examples:

4. The dreamer *"pulls a certain woman of his acquaintance
from behind a bed."* He finds the meaning of this dream element himself by his first association. It means: This woman
"has a pull" with him.[1]

[1] "Vorzug." "Vom Bett hervorziehen."

5. Another man dreams that *"his brother is in a closet."*
The first association substitutes *clothes-press* for closet, and the
second gives the meaning: his brother is *close-pressed* for
money.[3]

6. The dreamer *"climbs a mountain from the top of which
he has an extraordinarily distant view."* This sounds quite
sensible; perhaps there is nothing about it that needs interpretation, and it is simply necessary to find out which reminiscence
this dream touches upon and why it was recalled. But you are
mistaken; it is evident that this dream requires interpretation
as well as any other which is confused. For no previous
mountain climbing of his own occurs to the dreamer, but he
remembers that an acquaintance of his is publishing a *"Rund-
schau,"* which deals with our relation to the furthermost parts
of the earth. The latent dream thought is therefore in this case
an identification of the dreamer with the *"Rundschauer."*

Here you find a new type of connection between the manifest
content and the latent dream element. The former is not so much
a distortion of the latter as a representation of it, a plastic
concrete perversion that is based on the sound of the word.
However, it is for this very reason again a distortion, for we
have long ago forgotten from which concrete picture the word
has arisen, and therefore do not recognize it by the image which
is substituted for it. If you consider that the manifest dream
consists most often of visual images, and less frequently of
thoughts and words, you can imagine that a very particular
significance in dream formation is attached to this sort of relation. You can also see that in this manner it becomes possible
to create substitute formations for a great number of abstract
thoughts in the manifest dream, substitutions that serve the purpose of further concealment all the same. This is the technique
of our picture puzzle. What the origin is of the semblance of
wit which accompanies such representations is a particular question which we need not touch upon at this time.

A fourth type of relation between the manifest and the latent
dream cannot be dealt with until its cue in the technique has
been given. Even then I shall not have given you a complete
enumeration, but it will be sufficient for our purpose.

Have you the courage to venture upon the interpretation of

[3] *"Schränkt sich ein."*

an entire dream? Let us see if we are well enough equipped
for this undertaking. Of course, I shall not choose one of the
most obscure, but one nevertheless that shows in clear outline
the general characteristics of a dream.

A young woman who has been married for many years dreams:
*"She is sitting in the theatre with her husband; one side of the
orchestra is entirely unoccupied. Her husband tells her that
Elise L. and her bridegroom had also wished to come, but had
only been able to procure poor seats, three for 1 Fl., 50 Kr.
and those of course they could not take. She thinks this is no
misfortune for them."*

The first thing that the dreamer has to testify is that the
occasion for the dream is touched upon in its manifest content.
Her husband had really told her that Elise L., an acquaintance
of about her age, had become engaged. The dream is the reaction to this news. We already know that in the case of many
dreams it is easy to trace such a cause to the preceding day, and
that the dreamer often gives these deductions without any
difficulty. The dreamer also places at our disposal further
information for other parts of the manifest dream content.
Whence the detail that one side of the orchestra is unoccupied?
It is an allusion to an actual occurrence of the previous week.
She had made up her mind to go to a certain performance and
had procured tickets in advance, so much in advance that she
had been forced to pay a preference tax.[2] When she arrived at
the theatre, she saw how needless had been her anxiety, for *one
side of the orchestra was almost empty*. She could have bought
the tickets on the day of the performance itself. Her husband
would not stop teasing her about her excessive haste. Whence
the 1 Fl. 50 Kr.? From a very different connection that
has nothing to do with the former, but which also alludes to an
occurrence of the previous day. Her sister-in-law had received
150 florins as a present from her husband, and knew no better,
the poor goose, than to hasten to the jeweler and spend the
money on a piece of jewelry. Whence the number 3? She can
think of nothing in connection with this unless one stresses the
association that the bride, Elise L., is only three months younger

[2] In Germany tickets may be bought before the day of the performance
only upon additional payment, over and above the regular cost of the
ticket. This is called " Vorverkaufsgebühr."

than she herself, who has been married for almost ten years. And the absurdity of buying three tickets for two people? She says nothing of this, and indeed denies all further associations or information.

But she has given us so much material in her few associations, that it becomes possible to derive the latent dream thought from it. It must strike us that in her remarks concerning the dream, time elements which constitute a common element in the various parts of this material appear at several points. She attended to the tickets *too soon*, took them *too hastily*, so that she had to pay more than usual for them; her sister-in-law likewise *hastened* to carry her money to the jeweler's to buy a piece of jewelry, just as if she might *miss* it. Let us add to the expressions *"too early," "precipitately,"* which are emphasized so strongly, the occasion for the dream, namely, that her friend only three months younger than herself had even now gotten a good husband, and the criticism expressed in the condemnation of her sister-in-law, that it was *foolish* to hurry so. Then the following construction of the latent dream thought, for which the manifest dream is a badly distorted substitute, comes to us almost spontaneously:

"How *foolish* it was of me to hurry so in marrying! Elise's example shows me that I could have gotten a husband later too." (The precipitateness is represented by her own behavior in buying the tickets, and that of her sister-in-law in purchasing jewelry. Going to the theatre was substituted for getting married. This appears to have been the main thought; and perhaps we may continue, though with less certainty, because the analysis in these parts is not supported by statements of the dreamer.) "And I would have gotten 100 times as much for my money." (150 Fl. is 100 times as much as 1 Fl. 50 Kr.). If we might substitute the dowry for the money, then it would mean that one buys a husband with a dowry; the jewelry as well as the poor seats would represent the husband. It would be even more desirable if the fragment "3 seats" had something to do with a husband. But our understanding does not penetrate so far. We have only guessed that the dream expresses her *disparagement* of her own husband, and her regret at having *married so early*.

It is my opinion that we are more surprised and confused than satisfied by the result of this first dream interpretation. We are swamped by more impressions than we can master. We see that the teachings of dream interpretation are not easily exhausted. Let us hasten to select those points that we recognize as giving us new, sound insight.

In the first place, it is remarkable that in the latent thought the main emphasis falls on the element of haste; in the manifest dream there is absolutely no mention of this to be found. Without the analysis we should not have had any idea that this element was of any importance at all. So it seems possible that just the main thing, the central point of the unconscious thoughts, may be absent in the manifest dream. Because of this, the original impression in the dream must of necessity be entirely changed. Secondly: In the dream there is a senseless combination, 3 for 1 Fl. 50 Kr.; in the dream thought we divine the sentence, "It was senseless (to marry so early)." Can one deny that this thought, "It was senseless," was represented in the manifest dream by the introduction of an absurd element? Thirdly: Comparison will show that the relation between the manifest and latent elements is not simple, certainly not of such a sort that a manifest element is always substituted for the latent. There must rather be a quantitative relationship between the two groups, according to which a manifest element may represent several latent ones, or a latent element represented by several manifest elements.

Much that is surprising might also be said of the sense of the dream and the dreamer's reaction to it. She acknowledges the interpretation but wonders at it. She did not know that she disparaged her husband so, and she did not know why she should disparage him to such a degree. There is still much that is incomprehensible. I really believe that we are not yet fully equipped for dream interpretation, and that we must first receive further instruction and preparation.

EIGHTH LECTURE

Dreams of Childhood

WE think we have advanced too rapidly. Let us go back a little. Before our last attempt to overcome the difficulties of dream distortion through our technique, we had decided that it would be best to avoid them by limiting ourselves only to those dreams in which distortion is either entirely absent or of trifling importance, if there are such. But here again we digress from the history of the evolution of our knowledge, for as a matter of fact we become aware of dreams entirely free of distortion only after the consistent application of our method of interpretation and after complete analysis of the distorted dream.

The dreams we are looking for are found in children. They are short, clear, coherent, easy to understand, unambiguous, and yet unquestionable dreams. But do not think that all children's dreams are like this. Dream distortion makes its appearance very early in childhood, and dreams of children from five to eight years of age have been recorded that showed all the characteristics of later dreams. But if you will limit yourselves to the age beginning with conscious psychic activity, up to the fourth or fifth year, you will discover a series of dreams that are of a so-called infantile character. In a later period of childhood you will be able to find some dreams of this nature occasionally. Even among adults, dreams that closely resemble the typically infantile ones occur under certain conditions.

From these children's dreams we gain information concerning the nature of dreams with great ease and certainty, and we hope it will prove decisive and of universal application.

1. For the understanding of these dreams we need no analysis, no technical methods. We need not question the child that is giving an account of his dream. But one must add to this a

101

story taken from the life of the child. An experience of the previous day will always explain the dream to us. The dream is a sleep-reaction of psychic life upon these experiences of the day.

We shall now consider a few examples so that we may base our further deductions upon them.

a). A boy of 22 months is to present a basket of cherries as a birthday gift. He plainly does so very unwillingly, although they promise him that he will get some of them himself. The next morning he relates as his dream, *"Hermann eat all cherries."*

b). A little girl of three and a quarter years makes her first trip across a lake. At the landing she does not want to leave the boat and cries bitterly. The time of the trip seems to her to have passed entirely too rapidly. The next morning she says, *"Last night I rode on the lake."* We may add the supplementary fact that this trip lasted longer.

c). A boy of five and a quarter years is taken on an excursion into the Escherntal near Hallstatt. He had heard that Hallstatt lay at the foot of the Dachstein, and had shown great interest in this mountain. From his home in Aussee there was a beautiful view of the Dachstein, and with a telescope one could discern the Simonyhütte upon it. The child had tried again and again to see it through the telescope, with what result no one knew. He started on the excursion in a joyously expectant mood. Whenever a new mountain came in sight the boy asked, "Is that the Dachstein?" The oftener this question was answered in the negative, the more moody he became; later he became entirely silent and would not take part in a small climb to a waterfall. They thought he was overtired, but the next morning, he said quite happily, *"Last night I dreamed that we were in the Simonyhütte."* It was with this expectation, therefore, that he had taken part in the excursion. The only detail he gave was one he had heard before, "you had to climb steps for six hours."

These three dreams will suffice for all the information we desire.

2. We see that children's dreams are not meaningless; they are *intelligible, significant, psychic acts.* You will recall what I represented to you as the medical opinion concerning the dream, the simile of untrained fingers wandering aimlessly over the

keys of the piano. You cannot fail to see how decidedly these dreams of childhood are opposed to this conception. But it would be strange indeed if the child brought forth complete psychic products in sleep, while the adult in the same condition contents himself with spasmodic reactions. Indeed, we have every reason to attribute the more normal and deeper sleep to the child.

3. Dream distortion is lacking in these dreams, therefore they need no interpretation. The manifest and latent dreams are merged. *Dream distortion is therefore not inherent in the dream.* I may assume that this relieves you of a great burden. But upon closer consideration we shall have to admit of a tiny bit of distortion, a certain differentiation between manifest dream content and latent dream thought, even in these dreams.

4. The child's dream is a reaction to an experience of the day, which has left behind it a regret, a longing or an unfulfilled desire. *The dream brings about the direct unconcealed fulfillment of this wish.* Now recall our discussions concerning the importance of the role of external or internal bodily stimuli as disturbers of sleep, or as dream producers. We learned definite facts about this, but could only explain a very small number of dreams in this way. In these children's dreams nothing points to the influence of such somatic stimuli; we cannot be mistaken, for the dreams are entirely intelligible and easy to survey. But we need not give up the theory of physical causation entirely on this account. We can only ask why at the outset we forgot that besides the physical stimuli there are also psychic sleep-disturbing stimuli. For we know that it is these stimuli that commonly cause the disturbed sleep of adults by preventing them from producing the ideal condition of sleep, the withdrawal of interest from the world. The dreamer does not wish to interrupt his life, but would rather continue his work with the things that occupy him, and for this reason he does not sleep. The unfulfilled wish, to which he reacts by means of the dream, is the psychic sleep-disturbing stimulus for the child.

5. From this point we easily arrive at an explanation of the function of the dream. The dream, as a reaction to the psychic stimulus, must have the value of a release of this stimulus which results in its elimination and in the continuation of sleep. We do not know how this release is made possible by the dream, bu⁺

we note that *the dream is not a disturber of sleep*, as calumny says, *but a guardian of sleep, whose duty it is to quell disturbances.* It is true, we think we would have slept better if we had not dreamt, but here we are wrong; as a matter of fact, we would not have slept at all without the help of the dream. That we have slept so soundly is due to the dream alone. It could not help disturbing us slightly, just as the night watchman often cannot avoid making a little noise while he drives away the rioters who would awaken us with their noise.

6. One main characteristic of the dream is that a wish is its source, and that the content of the dream is the gratification of this wish. Another equally constant feature is that the dream does not merely express a thought, but also represents the fulfillment of this wish in the form of a hallucinatory experience. *"I should like to travel on the lake,"* says the wish that excites the dream; the dream itself has as its content *"I travel on the lake."* One distinction between the latent and manifest dream, a distortion of the latent dream thought, therefore remains even in the case of these simple children's dreams, namely, *the translation of the thought into experience.* In the interpretation of the dream it is of utmost importance that this change be traced back. If this should prove to be an extremely common characteristic of the dream, then the above mentioned dream fragment, *"I see my brother in a closet"* could not be translated, *"My brother is close-pressed,"* but rather, "I wish that my brother were close-pressed, *my brother should be close-pressed."* Of the two universal characteristics of the dream we have cited, the second plainly has greater prospects of unconditional acknowledgment than the first. Only extensive investigation can ascertain that the cause of the dream must always be a wish, and cannot also be an anxiety, a plan or a reproach; but this does not alter the other characteristic, that the dream does not simply reproduce the stimulus but by experiencing it anew, as it were, removes, expells and settles it.

7. In connection with these characteristics of the dream we can again resume the comparison between the dream and the error. In the case of the latter we distinguish an interfering tendency and one interfered with, and the error is the compromise between the two. The dream fits into the same scheme. The tendency

interfered with, in this case, can be no other than that of sleep. For the interfering tendency we substitute the psychic stimulus, the wish which strives for its fulfillment, let us say, for thus far we are not familiar with any other sleep-disturbing psychic stimulus. In this instance also the dream is the result of compromise. We sleep, and yet we experience the removal of a wish; we gratify the wish, but at the same time continue to sleep. Both are partly carried out and partly given up.

8. You will remember that we once hoped to gain access to the understanding of the dream problem by the fact that certain very transparent phantasy formations are called *day dreams*. Now these day dreams are actual wish fulfillments, fulfillments of ambitious or erotic wishes with which we are familiar; but they are conscious, and though vividly imagined, they are never hallucinatory experiences. In this instance, therefore, the less firmly established of the two main characteristics of the dream holds, while the other proves itself entirely dependent upon the condition of sleep and impossible to the waking state. In colloquial usage, therefore, there is a presentment of the fact that the fulfillment of a wish is a main characteristic of the dream. Furthermore, if the experience in the dream is a transformed representation only made possible by the condition of sleep—in other words, a sort of nocturnal day dream—then we can readily understand that the occurrence of phantasy formations can release the nocturnal stimulus and bring satisfaction. For day dreaming is an activity closely bound up in gratification and is, indeed, pursued only for this reason.

Not only this but other colloquial usages also express the same feeling. Well-known proverbs say, "The pig dreams of acorns, the goose of maize," or ask, "Of what does the hen dream? Of millet." So the proverb descends even lower than we do, from the child to the animal, and maintains that the content of a dream is the satisfaction of a need. Many turns of speech seem to point to the same thing—"dreamlike beauty," "I should never have dreamed of that," "in my wildest dreams I hadn't imagined that." This is open partisanship on the part of colloquial usage. For there are also dreams of fear and dreams of embarrassing or indifferent content, but they have not been drawn into common usage. It is true that common usage recognizes "bad" dreams, but still the dream plainly connotates to it only the beautiful wish fulfillment. There is indeed no proverb that tells us that the pig or the goose dreams of being slaughtered.

Of course it is unbelievable that the wish-fulfillment characteristic has not been noted by writers on the dream. Indeed, this was very often the case, but none of them thought of acknowledging this characteristic as universal and of making it the basis of an explanation of the dream. We can easily imagine what may have deterred them and shall discuss it subsequently.

See what an abundance of information we have gained, with almost no effort, from the consideration of children's dreams—the function of the dream as a guardian of sleep; its origin from two rival tendencies, of which the one, the longing for sleep, remains constant, while the other tries to satisfy a psychic stimulus; the proof that the dream is a significant psychic act; its two main characteristics: wish fulfillment and hallucinatory experience. And we were almost able to forget that we are engaged in psychoanalysis. Aside from its connection with errors our work has no specific connotation. Any psychologist, who is entirely ignorant of the claims of psychoanalysis, could have given this explanation of children's dreams. Why has no one done so?

If there were only infantile dreams, our problem would be solved, our task accomplished, and that without questioning the dreamer, or approaching the unconscious, and without taking free association into consideration. The continuation of our task plainly lies in this direction. We have already repeatedly had the experience that characteristics that at first seemed universally true, have subsequently held good only for a certain kind and for a certain number of dreams. It is therefore for us to decide whether the common characteristics which we have gathered from children's dreams can be applied universally, whether they also hold for those dreams that are not transparent, whose manifest content shows no connection with wishes left over from the previous day. We think that these dreams have undergone considerable distortion and for this reason are not to be judged superficially. We also suspect that for the explanation of this distortion we shall need the psychoanalytic method which we could dispense with in the understanding of children's dreams.

There is at any rate a class of dreams that are undistorted, and, just like children's dreams, are easily recognizable as wish fulfillments. It is those that are called up throughout life by the imperative needs of the body—hunger, thirst, sexual desire— hence wish fulfillments in reaction to internal physical stimuli. For this reason, I have noted the dream of a young girl, that consisted of a menu following her name (Anna F......, strawberry, huckleberry, egg-dish, pap), as a reaction to an enforced day of fasting on account of a spoiled stomach, which was directly traceable to the eating of the fruits twice mentioned in the dream. At the same time, the grandmother, whose age added to that of her grandchild would make a full seventy, had to go without food for a day on account of kidney-trouble, and dreamed the same night that she had been invited out and that the finest tid-bits had been set before her. Observations with prisoners who are allowed to go hungry, or with people who suffer privations on travels or expeditions, show that under these conditions the dreams regularly deal with the satisfaction of these needs. Otto Nordenskjold, in his book *Antarctic* (1904), testifies to the same thing concerning his crew, who were ice-bound with him during the winter (Vol. 1, page 336). "Very significant in determining the trend of our inmost thoughts were our dreams, which were never more vivid and numerous than just at this time. Even those of our comrades who ordinarily dreamed but seldom, now had long stories to tell, when in the morning we exchanged our latest experiences in that realm of phantasy. All of them dealt with that outside world that now was so far away from us, but often they fitted into our present condition. Food and drink were most often the pivots about which our dreams revolved. One of us, who excelled in going to great dinners in his sleep, was most happy whenever he could tell us in the morning that he attended a dinner of three courses; another one dreamed of tobacco, whole mountains of tobacco; still another dreamed of a ship that came along on the open sea, under full sail. One other dream deserves mention: The postman comes with the mail and gives a long explanation of why it is so late; he had delivered it to the wrong address and only after great trouble on his part had succeeded in getting it back. Of course occupies himself with even more impossible things in sleep, but in nearly all the dreams that I myself dreamed or heard tell of, the lack of phantasy was quite striking. It would surely be of great psychological interest if all these dreams were recorded. It is easy to understand how we longed for sleep, since it could offer us everything for which each one of us felt the most burning desire." I quote further from Du Prel. "Mungo Park, who during a trip in Africa was almost exhausted, dreamed without interruption of the fertile valleys and fields of his home. Trenck, tortured by hunger in the redoubt at Magdeburg, likewise saw himself surrounded by wonderful meals, and George Back, who took part in Franklin's first expedition, dreamed regularly and consistently of luxurious meals when, as a result of terrible privations, he was nearly dead of hunger."

A man who feels great thirst at night after enjoying highly seasoned food for supper, often dreams that he is drinking. It is of course impossible to satisfy a rather strong desire for food or drink by means of the dream; from such a dream one awakes thirsty and must now drink real water. The effect of the dream is in this case practically trifling, but it is none the less clear that it was called up for the purpose of maintaining the sleep in spite of the urgent impulse to awake and to act. Dreams of satisfaction often overcome needs of a lesser intensity.

In a like manner, under the influence of sexual stimuli, the dream brings about satisfaction that shows noteworthy peculiarities. As a result of the characteristic of the sexual urge which makes it somewhat less dependent upon its object than hunger and thirst, satisfaction in a dream of pollution may be an actual one, and as a result of difficulties to be mentioned later in connection with the object, it happens especially often that the actual satisfaction is connected with confused or distorted dream content. This peculiarity of the dream of pollution, as O. Rank has observed, makes it a fruitful subject to pursue in the study of dream distortion. Moreover, all dreams of desire of adults usually contain something besides satsfaction, something that has its origin in the sources of the purely psychic stimuli, and which requires interpretation to render it intelligible.

Moreover we shall not maintain that the wish-fulfillment dreams of the infantile kind occur in adults only as reactions to the known imperative desires. We also know of short clear dreams of this sort under the influence of dominating situations that arise from unquestionably psychic sources. As, for example, in dreams of impatience, whenever a person has made preparations for a journey, for a theatrical performance, for a lecture or for a visit, and now dreams of the anticipated fulfillment of his expectations, and so arrives at his goal the night before the actual experience, in the theatre or in conversation with his host. Or the well-named dreams of comfort, when a person who likes to prolong his sleep, dreams that he is already up, is washing himself, or is already in school, while as a matter of fact he continues sleeping, hence would rather get up in a dream than in reality. The desire for sleep which we have recognized as a regular part of the dream structure becomes intense in these dreams and appears in them as the actual shaping force of the dream. The wish for sleep properly takes its place beside other great physical desires.

At this point I refer you to a picture by Schwind, from the Schack Gallery in Munich, so that you may see how rightly the artist has conceived the origin of a dream from a dominating situation. It is the *Dream of a Prisoner,*[1] which can have no other subject than his release. It is a very neat stroke that the release should be effected through the window, for the ray of light that awakens the prisoner comes through the same window. The gnomes standing one above the other probably represent the successive positions which he himself had to take in climbing to the height of the window, and I do not think I am mistaken or that I attribute too much preconcerted design to the artist, by noting that the uppermost of the gnomes, who is filing the grating (and so does what the prisoner would like to do) has the features of the prisoner.

In all other dreams except those of children and those of the infantile type, distortion, as we have said, blocks our way. At the outset we cannot ascertain whether they are also wish fulfillments, as we suspect; from their manifest content we cannot determine from what psychic stimulus they derive their origin, and we cannot prove that they also are occupied in doing away with the stimulus and in satisfying it. They must probably be interpreted, that is, translated; their distortion must be annulled; their manifest content replaced by their latent thought before we can judge whether what we have found in childr dreams may claim a universal application for all dreams.

NINTH LECTURE

THE DREAM

The Dream Censor

WE have learned to know the origin, nature and function of the dream from the study of children's dreams. *Dreams are the removal of sleep-disturbing psychic stimuli by way of hallucinated satisfaction.* Of adults' dreams, to be sure, we could explain only one group, what we characterized as dreams of an infantile type. As to the others we know nothing as yet, nor do we understand them. For the present, however, we have obtained a result whose significance we do not wish to under-estimate. Every time a dream is completely comprehensible to us, it proves to be an hallucinated wish-fulfillment. This coincidence cannot be accidental, nor is it an unimportant matter.

We conclude, on the basis of various considerations and by analogy to the conception of mistakes, that another type of dream is a distorted substitute for an unknown content and that it must first be led back to that content. Our next task is the investigation and the understanding of this dream distortion.

Dream distortion is the thing which makes the dream seem strange and incomprehensible to us. We want to know several things about it; firstly, whence it comes, its dynamics; secondly, what it does; and finally, how it does it. We can say at this point that dream distortion is the product of the dream work, that is, of the mental functioning of which the dream itself is the conscious symptom. Let us describe the dream work and trace it back to the forces which work upon it.

And now I shall ask you to listen to the following dream. It was recorded by a lady of our profession, and according to her, originated with a highly cultivated and respected lady of advanced age. No analysis of this dream was made. Our informant remarks that to a psychoanalyst it needs no interpretation. The dreamer herself did not interpret it, but she judged and condemned it as if she understood its interpretation. For she said concerning it: "That a woman of fifty should dream such abominable, stupid stuff—a woman who has no other thought, day and night, than to care for her child!"

And now follows the dreams of the *"services of love."* "She goes into Military Hospital No. 1, and says to the sentry at the gate, that she must speak to the chief physician . . . (she mentions a name which is not familiar to her), as she wants to offer her service to the hospital. She stresses the word 'service,' so love services. Since she is an old lady he lets her pass after some hesitation. But instead of reaching the chief physician, she finds herself in a large somber room in which there are many officers and army doctors sitting and standing around a long table. She turns with her proposal to a staff doctor who, after a few words, soon understands her. The words of her speech in the dream are, 'I and numerous other women and girls of Vienna are ready for the soldiers, troops, and officers, without distinction . . .' Here in the dream follows a murmuring. That the idea is, however, correctly understood by those present she sees from the semi-embarrassed, somewhat malicious expressions of the officers. The lady then continues, 'I know that our decision sounds strange, but we are in bitter earnest. The soldier in the field is not asked either whether or not he wants to die.' A moment of painful silence follows. The staff doctor puts his arm around her waist and says, 'Madame, let us assume that it really came to that . . .' (murmurs). She withdraws from his arm with the thought, 'They are all alike!' and answers, 'My heavens, I am an old woman, and perhaps will never be confronted with that situation; one consideration, moreover, must be kept in mind: the consideration of age, which prevents an older woman from . . . with a very young boy . . . (murmurs) . . . that would be horrible.' The staff doctor, 'I understand perfectly.' Several officers, among them one who had paid court to her in her youth, laugh loudly, and the lady asks to be conducted to the chief physician, whom she knows, so that everything may be arranged. At this she realizes with great dismay that she does not know his name. The staff officer, nevertheless, very politely and respectfully shows her the wrto the second story, up a very narrow winding iron stairway which leads to the upper story directly from the door of the room. In going up she hears an officer say, 'That is a tremendous decision irrespective of whether a woman is young or old; all honor to her!'

"With the feeling that she is merely doing her duty, she goes up an endless staircase."

This dream she repeats twice in the course of a few weeks, with—as the lady notices—quite insignificant and very senseless changes.

This dream corresponds in its structure to a day dream. It has few gaps, and many of its individual points might have been elucidated as to content through inquiry, which, as you know, was omitted. The conspicuous and interesting point for us, however, is that the dream shows several gaps, gaps not of recollection, but of original content. In three places the content is apparently obliterated, the speeches in which these gaps occur are interrupted by murmurs. Since we have performed no analysis, we have, strictly speaking, also no right to make any assertion about the meaning of the dream. Yet there are intimations given from which something may be concluded. For example, the phrase "services of love," and above all the bits of speech which immediately precede the murmurs, demand a completion which can have but one meaning. If we interpolate these, then the phantasy yields as its content the idea that the dreamer is ready, as an act of patriotic duty, to offer her person for the satisfaction of the erotic desires of the army, officers as well as troops. That certainly is exceedingly shocking, it is an impudent libidinous phantasy, but—it does not occur in the dream at all. Just at the point where consistency would demand this confession, there is a vague murmur in the manifest dream, something is lost or suppressed.

I hope you will recognize the inevitability of the conclusion that it is the shocking character of these places in the dream that was the motive for their suppression. Yet where do you find a parallel for this state of affairs? In these times you need not seek far. Take up any political paper and you will find that the text is obliterated here and there, and that in its place shimmers the white of the paper. You know that that is the work of the newspaper censor. In these blank spaces something

was printed which was not to the liking of the censorship authorities, and for that reason it was crossed out. You think that it
is a pity, that it probably was the most interesting part, it was
"the best part."

In other places the censorship did not touch the completed
sentence. The author foresaw what parts might be expected to
meet with the objection of the censor, and for that reason he
softened them by way of prevention, modified them slightly, or
contented himself with innuendo and allusion to what really
wanted to flow from his pen. Thus the sheet, it is true, has no
blank spaces, but from certain circumlocutions and obscurities of
expression you will be able to guess that thoughts of the censorship were the restraining motive.

Now let us keep to this parallel. We say that the omitted
dream speeches, which were disguised by a murmuring, were
also sacrifices to a censorship. We actually speak of a *dream
censor* to which we may ascribe a contributing part in the dream
distortion. Wherever there are gaps in the manifest dream, it
is the fault of the dream censor. Indeed, we should go further,
and recognize each time as a manifestation of the dream censor,
those places at which a dream element is especially faint, indefinitely and doubtfully recalled among other, more clearly delineated portions But it is only rarely that this censorship
manifests itself so undisguisedly, so naively one may say, as in
the example of the dream of the "services of love." Far more
frequently the censorship manifests itself according to the
second type, through the production of weakenings, innuendoes,
allusions instead of direct truthfulness.

For a third type of dream censorship I know of no parallel
in the practice of newspaper censorship, yet it is just this type
that I can demonstrate by the only dream example which we
have so far analyzed. You will remember the dream of the
"three bad theatre tickets for one florin and a half." In the
latent thoughts of this dream, the element *"precipitately, too
soon,"* stood in the foreground. It means: "It was foolish to
marry so *early*, it was also foolish to buy theatre tickets so *early;*
it was ridiculous of the sister-in-law to spend her money so
hastily, merely to buy an ornament." Nothing of this central
element of the dream thought was evident in the manifest dream.
In the latter, going to the theatre and getting the tickets were

shoved into the foreground. Through this displacement of the emphasis, this regrouping of the elements of the content, the manifest dream becomes so dissimilar from the latent dream thoughts that no one would suspect the latter behind the former. This displacement of emphasis is a favorite device of the dream distortion and gives the dream that strangeness which makes the dreamer himself unwilling to recognize it as his own production.

Omission, modification, regrouping of the material, these, then, are the effects of the dream censor and the devices of dream distortion. The dream censorship itself is the author, or one of the authors, of the dream distortion whose investigation now occupies us. Modification and rearrangement we are already accustomed to summarize as *displacement*.

After these remarks concerning the effects of the dream censor, let us now turn to their dynamics. I hope you will not consider the expression too anthropomorphically, and picture the dream censor as a severe little manikin who lives in a little brain chamber and there performs his duties; nor should you attempt to localize him too much, to think of a brain center from which his censoring influence emanates, and which would cease with the injury or extirpation of this center. For the present, the term "dream censor" is no more than a very convenient phrase for a dynamic relationship. This phrase does not prevent us from asking by what tendencies such influence is exerted and upon which tendencies it works; nor will we be surprised to discover that we have already encountered the dream censor before, perhaps without recognizing him.

For such was actually the case. You will remember that we had a surprising experience when we began to apply our technique of free association. We then began to feel that some sort of a resistance blocked our efforts to proceed from the dream element to the unconscious element for which the former is the substitute. This resistance, we said, may be of varying strength, enormous at one time, quite negligible at another. In the latter case we need cross only a few intermediate steps in our work of interpretation. But when the resistance is strong, then we must go through a long chain of associations, are taken far afield and must overcome all the difficulties which present themselves as critical objections to the association technique. What we met with in the work of interpretation, we must now bring into the dream work as the dream censor. The resistance to interpretation is nothing but the objectivation of the dream censor. The latter proves to us that the force of the censor has not spent itself in causing the dream distortion, has not since been extinguished, but that this censorship continues as a permanent institution with the purpose of preserving the distortion. Moreover, just as in the interpretation the strength of the resistance varied with each element, so also the distortion produced by the censor in the same dream is of varying magnitude for each element. If one compares the manifest with the latent dream one sees that certain isolated latent elements have been practically eliminated, others more or less modified, and still others left unchanged, indeed, have perhaps been taken over into the dream content with additional strength.

But we wanted to discover what purposes the censorship serves and against which tendencies it acts. This question, which is fundamental to the understanding of the dream, indeed perhaps to human life, is easily answered if we look over a series of those dreams which have been analyzed. The tendencies which the censorship exercises are those which are recognized by the waking judgment of the dreamer, those with which he feels himself in harmony. You may rest assured that when you reject an accurate interpretation of a dream of your own, you do so with the same motives with which the dream censor works, the motives with which it produces the dream distortion and makes the interpretation necessary. Recall the dream of our fifty-year old lady. Without having interpreted it, she considers her dream abominable, would have been still more outraged if our informant had told her anything about the indubitable meaning; and it is just on account of this condemnation that the shocking spots in her dream were replaced by a murmur.

The tendencies, however, against which the dream censor directs itself, must now be described from the standpoint of this instance. One can say only that these tendencies are of an objectionable nature throughout, that they are shocking from an ethical, aesthetic and social point of view, that they are things one does not dare even to think, or thinks of only with abhorrence. These censored wishes which have attained to a distorted expression in the dream, are above all expressions of a boundless, reckless egoism. And indeed, the personal ego occurs in every dream to play the major part in each of them, even if it can successfully disguise itself in the manifest content. This *sacro egoismo* of the dream is surely not unconnected with the sleep-inducing cessation of psychic activity which consists, it should be noted, in the withdrawal of interest from the entire external world.

The ego which has been freed of all ethical restraints feels itself in accord with all the demands of the sexual striving, with those demands which have long since been condemned by our aesthetic rearing, demands of such a character that they resist all our moral demands for restraint. The pleasure-striving—the libido, as we term it—chooses its objects without inhibitions, and indeed, prefers those that are forbidden. It chooses not only the wife of another, but, above all, those incestuous objects declared sacred by the agreement of mankind—the mother and sister in the man's case, the father and brother in the woman's. Even the dream of our fifty-year old lady is an incestuous one, its libido unmistakably directed toward her son. Desires which we believe to be far from human nature show themselves strong enough to arouse dreams. Hate, too, expends itself without restraint. Revenge and murderous wishes toward those standing closest to the dreamer are not unusual, toward those best beloved in daily life, toward parents, brothers and sisters, toward one's spouse and one's own children. These censored wishes seem to arise from a veritable hell; no censorship seems too harsh to be applied against their waking interpretation.

But do not reproach the dream itself for this evil content. You will not, I am sure, forget that the dream is charged with the harmless, indeed the useful function of guarding sleep from disturbance. This evil content, then, does not lie in the nature of the dream. You know also that there are dreams which can be recognized as the satisfaction of justified wishes and urgent bodily needs. These, to be sure, undergo no dream distortion. They need none. They can satisfy their function without offending the ethical and aesthetic tendencies of the ego. And will you also keep in mind the fact that the amount of dream distortion is proportional to two factors. On the one hand, the worse the censorable wish, the greater the distortion; on the other hand, however, the stricter the censor himself is at any particular time the greater the distortion will be also. A young strictly reared and prudish girl will, by reason of those factors, disfigure with an inexorable censorship those dream impulses which we physicians, for example, and which the dreamer herself ten years later, would recognize as permissible, harmless, libidinous desires.

Besides, we are far from being at the point where we can allow ourselves to be shocked by the results of our work of interpretation. I think we are not yet quite adept at it; and above all there lies upon us the obligation to secure it against certain attacks. It is not at all difficult to "find a hitch" in it. Our dream interpretations were made on the hypotheses we accepted a little while ago, that the dream has some meaning, that from the hypnotic to the normal sleep one may carry over the idea of the existence at such times of an unconscious psychic activity, and that all associations are predetermined. If we had come to plausible results on the basis of these hypotheses, we would have been justified in concluding that the hypotheses were correct. But what is to be done when the results are what I have just pictured them to be? Then it surely is natural to say, "These results are impossible, foolish, at least very improbable, hence there must have been something wrong with the hypotheses. Either the dream is no psychic phenomenon after all, or there is no such thing as unconscious mental activity in the normal condition, or our technique has a gap in it somewhere. Is that not a simpler and more satisfying conclusion than the abominations which we pretend to have disclosed on the basis of our suppositions?"

Both, I answer. It is a simpler as well as a more satisfying conclusion, but not necessarily more correct for that reason. Let us take our time, the matter is not yet ripe for judgment. Above all we can strengthen the criticism against our dream interpretation still further. That its conclusions are so unpleasant and unpalatable is perhaps of secondary importance. A stronger argument is the fact that the dreamers to whom we ascribe such wish-tendencies from the interpretation of their dreams reject the interpretations most emphatically, and with good reason. "What," says the one, "you want to prove to me by this dream that I begrudged the sums which I spent for my sister's trousseau and my brother's education? But indeed that can't be so. Why I work only for my sister, I have no interest in life but to fulfill my duties toward her. as being the oldest child. I,

promised our blessed mother I would." Or a woman says of
her dream, "You mean to say that I wish my husband were
dead! Why, that is simply revolting, nonsense. It isn't only
that we have the happiest possible married life, you probably
won't believe me when I tell you so, but his death would deprive me of everything else that I own in the world." Or
another will tell us, "You mean that I have sensual desires
toward my sister? That is ridiculous. I am not in the least
fond of her. We don't get along and I haven't exchanged a
word with her in years." We might perhaps ignore this sort of
thing if the dreamers did not confirm or deny the tendencies
ascribed to them; we could say that they are matters which
the dreamers do not know about themselves. But that the
dreamers should feel the exact opposite of the ascribed wish, and
should be able to prove to us the dominance of the opposite
tendency—this fact must finally disconcert us. Is it not time
to lay aside the whole work of the dream interpretation as
something whose results reduce it to absurdity?

By no means; this stronger argument breaks down when we
attack it critically. Assuming that there are unconscious tendencies in the psychic life, nothing is proved by the ability of
the subject to show that their opposites dominate his conscious
life. Perhaps there is room in the psychic life even for antithetical tendencies, for contradictions which exist side by side,
yes, possibly it is just the dominance of the one impulse which
is the necessary condition for the unconsciousness of its opposite.
The first two objections raised against our work hold merely
that the results of dream interpretation are not simple, and very
unpleasant. In answer to the first of these, one may say that
for all your enthusiasm for the simple solution, you cannot
thereby solve a single dream problem. To do so you must make
up your mind to accept the fact of complicated relationships.
And to the second of these objections one may say that you
are obviously wrong to use a preference or a dislike as the basis
for a scientific judgment. What difference does it make if the
results of the dream interpretation seem unpleasant, even embarrassing and disgusting to you? "That doesn't prevent them
from existing," as I used to hear my teacher Charcot say in
similar cases, when I was a young doctor. One must be humble,
one must keep personal preferences and antipathies in the back-

ground, if one wishes to discover the realities of the world. If a physicist can prove to you that the organic life of this planet must, within a short period of time, become completely extinct, do you also venture to say to him, "That cannot be so. This prospect is too unpleasant." On the contrary, you will be silent until another physicist proves some error in the assumptions or calculations of the first. If you reject the unpleasant, you are repeating the mechanism of dream construction instead of under·standing and mastering it.

Perhaps you will promise to overlook the repulsive character of the censored dream-wishes, and will take refuge in the argument that it is improbable, after all, that so wide a field be given over to the evil in the constitution of man. But does your own experience justify you in saying that? I will not discuss the question of how you may estimate yourselves, but have you found so much good will among your superiors and rivals, so much chivalry among your enemies, so little envy in their company, that you feel yourselves in duty bound to enter a protest against the part played by the evil of egoism in human nature? Are you ignorant of how uncontrolled and undependable the average human being is in all the affairs of sex life? Or do you not know that all the immoralities and excesses of which we dream nightly are crimes commited daily by waking persons? What else does psychoanalysis do here but confirm the old saying of Plato, that the good people are those who content themselves with dreaming what the others, the bad people, really do?

And now turn your attention from the individual case to the great war devastating Europe. Think of the amount of brutality, the cruelty and the lies allowed to spread over the civilized world. Do you really believe that a handful of conscienceless egoists and corruptionists could have succeeded in setting free all these evil spirits, if the millions of followers did not share in the guilt? Do you dare under these circumstances to break a lance for the absence of evil from the psychic constitution of mankind?

You will reproach me with judging the war one-sidedly, you will say that it has also brought forth all that is most beautiful and noble in mankind, its heroic courage, its self-sacrifice, its social feeling. Certainly, but do not at this point allow yourselves to become guilty of the injustice which has so often been

perpetrated against psychoanalysis, of reproaching it with denying one thing because it was asserting another. It is not our
intention to deny the noble strivings of human nature, nor have
we ever done anything to deprecate their value. On the contrary, I show you not only the censored evil dream-wishes, but
also the censor which suppresses them and renders them unrecognizable. We dwell on the evil in mankind with greater
emphasis only because others deny it, a method whereby the
psychic life of mankind does not become better, but merely
incomprehensible. When, however, we give up this one-sided
ethical estimate, we shall surely be able to find a more accurate
formula for the relationship of the evil to the good in human
nature.

And thus the matter stands. We need not give up the conclusions to which our labors in dream interpretation lead us
even though we must consider those conclusions strange. Perhaps we can approach their understanding later by another
path. For the present, let us repeat: dream distortion is a
consequence of the censorship practised by accredited tendencies
of the ego against those wish-impulses that are in any way
shocking, impulses which stir in us nightly during sleep. Why
these wish-impulses come just at night, and whence they come—
these are questions which will bear considerable investigation.

It would be a mistake, however, to omit to mention, with fitting
emphasis, another result of these investigations. The dream
wishes which try to disturb our sleep are not known to us, in
fact we learn of them first through the dream interpretation.
Therefore, they may be described as "at that time" unconscious
in the sense above defined. But we can go beyond this and say
that they are more than merely "at that time" unconscious.
The dreamer to be sure denies their validity, as we have seen
in so many cases, even after he has learned of their existence by
means of the interpretation. The situation is then repeated
which we first encountered in the interpretation of the tongue
slip "hiccough" where the toastmaster was outraged and assured us that neither then nor ever before had he been conscious
of disrespectful impulse toward his chief. This is repeated with
every interpretation of a markedly distorted dream, and for
that reason attains a significance for our conception. We are
now prepared to conclude that there are processes and tendencies

in the psychic life of which one knows nothing at all, has known nothing for some time, might, in fact, perhaps never have known anything. The unconscious thus receives a new meaning for us; the idea of "at present" or "at a specific time" disappears from its conception, for it can also mean *permanently* unconscious, not merely *latent at the time*. Obviously we shall have to learn more of this at another session.

Symbolism in the Dream

WE have discovered that the distortion of dreams, a disturbing element in our work of understanding them, is the result of a censorious activity which is directed against the unacceptable of the unconscious wish-impulses. But, of course, we have not maintained that censorship is the only factor which is to blame for the dream distortion, and we may actually make the discovery in a further study of the dream that other items play a part in this result. That is, even if the dream censorship were eliminated we might not be in a position to understand the dreams; the actual dream still might not be identical with the latent dream thought.

This other item which makes the dream unintelligible, this new addition to dream distortion, we discover by considering a gap in our technique. I have already admitted that for certain elements of the dream, no associations really occur to the person being analyzed. This does not happen so often as the dreamers maintain; in many cases the association can be forced by persistence. But still there are certain instances in which no association is forthcoming, or if forced does not furnish what we expected. When this happens in the course of a psychoanalytic treatment, then a particular meaning may be attached thereto, with which we have nothing to do here. It also occurs, however, in the interpretation of the dreams of a normal person or in interpreting one's own dreams. Once a person is convinced that in these cases no amount of forcing of associations will avail, he will finally make the discovery that the unwished-for contingency occurs regularly in certain dream elements, and he will begin to recognize a new order of things there, where at first he believed he had come across a peculiar exception to our technique.

In this way we are tempted to interpret these silent dream elements ourselves, to undertake their translation by the means at hand. The fact that every time we trust to this substitution we obtain a satisfactory meaning is forced upon us; until we resolve upon this decision the dream remains meaningless, its continuity is broken. The accumulation of many similar cases tends to give the necessary certainty to our first timid attempts.

I am expounding all this in rather a schematic manner, but this is permissible for purposes of instruction, and I am not trying to misstate, but only to simplify matters.

In this manner we derive constant translations for a whole series of dream elements just as constant translations are found in our popular dream books for all the things we dream. But do not forget that in our association technique we never discover constant substitutes for the dream elements.

You will say at once that this road to interpretation appears far more uncertain and open to objection than the former methods of free association. But a further fact is to be taken into consideration. After one has gathered a sufficient number of such constant substitutes empirically, he will say that of his own knowledge he should actually have denied that these items of dream interpretation could really be understood without the associations of the dreamer. The facts that force us to recognize their meaning will appear in the second half of our analysis.

We call such a constant relationship between a dream element and its interpretation *symbolic*. The dream element is itself a *symbol* of the unconscious dream thought. You will remember that previously, when we were investigating the relationship between dream elements and their actuality, I drew three distinctions, viz., that of the part of the whole, that of the allusion, and that of the imagery. I then announced that there was a fourth, but did not name it. This fourth is the symbolic relationship here introduced. Very interesting discussions center about this, and we will now consider them before we express our own particular observations on symbolism. Symbolism is perhaps the most noteworthy chapter of dream study.

In the first place, since symbols are permanent or constant translations, they realize, in a certain measure, the ideal of ancient as well as popular dream interpretation, an ideal which by means of our technique we had left behind. They permit us in certain cases to interpret a dream without questioning the dreamer who, aside from this, has no explanation for the symbol. If the interpreter is acquainted with the customary dream symbols and, in addition, with the dreamer himself, the conditions under which the latter lives and the impressions he received before having the dream, it is often possible to interpret a dream without further information—to translate it "right off the bat." Such a trick flatters the interpreter and impresses the dreamer; it stands out as a pleasurable incident in the usual arduous course of cross-examining the dreamer. But do not be misled. It is not our function to perform tricks. Interpretation based on a knowledge of symbols is not a technique that can replace the associative technique, or even compare with it. It is a supplement to the associative technique, and furnishes the latter merely with transplanted, usable results. But as regards familiarity with the dreamer's psychic situation, you must consider the fact that you are not limited to interpreting the dreams of acquaintances; that as a rule you are not acquainted with the daily occurrences which act as the stimuli for the dreams, and that the associations of the subject furnish you with a knowledge of that very thing we call the psychic situation.

Furthermore, it is very extraordinary, particularly in view of circumstances to be mentioned later, that the most vehement opposition has been voiced against the existence of the symbolic relationship between the dream and the unconscious. Even persons of judgment and position, who have otherwise made great progress in psychoanalysis, have discontinued their support at this point. This is the more remarkable since, in the first place, symbolism is neither peculiar to the dream nor characteristic of it, and since in the second place, symbolism in the dream was not discovered through psychoanalysis, although the latter is not poor otherwise in making startling discoveries. The discoverer of dream symbolism, if we insist on a discovery in modern times, was the philosopher K. A. Scherner (1861). Psychoanalysis affirmed Scherner's discovery and modified it considerably.

Now you will want to know something of the nature of dream symbolism, and to hear some examples. I shall gladly impart to you what I know, but I admit that our knowledge is not so complete as we could desire it to be.

The nature of the symbol relationship is a comparison, but not any desired comparison. One suspects a special prerequisite for this comparison, but is unable to say what it is. Not everything to which we are able to compare an object or an occurrence occurs in the dream as its symbol; on the other hand, the dream does not symbolize anything we may choose, but only specific elements of the dream thought. There are limitations on both sides. It must be admitted that the idea of the symbol cannot be sharply delimited at all times—it mingles with the substitution, dramatization, etc., even approaches the allusion. In one series of symbols the basic comparison is apparent to the senses. On the other hand, there are other symbols which raise the question of where the similarity, the "something intermediate" of this suspected comparison is to be sought. We may discover it by more careful consideration, or it may remain hidden to us. Furthermore, it is extraordinary, if the symbol is a comparison, that this comparison is not revealed by the association, that the dreamer is not acquainted with the comparison, that he makes use of it without knowing of its existence. Indeed, the dreamer does not even care to admit the validity of this comparison when it is pointed out to him. So you see, a symbolic relationship is a comparison of a very special kind, the origin of which is not yet clearly understood by us. Perhaps later we may find references to this unknown factor.

The number of things that find symbolic representation in the dream is not great—the human body as a whole, parents, children, brothers and sisters, birth, death, nakedness and a few others. The only typical, that is, regular representation of the human person as a whole is in the form of a *house*, as was recognized by Scherner who, indeed, wished to credit this symbol with an overwhelming significance which it does not deserve. It occurs in dreams that a person, now lustful, now frightened, climbs down the fronts of houses. Those with entirely smooth walls are men; but those which are provided with projections and balconies to which one can hold on, are women. Parents appear in the dream as *king* and *queen*, or other persons highly respected. The dream in this instance is very pious. It treats children, and brothers and sisters, less tenderly; they are symbolized as *little animals* or *vermin*. Birth is almost regularly represented by some reference to *water;* either one plunges into the water or climbs out of it, or rescues someone from the water, or is himself rescued from it, i.e., there is a mother-relation to the person. Death is replaced in the dream by *taking a journey, riding in a train; being dead, by various darksome, timid suggestions; nakedness, by clothes* and *uniforms.* You see here how the lines between symbolic and suggestive representa tion merge one into another.

In contrast to the paucity of this enumeration, it is a striking fact that the objects and subject matter of another sphere are represented by an extraordinarily rich symbolism. This is the sphere of the sexual life, the genitals, the sex processes and sexual intercourse. The great majority of symbols in the dream are sex symbols. A remarkable disproportion results from this fact. The designated subject matters are few, their symbols extraordinarily profuse, so that each of these objects can be expressed by any number of symbols of almost equal value. In the interpretation something is disclosed that arouses universal objection. The symbol interpretations, in contrast to the many-sidedness of the dream representations, are very monotonous—this displeases all who deal with them; but what is one to do?

Since this is the first time in these lectures that we speak of the sexual life, I must tell you the manner in which I intend to handle this theme. Psychoanalysis sees no reason for hiding matters or treating them by innuendo, finds no necessity of being ashamed of dealing with this important subject, believes it is proper and decent to call everything by its correct name, and hopes most effectively in this manner to ward off disturbing or salacious thoughts. The fact that I am talking before a mixed audience can make no difference on this point. Just as there is no special knowledge either for the Delphic oracle or for flappers, so the ladies present among you have, by their appearance in this lecture hall, made it clear that they wish to be considered on the same basis as the men.

The dream has a number of representations for the male genital that may be called symbolic, and in which the similarity of the comparison is, for the most part, very enlightening. In the first place, the holy figure 3 is a symbolical substitute for the entire male genital. The more conspicuous and more inter-esting part of the genital to both sexes, the male organ, has symbolical substitute in objects of like form, those which are long and upright, such as *sticks, umbrellas, poles, trees,* etc. It is also symbolized by objects that have the characteristic, in common with it, of penetration into the body and consequent injury, hence pointed *weapons* of every type, *knives, daggers, lances, swords,* and in the same manner *firearms, guns, pistols* and the *revolver,* which is so suitable because of its shape. In the troubled dream of the young girl, pursuit by a man with a knife or a firearm plays a big role. This, probably the most frequent dream symbolism, is easily translatable. Easily comprehensible, too, is the substitution for the male member of objects out of which water flows: *faucets, water cans, fountains,* as well as its representation by other objects that have the power of elongation, such as *hanging lamps, collapsible 'pencils,* etc. That *pencils, quills, nail files, hammers* and other *instruments* are undoubtedly male symbols is a fact connected with a conception of the organ, which likewise is not far to seek.

The extraordinary characteristic of the member of being able to raise itself against the force of gravity, one of the phenomena of erection, leads to symbolic representations by *balloons, aeroplanes,* and more recently, *Zeppelins.* The dream has another far more expressive way of symbolizing erection. It makes the sex organ the essential part of the whole person and pictures the person himself as *flying.* Do not feel disturbed because the dreams of flying, often so beautiful, and which we all have had, must be interpreted as dreams of general sexual excitement, as erection dreams. P. Federn, among the psychoanalytical students, has confirmed this interpretation beyond any doubt, and even Mourly Vold, much praised for his sobriety, who carried on his dream experiments with artificial positions of the arms and legs, and who was really opposed to psychoanalysis — perhaps knew nothing about psychoanalysis — has come to the same conclusion as a result of his research. It is no objection to this conclusion that women may have the same dreams of flying. Remember that our dreams act as wish-fulfillments, and that the wish to be a man is often present in women, consciously or unconsciously. And the fact that it is possible for a woman to realize this wish by the same sensation as a man does, will not mislead anyone acquainted with anatomy. There is a small organ in the genitals of a woman similar to that of the male, and this small organ, the clitoris, even in childhood, and in the years before sexual intercourse, plays the same role as does the large organ of the male.

To the less comprehensible male sex-symbols belong certain *reptiles* and *fish*, notably the famous symbol of the *snake*. Why *hats* and *cloaks* should have been turned to the same use is certainly difficult to discover, but their symbolic meaning leaves no room for doubt. And finally the question may be raised whether possibly the substitution of some other member as a representation for the male organ may not be regarded as symbolic. I believe that one is forced to this conclusion by the context and by the female counterparts.

The female genital is symbolically represented by all those objects which share its peculiarity of enclosing a space capable of being filled by something—viz., by *pits, caves*, and *hollows*, by *pitchers* and *bottles*, by *boxes* and *trunks, jars, cases, pockets*, etc. The *ship*, too, belongs in this category. Many symbols represent the womb of the mother rather than the female genital, as *wardrobes, stoves*, and primarily a *room*. The room-symbolism is related to the house-symbol, *doors* and *entrances* again become symbolic of the genital opening. But materials, too, are symbols of the woman—*wood, paper*, and objects that are made of these materials, such as *tables* and *books*. Of animals, at least the *snail* and *mussel* are unmistakably recognizable as symbols for the female; of parts of the body the *mouth* takes the place of the genital opening, while *churches* and *chapels* are structural symbolisms. As you see, all of these symbols are not equally comprehensible.

The breasts must be included in the genitals, and like the larger hemispheres of the female body are represented by *apples, peaches* and *fruits* in general. The pubic hair growth of both sexes appears in the dream as *woods* and *bushes*. The complicated topography of the female genitals accounts for the fact that they are often represented as scenes with *cliffs, woods* and *water*, while the imposing mechanism of the male sex apparatus leads to the use of all manner of very complicated *machinery*, difficult to describe.

A noteworthy symbol of the female genital is also the *jewel-casket; jewels* and *treasure* are also representatives of the beloved person in the dream; *sweets* frequently occur as representatives of sexual delights. The satisfaction in one's own genital is suggested by all types of *play*, in which may be included *piano-playing*. Exquisite symbolic representations of *onanism* are *sliding* and *coasting* as well as *tearing off a branch*. A particularly remarkable dream symbol is that of having *one's teeth fall out*, or *having them pulled*. Certainly its most immediate interpretation is castration as a punishment for onanism. Special representations for the relations of the sexes are less numerous in the dream than we might have expected from the foregoing. Rhythmic activities, such as *dancing, riding* and *climbing* may be mentioned, also harrowing experiences, such as *being run over*. One may include certain *manual activities*, and, of course, *being threatened with weapons*.

You must not imagine that either the use or the translation of these symbols is entirely simple. All manner of unexpected things are continually happening. For example, it seems hardly believable that in these symbolic representations the sex differences are not always sharply distinguished. Many symbols represent a genital in general, regardless of whether male or female, e.g., the *little child*, the *small son* or *daughter*. It sometimes occurs that a predominantly male symbol is used for a female genital, or vice versa. This is not understood until one has acquired an insight into the development of the sexual representations of mankind. In many instances this double meaning of symbols may be only apparent; the most striking of the symbols, such as *weapons, pockets* and *boxes* are excluded from this bisexual usage.

I should now like to give a summary, from the point of view of the symbols rather than of the thing represented, of the field out of which the sex symbols are for the most part taken, and then to make a few remarks about the symbols which have points in common that are not understood. An obscure symbol of this type is the *hat*, perhaps headdress on the whole, and is usually employed as a male representation, though at times as a female. In the same way the *cloak* represents a man, perhaps not always the genital aspect. You are at liberty to ask, why? The *cravat*, which is suspended and is not worn by women, is an unmistakable male symbol. *White laundry*, all *linen*, in fact, is female. *Dresses, uniforms* are, as we have already seen, substitutes for nakedness, for body-formation; the *shoe* or *slipper* is a female genital. *Tables* and *wood* have already been mentioned as puzzling but undoubtedly female symbols. *Ladders, ascents, steps* in relation to their mounting, are certainly symbols of sexual intercourse. On closer consideration we see that they have the rhythm of walking as a common characteristic; perhaps, too, the heightening of excitement and the shortening of the breath, the higher one mounts.

We have already spoken of *natural scenery* as a representation of the female genitals. *Mountains* and *cliffs* are symbols of the male organ; the *garden* a frequent symbol of the female genitals. *Fruit* does not stand for the child, but for the breasts. *Wild animals* signify sensually aroused persons, or further, base impulses, passions. *Blossoms* and *flowers* represent the female genitals, or more particularly, virginity. Do not forget that the blossoms are really the genitals of the plants.

We already know the *room* as a symbol. The representation may be extended in that the windows, entrances and exits of the room take on the meaning of the body openings. Whether the room is *open* or *closed* is a part of this symbolism, and the *key* that opens it is an unmistakable male symbol.

This is the material of dream symbolism. It is not complete and might be deepened as well as extended. But I am of the opinion it will seem more than enough to you, perhaps will make you reluctant. You will ask, "Do I really live in the midst of sex symbols? Are all the objects that surround me, all the clothes I put on, all the things that I touch, always sex symbols, and nothing else?" There really are sufficient grounds for such questions, and the first is, "Where, in fact, are we to find the meaning of these dream symbols if the dreamer himself can give no information concerning them, or at best can give only incomplete information?"

My answer is: "From many widely different sources, from fairy tales and myths, jokes and farces, from folklore, that is, the knowledge of the customs, usages, sayings and songs of peoples, from the poetic and vulgar language. Everywhere we find the same symbolism and in many of these instances we understand them without further information. If we follow up each of these sources separately we shall find so many parallels to the dream symbolism that we must believe in the correctness of our interpretations."

The human body, we have said, is, according to Scherner,

frequently symbolized in the dream by the house. Continuing this representation, the windows, doors and entrances are the entrances into the body cavities, the facades are smooth or provided with balconies and projections to which to hold. The same symbolism is to be found in our daily speech when we greet a good friend as *"old house"* or when we say of someone, "We'll hit him in the *belfry*," or maintain of another that he's not quite right in the *upper story*. In anatomy the body openings are sometimes called the *body-portals*.

The fact that we meet our parents in the dream as imperial or royal persons is at first surprising. But it has its parallel in the fairy tale. Doesn't it begin to dawn upon us that the many fairy tales which begin "Once upon a time there was a *king* and a *queen*" intend nothing else than, "Once there was a *father* and a *mother?*" In our families we refer to our children as *princes*, the eldest as the *crown-prince*. The king usually calls himself the *father of the country*. We playfully designate little children as *worms*, and say, sympathetically, *"poor little worm."*

Let us return to the symbolism of the house. When we use the projections of the house to hold ourselves on to in the dream, are we not reminded of the familiar colloquialism about persons with well-developed breasts: "She has something *to hold on to*"? The folk express this in still another way when it says, "there's lots of *wood in front of her house*"; as though it wished to come to the aid of our interpretation that wood is a feminine, maternal symbol.

In addition to wood there are others. We might not understand how this material has come to be a substitute for the maternal, the feminine. Here our comparison of languages may be helpful. The German word *Holz* (wood) is said to be from the same stem as the Greek word, νλη, which means stuff, raw material. This is an example of the case, not entirely unusual, where a general word for material finally is exclusively used for some special material. There is an island in the ocean, known by the name of Madeira. The Portuguese gave it this name at the time of its discovery because it was at that time entirely covered with forests, for in the language of the Portuguese, Madeira means *wood*. You will recognize, however, that Madeira is nothing else than the slightly changed Latin word *materia* which again has the general meaning of *material.* Material is derived from *mater,* mother. The material out of which something is made, is at the same time its mother-part. In the symbolic use of wood for woman, mother, this ancient conception still lives.

Birth is regularly expressed in dreams by some connection with water; one plunges into the water, or comes out of the water, which means one gives birth to, or is born. Now let us not forget that this symbol may refer in two ways to the truths of evolutionary history. Not alone have all land-mammals, including the ancestors of man, developed out of water animals— this is the ultimate fact—but every single mammal, every human being, lived the first part of his existence in the water— namely, lived in the body of his mother as an embryo in the amnotic fluid and came out of the water at the time of his birth. I do not wish to maintain that the dreamer knows this, on the contrary I hold that he does not have to know. The dreamer very likely knows some things because of the fact that he was told about them in his childhood, and for that very reason I maintain that this knowledge has played no part in the construction of his symbols. He was told in childhood that the stork brought him—but where did it get him? Out of a lake, out of the well —again, out of the water. One of my patients to whom such information had been given, a little count, disappeared for a whole afternoon. Finally he was discovered lying at the edge of the palace lake, his little face bent above the water and earnestly peering into it to see if he could not see the little children at the bottom.

In the myths of the birth of the hero, which O. Rank submitted to comparative examination,—the oldest is that of King Sargon of Agade, about 2800 B.C.—exposure in the water and rescue from water play a predominating role. Rank has recognized that these are representations of birth, analogous to those customary in dreams. When a person in his dream rescues another from the water, the latter becomes his mother, or just plainly mother; in the myth a person who rescues a child out of the water professes herself as the real mother of the child. In a well-known joke the intelligent Jewish boy is asked who was the mother of Moses. He answered without hesitation, the Princess. But no, he is told, she only took him out of the water.

"That's what *she says*," is his reply, and thereby he shows that he has found the correct interpretation of the myth.

Leaving on a trip represents death in the dream. Likewise it is the custom in the nursery when a child asks where someone who has died, and whom he misses, may be, to say to him that the absent one has taken a trip. Again I should like to deny the truth of the belief that the dream symbol originates in this evasion used for the benefit of children. The poet makes use of the same symbol when he speaks of the Hereafter as "that undiscovered bourne from which no *traveler* returns." Even in everyday speech it is customary to refer to the last journey. Every person acquainted with ancient rite knows how seriously, for example, the Egyptians considered the portrayal of a journey to the land of the dead. There still exist many copies of the "death book" which was given to the mummy for this journey as a sort of Baedeker. Since the burial places have been separated from the living quarters, the last journey of the dead person has become a reality.

In the same manner the genital symbolism is just as little peculiar to the dream alone. Every one of you has perhaps at some time or other been so unkind as to call some woman an *"old casket"* without perhaps being aware that he was using a genital symbol. In the New Testament one may read "Woman is a weak *vessel.*" The Holy Scriptures of the Jews, so nearly poetic in their style, are filled with sex-symbolic expressions which have not always been correctly understood, and the true construction of which, in the *Song of Songs,* for example, has led to many misunderstandings. In the later Hebraic literature the representation of woman as a house, the door taking the place of the sex opening, is very widespread. The man complains, for instance, when he discovers a lack of virginity, that he has found *the door open.* The symbol of the table for woman is also known to this literature. The woman says of her husband, "I set the table for him, *but he upset it.*" Lame children are supposed to result from the fact that the man has *overturned the table.* I take these examples from a work by L. Levy of Brünn, *The Sexual Symbolism of the Bible and the Talmud.*

That ships, too, represent women in dreams is a belief derived from the etymologists, who maintain "ship" was originally the name of an earthen vessel and is the same word as *Schaff* (to create). The Greek myth of Periander of Corinth and his wife Melissa is proof that the stove or oven is a woman, and a womb. When, according to Herodotus, the tyrant entreated the shade of his beloved wife, whom, however, he had murdered in a fit of jealousy, for some sign of its identity, the deceased identified herself by the reminder that he, *Periander, had thrust his bread into a cold oven,* as a disguise for an occurrence that could have been known to no other person. In the *Anthropophyteia* published by F. S. Krauss, an indispensable source book for everything that has to do with the sex life of nations, we read that in a certain German region it is commonly said of a woman who has just been delivered of a child, *"Her oven has caved in."* The making of a fire and everything connected therewith is filled through and through with sex symbolism. The flame is always the male genital, the fireplace, the hearth, is the womb of the woman.

If you have often wondered why it is that landscapes are so often used to represent the female genitals in the dream, then let the mythologist teach you the role Mother Earth has played in the symbolisms and cults of ancient times. You may be tempted to say that a room represents a woman in the dream because of the German colloquialism which uses the term *Frauenzimmer* instead of *Frau,* in other words, it substitutes for the human person the idea of that room that is set aside for her exclusive use. In like manner we speak of the *Sublim Porte,* and mean the Sultan and his government; furthermore, the name of the ancient Egyptian ruler, Pharaoh, means nothing other than "great court room." (In the ancient Orient the court yards between the double gates of the town were the gathering places of the people, in the same manner as the market place was in the classical world.) What I mean is, this derivation is far too superficial. It seems more probable to me that the room, as the space surrounding man, came to be the symbol of woman. We have seen that the house is used in such a representation; from mythology and poetry we may take the *city, fortress, palace, citadel,* as further symbols of woman. The question may easily be decided by the dreams of those persons who do not speak German and do not understand it. In the last few years my patients have been predominantly foreign-language speaking, and I think I can recall that in their dreams as well the room represents woman, even where they had no analogous usages in their languages. There are still other signs which show that the symbolization is not limited by the bounds of language, a fact that even the old dream investigator, Schubert (1862) maintained. Since none of my dreamers were totally ignorant of German I must leave this differentiation to those psychoanalysts who can gather examples in other lands where the people speak but one language.

Among the symbol-representations of the male genital there is scarcely one that does not recur in jokes or in vulgar or poetical usage, especially among the old classical poets. Not alone do those symbols commonly met with in dreams appear here, but also new ones, e.g., the working materials of various performances, foremost of which is the incantation. Furthermore, we approach in the symbolic representation of the male a very extended and much discussed province, which we shall avoid for economic reasons. I should like to make a few remarks, however, about one of the unclassified symbols—the figure 3. Whether or not this figure derives its holiness from its symbolic meaning may remain undecided. But it appears certain that many objects which occur in nature as three-part things derive their use as coats-of-arms and emblems from such symbolic meaning, e.g., the clover, likewise the three-part French lily, (fleur-de-lys), and the extraordinary coats-of-arms of two such widely separated islands as Sicily and the Isle of Man, where the Triskeles (three partly bended knees, emerging from a central point) are merely said to be the portrayal in a different form of the male genitals. Copies of the male member were used in antiquity as the most powerful charms (*Apotropaea*) against evil influences, and this is connected with the fact that the lucky amulets of our own time may one and all be recognized as genital or sex-symbols. Let us study such a collection, worn in the form of little silver pendants: the four-leaf clover, a pig, a mushroom, a horse-shoe, a ladder, a chimney-sweep. The four-leaf clover, it seems, has usurped the place of the three-leaf clover, which is really more suitable as a symbol; the pig is an ancient symbol of fertility; the mushroom is an unquestionable penis symbol—there are mushrooms that derive their systematic names from their unmistakable similarity to the male member (Phallus impudicus); the horseshoe recalls the contour of the female genital opening; and the chimney sweep who carries a ladder belongs in this company because he carries on that trade with which the sex-intercourse is vulgarly compared (*cf.* the *Anthropophyteia*). We have already become acquainted with his ladder as a sex symbol in the dream; the German usage is helpful here, it shows us how the verb "to mount"[1] is made use of in an exquisite sexual sense. We use the expressions "*to run after women,*" which literally translated would be "*to climb after women,*" and "*an old climber.*"[2] In French, where "*step*" is "*la marche*" we find that the analogous expression for a man about town is "*un vieux marcheur.*" It is apparently not unknown in this connection that the sexual intercourse of many of the larger animals requires a mounting, *a climbing upon* the female.

The tearing off of a branch as the symbolic representation of onanism is not alone in keeping with the vulgar representation of the fact of onanism, but has far-reaching mythological parallels. Especially noteworthy, however, is the representation of onanism, or rather the punishment therefor, castration, by the falling out or pulling out of teeth, because there is a parallel in folk-lore which is probably known to the fewest dreamers. It does not seem at all questionable to me that the practice of circumcision common among so many peoples is an equivalent and a substitute for castration. And now we are informed that in Australia certain primitive tribes practice circumcision as a rite of puberty (the ceremony in honor of the boy's coming of age), while others, living quite near, have substituted for this act the striking out of a tooth.

I end my exposition with these examples. They are only examples. We know more about these matters, and you may well imagine how much richer and how much more interesting such a collection would appear if made, not by amateurs like ourselves, but by real experts in mythology, anthropology, philology and folk-lore. We are compelled to draw a few conclusions which cannot be exhaustive, but which give us much food for thought.

In the first place, we are faced by the fact that the dreamer has at his disposal a symbolic means of expression of which he

[1] " steigen."

[2] " den Frauen nachsteigen," and " ein alter Steiger."

is unconscious while awake, and does not recognize when he sees. That is as remarkable as if you should make the discovery that your chambermaid understands Sanskrit, although you know she was born in a Bohemian village and never learned the language. It is not easy to harmonize this fact with our psychological views. We can only say that the dreamer's knowledge of symbolism is unconscious, that it is a part of his unconscious mental life. We make no progress with this assumption. Until now it was only necessary to admit of unconscious impulses, those about which one knew nothing, either for a period of time or at all times. But now we deal with something more; indeed, with unknown knowledge, with thought relationships, comparisons between unlike objects which lead to this, that one constant may be substituted for another. These comparisons are not made anew each time, but they lie ready, they are complete for all time. That is to be concluded from the fact of their agreement in different persons, agreement despite differences in language.

But whence comes the knowledge of these symbol-relationships? The usages of language cover only a small part of them. The dreamer is for the most part unacquainted with the numerous parallels from other sources; we ourselves must first laboriously gather them together.

Secondly, these symbolic representations are peculiar neither to the dreamer nor to the dream work by means of which they become expressed. We have learned that mythology and fairytales make use of the same symbolism, as well as do the people in their sayings and songs, the ordinary language of every day, and poetic phantasy. The field of symbolism is an extraordinarily large one, and dream symbolism is but a small part thereof. It is not even expedient to approach the whole problem from the dream side. Many of the symbols that are used in other places do not occur in the dream at all, or at best only very seldom. Many of the dream symbols are to be found in other fields only very rarely, as you have seen. One gets the impression that he is here confronted with an ancient but no longer existent method of expression, of which various phases, however, continue in different fields, one here, one there, a third, perhaps in a slightly altered form, in several fields. I am reminded of the phantasy of an interesting mental defective, who had imagined a fundamental language, of which all these symbolic representations were the remains.

Thirdly, you must have noticed that symbolism in these other fields is by no means sex symbolism solely, while in the dream the symbols are used almost entirely to express sexual objects and processes. Nor is this easily explained. Is it possible that symbols originally sexual in their meaning later came to have other uses, and that this was the reason perhaps for the weakening of the symbolic representation to one of another nature? These questions are admittedly unanswerable if one has dealt only with dream-symbolism. One can only adhere to the supposition that there is an especially intimate connection between true symbols and things sexual.

An important indication of this has been given us recently. A philologist, H. Sperber (Upsala) who works independently of psychoanalysis, advanced the theory that sexual needs have played the largest part in the origin and development of languages. The first sounds served as means of communication, and called the sexual partner; the further development of the roots of speech accompanied the performance of the primitive man's work. This work was communal and progressed to the accompaniment of rhythmically repeated word sounds. In that way a sexual interest was transferred to the work. The primitive man made work acceptable at the same time that he used it as an equivalent and substitute for sex-activity. The word thus called forth by the common labor had two meanings, designating the sex-act as well as the equivalent labor-activity. In time the word became disassociated from its sexual significance and became fixed on this work. Generations later the same thing happened to a new word that once had sexual significance and came to be used for a new type of work. In this manner a number of word-roots were formed, all of sexual origin, and all of which had lost their sexual significance. If the description sketched here approximates the truth, it opens up the possibility for an understanding of the dream symbolism. We can understand how it is that in the dream, which preserves something of these most ancient conditions, there are so extraordinarily many symbols for the sexual, and why, in general, weapons and implements always stand for the male, materials and things manufactured, for the female. Symbolic relationships would be the remnants of the old word-identity; things which once were called by the same names as the genitals can now appear in the dream as symbols for them.

From our parallels to dream symbolization you may also learn to appreciate what is the character of psychoanalysis which makes it a subject of general interest, which is true of neither psychology nor psychiatry. Psychoanalytic work connects with so many other scientific subjects, the investigation of which promises the most pertinent discoveries, with mythology, with folk-lore, with racial psychology and with religion. You will understand how a journal can have grown on psychoanalytic soil, the sole purpose of which is the furtherance of these relationships. This is the *Imago* founded in 1912 and edited by Hanns Sachs and Otto Rank. In all of these relations, psychoanalysis is first and foremost the giving, less often the receiving, part. Indeed it derives benefit from the fact that its unusual teachings are substantiated by their recurrence in other fields, but on the whole it is psychoanalysis that provides the technical procedure and the point of view, the use of which will prove fruitful in those other fields. The psychic life of the human individual provides us, upon psychoanalytic investigation, with explanations with which we are able to solve many riddles in the life of humanity, or at least show these riddles in their proper light.

Furthermore, I have not even told you under what conditions we are able to get the deepest insight into that supposititious "fundamental language," or from which field we gain the most information. So long as you do not know this you cannot appreciate the entire significance of the subject. This field is the neurotic, its materials, the symptoms and other expressions of the nervous patient, for the explanation and treatment of which psychoanalysis was devised.

My fourth point of view returns to our premise and connects up with our prescribed course. We said, even if there were no such thing as dream censorship, the dream would still be hard to understand, for we would then be confronted with the task of translating the symbol-language of the dream into the thought of our waking hours. Symbolism is a second and independent item of dream distortion, in addition to dream censorship. It is not a far cry to suppose that it is convenient for the dream censorship to make use of symbolism since both lead to the same end, to making the dream strange and incomprehensible.

Whether or not in the further study of the dream we shall hit upon a new item that influences dream distortion, remains to be seen. I should not like to leave the subject of dream symbolism without once more touching upon the curious fact that it arouses such strong opposition in the case of educated persons, in spite of the fact that symbolism in myth, religion, art and speech is undoubtedly so prevalent. Is not this again because of its relationship to sexuality?

ELEVENTH LECTURE

THE DREAM

The Dream-Work

IF you have mastered dream censorship and symbolic representation, you are, to be sure, not yet adept in dream distortion, but you are nevertheless in a position to understand most dreams. For this you employ two mutually supplementary methods, call up the associations of the dreamer until you have penetrated from the substitute to the actual, and from your own knowledge supply the meaning for the symbol. Later we shall discuss certain uncertainties which show themselves in this process.

We are now in a position to resume work which we attempted, with very insufficient means at an earlier stage, when we studied the relation between the manifest dream elements and their latent actualities, and in so doing established four such main relationships: that of a part of the whole, that of approach or allusion, the symbolic relationship and plastic word representation. We shall now attempt the same on a larger scale, by comparing the manifest dream content as a whole, with the latent dream which we found by interpretation.

I hope you will never again confuse these two. If you have achieved this, you have probably accomplished more in the understanding of the dream than the majority of the readers of my *Interpretation of Dreams*. Let me remind you once more that this process, which changes the latent into the manifest dream, is called *dream-work*. Work which proceeds in the opposite direction, from the manifest dream to the latent, is our *work of interpretation*. The work of interpretation attempts to undo the dream-work. Infantile dreams that are recognized as evident wish fulfillments nevertheless have undergone some dream-work, namely, the transformation of the wish into reality, and generally, too, of thoughts into visual pictures. Here we

need no interpretation, but only a retracing of these transformations. Whatever dream-work has been added to other dreams,
we call *dream distortion*, and this can be annulled by our work
of interpretation.

The comparison of many dream interpretations has rendered
it possible for me to give you a coherent representation of what
the dream-work does with the material of the latent dream. I
beg of you, however, not to expect to understand too much of
this. It is a piece of description that should be listened to with
calm attention.

The first process of the dream-work is *condensation*. By this
we understand that the manifest dream has a smaller content
than the latent one, that is, it is a sort of abbreviated translation of the latter. Condensation may occasionally be absent,
but as a rule it is present, often to a very high degree. The
opposite is never true, that is, it never occurs that the manifest
dream is more extensive in scope and content than the latent.
Condensation occurs in the following ways: 1. Certain latent
elements are entirely omitted; 2. only a fragment of the many
complexes of the latent dream is carried over into the manifest
dream; 3. latent elements that have something in common
are collected for the manifest dream and are fused into a whole.

If you wish, you may reserve the term "condensation" for
this last process alone. Its effects are particularly easy to
demonstrate. From your own dreams you will doubtless recall
the fusion of several persons into one. Such a compound person
probably looks like A., is dressed like B., does something that
one remembers of C., but in spite of this one is conscious that
he is really D. By means of this compound formation something
common to all four people is especially emphasized. One can
make a compound formation of events and of places in the same
way as of people, provided always that the single events and
localities have something in common which the latent dream
emphasizes. It is a sort of new and fleeting concept of formation, with the common element as its kernel. This jumble of
details that has been fused together regularly results in a vague
indistinct picture, as though you had taken several pictures
on the same film.

The shaping of such compound formations must be of great
importance to the dream-work, for we can prove, (by the choice

of a verbal expression for a thought, for instance) that the common elements mentioned above are purposely manufactured where they originally do not exist. We have already become acquainted with such condensation and compound formations; they played an important part in the origin of certain cases of slips of the tongue. You recall the young man who wished to *inscort* a woman. Furthermore, there are jokes whose technique may be traced to such a condensation. But entirely aside from this, one may maintain that this appearance of something quite unknown in the dream finds its counterpart in many of the creations of our imagination which fuse together component parts that do not belong together in experience, as for example the centaurs, and the fabulous animals of old mythology or of Boecklin's pictures. For creative imagination can invent nothing new whatsoever, it can only put together certain details normally alien to one another. The peculiar thing, however, about the procedure of the dream-work is the following: The material at the disposal of the dream-work consists of thoughts, thoughts which may be offensive and unacceptable, but which are nevertheless correctly formed and expressed. These thoughts are transformed into something else by the dream-work, and it is remarkable and incomprehensible that this translation, this rendering, as it were, into another script or language, employs the methods of condensation and combination. For a translation usually strives to respect the discriminations expressed in the text, and to differentiate similar things. The dream-work, on the contrary, tries to fuse two different thoughts by looking, just as the joke does, for an ambiguous word which shall act as a connecting link between the two thoughts. One need not attempt to understand this feature of the case at once, but it may become significant for the conception of the dream-work.

Although condensation renders the dream opaque, one does not get the impression that it is an effect of dream censorship. One prefers to trace it back to mechanical or economic conditions; but censorship undoubtedly has a share in the process.

The results of condensation may be quite extraordinary. With its help, it becomes possible at times to collect quite unrelated latent thought processes into one manifest dream, so that one can arrive at an apparently adequate interpretation, and at the same time conceive a possible further interpretation.

The consequence of condensation for the relation between latent and manifest dreams is the fact that no simple relations can exist between the elements of the one and the other. A manifest element corresponds simultaneously to several latent ones, and vice versa, a latent element may partake of several manifest ones, an interlacing, as it were. In the interpretation of the dream it also becomes evident that the associations to a single element do not necessarily follow one another in orderly sequence. Often we must wait until the entire dream is interpreted.

Dream-work therefore accomplishes a very unusual sort of transcription of dream thoughts, not a translation word for word, or sign for sign, not a selection according to a set rule, as if all the consonants of a word were given and the vowels omitted; nor is it what we might call substitution, namely, the choice of one element to take the place of several others. It is something very different and much more complicated.

The second process of the dream-work is *displacement*. Fortunately we are already prepared for this, since we know that it is entirely the work of dream censorship. The two evidences of this are firstly, that a latent element is not replaced by one of its constituent parts but by something further removed from it, that is, by a sort of allusion; secondly, that the psychic accent is transferred from an important element to another that is unimportant, so that the dream centers elsewhere and seems strange.

Substitution by allusion is known to our conscious thinking also, but with a difference. In conscious thinking the allusion must be easily intelligible, and the substitute must bear a relation to the actual content. Jokes, too, often make use of allusion; they let the condition of content associations slide and replace it by unusual external associations, such as resemblances in sound, ambiguity of words, etc. They retain, however, the condition of intelligibility; the joke would lose all its effect if the allusion could not be traced back to the actual without any effort whatsoever. The allusion of displacement has freed itself of both these limitations. Its connection with the element which it replaces is most external and remote, is unintelligible for this reason, and if it is retraced, its interpretation gives the impression of an unsuccessful joke or of a forced, far-fetched explanation. For the dream censor has only then accomplished its purpose, when it has made the path of return from the allusion to the original undiscoverable.

The displacement of emphasis is unheard of as a means of expressing thoughts. In conscious thinking we occasionally admit it to gain a comic effect. I can probably give you an idea of the confusion which this produces by reminding you of the story of the blacksmith who had committed a capital crime. The court decided that the penalty for the crime must be paid, but since he was the only blacksmith in the village and therefore indispensable, while there were three tailors, one of the latter was hung in his stead.

The third process of the dream-work is the most interesting from a psychological point of view. It consists of the *translation* of thoughts into visual images. Let us bear in mind that by no means all dream thoughts undergo this translation; many of them retain their form and appear in the manifest dream also as thought or consciousness; moreover, visual images are not the only form into which thoughts are translated. They are, however, the foundation of the dream fabric; this part of the dream work is, as we already know, the second most constant, and for single dream elements we have already learned to know "plastic word representation."

It is evident that this process is not simple. In order to get an idea of its difficulties you must pretend that you have undertaken the task of replacing a political editorial in a newspaper by a series of illustrations, that you have suffered an atavistic return from the use of the alphabet to ideographic writing. Whatever persons or concrete events occur in this article you will be able to replace easily by pictures, perhaps to your advantage, but you will meet with difficulties in the representation of all abstract words and all parts of speech denoting thought relationships, such as particles, conjunctions, etc. With the abstract words you could use all sorts of artifices. You will, for instance, try to change the text of the article into different words which may sound unusual, but whose components will be more concrete and more adapted to representation. You will then recall that most abstract words were concrete before their meaning paled, and will therefore go back to the original concrete significance of these words as often as possible, and so you will be glad to learn that you can represent the "possession" of an object by the actual physical straddling of it.¹ The dream work does the same thing. Under such circumstances you can hardly demand accuracy of representation. You will also have to allow the dream-work to replace an element that is as hard to depict as for instance, broken faith, by another kind of rupture, a broken leg.² In this way you will be able to smooth away to some extent the crudity of imagery when the latter is endeavoring to replace word expression.

In the representation of parts of speech that denote thought relations, such as *because, therefore, but*, etc., you have no such aids; these constituent parts of the text will therefore be lost in your translation into images. In the same way, the dream-work resolves the content of the dream thought into its raw

¹ " besitzen," to straddle.
² While revising these pages I chanced upon a newspaper article that I quote here as an unexpected supplement to the above lines.

THE PUNISHMENT OF GOD

A BROKEN ARM FOR BROKEN FAITH

Mrs. Anna M. the wife of a soldier in the reserve accused Mrs. Clementine C. of being untrue to her husband. The accusation reads that Mrs. C. had carried on an illicit relationship with Karl M. while her own husband was on the battlefiel', from which he even sent her 70 Kronen a month. Mrs. C. had received *quite a lot of money* from the husband of the plaintiff, while she and her children had to live in *hunger* and in misery. Friends of her husband had told her that Mrs. C. had visited inns with M. and had caroused there until late at night. The accused had even asked the husband of the plaintiff before several infantrymen whether he would not soon get a divorce from his "old woman" and live with her. Mrs. C.'s housekeeper had also repeatedly seen the husband of the plaintiff in her (Mrs. C.'s) apartment, in complete negligée.

Yesterday Mrs. C. *denied* before a judge in Leopoldstadt that she even knew M; there could be no question of intimate relation between them.

The witness, Albertine M., however, testified that Mrs. C. had kissed the husband of the plaintiff and that she had surprised them at it.

When M. was called as a witness in an earlier proceeding he had denied any intimate relation to the accused. Yesterday the judge received a *letter* in which the witness retracts the statement he made in the first proceeding and *admits* that he had carried on a love affair with Mrs. C., until last June. He says that he only denied this relationship in the former proceeding for the sake of the accused because before the proceeding she had come to him and begged on her knees that he should save her and not confess. " To-day," wrote the witness, " I felt impelled to make a full confession to the court, since I have *broken my left arm* and this appears to me as the *punishment of God* for my transgression."

The judge maintained the penal offense had already become null and void, whereupon the plaintiff withdrew her accusation and the liberation of the accused followed.

material of objects and activities. You may be satisfied if the possibility is vouchsafed you to suggest certain relations, not representable in themselves, in a more detailed elaboration of the image. In quite the same way the dream-work succeeds in expressing much of the content of the latent dream thought in the formal peculiarities of the manifest dream, in its clearness or vagueness, in its division into several parts, etc. The number of fragmentary dreams into which the dream is divided corresponds as a rule to the number of main themes, of thought sequences in the latent dream; a short preliminary dream often stands as an introduction or a motivation to the complementary dream which follows; a subordinate clause in dream thought is represented in the manifest dream as an interpolated change of scene, etc. The form of the dream is itself, therefore, by no means without significance and challenges interpretation. Different dreams of the same night often have the same meaning, and testify to an increasing effort to control a stimulus of growing urgency. In a single dream a particularly troublesome element may be represented by "duplicates," that is, by numerous symbols.

By continually comparing dream thought with the manifest dream that replaces it, we learn all sorts of things for which we were not prepared, as for instance, the fact that even the nonsense and absurdity of the dream have meaning. Yes, on this point the opposition between the medical and psychoanalytic conception of the dream reaches a climax not previously achieved. According to the former, the dream is senseless because the dreaming psychic activity has lost all power of critical judgment; according to our theory, on the other hand, the dream becomes senseless, whenever a critical judgment, contained in the dream thought, wishes to express the opinion: "It is nonsense." The dream which you all know, about the visit to the theatre (three tickets 1 Fl. 50 Kr.) is a good example of this. The opinion expressed here is: "It was *nonsense* to marry so early."

In the same way, we discover in interpretation what is the significance of the doubts and uncertainties so often expressed by the dreamer as to whether a certain element really occurred in the dream; whether it was this or something else. As a rule these doubts and uncertainties correspond to nothing in the latent dream thought; they are occasioned throughout by the working of the dream censor and are equivalent to an unsuccessful attempt at suppression.

One of the most surprising discoveries is the manner in which the dream-work deals with those things which are opposed to one another in the latent dream. We already know that agreements in the latent material are expressed in the manifest dream by condensations. Now oppositions are treated in exactly the same way as agreements and are, with special preference, expressed by the same manifest element. An element in a manifest dream, capable of having an opposite, may therefore represent itself as well as its opposite, or may do both simultaneously; only the context can determine which translation is to be chosen. It must follow from this that the particle "no" cannot be represented in the dream, at least not unambiguously.

The development of languages furnishes us with a welcome analogy for this surprising behavior on the part of the dream work. Many scholars who do research work in languages have maintained that in the oldest languages opposites—such as strong, weak; light, dark; big, little—were expressed by the same root word. (*The Contradictory Sense of Primitive Words.*) In old Egyptian, *ken* originally meant both strong and weak. In conversation, misunderstanding in the use of such ambiguous words was avoided by the tone of voice and by accompanying gestures, in writing by the addition of so-called determinatives, that is, by a picture that was itself not meant to be expressed. Accordingly, if *ken* meant strong, the picture of an erect little man was placed after the alphabetical signs, if *ken, weak,* was meant, the picture of a cowering man followed. Only later, by slight modifications of the original word, were two designations developed for the opposites which it denoted. In this way, from *ken* meaning both strong and weak, there was derived a *ken,* strong, and a *ken,* weak. It is said that not only the most primitive languages in their last developmental stage, but also the more recent ones, even the living tongues of to-day have retained abundant remains of this primitive opposite meaning. Let me give you a few illustrations of this taken from C. Abel (1884).

In Latin there are still such words of double meaning: *altus*—high, deep, and *sacer,* sacred, accursed.

As examples of modifications of the same root, I cite:

clamare—to scream, *clam*—quiet, still, secret;

siccus—dry, *succus*—juice.

And from the German:

Stimme—voice, *stumm*—dumb.

The comparison of related tongues yields a wealth of examples:

English: *lock;* German: *Loch*—hole, *Lücke*—gap.

English: *cleave;* German: *kleben*—to stick, to adhere.

The English *without,* is to-day used to mean "not with"; that "with" had the connotation of deprivation as well as that of apportioning, is apparent from the compounds: *withdraw, withhold.* The German *wieder,* again, closely resembles this.

Another peculiarity of dream-work finds it prototype in the development of language. It occurred in ancient Egyptian as well as in other later languages that the sequence of sounds of the words was transposed to denote the same fundamental idea. The following are examples from English and German:

Topf—*pot; boat*—*tub; hurry*—*Ruhe* (rest, quiet).

Balken (beam)—*Kloben* (mallet)—*club.*

From the Latin and the German:

capere (to seize)—*packen* (to seize, to grasp).

Inversions such as occur here in the single word are effected in a very different way by the dream-work. We already know the inversion of the sense, substitution by the opposite. Besides there are inversions of situations, of relations between two people, and so in dreams we are in a sort of topsy-turvy world. In a dream it is frequently the rabbit that shoots the hunter. Further inversion occurs in the sequence of events, so that in the dream the cause is placed after the effect. It is like a performance in a third-rate theatre, where the hero falls before the shot which kills him is fired from the wings. Or there are dreams in which the whole sequence of the elements is inverted, so that in the interpretation one must take the last first, and the first last, in order to obtain a meaning. You will recall from our study of dream symbolism that to go or fall into the water means the same as to come out of it, namely, to give birth to, or to be born, and that mounting stairs or a ladder means the same as going down. The advantage that dream distortions may gain from such freedom of representation, is unmistakable.

These features of the dream-work may be called *archaic*. They are connected with ancient systems of expression, ancient languages and literatures, and involve the same difficulties which .we shall deal with later in a critical connection.

Now for some other aspects of the matter. In the dream-work .it is plainly a question of translating the latent thoughts, expressed in words, into psychic images, in the main, of a visual kind. Now our thoughts were developed from such psychic images; their first material and the steps which led up to them were psychic impressions, or to be more exact, the memory images of these psychic impressions. Only later were words attached to these and then combined into thoughts. The dream-work therefore puts the thoughts through a *regressive* treatment, that is, one that retraces the steps in their development. In this regression, all that has been added to the thoughts as a new contribution in the course of the development of the memory pictures must fall away.

This, then, is the dream-work. In view of the processes that we have discovered about it, our interest in the manifest dream was forced into the background. I shall, however, devote a few remarks to the latter, since it is after all the only thing that is positively known to us.

It is natural that the manifest dream should lose its importance for us. It must be a matter of indifference to us whether it is well composed or resolved into a series of disconnected single images. Even when its exterior seems to be significant, we know that it has been developed by means of dream distortion and may have as little organic connection with the inner content of the dream as the facade of an Italian church has with its structure and ground plan. At other times this facade of the dream, too, has its significance, in that it reproduces with little or no distortion an important part of the latent dream thought. But we cannot know this before we have put the dream through a process of interpretation and reached a decision as to what amount of distortion has taken place. A similar doubt prevails when two elements in the dream seem to have been brought into close relations to one another. This may be a valuable hint, suggesting that we may join together those manifest thoughts which correspond to the elements in the latent dream; yet at other times we are convinced that what belongs together in thought has been torn apart in the dream.

As a general rule we must refrain from trying to explain one ' part of the manifest dream by another, as if the dream were coherently conceived and pragmatically represented. At the most it is comparable to a Breccian stone, produced by the fusion of various minerals in such a way that the markings it shows are entirely different from those of the original mineral constituents. There is actually a part of the dream-work, the so-called *secondary treatment,* whose function it is to develop something unified, something approximately coherent from the final products of the dream-work. In so doing the material is often arranged in an entirely misleading sense and insertions are made wherever it seems necessary.

On the other hand, we must not over-estimate the dream-work, nor attribute too much to it. The processes which we have enumerated tell the full tale of its functioning; beyond condensing, displacing, representing plastically, and then subjecting the whole to a secondary treatment, it can do nothing. Whatever of judgment, of criticism, of surprise, and of deduction are to be found in the dream are not products of the dream-work and are only very seldom signs of afterthoughts about the dream, but are generally parts of the latent dream thought, which have passed over into the manifest dream, more or less modified and adapted to the context. In the matter of composing speeches, the dream-work can also do nothing. Except for a few examples, the speeches in the dream are imitations and combinations of speeches heard or made by oneself during the day, and which have been introduced into the latent thought, either as material or as stimuli for the dream. Neither can the dream pose problems; when these are found in the dream, they are in the main combinations of numbers, semblances of examples that are quite absurd or merely copies of problems in the latent dream thought. Under these conditions it is not surprising that the interest which has attached itself to the dream-work is soon deflected from it to the latent dream thoughts which are revealed in more or less distorted form in the manifest dream. It is not justifiable, however, to have this change go so far that in a theoretical consideration one regularly substitutes the latent dream thought for the dream itself, and maintains of the latter what can hold only for the former. It is odd that the results of psychoanalysis should be misused for such an exchange. "Dream" can mean nothing but the result of the dream-work, that is, the *form* into which the latent dream thoughts have been translated by the dream-work.

Dream-work is a process of a very peculiar sort, the like of which has hitherto not been discovered in psychic life. These condensations, displacements, regressive translations of thoughts into pictures, are new discoveries which richly repay our efforts in the field of psychoanalysis. You will realize from the parallel to the dream-work, what connections psychoanalytic studies will reveal with other fields, especially with the development of speech and thought. You can only surmise the further significance of these connections when you hear that the mechanism of the dream structure is the model for the origin of neurotic symptoms.

I know too that we cannot as yet estimate the entire contribution that this work has made to psychology. We shall only indicate the new proofs that have been given of the existence of unconscious psychic acts—for such are the latent dream thoughts—and the unexpectedly wide approach to the understanding of the unconscious psychic life that dream interpretation opens up to us.

The time has probably come, however, to illustrate separately, by various little examples of dreams, the connected facts for which you have been prepared.

Analysis of Sample Dreams

I HOPE you will not be disappointed if I again lay before you excerpts from dream analyses instead of inviting you to participate in the interpretation of a beautiful long dream. You will say that after so much preparation you ought to have this right, and that after the successful interpretation of so many thousands of dreams it should long ago have become possible to assemble a collection of excellent dream samples with which we could demonstrate all our assertions concerning dream-work and dream thoughts. Yes, but the difficulties which stand in the way of the fulfillment of your wish are too many.

First of all, I must confess to you that no one practices dream interpretation as his main occupation. When does one interpret dreams? Occasionally one can occupy himself with the dream of some friend, without any special purpose, or else he may work with his own dreams for a time in order to school himself in psychoanalytic method; most often, however, one deals with the dreams of nervous individuals who are undergoing analytic treatment. These latter dreams are excellent material, and in no way inferior to those of normal persons, but one is forced by the technique of the treatment to subordinate dream analysis to therapeutic aims and to pass over a large number of dreams after having derived something from them that is of use in the treatment. Many dreams we meet with during the treatment are, as a matter of fact, impossible of complete analysis. Since they spring from the total mass of psychic material which is still unknown to us, their understanding becomes possible only after the completion of the cure. Besides, to tell you such dreams would necessitate the disclosure of all the secrets concerning a neurosis. That will not do for us, since we have taken the dream as preparation for the study of the neuroses.

I know you would gladly leave this material, and would prefer to hear the dreams of healthy persons, or your own dreams explained. But that is impossible because of the content of these dreams. One can expose neither himself, nor another whose confidence he has won, so inconsiderately as would result from a thorough interpretation of his dreams—which, as you already know, refer to the most intimate things of his personality, In addition to this difficulty, caused by the nature of the material, there is another that must be considered when communicating a dream. You know the dream seems strange even to the dreamer himself, let alone to one who does not know the dreamer. Our literature is not poor in good and detailed dream analyses. I myself have published some in connection with case histories. Perhaps the best example of a dream interpretation is the one published by O. Rank, being two related dreams of a young girl, covering about two pages of print, the analysis covering seventy-six pages. I would need about a whole semester in order to take you through such a task. If we select a longer or more markedly distorted dream, we have to make so many explanations, we must make use of so many free associations and recollections, must go into so many by-paths, that a lecture on the subject would be entirely unsatisfactory and inconclusive. So I must ask you to be content with what is more easily obtained, with the recital of small bits of dreams of neurotic persons, in which we may be able to recognize this or that isolated fact. Dream symbols are the most easily demonstrable, and after them, certain peculiarities of regressive dream representations.[1] I shall tell you why I considered each of the following dreams worthy of communication.

1. A dream, consisting of only two brief pictures: *"The dreamer's uncle is smoking a cigarette, although it is Saturday. A woman caresses him as though he were her child."*

In commenting on the first picture, the dreamer (a Jew) remarks that his uncle is a pious man who never did, and never would do, anything so sinful as smoking on the Sabbath. As to the woman of the second picture, he has no free associations other than his mother. These two pictures or thoughts should

[1] This highly technical concept is explained in *The Interpretation of Dreams*, Chap. VII, Sec. (b) pp. 422 et seq.

obviously be brought into connection with each other, but how? Since he expressly rules out the reality of his uncle's action, then it is natural to interpolate an "if." "*If* my uncle, that pious man, should smoke a cigarette on Saturday, then I could also permit my mother's caresses." This obviously means that the mother's caresses are prohibited, in the same manner as is smoking on Saturday, to a pious Jew. You will recall, I told you that all relations between the dream thoughts disappear in the dream-work, that these relations are broken up into their raw material, and that it is the task of interpretation to re-interpolate the omitted connections.

2. Through my publications on dreams I have become, in certain respects, the public consultant on matters pertaining to dreams, and for many years I have been receiving communications from the most varied sources, in which dreams are related to me or presented to me for my judgment. I am of course grateful to all those persons who include with the story of the dream, enough material to make an interpretation possible, or who give such an interpretation themselves. It is in this category that the following dream belongs, the dream of a Munich physician in the year 1910. I select it because it goes to show how impossible of understanding a dream generally is before the dreamer has given us what information he has about it. I suspect that at bottom you consider the ideal dream interpretation that in which one simply inserts the meaning of the symbols, and would like to lay aside the technique of free association to the dream elements. I wish to disabuse your minds of this harmful error.

"On July 13, 1910, toward morning, I dreamed *that I was bicycling down a street in Tübingen, when a brown Dachshund tore after me and caught me by the heel. A bit further on I get off, seat myself on a step, and begin to beat the beast, which has clenched its teeth tight. (I feel no discomfort from the biting or the whole scene.) Two elderly ladies are sitting opposite me and watching me with grins on their faces. Then I wake up and, as so often happens to me, the whole dream becomes perfectly clear to me in this moment of transition to the waking state.*"

Symbols are of little use in this case. The dreamer, however, informs us, "I lately fell in love with a girl, just from seeing h* on the street, but had no means of becoming acquainted with her. The most pleasant means might have been the Dachshund, since I am a great lover of animals, and also felt that the girl was in sympathy with this characteristic." He also adds that he repeatedly interfered in the fights of scuffling dogs with great dexterity and frequently to the great amazement of the spectators. Thus we learn that the girl, who pleased him, was always accompanied by this particular dog. This girl, however, was disregarded in the manifest dream, and there remained only the dog which he associates with her. Perhaps the elderly ladies who simpered at him took the place of the girl. The remainder of what he tells us is not enough to explain this point. Riding a bicycle in the dream is a direct repetition of the remembered situation. He had never met the girl with the dog except when he was on his bicycle.

3. When anyone has lost a loved one, he produces dreams of a special sort for a long time afterward, dreams in which the knowledge of death enters into the most remarkable compromises with the desire to have the deceased alive again. At one time the deceased is dead and yet continues to live on because he does not know that he is dead, and would die completely only if he knew it; at another time he is half dead and half alive, and each of these conditions has its particular signs. One cannot simply label these dreams nonsense, for to come to life again is no more impossible in the dream than, for example, it is in the fairy story, in which it occurs as a very frequent fate. As far as I have been able to analyze such dreams, I have always found them to be capable of a sensible solution, but that the pious wish to recall the deceased to life goes about expressing itself by the oddest methods. Let me tell you such a dream, which seems queer and senseless enough, and analysis of which will show you many of the points for which you have been prepared by our theoretical discussions. The dream is that of a man who had lost his father many years previously.

"Father is dead, but has been exhumed and looks badly. He goes on living, and the dreamer does everything to prevent him from noticing that fact." Then the dream goes on to other things, apparently irrelevant.

The father is dead, that we know. That he was exhumed is not really true, nor is the truth of the rest of the dream important. But the dreamer tells us that when he came back from his father's funeral, one of his teeth began to ache. He wanted to treat this tooth according to the Jewish precept, "If thy tooth offend thee, pluck it out," and betook himself to the dentist. But the latter said, "One does not simply pull a tooth out, one must have patience with it. I shall inject something to kill the nerve. Come again in three days and then I will take it out."

"This 'taking it out'," says the dreamer suddenly, "is the exhuming."

Is the dreamer right? It does not correspond exactly, only approximately, for the tooth is not taken out, but something that has died off is taken out of it. But after our other experiences we are probably safe in believing that the dream work is capable of such inaccuracies. It appears that the dreamer condensed, fused into one, his dead father and the tooth that was killed but retained. No wonder then, that in the manifest dream something senseless results, for it is impossible for everything that is said of the tooth to fit the father. What is it that serves as something intermediate between tooth and father and makes this condensation possible?

This interpretation must be correct, however, for the dreamer says that he is acquainted with the saying that when one dreams of losing a tooth it means that one is going to lose a member of his family.

We know that this popular interpretation is incorrect, or at least is correct only in a scurrilous sense. For that reason it is all the more surprising to find this theme thus touched upon in the background of other portions of the dream content.

Without any further urging, the dreamer now begins to tell of his father's illness and death as well as of his relations with him. The father was sick a long time, and his care and treatment cost him, the son, much money. And yet it was never too much for him, he never grew impatient, never wished it might end soon. He boasts of his true Jewish piety toward his father, of rigid adherence to the Jewish precepts. But are you not struck by a contradiction in the thoughts of the dream? He had identified tooth with father. As to the tooth he wanted to follow the Jewish precept that carries out its own judgment, "pull it out if it causes pain and annoyance." He had also been anxious to follow the precept of the law with regard to his father, which in this case, however, tells him to disregard trouble and expense, to take all the burdens upon himself and to let no hostile intent arise toward the object which causes the pain. Would not the agreement be far more compelling if he had really developed feelings toward his father similar to those about his sick tooth; that is, had he wished that a speedy death should put an end to that superfluous, painful and expensive existence?

I do not doubt that this was really his attitude toward his father during the latter's extended illness, and that his boastful assurances of filial piety were intended to distract his attention from these recollections. Under such circumstances, the death-wish directed toward the parent generally becomes active, and disguises itself in phrases of sympathetic consideration such as, "It would really be a blessed release for him." But note well that we have here overcome an obstacle in the latent dream thoughts themselves. The first part of these thoughts was surely unconscious only temporarily, that is to say, during the dream-work, while the inimical feelings toward the father might have been permanently unconscious, dating perhaps from childhood, occasionally slipping into consciousness, shyly and in disguise, during his father's illness. We can assert this with even greater certainty of other latent thoughts which have made unmistakable contributions to the dream content. To be sure, none of these inimical feelings toward the father can be discovered in the dream. But when we search a childhood history for the root of such enmity toward the father, we recollect that fear of the father arises because the latter, even in the earliest years, opposes the boy's sex activities, just as he is ordinarily forced to oppose them again, after puberty, for social motives. This relation to the father applies also to our dreamer; there had been mixed with his love for him much respect and fear, having its source in early sex intimidation.

From the onanism complex we can now explain the other parts of the manifest dream. "He looks badly" does, to be sure, allude to another remark of the dentist, that it looks badly to have a tooth missing in that place; but at the same time it refers to the "looking badly" by which the young man betrayed, or feared to betray, his excessive sexual activity during puberty. It was not without lightening his own heart that the dreamer transposed the bad looks from himself to his father in the manifest content, an inversion of the dream work with which you are familiar. *"He goes on living since then,"* disguises itself with the wish to have him alive again as well as with the promise of the dentist that the tooth will be preserved. A very subtle phrase, however, is the following: "The dreamer does everything *to prevent him (the father) from noticing the fact,"* a phrase calculated to lead us to conclude that he is dead. Yet the only meaningful conclusion is again drawn from the onanism complex, where it is a matter of course for the young man to do everything in order to hide his sex life from his father. Remember, in conclusion, that we were constantly forced to interpret the so-called tooth-ache dreams as dreams dealing with the subject of onanism and the punishment that is feared.

You now see how this incomprehensible dream came into being, by the creation of a remarkable and misleading condensation, by the fact that all the ideas emerge from the midst of the latent thought process, and by the creation of ambiguous substitute formations for the most hidden and, at the time, most remote of these thoughs.

4. We have tried repeatedly to understand those prosaic and banal dreams which have nothing foolish or repulsive about them, but which cause us to ask: "Why do we dream such unimportant stuff!" So I shall give you a new example of this kind, three dreams belonging together, all of which were dreamed in the same night by a young woman.

(a). *"She is going through the hall of her house and strikes her head against the low-hanging chandelier, so that her head bleeds."*

She has no reminiscence to contribute, nothing that really happened. The information she gives leads in quite another direction. "You know how badly my hair is falling out. Mother said to me yesterday, 'My child, if it goes on like this, you will have a head like the cheek of a buttock.' " Thus the head here stands for the other part of the body. We can understand the chandelier symbolically without other help; all objects that can be lengthened are symbols of the male organ. Thus the dream deals with a bleeding at the lower end of the body, which results from its collision with the male organ. This might still be ambiguous; her further associations show that it has to do with her belief that menstrual bleeding results from sexual intercourse with a man, a bit of sexual theory believed by many immature girls.

(*b*). "*She sees a deep hole in the vineyard which she knows was made by pulling out a tree.*" Herewith her remark that "*she misses the tree.*" She means that she did not see the tree in the dream, but the same phrase serves to express another thought which symbolic interpretation makes completely certain. The dream deals with another bit of the infantile sex theory, namely, with the belief that girls originally had the same genitals as boys and that the later conformation resulted from castration (pulling out of a tree).

(*c*). "*She is standing in front of the drawer of her writing table, with which she is so familiar that she knows immediately if anybody has been through it.*" The writing-table drawer, like every drawer, chest, or box, stands for the female genital. She knows that one can recognize from the genital the signs of sexual intercourse (and, as she thinks, even of any contact at all) and she has long been afraid of such a conviction. I believe that the accent in all these dreams is to be laid upon the idea of *knowing*. She is reminded of the time of her childish sexual investigations, the results of which made her quite proud at the time.

5. Again a little bit of symbolism. But this time I must first describe the psychic situation in a short preface. A man who spent the night with a woman describes his partner as one of those motherly natures whose desire for a child irresistibly breaks through during intercourse. The circumstances of their meeting, however, necessitated a precaution whereby the fertilizing discharge of semen is kept away from the womb. Upon awaking after this night, the woman tells the following dream:

"*An officer with a red cap follows her on the street. She flees from him, runs up the staircase, and he follows after her. Breathlessly she reaches her apartment and slams and locks the door behind her. He remains outside and as she looks through a peephole she sees him sitting outside on a bench and weeping.*"

You undoubtedly recognize in the pursuit by an officer with a red cap, and the breathless stair climbing, the representation of the sexual act. The fact that the dreamer locks herself in against the pursuer may serve as an example of that inversion which is so frequently used in dreams, for in reality it was the man who withdrew before the completion of the act. In the same way her grief has been transposed to the partner, it is he who weeps in the dream, whereby the discharge of the semen is also indicated.

You must surely have heard that in psychoanalysis it is always maintained that all dreams have a sexual meaning. Now you yourselves are in a position to form a judgment as to the incorrectness of this reproach. You have become acquainted with the wish-fulfillment dreams, which deal with the satisfying of the plainest needs, of hunger, of thirst, of longing for freedom, the dreams of convenience and of impatience and likewise the purely covetous and egoistic dreams. But that the markedly distorted dreams preponderantly—though again not exclusively —give expression to sex wishes, is a fact you may certainly keep in mind as one of the results of psychoanalytical research.

6. I have a special motive for piling up examples of the use of symbols in dreams. At our first meeting I complained of how hard it is, when lecturing on psychoanalysis, to demonstrate the facts in order to awaken conviction; and you very probably have come to agree with me since then. But the various assertions of psychoanalysis are so closely linked that one's conviction can easily extend from one point to a larger part of the whole. We might say of psychoanalysis that if we give it our little finger it promptly demands the whole hand. Anyone who was convinced by the explanation of errors can no longer logically disbelieve in all the rest of psychoanalysis. A second equally accessible point of approach is furnished by dream symbolism. I shall give you a dream, already published, of a peasant woman, whose husband is a watchman and who has certainly never heard anything about dream symbolism and psychoanalysis. You may then judge for yourselves whether its explanation with the help of sex symbols can be called arbitrary and forced.

"*Then someone broke into her house and she called in fright for a watchman. But the latter had gone companionably into a church together with two 'beauties.' A number of steps led up to the church. Behind the church was a hill, and on its crest a thick forest. The watchman was fitted out with a helmet, gorget and a cloak. He had a full brown beard. The two were going along peacefully with the watchman, had sack-like aprons bound around their hips. There was a path from the church to the hill. This was overgrown on both sides with grass and under-brush that kept getting thicker and that became a regular forest on the crest of the hill."*

You will recognize the symbols without any difficulty. The male genital is represented by a trinity of persons, the female by a landscape with a chapel, hill and forest. Again you en-counter steps as the symbol of the sexual act. That which is called a hill in the dream has the same name in anatomy, namely, *mons veneris,* the mount of Venus.

7. I have another dream which can be solved by means of inserting symbols, a dream that is remarkable and convincing because the dreamer himself translated all the symbols, even though he had had no preliminary knowledge of dream interpre-tation. This situation is very unusual and the conditions essen-tial to its occurrence are not clearly known.

"He is going for a walk with his father in some place which must be the Prater,[1] for one can see the rotunda and before it a smaller building to which is anchored a captive balloon, which, however, seems fairly slack. His father asks him what all that is for; he wonders at it himself but explains it to his father. Then they come to a courtyard in which there lies spread out a big sheet of metal. His father wants to break off a big piece of it for himself but first looks about him to see if anyone might see him. He says to him that all he needs to do is to tell the inspector and then he can take some without more ado. There are steps leading from this courtyard down into a pit, the walls of which are upholstered with some soft material rather like a leather arm chair. At the end of this pit is a longish platform and then a new pit begins . . ."

The dreamer himself interprets as follows: "The rotunda is my genital, the balloon in front of it is my penis, of whose slackness I have been complaining." Thus one may translate in more detail, that the rotunda is the posterior—a part of the body which the child regularly considers as part of the genital—while the smaller building before it is the scrotum. In the dream his father asks him what all that is for; that is to say, he asks the object and function of the genitals. It is easy to turn this situation around so that the dreamer is the one who does the

[1]The principal street of Vienna.

asking. Since no such questioning of the father ever took place in real life, we must think of the thought of this dream as a wish or consider it in the light of a supposition, "If I had asked father for sexual enlightenment." We will find the continuation of this idea in another place shortly.

The courtyard, in which the sheet metal lies spread out, is not to be considered primarily as symbolical but refers to the father's place of business. For reasons of discretion I have substituted the "sheet metal" for another material with which the father deals, without changing anything in the literal wording of the dream. The dreamer entered his father's business and took great offense at the rather dubious practices upon which the profits depended to a large extent. For this reason the continuation of the above idea of the dream might be expressed as "if I had asked him, he would only have deceived me as he deceives his customers." The dreamer himself gives us the second meaning of "breaking off the metal," which serves to represent the commercial dishonesty. He says it means masturbation. Not only have we long since become familiar with this symbol, but the fact also is in agreement. The secrecy of masturbation is expressed by means of its opposite—"It can be safely done openly." Again our expectations are fulfilled by the fact that masturbatory activity is referred to as the father's, just as the questioning was in the first scene of the dream. Upon being questioned he immediately gives the interpretation of the pit as the vagina on account of the soft upholstering of its walls. I will add arbitrarily that the "going down" like the more usual "going up" is meant to describe the sexual intercourse in the vagina.

Such details as the fact that the first pit ends in a platform and then a new one begins, he explains himself as having been taken from his own history. He practiced intercourse for a while, then gave it up on account of inhibitions, and now hopes to be able to resume it as a result of the treatment.

8. The two following dreams are those of a foreigner, of very polygamous tendencies, and I give them to you as proof for the claim that one's ego appears in every dream, even in those in which it is disguised in the manifest content. The trunks in the dream are a symbol for woman.

(a). *"He is to take a trip, his luggage is placed on a carriage*

*to be taken to the station, and there are many trunks piled up,
among which are two big black ones like sample trunks. He
says, consolingly, to someone, 'Well, they are only going as far
as the station with us.' "*

In reality he does travel with a great deal of luggage, but he
also brings many tales of women with him when he comes for
treatment. The two black trunks stand for two dark women
who play the chief part in his life at present. One of them
wanted to travel to Vienna after him, but he telegraphed her
not to, upon my advice.

(*b*). A scene at the customs house: *"A fellow traveler opens
his trunk and says indifferently while puffing a cigarette,
'There's nothing in here.' The customs official seems to believe
him but delves into the trunk once more and finds something
particularly forbidden. The traveler then says resignedly,
'Well, there's no help for it.' "*

He himself is the traveler, I the customs official. Though
otherwise very frank in his confessions, he has on this occasion
tried to conceal from me a new relationship which he had struck
up with a lady whom he was justified in believing that I knew.
The painful situation of being convicted of this is transposed
into a strange person so that he himself apparently is not present
in the dream.

9. The following is an example of a symbol which I have not
yet mentioned:

*"He meets his sister in company with two friends who are
themselves sisters. He extends his hand to both of them but not
to his sister."*

This is no allusion to a real occurrence. His thoughts instead
lead him back to a time when his observations made him wonder
why a girl's breasts develop so late. The two sisters, therefore,
are the breasts. He would have liked to touch them if only it
had not been his sister.

10. Let me add an example of a symbol of death in a dream:

*"He is walking with two persons whose name he knows but
has forgotten. By the time he is awake, over a very high, steep
iron bridge. Suddenly the two people are gone and he sees a
ghostly man with a cap, and clad in white. He asks this man
whether he is the telegraph messenger . . . , No. Or is he a
coachman? No. Then he goes on,"* and even in the dream he is

in great fear. After waking he continues the dream by a phantasy in which the iron bridge suddenly breaks, and he plunges into the abyss.

When the dreamer emphasizes the fact that certain individuals in a dream are unknown, that he has forgotten their names, they are generally persons standing in very close relationship to the dreamer. This dreamer has two sisters; if it be true, as his dream indicates, that he wished these two dead, then it would only be justice if the fear of death fell upon him for so doing. In connection with the telegraph messenger he remarks that such people always bring bad news. Judged by his uniform he might also have been the lamp-lighter, who, however, also extinguishes the lamps—in other words, as the spirit of death extinguishes the flame of life. The coachman reminds him of Uhland's poem of King Karl's ocean voyage and also of a dangerous lake trip with two companions in which he played the role of the king in the poem. In connection with the iron bridge he remembers a recent accident and the stupid saying "Life is a suspension bridge."

11. The following may serve as another example of the representation of death in a dream: *"An unknown man leaves a black bordered visiting card for him."*

12. The following dream will interest you for several reasons, though it is one arising from a neurotic condition among other things:

"He is traveling in a train. The train stops in an open field. He thinks it means that there is going to be an accident, that he must save himself, and he goes through all the compartments of the train and strikes dead everyone whom he meets, conductors, engine drivers, etc."

In connection with this he tells a story that one of his friends told him. An insane man was being transported in a private compartment in a certain place in Italy, but through some mistake another traveler was put in the same compartment. The insane man murdered his fellow passenger. Thus he identifies himself with this insane person and bases his right so to do upon a compulsive idea which was then torturing him, namely, he must "do away with all persons who knew of his failings." But then he himself finds a better motivation which gave rise to the dream. The day before, in the theatre, he again saw the girl whom he had expected to marry but whom he had left because she had given him cause for jealousy. With a capacity for intense jealousy such as he has, he would really be insane if he married. In other words, he considers her so untrustworthy that out of jealousy he would have to strike dead all the persons who stood in his way. Going through a series of rooms, of compartments in this case, we have already learned to recognize as the symbol of marriage (the opposite of monogamy).

In connection with the train stopping in the open country and his fear of an accident, he tells the following: Once, when he was traveling in a train and it came to a sudden stop outside of a station, a young lady in the compartment remarked that perhaps there was going to be a collision, and that in that case the best precaution would be to pull one's legs up. But this "legs up" had also played a role in the many walks and excursions into the open which he had taken with the girl in that happy period in their first love. Thus it is a new argument for the idea that he would have to be crazy in order to marry her now. But from my knowledge of the situation I can assume with certainty that the wish to be as crazy as that nevertheless exists in him.

THIRTEENTH LECTURE

THE DREAM

Archaic Remnants and Infantilism in the Dream

LET us revert to our conclusion that the dream-work, under the influence of the dream censorship, transforms the latent dream thoughts into some other form of expression. The latent thoughts are no other than the conscious thoughts known to us in our waking hours; the new mode of expression is incomprehensible to us because of its many-sided features. We have said it extends back to conditions of our intellectual development which we have long progressed beyond, to the language of pictures, the symbol-representations, perhaps to those conditions which were in force before the development of our language of thought. So we called the mode of expression of the dream-work the archaic or regressive.

You may conclude that as a result of the deeper study of the dream-work we gain valuable information about the rather unknown beginnings of our intellectual development. I trust this will be true, but this work has not, up to the present time, been undertaken. The antiquity into which the dream-work carries us back is of a double aspect, firstly, the individual antiquity, childhood; and, secondly (in so far as every individual in his childhood lives over again in some more or less abbreviated manner the entire development of the human race), also this antiquity, the philogenetic. That we shall be able to differentiate which part of the latent psychic proceeding has its source in the individual, and which part in the philogenetic antiquity is not improbable. In this connection it appears to me, for example, that the symbolic relations which the individual has never learned are ground for the belief that they should be regarded as a philogenetic inheritance.

However, this is not the only archaic characteristic of the

dream. You probably all know from your own experiences the peculiar amnesia, that is, loss of memory, concerning childhood. I mean the fact that the first years, to the fifth, sixth or eighth, have not left the same traces in our memory as have later experiences. One meets with individual persons, to be sure, who can boast of a continuous memory from the very beginning to the present day, but the other condition, that of a gap in the memory, is far more frequent. I believe we have not laid enough stress on this fact. The child is able to speak well at the age of two, it soon shows that it can become adjusted to the most complicated psychic situations, and makes remarks which years later are retold to it, but which it has itself entirely forgotten. Besides, the memory in the early years is more facile, because it is less burdened than in later years. Nor is there any reason for considering the memory-function as a particularly high or difficult psychic performance; in fact, the contrary is true, and you can find a good memory in persons who stand very low intellectually.

As a second peculiarity closely related to the first, I must point out that certain well-preserved memories, for the most part formatively experienced, stand forth in this memory-void which surrounds the first years of childhood and do not justify this hypothesis. Our memory deals selectively with its later materials, with impressions which come to us in later life. It retains the important and discards the unimportant. This is not true of the retained childhood memories. They do not bespeak necessarily important experiences of childhood, not even such as from the viewpoint of the child need appear of importance. They are often so banal and intrinsically so meaningless that we ask ourselves in wonder why just these details have escaped being forgotten. I once endeavored to approach the riddle of childhood amnesia and the interrupted memory remnants with the help of analysis, and I arrived at the conclusion that in the case of the child, too, only the important has remained in the memory, except that by means of the process of condensation already known to you, and especially by means of distortion, the important is represented in the memory by something that appears unimportant. For this reason I have called these childhood memories "disguise-memories," memories used to conceal; by means of careful analysis one is able to develop out of them everything that is forgotten.

In psychoanalytic treatment we are regularly called upon to fill out the infantile memory gaps, and in so far as the cure is to any degree successful, we are able again to bring to light the content of the childhood years thus clouded in forgetfulness. These impressions have never really been forgotten, they have only been inaccessible, latent, have belonged to the unconscious. But sometimes they bob up out of the unconscious spontaneously, and, as a matter of fact, this is what happens in dreams. It is apparent that the dream life knows how to find the entrance to these latent, infantile experiences. Beautiful examples of this occur in literature, and I myself can present such an example. I once dreamed in a certain connection of a person who must have performed some service for me, and whom I clearly saw. He was a one-eyed man, short in stature, stout, his head deeply sunk into his neck. I concluded from the content that he was a physician. Luckily I was able to ask my mother, who was still living, how the physician in my birth-place, which I left when I was three years old, looked, and I learned from her that he had one eye, was short and stout, with his head sunk into his neck, and also learned at what forgotten mishap he had been of service to me. This control over the forgotten material of childhood years is, then, a further archaic tendency of the dream.

The same information may be made use of in another of the puzzles that have presented themselves to us. You will recall how astonished people were when we came to the conclusion that the stimuli which gave rise to dreams were extremely bad and licentious sexual desires which have made dream-censorship and dream-distortion necessary. After we have interpreted such a dream for the dreamer and he, in the most favorable circumstances does not attack the interpretation itself, he almost always asks the question whence such a wish comes, since it seems foreign to him and he feels conscious of just the opposite sensations. We need not hesitate to point out this origin. These evil wish-impulses have their origin in the past, often in a past which is not too far away. It can be shown that at one time they were known and conscious, even if they no longer are so. The woman, whose dream is interpreted to mean that she would like to see her seventeen-year old daughter dead, discovers under our ance that she in fact at one time entertained this wish. The child is the fruit of an unhappy marriage, which early ended in a separation. Once, while the child was still in the womb, and after a tense scene with her husband, she beat her body with her fists in a fit of anger, in order to kill the child. How many mothers who to-day love their children tenderly, perhaps too tenderly, received them unwillingly, and at the time wished that the life within them would not develop further; indeed, translated this wish into various actions, happily harmless. The later death-wish against some loved one, which seems so strange, also has its origin in early phases of the relationship to that person.

The father, the interpretation of whose dream shows that he wishes for the death of his eldest and favorite child, must be reminded of the fact that at one time this wish was no stranger to him. While the child was still a suckling, this man, who was unhappy in his choice of a wife, often thought that if the little being that meant nothing to him would die, he would again be free, and would make better use of his freedom. A like origin may be found for a large number of similar hate impulses; they are recollections of something that belonged to the past, were once conscious and played their parts in the psychic life. You will wish to conclude therefrom that such wishes and such dreams cannot occur if such changes in the relationship to a person have not taken place; if such relationship was always of the same character. I am ready to admit this, only wish to warn you that you are to take into consideration not the exact terms of the dream, but the meaning thereof according to its interpretation. It may happen that the manifest dream of the death of some loved person has only made use of some frightful mask, that it really means something entirely different, or that the loved person serves as a concealing substitute for some other.

But the same circumstances will call forth another, more difficult question. You say: "Granted this death wish was present at some time or other, and is substantiated by memory, yet this is no explanation. It is long outlived, to-day it can be present only in the unconscious and as an empty, emotionless memory, but not as a strong impulse. Why should it be recalled by the dream at all?" This question is justified. The attempt to answer it would lead us far afield and necessitate taking up a position in one of the most important points of dream study.

But I must remain within the bounds of our discussion and practice restraint. Prepare yourselves for the temporary abstention. Let us be satisfied with the circumstantial proof that this outlived wish can be shown to act as a dream stimulator and let us continue the investigation to see whether or not other evil wishes admit of the same derivation out of the past.

Let us continue with the removal or death-wish which most frequently can be traced back to the unbounded egoism of the dreamer. Such a wish can very often be shown to be the inciting cause of the dream. As often as someone has been in our way in life—and how often must this happen in the complicated relationships of life—the dream is ready to do away with him, be he father, mother, brother, sister, spouse, etc. We have wondered sufficiently over this evil tendency of human nature, and certainly were not predisposed to accept the authenticity of this result of dream interpretation without question. After it has once been suggested to us to seek the origin of such wishes in the past, we disclose immediately the period of the individual past in which such egoism and such wish-impulses, even as directed against those closest to the dreamer, are no longer strangers. It is just in these first years of childhood which later are hidden by amnesia, that this egoism frequently shows itself in most extreme form, and from which regular but clear tendencies thereto, or real remnants thereof, show themselves. For the child loves itself first, and later learns to love others, to sacrifice something of its ego for another. Even those persons whom the child seems to love from the very beginning, it loves at the outset because it has need of them, cannot do without them, in others words, out of egoistical motives. Not until later does the love impulse become independent of egoism. *In brief, egoism has taught the child to love.*

In this connection it is instructive to compare the child's regard for his brothers and sisters with that which he has for his parents. The little child does not necessarily love his brothers and sisters, often, obviously, he does not love them at all. There is no doubt that in them he hates his rivals and it is known how frequently this attitude continues for many years until maturity, and even beyond, without interruption. Often enough this attitude is superseded by a more tender feeling, or rather let us say, glossed over, but the hostile feeling appears regularly

have been the earlier. It is most noticeable in children of from
two and one-half to four or five years of age, when a new little
brother or sister arrives. The latter is usually received in a
far from friendly manner. Expressions such as "I don't want
him! Let the stork take him away again," are very usual.
Subsequently every opportunity is made use of to disparage the
new arrival, and even attempts to do him bodily harm, direct
attacks, are not unheard of. If the difference in age is less, the
child learns of the existence of the rival with intense psychic
activity, and accommodates himself to the new situation. If the
difference in age is greater, the new child may awaken certain
sympathies as an interesting object, as a sort of living doll, and
if the difference is eight years or more, motherly impulses,
especially in the case of girls, may come into play. But to be
truthful, when we disclose in a dream the wish for the death
of a mother or sister we need seldom find it puzzling and may
trace its origin easily to early childhood, often enough, also,
to the propinquity of later years.

Probably no nurseries are free from mighty conflicts among
the inhabitants. The motives are rivalry for the love of the
parents, articles owned in common, the room itself. The hostile
impulses are called forth by older as well as younger brothers
and sisters. I believe it was Bernard Shaw who said: "If there
is anyone who hates a young English lady more than does her
mother, it is her elder sister." There is something about this
saying, however, that arouses our antipathy. We can, at a
pinch, understand hatred of brothers and sisters, and rivalry
among them, but how may feelings of hatred force their way
into the relationship between daughter and mother, parents and
children?

This relationship is without doubt the more favorable, even
when looked at from the viewpoint of the child. This is in
accord with our expectation; we find it much more offensive for
love between parents and children to be lacking than for love
between brothers and sisters. We have, so to speak, made something holy in the first instance which in the other case we permitted to remain profane. But daily observation can show us
how frequently the feelings between parents and their grown
children fail to come up to the ideal established by society, how
much enmity exists and would find expression did not accumula-

tions of piety and of tender impulse hold them back. The motives for this are everywhere known and disclose a tendency to separate those of the same sex, daughter from mother, father from son. The daughter finds in her mother the authority that hems in her will and that is entrusted with the task of causing her to carry out the abstention from sexual liberty which society demands; in certain cases also she is the rival who objects to being displaced. The same type of thing occurs in a more glaring manner between father and son. To the son the father is the embodiment of every social restriction, borne with such great opposition; the father bars the way to freedom of will, to early sexual satisfaction, and where there is family property held in common, to the enjoyment thereof. Impatient waiting for the death of the father grows to heights approximating tragedy in the case of a successor to the throne. Less strained is the relationship between father and daughter, mother and son. The latter affords the purest examples of an unalterable tenderness, in no way disturbed by egoistical considerations.

Why do I speak of these things, so banal and so well known? Because there is an unmistakable disposition to deny their significance in life, and to set forth the ideal demanded by society as a fulfilled thing much oftener than it really is fulfilled. But it is preferable for psychology to speak the truth, rather than that this task should be left to the cynic. In any event, this denial refers only to actual life. The arts of narrative and dramatic poetry are still free to make use of the motives that result from a disturbance of this ideal.

It is not to be wondered at that in the case of a large number of people the dream discloses the wish for the removal of the parents, especially the parent of the same sex. We may conclude that it is also present during waking hours, and that it becomes conscious even at times when it is able to mask itself behind another motive, as in the case of the dreamer's sympathy for his father's unnecessary sufferings in example 3. It is seldom that the enmity alone controls the relationship; much more often it recedes behind more tender impulses, by which it is suppressed, and must wait until a dream isolates it. That which the dream shows us in enlarged form as a result of such isolation, shrinks together again after it has been properly docketed in its relation to life as a result of our interpretation (H. Sachs). But we

also find this dream wish in places where it has no connection
with life, and where the adult, in his waking hours, would
never recognize it. The reason for this is that the deepest and
most uniform motive for becoming unfriendly, especially between
persons of the same sex, has already made its influence felt in
earliest childhood.

I mean the love rivalry, with the especial emphasis of the sex
character. The son, even as a small child, begins to develop an
especial tenderness for his mother, whom he considers as his
own property, and feels his father to be a rival who puts into
question his individual possession; and in the same manner the
little daughter sees in her mother a person who is a disturbing
element in her tender relationship with her father, and who
occupies a position that she could very well fill herself. One
learns from these observations to what early years these ideas
extend back—ideas which we designate as the *Oedipus-complex*,
because this myth realizes with a very slightly weakened effect
the two extreme wishes which grow out of the situation of the
son—to kill his father and take his mother to wife. I do not
wish to maintain that the Oedipus-complex covers entirely the
relation of the child to its parents; this relation can be much
more complicated. Furthermore, the Oedipus-complex is more
or less well-developed; it may even experience a reversal, but
it is a customary and very important factor in the psychic life
of the child; and one tends rather to underestimate than to
overestimate its influence and the developments which may follow from it. In addition, children frequently react to the
Oedipus-idea through stimulation by the parents, who in the
placing of their affection are often led by sex-differences, so that
the father prefers the daughter, the mother the son; or again,
where the marital affection has cooled, and this love is substituted
for the outworn love.

One cannot maintain that the world was very grateful to
psychoanalytic research for its discovery of the Oedipus-complex.
On the contrary, it called forth the strongest resistance on the
part of adults; and persons who had neglected to take part in
denying this proscribed or tabooed feeling-relationship later
made good the omission by taking all value from the complex
through false interpretations. According to my unchanged conviction there is nothing to deny and nothing to make more

palatable. One should accept the fact, recognized by the Greek myth itself, as inevitable destiny. On the other hand, it is interesting that this Oedipus-complex, cast out of life, was yielded up to poetry and given the freest play. O. Rank has shown in a careful study how this very Oedipus-complex has supplied dramatic literature with a large number of motives in unending variations, derivations and disguises, also in distorted forms such as we recognize to be the work of a censor. We may also ascribe this Oedipus-complex to those dreamers who were so fortunate as to escape in later life these conflicts with their parents, and intimately associated therewith we find what we call the *castration complex,* the reaction to sexual intimidation or restriction, ascribed to the father, of early infantile sexuality.

By applying our former researches to the study of the psychic life of the child, we may expect to find that the origin of other forbidden dream-wishes, of excessive sexual impulses, may be explained in the same manner. Thus we are moved to study the development of sex-life in the child also, and we discover the following from a number of sources: In the first place, it is a mistake to deny that the child has a sexual life, and to take it for granted that sexuality commences with the ripening of the genitals at the time of puberty. On the contrary—the child has from the very beginning a sexual life rich in content and differing in numerous respects from that which is later considered normal. What we call "perverse" in the life of the adult, differs from the normal in the following respects: first, in disregard for the dividing line of species (the gulf between man and animal); second, being insensible to the conventional feeling of disgust; third, the incest-limitation (being prohibited from seeking sexual satisfaction with near blood-relations); fourth, homosexuality, and fifth, transferring the role of the genitals to other organs and other parts of the body. None of these limitations exist in the beginning, but are gradually built up in the course of development and education. The little child is free from them. He knows no unbridgable chasm between man and animal; the arrogance with which man distinguishes himself from the animal is a later acquisition. In the beginning he is not disgusted at the sight of excrement, but slowly learns to be so disgusted under the pressure of education; he lays no special stress on the difference between the sexes, rather accredi- to both the same genital formation; he directs his earliest sexual desires and his curiosity toward those persons closest to him, and who are dear to him for various reasons—his parents, brothers and sisters, nurses; and finally, you may observe in him that which later breaks through again, raised now to a love attraction, viz., that he does not expect pleasure from his sexual organs alone, but that many other parts of the body portray the same sensitiveness, are the media of analogous sensations, and are able to play the role of the genitals. The child may, then, be called "polymorphus perverse," and if he makes but slight use of all these impulses, it is, on the one hand, because of their lesser intensity as compared to later life, and on the other hand, because the bringing up of the child immediately and energetically suppresses all his sexual expressions. This suppression continues in theory, so to say, since the grown-ups are careful to control part of the childish sex-expressions, and to disguise another part by misrepresenting its sexual nature until they can deny the whole business. These are often the same persons who discourse violently against all the sexual faults of the child and then at the writing table defend the sexual purity of the same children. Where children are left to themselves or are under the influence of corruption, they often are capable of really conspicuous performances of perverse sexual activity. To be sure, the grown-ups are right in looking upon these things as "childish performances," as "play," for the child is not to be judged as mature and answerable either before the bar of custom or before the law, but these things do exist, they have their significance as indications of innate characteristics as well as causes and furtherances of later developments, they give us an insight into childhood sex-life and thereby into the sex life of man. When we rediscover in the background of our distorted dreams all these perverse wish-impulses, it means only that the dream has in this field traveled back to the infantile condition.

Especially noteworthy among these forbidden wishes are those of incest, i.e., those directed towards sexual intercourse with parents and brothers and sisters. You know what antipathy society feels toward such intercourse, or at least pretends to feel, and what weight is laid on the prohibitions directed against it. The most monstrous efforts have been made to explain this fear of incest. Some have believed that it is due to evolutionary foresight on the part of nature, which is psychically represented by this prohibition, because inbreeding would deteriorate the race-character; others maintained that because of having lived together since early childhood the sexual desire is diverted from the persons under consideration. In both cases, furthermore, the incest-avoidance would be automatically assured, and it would be difficult to understand the need of strict prohibitions, which rather point to the presence of a strong desire. Psycho-analytic research has incontrovertibly shown that the incestuous love choice is rather the first and most customary choice, and that not until later is there any resistance, the source of which probably is to be found in the individual psychology.

Let us sum up what our plunge into child psychology has given us toward the understanding of the dream. We found not only that the materials of forgotten childhood experiences are accessible to the dream, but we saw also that the psychic life of children, with all its peculiarities, its egoism, its incestuous love-choice, etc., continues, for the purposes of the dream, in the unconscious, and that the dream nightly leads us back to this infantile stage. Thus it becomes more certain *that the unconscious in our psychic life is the infantile*. The estranging impression that there is so much evil in man, begins to weaken. This frightful evil is simply the original, primitive, infantile side of psychic life, which we may find in action in children, which we overlook partly because of the slightness of its dimensions, partly because it is lightly considered, since we demand no ethical heights of the child. Since the dream regresses to this stage, it seems to have made apparent the evil that lies in us. But it is only a deceptive appearance by which we have allowed ourselves to be frightened. We are not so evil as we might suspect from the interpretation of dreams.

If the evil impulses of the dream are merely infantilism, a return to the beginnings of our ethical development, since the dream simply makes children of us again in thinking and in feeling, we need not be ashamed of these evil dreams if we are reasonable. But being reasonable is only a part of psychic life. Many things are taking place there that are not reasonable, and so it happens that we are ashamed of such dreams, and unreasonably. We turn them over to the dream-censorship, are ashamed and angry if one of these dreams has in some unu

manner succeeded in penetrating into consciousness in an undistorted form, so that we must recognize it—in fact, we are at
times just as ashamed of the distorted dream as we would be
if we understood it. Just think of the scandalized opinion of
the fine old lady about her uninterpreted dream of "services
of love." The problem is not yet solved, and it is still possible
that upon further study of the evil in the dream we shall come
to some other decision and arrive at another valuation of human
nature.

As a result of the whole investigation we grasp two facts,
which, however, disclose only the beginnings of new riddles,
new doubts. First: the regression of dream-work is not only
formal, it is also of greater import. It not only translates our
thoughts into a primitive form of expression, but it reawakens
the peculiarities of our primitive psychic life, the ancient predominance of the ego, the earliest impulses of our sexual life,
even our old intellectual property, if we may consider the symbolic relations as such. And second: We must accredit all these
infantilisms which once were governing, and solely governing,
to the unconscious, about which our ideas now change and are
broadened. Unconscious is no longer a name for what is at
that time latent, the unconscious is an especial psychic realm
with wish-impulses of its own, with its own method of expression and with a psychic mechanism peculiar to itself, all of
which ordinarily are not in force. But the latent dream-
thoughts, which we have solved by means of the dream-interpretation, are not of this realm. They are much more nearly the
same as any we may have thought in our waking hours. Still
they are unconscious; how does one solve this contradiction?
We begin to see that a distinction must be made. Something
that originates in our conscious life, and that shares its characteristics—we call it the day-remnants—combines in the dream-
fabrication with something else out of the realm of the unconscious. Between these two parts the dream-work completes
itself. The influencing of the day-remnants by the unconscious
necessitates regression. This is the deepest insight into the
nature of the dream that we are able to attain without having
searched through further psychic realms. The time will soon
come, however, when we shall clothe the unconscious character of
the latent dream-thought with another name, which shall differ-

entiate it from the unconscious out of the realm of the infantile.

We may, to be sure, propound the question: what forces the psychological activity during sleep to such regression? Why do not the sleep disturbing psychic stimuli do the job without it? And if they must, because of the dream censorship, disguise themselves through old forms of expression which are no longer comprehensible, what is the use of giving new life to old, long-outgrown psychic stimuli, wishes and character types, that is, why the material regression in addition to the formal? The only satisfactory answer would be this, that only in this manner can a dream be built up, that dynamically the dream-stimulus can be satisfied only in this way. But for the time being we have no right to give such an answer.

FOURTEENTH LECTURE

THE DREAM

Wish Fulfillment

MAY I bring to your attention once more the ground we have already covered? How, when we met with dream distortion in the application of our technique, we decided to leave it alone for the time being, and set out to obtain decisive information about the nature of the dream by way of infantile dreams? How, then, armed with the results of this investigation, we attacked dream distortion directly and, I trust, in some measure overcame it? But we must remind ourselves that the results we found along the one way and along the other do not fit together as well as might be. It is now our task to put these two results together and balance them against one another.

From both sources we have seen that the dream-work consists essentially in the transposition of thoughts into an hallucinatory experience. How that can take place is puzzling enough, but it is a problem of general psychology with which we shall not busy ourselves here. We have learned from the dreams of children that the purpose of the dream-work is the satisfaction of one of the sleep-disturbing psychic stimuli by means of a wish fulfillment. We were unable to make a similar statement concerning distorted dreams, until we knew how to interpret them. But from the very beginning we expected to be able to bring the distorted dreams under the same viewpoint as the infantile. The earliest fulfillment of this expectation led us to believe that as a matter of fact all dreams are the dreams of children and that they all work with infantile materials, through childish psychic stimuli and mechanics. Since we consider that we have conquered dream-distortion, we must continue the investigation to see whether our hypothesis of wish-fulfillment holds good for distorted dreams also.

We very recently subjected a number of dreams to interpretation, but left wish-fulfillment entirely out of consideration. I am convinced that the question again and again occurred to you: "What about wish-fulfillment, which ostensibly is the goal of dream-work?" This question is important. It was, in fact, the question of our lay-critics. As you know, humanity has an instinctive antagonism toward intellectual novelties. The expression of such a novelty should immediately be reduced to its narrowest limits, if possible, comprised in a commonplace phrase. Wish-fulfillment has become that phrase for the new dream-science. The layman asks: "Where is the wish-fulfillment?" Immediately, upon having heard that the dream is supposed to be a wish-fulfillment, and indeed, by the very asking of the question, he answers it with a denial. He is at once reminded of countless dream-experiences of his own, where his aversion to the dream was enormous, so that the proposition of psychoanalytic dream-science seems very improbable to him. It is a simple matter to answer the layman that wish-fulfillment cannot be apparent in distorted dreams, but must be sought out, so that it is not recognized until the dream is interpreted. We know, too, that the wishes in these distorted dreams are prohibited wishes, are wishes rejected by the censor and that their existence is the very cause of the dream distortion and the reason for the intrusion of the dream censor. But it is hard to convince the lay-critic that one may not seek the wish-fulfillment in the dream before the dream has been interpreted. This is continually forgotten. His sceptical attitude toward the theory of wish-fulfillment is really nothing more than a consequence of dream-censorship, a substitute and a result of the denial of this censored dream-wish.

To be sure, even we shall find it necessary to explain to ourselves why there are so many dreams of painful content, and especially dreams of fear. We see here, for the first time, the problem of the affects in the dream, a problem worthy of separate investigation, but which unfortunately cannot be considered here. If the dream is a wish-fulfillment, painful experiences ought to be impossible in the dream; in that the lay-critics apparently are right. But three complications, not thought of by them, must be taken into consideration.

First: It may be that the dream work has not been successful in creating a wish-fulfillment, so that a part of the painful effect of the dream-thought is left over for the manifest dream. Analysis should then show that these thoughts were far more painful even than the dream which was built out of them. This much may be proved in each instance. We admit, then, that the dream work has not achieved its purpose any more than the drink-dream due to the thirst-stimulus has achieved its purpose of satisfying the thirst. One remains thirsty, and must wake up in order to drink. But it was a real dream, it sacrificed nothing of its nature. We must say: "Although strength be lacking, let us praise the will to do." The clearly recognizable intention, at least, remains praiseworthy. Such cases of miscarriage are not unusual. A contributory cause is this, that it is so much more difficult for the dream work to change affect into content in its own sense; the affects often show great resistance, and thus it happens that the dream work has worked the painful content of the dream-thoughts over into a wish-fulfillment, while the painful affect continues in its unaltered form. Hence in dreams of this type the affect does not fit the content at all, and our critics may say the dream is so little a wish-fulfillment that a harmless content may be experienced as painful. In answer to this unintelligible remark we say that the wish-fulfillment tendency in the dream-work appears most prominent, because isolated, in just such dreams. The error is due to the fact that he who does not know neurotics imagines the connection between content and affect as all too intimate, and cannot, therefore, grasp the fact that a content may be altered without any corresponding change in the accompanying affect-expression.

A second, far more important and more extensive consideration, equally disregarded by the layman, is the following: A wish-fulfillment certainly must bring pleasure—but to whom? Naturally, to him who has the wish. But we know from the dreamer that he stands in a very special relationship to his wishes. He casts them aside, censors them, he will have none of them. Their fulfillment gives him no pleasure, but only the opposite. Experience then shows that this opposite, which must still be explained, appears in the form of fear. The dreamer in his relation to his dream-wishes can be compared only to a combination of two persons bound together by some strong common quality. Instead of further explanations, I shall give you a well-known fairy tale, in which you will again find the relationships I have mentioned. A good fairy promises a poor couple, husband and wife, to fulfill their first three wishes. They are overjoyed, and determine to choose their three wishes with great care. But the woman allows herself to be led astray by the odor of cooking sausages emanating from the next cottage, and wishes she had a couple of such sausages. Presto! they are there. This is the first wish-fulfillment. Now the husband becomes angry, and in his bitterness wishes that the sausages might hang from the end of her nose. This, too, is accomplished, and the sausages cannot be removed from their new location. So this is the second wish-fulfillment, but the wish is that of the husband. The wife is very uncomfortabe because of the fulfillment of this wish. You know how the fairy tale continues. Since both husband and wife are fundamentally one, the third wish must be that the sausages be removed from the nose of the wife. We could make use of this fairy tale any number of times in various connections; here it serves only as an illustration of the possibility that the wish-fulfillment for the one personality may lead to an aversion on the part of the other, if the two do not agree with one another.

It will not be difficult now to come to a better understanding of the anxiety-dream. We shall make one more observation, then we shall come to a conclusion to which many things lead. The observation is that the anxiety dreams often have a content which is entirely free from distortion and in which the censorship is, so to speak, eluded. The anxiety dream is ofttimes an undisguised wish-fulfillment, not, to be sure, of an accepted, but of a discarded wish. The anxiety development has stepped into the place of the censorship. While one may assert of the infantile dream that it is the obvious fulfillment of a wish that has gained admittance, and of the distorted dream that it is the disguised fulfillment of a suppressed wish, he must say of the anxiety dream that the only suitable formula is this, that it is the obvious fulfillment of a suppressed wish. Anxiety is the mark which shows that the suppressed wish showed itself stronger than the censorship, that it put through its wish-fulfillment despite the censorship, or was about to put it through. We understand that what is wish-fulfillment for the suppr---- wish is for us, who are on the side of the dream-censor, painful sensation and a cause for antagonism. The anxiety which occurs in dreams is, if you wish, anxiety because of the strength of these otherwise suppressed wishes. Why this antagonism arises in the form of anxiety cannot be discovered from a study of the dream alone; one must obviously study anxiety from other sources.

What holds true for the undistorted anxiety dream we may assume to be true also of those dreams which have undergone partial distortion, and of the other dreams of aversion whose painful impressions very probably denote approximations of anxiety. The anxiety dream is usually also a dream that causes waking; we habitually interrupt sleep before the suppressed wish of the dream has accomplished its entire fulfillment in opposition to the censorship. In this case the execution of the dream is unsuccessful, but this does not change its nature. We have likened the dream to the night watchman or sleep-defender who wishes to protect our sleep from being disturbed. The night watchman, too, sometimes wakes the sleeper when he feels himself too weak to drive away the disturbance or danger all by himself. Yet we are often able to remain asleep, even when the dream begins to become suspicious, and begins to assume the form of anxiety. We say to ourselves in our sleep: "It's only a dream," and we sleep on.

When does it happen that the dream-wish is in a position to overpower this censorship? The conditions for this may be just as easily furnished by the dream-wish as by the dream-censorship. The wish may, for unknown reasons, become irresistible; but one gets the impression that more frequently the attitude of the dream censorship is to blame for this disarrangement in the relations of the forces. We have already heard that the censorship works with varying intensity in each single instance, that it handles each element with a different degree of strictness; now we should like to add the proposition that it is an extremely variable thing and does not exert equal force on every occasion against the same objectionable element. If on occasion the censorship feels itself powerless with respect to a dream-wish which threatens to over-ride it, then, instead of distortion, it makes use of the final means at its disposal, it destroys the sleep condition by the development of anxiety.

And now it occurs to us that we know absolutely nothing yet

as to why these evil, depraved wishes are aroused just at night, in order that they may disturb our sleep. The answer can only be an assumption which is based on the nature of the condition of sleep. During the day the heavy pressure of a censorship weighs upon these wishes, making it impossible, as a rule, for them to express themselves in any manner. At night, evidently, this censorship is withdrawn for the benefit of the single sleep-wish, in the same manner as are all the other interests of psychic life, or at least placed in a position of very minor importance. The forbidden wishes must thank this noctural deposition of the censor for being able to raise their heads again. There are nervous persons troubled with insomnia who admit that their sleeplessness was in the beginning voluntary. They did not trust themselves to fall asleep, because they were afraid of their dreams, that is, of the results due to a slackening of the censorship. So you can readily see that this withdrawal of the censor does not in itself signify rank carelessness. Sleep weakens our power to move; our evil intentions, even if they do begin to stir, can accomplish nothing but a dream, which for practical purposes is harmless, and the highly sensible remark of the sleepers, a night-time remark indeed, but not a part of the dream life, "it is only a dream," is reminiscent of this quieting circumstance. So let us grant this, and sleep on.

If, thirdly, you recall the concept that the dreamer, struggling against his wishes, is to be compared to a summation of two separate persons, in some manner closely connected, you will be able to grasp the further possibility of how a thing which is highly unpleasant, namely, punishment, may be accomplished by wish-fulfillment. Here again the fairy tale of the three wishes can be of service to us: the sausages on the plate are the direct wish-fulfillment of the first person, the woman; the sausages at the end of her nose are the wish-fulfillment of the second person, the husband, but at the same time the punishment for the stupid wish of the woman. Among the neurotics we find again the motivation of the third wish, which remains in fairy tales only. There are many such punishment-tendencies in the psychic life of man; they are very powerful, and we may make them responsible for some of our painful dreams. Perhaps you now say that at this rate, not very much of the famed wish-fulfillment is left. But upon closer view you will admit th you are wrong. In contrast to the manysided aspects, later to be discussed, of what the dream might be—and, according to numerous authors, is—the solution (wish-fulfillment, anxiety-fulfillment, punishment-fulfillment) is indeed very restricted. That is why anxiety is the direct antithesis of the wish, why antitheses are so closely allied in association and why they occur together in the unconscious, as we have heard; and that is why punishment, too, is a wish-fulfillment of the other, the censoring person.

On the whole, then, I have made no concessions to your protestation against the theory of wish-fulfillment. We are bound, however, to establish wish-fulfillment in every dream no matter how distorted, and we certainly do not wish to withdraw from this task. Let us go back to the dream, already interpreted, of the three bad theatre tickets for 1 Fl. 50 Kr. from which we have already learned so much. I hope you still remember it. A lady who tells her husband during the day that her friend Elise, only three months younger than herself, has become engaged, dreams she is in the theatre with her husband. Half the parquet is empty. Her husband says, " Elise and her fiancé wanted to go to the theatre, too, but couldn't because they could get only poor seats, three for one gulden and a half." She was of the opinion that that wasn't so unfortunate. We discovered that the dream-thought originated in her discontent at having married too soon, and the fact that she was dissatisfied with her husband. We may be curious as to the manner in which these thoughts have been worked over into a wish-fulfillment, and where their traces may be found in the manifest content. Now we know that the element "too soon, premature" is eliminated from the dream by the censor. The empty parquet is a reference to it. The puzzling "three for 1 Fl. 50 Kr." is now, with the help of symbolism which we have since learned, more understandable.[1] The "3" really means a husband, and the manifest element is easy to translate: to buy a husband for her dowry ("I could have bought one ten times better for my dowry"). The marriage is obviously replaced by going into the theatre. "Buying the tickets too soon" directly takes the place of the premature mar-

[1] I do not mention another obvious interpretation of this "3" in the case of this childless woman, because it is not material to this analysis.

riage. This substitution is the work of the wish-fulfillment. Our dreamer was not always so dissatisfied with her early marriage as she was on the day she received news of the engagement of her friend. At the time she was proud of her marriage and felt herself more favored than her friend. Naive girls have frequently confided to their friends after their engagement that soon they, too, will be able to go to all the plays hitherto forbidden, and see everything. The desire to see plays, the curiosity that makes its appearance here, was certainly in the beginning directed towards sex matters, the sex-life, especially the sex-life of the parents, and then became a strong motive which impelled the girl to an early marriage. In this way the visit to the theatre becomes an obvious representative substitute for being married. In the momentary annoyance at her early marriage she recalls the time when the early marriage was a wish-fulfillment for her, because she had satisfied her curiosity; and she now replaces the marriage, guided by the old wish-impulse, with the going to the theatre.

We may say that we have not sought out the simplest example as proof of a hidden wish-fulfillment. We would have to proceed in analogous manner with other distorted dreams. I cannot do that for you, and simply wish to express the conviction that it will be successful everywhere. But I wish to continue along this theoretical line. Experience has taught me that it is one of the most dangerous phases of the entire dream science, and that many contradictions and misunderstandings are connected therewith. Besides, you are perhaps still under the impression that I have retracted a part of my declaration, in that I said that the dream is a fulfilled wish or its opposite, an actualized anxiety or punishment, and you will think this is the opportunity to compel further reservations of me. I have also heard complaints that I am too abrupt about things which appear evident to me, and that for that reason I do not present the thing convincingly enough.

If a person has gone thus far with us in dream-interpretation, and accepted everything that has been offered, it is not unusual for him to call a halt at wish-fulfillment, and say, "Granted that in every instance the dream has a meaning, and that this meaning can be disclosed by psychoanalytic technique, why must this dream, despite all evidence to the contrary, always be force into the formula of wish-fulfillment? Why might not the meaning of this nocturnal thought be as many-sided as thought is by day; why may not the dream in one case express a fulfilled wish, in another, as you yourself say, the opposite thereof, an actualized anxiety; or why may it not correspond to a resolution, a warning, a reflection with its pro's and con's, a reproach, a goad to conscience, an attempt to prepare oneself for a contemplated performance, etc? Why always nothing more than a wish, or at best, its opposite?"

One might maintain that a difference of opinion on these points is of no great importance, so long as we are at one otherwise. We might say that it is enough to have discovered the meaning of the dream, and the way to recognize it; that it is a matter of no importance, if we have too narrowly limited this meaning. But this is not so. A misunderstanding of this point strikes at the nature of our knowledge of the dream, and endangers its worth for the understanding of neuroses. Then, too, that method of approach which is esteemed in the business world as genteel is out of place in scientific endeavors, and harmful.

My first answer to the question why the dream may not be many-sided in its meaning is the usual one in such instances: I do not know why it should not be so. I would not be opposed to such a state of affairs. As far as I am concerned, it could well be true. Only one small matter prevents this broader and more comfortable explanation of the dream—namely, that as a matter of fact it isn't so. My second answer emphasizes the fact that the assumption that the dream corresponds to numerous forms of thought and intellectual operations is no stranger to me. In a story about a sick person I once reported a dream that occurred three nights running and then stopped, and I explained this suppression by saying that the dream corresponded to a resolution which had no reason to recur after having been carried out. More recently I published a dream which corresponded to a confession. How is it possible for me to contradict myself, and maintain that the dream is always only a fulfilled wish?

I do that, because I do not wish to admit a stupid misunderstanding which might cost us the fruits of all our labors with regard to the dream, a misunderstanding which confuses the dream with the latent dream-thought and affirms of the dream something that applies specifically and solely to the latter. For it is entirely correct that the dream can represent, and be replaced by all those things we enumerated: a resolution, a warning, reflection, preparation, an attempt to solve a problem, etc. But if you look closely, you will recognize that all these things are true only of the latent dream thoughts, which have been changed about in the dream. You learn from the interpretation of the dreams that the person's unconscious thinking is occupied with such resolutions, preparations, reflections, etc., out of which the dream-work then builds the dream. If you are not at the time interested in the dream-work, but are very much interested in the unconscious thought-work of man, you eliminate the dream-work, and say of the dream, for all practical purposes quite correctly, that it corresponds to a warning, a resolution, etc. This often happens in psychoanalytic activity. People endeavor for the most part only to destroy the dream form, and to substitute in its place in the sequence the latent thoughts out, of which the dream was made.

Thus we learn, from the appreciation of the latent dream-thoughts, that all the highly complicated psychic acts we have enumerated can go on unconsciously, a result as wonderful as it is confusing.

But to return, you are right only if you admit that you have made use of an abbreviated form of speech, and if you do not believe that you must connect the many-sidedness we have mentioned with the essence of the dream. When you speak of the dream you must mean either the manifest dream, i.e., the product of the dream-work, or at most the dream-work itself— that psychic occurrence which forms the manifest dream out of the latent dream thought. Any other use of the word is a confusion of concept that can only cause trouble. If your assertions refer to the latent thoughts back of the dream, say so, and do not cloud the problem of the dream by using such a faulty means of expression. The latent dream thoughts are the material which the dream-work remolds into the manifest dream. Why do you insist upon confusing the material with the work that makes use of it? Are you any better off than those who knew only the product of this work, and could explain neither where it came from nor how it was produced?

The only essential thing in the dream is the dream-w'

has had its influence upon the thought-material. We have no right to disregard it theoretically even if, in certain practical situations, we may fail to take it into account. Analytic observation, too, shows that the dream-work never limits itself to translating these thoughts in the archiac or regressive mode of expression known to you. Rather it regularly adds something which does not belong to the latent thoughts of waking, but which is the essential motive of dream-formation. This indispensable ingredient is at the same time the unconscious wish, for the fulfillment of which the dream content is rebuilt. The dream may be any conceivable thing, if you take into account only the thoughts represented by it, warning, resolution, preparation, etc.; it is also always the fulfillment of an unknown wish, and it is this only if you look upon it as the result of the dream-work. A dream is never itself a resolution, a warning, and no more—but always a resolution, etc., translated into an archaic form of expression with the help of the unconscious wish, and changed about for the purpose of fulfilling this wish. The one characteristic, wish-fulfillment, is constant; the other may vary; it may itself be a wish at times, so that the dream, with the aid of an unconscious wish, presents as fulfilled a latent wish out of waking hours.

I understand all this very well, but I do not know whether or not I shall be successful in making you understand it as well. I have difficulties, too, in proving it to you. This cannot be done without, on the one hand, careful analysis of many dreams, and on the other hand this most difficult and most important point of our conception of the dream cannot be set forth convincingly without reference to things to follow. Can you, in fact, believe that taking into consideration the intimate relationship of all things, one is able to penetrate deeply into the nature of one thing without having carefully considered other things of a very similar nature? Since we know nothing as yet about the closest relatives of the dream, neurotic symptoms, we must once again content ourselves with what has already been accomplished. I want to explain one more example to you, and propose a new viewpoint.

Let us again take up that dream to which we have several times recurred, the dream of the three theatre tickets for 1 Fl. 50 Kr. I can assure you that I took this example

quite unpremeditatedly at first. You are acquainted with the
latent dream thoughts: annoyance, upon hearing that her friend
had just now become engaged, at the thought that she herself
had hurried so to be married; contempt for her husband; the
idea that she might have had a better one had she waited. We
also know the wish, which made a dream out of these thoughts—
it is "curiosity to see," being permitted to go to the theatre,
very likely a derivation from the old curiosity finally to know
just what happens when one is married. This curiosity, as is
well known, regularly directs itself in the case of children to
the sex-life of the parents. It is an impulse of childhood, and
in so far as it persists later, an impulse whose roots reach back
into the infantile. But that day's news played no part in awaking the curiosity, it awoke only annoyance and regret. This
wish impulse did not have anything to do immediately with the
latent dream thoughts, and we could fit the result of the dream
interpretation into the analysis without considering the wish
impulse at all. But then, the annoyance itself was not capable
of producing the dream; a dream could not be derived from the
thought: "It was stupid to marry so soon," except by reviving
the old wish finally to see what happens when one is married.
The wish then formed the dream content, in that it replaced
marriage by going to the theatre, and gave it the form of an
earlier wish-fulfillment: "so now I may go to the theatre and
see all the forbidden things, and you may not. I am married
and you must wait." In such a manner the present situation
was transposed into its opposite, an old triumph put into the
place of the recent defeat. Added thereto was a satisfied
curiosity amalgamated with a satisfied egoistic sense of rivalry.
This satisfaction determines the manifest dream content in
which she really is sitting in the theatre, and her friend was
unable to get tickets. Those bits of dream content are affixed
to this satisfaction situation as unfitting and inexplicable modifications, behind which the latent dream thoughts still hide.
Dream interpretation must take into consideration everything
that serves toward the representation of the wish-fulfillment and
must reconstruct from these suggestions the painful latent
dream-thought.

The observation I now wish to make is for the purpose of
drawing your attention to the latent dream thoughts, now

pushed to the fore. I beg of you not to forget first, that the dreamer is unconscious of them, second, they are entirely logical and continuous, so that they may be understood as a comprehensible reaction to the dream occasion, third, that they may have the value of any desired psychic impulse or intellectual operation. I shall now designate these thoughts more forcibly than before as "day-remnants"; the dreamer may acknowledge them or not. I now separate day-remnants and latent dream thoughts in accordance with our previous usage of calling everything that we discover in interpreting the dream "latent dream thoughts," while the day-remnants are only a part of the latent dream thoughts. Then our conception goes to show that something additional has been added to the day-remnants, something which also belonged to the unconscious, a strong but suppressed wish impulse, and it is this alone that has made possible the dream fabrication. The influence of this wish impulse on the day-remnants creates the further participation of the latent dream thoughts, thoughts which no longer appear rational and understandable in relation to waking life.

In explaining the relationship of the day-remnants to the unconscious wish I have made use of a comparison which I can only repeat here. Every undertaking requires a capitalist, who defrays the expenses, and an entrepreneur, who has the idea and understands how to carry it out. The role of the capitalist in the dream fabrication is always played by the unconscious wish; it dispenses the psychic energy for dream-building. The actual worker is the day-remnant, which determines how the expenditure is to be made. Now the capitalist may himself have the idea and the particularized knowledge, or the entrepreneur may have the capital. This simplifies the practical situation, but makes its theoretical comprehension more difficult. In economics we always distinguish between the capitalist and the entrepeneur aspect in a single person, and thus we reconstruct the fundamental situation which was the point of departure for our comparison. In dream-fabrication the same variations occur. I shall leave their further development to you.

We can go no further here, for you have probably long been disturbed by a reflection which deserves to be heard. Are the day-remnants, you ask, really unconscious in the same sense as the unconscious wish which is essential to making them suitable for the dream? You discern correctly. Here lies the salient point of the whole affair. They are not unconscious in the same sense. The dream wish belongs to a different unconsciousness, that which we have recognized as of infantile origin, fitted out with special mechanisms. It is entirely appropriate to separate these two types of unconsciousness and give them different designations. But let us rather wait until we have become acquainted with the field of neurotic symptoms. If people say one unconsciousness is fantastic, what will they say when we acknowledge that we arrived at our conclusions by using two kinds of unconsciousness?

Let us stop here. Once more you have heard something incomplete; but is there not hope in the thought that this science has a continuation which will be brought to light either by ourselves or by those to follow? And have not we ourselves discovered a sufficient number of new and surprising things?

Doubtful Points and Criticism

LET us not leave the subject of dreams before we have touched upon the most common doubts and uncertainties which have arisen in connection with the new ideas and conceptions we have discussed up to this point. The more attentive members of the audience probably have already accumulated some material bearing upon this.

1. You may have received the impression that the results of our work of interpretation of the dream have left so much that is uncertain, despite our close adherence to technique, that a true translation of the manifest dream into the latent dream thoughts is thereby rendered impossible. In support of this you will point out that in the first place, one never knows whether a specific element of the dream is to be taken literally or symbolically, since those elements which are used symbolically do not, because of that fact, cease to be themselves. But if one has no objective standard by which to decide this, the interpretation is, as to this point, left to the discretion of the dream interpreter. Moreover, because of the way in which the dream work combines opposites, it is always uncertain whether a specific dream element is to be taken in the positive or the negative sense, whether it is to be understood as itself or as its opposite. Hence this is another opportunity for the exercise of the interpreter's discretion. In the third place, in consequence of the frequency with which every sort of inversion is practised in the dream, the dream interpreter is at liberty to assume such an inversion at any point of the dream he pleases. And finally you will say, you have heard that one is seldom sure that the interpretation which is found is the only possible one. There is danger of overlooking a thoroughly admissible second inter-

pretation of the same dream. Under these circumstances, you will conclude there is a scope left for the discretion of the interpreter, the breadth of which seems incompatible with the objective accuracy of the results. Or you may also conclude that the fault does not rest with the dream but that the inadequacies of our dream interpretation result from errors in our conceptions and hypotheses.

All your material is irreproachable, but I do not believe that it justifies your conclusions in two directions, namely, that dream interpretation as we practice it is sacrificed to arbitrariness and that the deficiency of our results makes the justification of our method doubtful. If you will substitute for the arbitrariness of the interpreter, his skill, his experience, his comprehension, I agree with you. We shall surely not be able to dispense with some such personal factor, particularly not in difficult tasks of dream interpretation. But this same state of affairs exists also in other scientific occupations. There is no way in which to make sure that one man will not wield a technique less well, or utilize it more fully, than another. What might, for example, impress you as arbitrariness in the interpretation of symbols, is compensated for by the fact that as a rule the connection of the dream thoughts among themselves, the connection of the dream with the life of the dreamer, and the whole psychic situation in which the dream occurs, chooses just one of the possible interpretations advanced and rejects the others as useless for its purposes. The conclusion drawn from the inadequacies of dream interpretation, that our hypotheses are wrong, is weakened by an observation which shows that the ambiguity and indefiniteness of the dream is rather characteristic and necessarily to be expected.

Recollect that we said that the dream work translates the dream thoughts into primitive expressions analogous to picture writing. All these primitive systems of expression are, however, subject to such indefiniteness and ambiguities, but it does not follow that we are justified in doubting their usefulness. You know that the fusion of opposites by the dream-work is analogous to the so-called "antithetical meaning of primitive words," in the oldest languages. The philologist, R. Abel (1884), whom we have to thank for this point of view, admonishes us not to believe that the meaning of the communication which one person made to another when using such ambiguous words was necessarily unclear. Tone and gesture used in connection with the words would have left no room for doubt as to which of the two opposites the speaker intended to communicate. In writing, where gesture is lacking, it was replaced by a supplementary picture sign not intended to be spoken, as for example by the picture of a little man squatting lazily or standing erect, according to whether the ambiguous hieroglyphic was to mean "weak" or "strong." It was in this way that one avoided any misunderstanding despite the ambiguity of the sounds and signs.

We recognize in the ancient systems of expression, e.g., the writings of those oldest languages, a number of uncertainties which we would not tolerate in our present-day writings. Thus in many Semitic writings only the consonants of words are indicated. The reader had to supply the omitted vowels according to his knowledge and the context. Hieroglyphic writing does not proceed in exactly this way, but quite similarly, and that is why the pronunciation of old Egyptian has remained unknown to us. The holy writings of the Egyptians contain still other uncertainties. For example, it is left to the discretion of the writer whether or not he shall arrange the pictures from right to left or from left to right. To be able to read we have to follow the rule that we must depend upon the faces of the figures, birds, and the like. The writer, however, could also arrange the picture signs in vertical rows, and in inscriptions on small objects he was guided by considerations of beauty and proportion further to change the order of the signs. Probably the most confusing feature of hieroglyphic writing is to be found in the fact that there is no space between words. The pictures stretch over the page at uniform distances from one another, and generally one does not know whether a sign belongs to what has gone before or is the beginning of a new word. Persian cuneiform writing, on the other hand, makes use of an oblique wedge sign to separate the words.

The Chinese tongue and script is exceedingly old, but still used by four hundred million people. Please do not think I understand anything about it. I have only informed myself concerning it because I hoped to find analogies to the indefinite aspects of the dream. Nor was I disappointed. The Chinese

language is filled with so many vagaries that it strikes terror
into our hearts. It consists, as is well known, of a number of
syllable sounds which are spoken singly or are combined in
twos. One of the chief dialects has about four hundred such
sounds. Now since the vocabulary of this dialect is estimated at
about four thousand words, it follows that every sound has on an
average of ten different meanings, some less but others, consequently, more. Hence there are a great number of ways of
avoiding a multiplicity of meaning, since one cannot guess from
the context alone which of the ten meanings of the syllable sound
the speaker intended to convey to the hearer. Among them are
the combining of two sounds into a compounded word and the
use of four different "tones" with which to utter these syllables.
For our purposes of comparison, it is still more interesting to
note that this language has practically no grammar. It is impossible to say of a one-syllable word whether it is a noun, a
verb, or an adjective, and we find none of those changes in the
forms of the words by means of which we might recognize sex,
number, ending, tense or mood. The language, therefore, might
be said to consist of raw material, much in the same manner
as our thought language is broken up by the dream work into
its raw materials when the expressions of relationship are left
out. In the Chinese, in all cases of vagueness the decision is
left to the understanding of the hearer, who is guided by the
context. I have secured an example of a Chinese saying which,
literally translated, reads: "Little to be seen, much to wonder
at." That is not difficult to understand. It may mean, "The
less a man has seen, the more he finds to wonder at," or, "There
is much to admire for the man who has seen little." Naturally,
there is no need to choose between these two translations, which
differ only in grammar. Despite these uncertainties, we are
assured, the Chinese language is an extraordinarily excellent
medium for the expression of thought. Vagueness does not,
therefore, necessarily lead to ambiguity.

Now we must certainly admit that the condition of affairs
is far less favorable in the expression-system of the dream than
in these ancient languages and writings. For, after all, these
latter are really designed for communication, that is to say
they were always intended to be understood, no matter in wha
way and with what aids. But it is just this characteristic whicl

the dream lacks. The dream does not want to tell anyone anything, it is no vehicle of communication, it is, on the contrary,
constructed so as not to be understood. For that reason we
must not be surprised or misled if we should discover that a
number of the ambiguities and vagaries of the dream do not
permit of determination. As the one specific gain of our comparison, we have only the realization that such uncertainties as
people tried to make use of in objecting to the validity of our
dream interpretation, are rather the invariable characteristic of
all primitive systems of expression.

How far the dream can really be understood can be determined only by practice and experience. My opinion is, that
that is very far indeed, and the comparison of results which
correctly trained analysts have gathered confirms my view. The
lay public, even that part of the lay public which is interested
in science, likes, in the face of the difficulties and uncertainties
of a scientific task, to make what I consider an unjust show
of its superior scepticism. Perhaps not all of you are acquainted
with the fact that a similar situation arose in the history of
the deciphering of the Babylonian-Assyrian inscriptions.
There was a period then when public opinion went far in de-
claring the decipherors of cuneiform writing to be visionaries
and the whole research a "fraud." But in the year 1857 the
Royal Asiatic Society made a decisive test. It challenged the
four most distinguished decipherors of cuneiform writing, Raw-
linson, Hincks, Fox Talbot and Oppert, each to send to it in a
sealed envelope his independent translation of a newly discovered inscription, and the Society was then able to testify,
after having made a comparison of the four readings, that their
agreement was sufficiently marked to justify confidence in what
already had been accomplished, and faith in further progress.
At this the mockery of the learned lay world gradually came
to an end and the confidence in the reading of cuneiform documents has grown appreciably since then.

2. A second series of objections is firmly grounded in the
impression from which you too probably are not free, that a
number of the solutions of dream interpretations which we find
it necessary to make seem forced, artificial, far-fetched, in other
words, violent or even comical or jocose. These comments are
so frequent that I shall choose at random the latest example

which has come to my attention. Recently, in free Switzerland, the director of a boarding-school was relieved of his position on account of his active interest in psychoanalysis. He raised objections and a Berne newspaper made public the judgment of the school authorities. I quote from that article some sentences which apply to psychoanalysis: "Moreover, we are surprised at the many far-fetched and artificial examples as found in the aforementioned book of Dr. Pfister of Zurich. . . . Thus, it certainly is a cause of surprise when the director of a boarding-school so uncritically accepts all these assertions and apparent proofs." These observations are offered as the decisions of "one who judges calmly." I rather think this calm is "artificial." Let us examine these remarks more closely in the hope that a little reflection and knowledge of the subject can be no detriment to calm judgment.

It is positively refreshing to see how quickly and unerringly some individuals can judge a delicate question of abstruse psychology by first impressions. The interpretations seem to them far-fetched and forced, they do not please them, so the interpretations are wrong and the whole business of interpretation amounts to nothing. No fleeting thought ever brushes the other possibility, that these interpretations must appear as they are for good reasons, which would give rise to the further question of what these good reasons might be.

The content thus judged generally relates to the results of displacement, with which you have become acquainted as the strongest device of the dream censor. It is with the help of displacements that the dream censor creates substitute-formations which we have designated as allusions. But they are allusions which are not easily recognized as such, and from which it is not easy to find one's way back to the original and which are connected with this original by means of the strangest, most unusual, most superficial associations. In all of these cases, however, it is a question of matters which are to be hidden, which were intended for concealment; this is what the dream censor aims to do. We must not expect to find a thing that has been concealed in its accustomed place in the spot where it belongs. In this respect the Commissions for the Surveillance of Frontiers now in office are more cunning than the S school authorities. In their search for documents and maps

are not content to search through portfolios and letter cases
but they also take into account the possibility that spies and
smugglers might carry such severely proscribed articles in the
most concealed parts of their clothing, where they certainly do
not belong, as for example between the double soles of their
boots. If the concealed objects are found in such a place, they
certainly are very far-fetched, but nevertheless they have been
"fetched."

If we recognize that the most remote, the most extraordinary
associations between the latent dream element and its manifest
substitute are possible, associations appearing ofttimes comical,
ofttimes witty, we follow in so doing a wealth of experience
derived from examples whose solutions we have, as a rule, not
found ourselves. Often it is not possible to give such interpretations from our own examples. No sane person could guess
the requisite association. The dreamer either gives us the translation with one stroke by means of his immediate association—
he can do this, for this substitute formation was created by his
mind—or he provides us with so much material that the solution
no longer demands any special astuteness but forces itself upon
us as inevitable. If the dreamer does not help us in either of
these two ways, then indeed the manifest element in question
remains forever incomprehensible to us. Allow me to give you
one more such example of recent occurrence. One of my patients
lost her father during the time that she was undergoing treatment. Since then she has made use of every opportunity to
bring him back to life in her dreams. In one of her dreams her
father appears in a certain connection, of no further importance
here, and says, *"It is a quarter past eleven, it is half past eleven,
it is quarter of twelve."* All she can think of in connection
with this curious incident is the recollection that her father liked
to see his grown-up children appear punctually at the general
meal hour. That very thing probably had some connection with
the dream element, but permitted of no conclusion as to its
source. Judging from the situation of the treatment at that
time, there was a justified suspicion that a carefully suppressed
critical rebellion against her loved and respected father played
its part in this dream. Continuing her associations, and apparently far afield from topics relevant to the dream, the
dreamer relates that yesterday many things of a psychological

nature had been discussed in her presence, and that a relative made the remark: "The cave man (*Urmensch*) continues to live in all of us." Now we think we understand. That gave her an excellent opportunity of picturing her father as continuing to live. So in the dream she made of him a clockman (*Uhrmensch*) by having him announce the quarter-hours at noon time.

You may not be able to disregard the similarity which this examples bears to a pun, and it really has happened frequently that the dreamer's pun is attributed to the interpreter. There are still other examples in which it is not at all easy to decide whether one is dealing with a joke or a dream. But you will recall that the same doubt confronted us when we were dealing with slips of the tongue. A man tells us a dream of his, that his uncle, while they were sitting in the latter's *auto*mobile, gave him a kiss. He very quickly supplies the interpretation himself. It means "*auto*-eroticism," (a term taken from the study of the libido, or love impulse, and designating satisfaction of that impulse without an external object). Did this man permit himself to make fun of us and give out as a dream a pun that occurred to him? I do not believe so; he really dreamed it. Whence comes the astounding similarity? This question at one time led me quite a ways from my path, by making it necessary for me to make a thorough investigation of the problem of humor itself. By so doing I came to the conclusion that the origin of wit lies in a foreconscious train of thought which is left for a moment to unconscious manipulation, from which it then emerges as a joke. Under the influence of the unconscious it experiences the workings of the mechanisms there in force, namely, of condensation and displacement, that is, of the same processes which we found active in the dream work, and it is to this agreement that we are to ascribe the similarity between wit and the dream, wherever it occurs. The unintentional "dream joke" has, however, none of the pleasure-giving quality of the ordinary joke. Why that is so, greater penetration into the study of wit may teach you. The "dream joke" seems a poor joke to us, it does not make us laugh, it leaves us cold.

Here we are also following in the footsteps of ancient dream interpretation, which has left us, in addition to much that is useless, many a good example of dream interpretation v̄ we ourselves cannot surpass. I am now going to tell dream of historical importance which Plutarch and Artemidorus of Daldis both tell concerning Alexander the Great, with certain variations. When the King was engaged in besieging the city of Tyre (322 B.C.), which was being stubbornly defended, he once dreamed that he saw a dancing satyr. Aristandros, his dream interpreter, who accompanied the army, interpreted this dream for him by making of the word *Satyros*, σὰ Τύρος, "Thine is Tyre," and thus promising him a triumph over the city. Alexander allowed himself to be influenced by this interpretation to continue the siege, and finally captured Tyre. The interpretation, which seems artificial enough, was without doubt the correct one.

3. I can imagine that it will make a special impression on you to hear that objections to our conception of the dream have been raised also by persons who, as psychoanalysts, have themselves been interested in the interpretation of dreams. It would have been too extraordinary if so pregnant an opportunity for new errors had remained unutilized, and thus, owing to comprehensible confusions and unjustified generalizations, there have been assertions made which, in point of incorrectness are not far behind the medical conception of dreams. One of these you already know. It is the declaration that the dream is occupied with the dreamer's attempts at adaptation to his present environment, and attempts to solve future problems, in other words, that the dream follows a "prospective tendency" (A. Maeder). We have already shown that this assertion is based upon a confusion of the dream with the latent thoughts of the dream, that as a premise it overlooks the existence of the dream-work. In characterizing that psychic activity which is unconscious and to which the latent thoughts of the dream belong, the above assertion is no novelty, nor is it exhaustive, for this unconscious psychic activity occupies itself with many other things besides preparation for the future. A much worse confusion seems to underlie the assurance that back of every dream one finds the "death-clause," or death-wish. I am not quite certain what this formula is meant to indicate, but I suppose that back of it is a confusion of the dream with the whole personality of the dreamer.

An unjustified generalization, based on few good examples, is the pronouncement that every dream permits of two interpretations, one such as we have explained, the so-called psycho-analytic, and another, the so-called anagogical or mystical, which ignores the instinctive impulses and aims at a representation of the higher psychic functions (V. Silberer). There are such dreams, but you will try in vain to extend this conception to even a majority of the dreams. But after everything you have heard, the statement will seem very incomprehensible that all dreams can be interpreted bisexually, that is, as the concurrence of two tendencies which may be designated as male and female (A. Adler). To be sure, there are a few such dreams, and you may learn later that these are built up in the manner of certain hysterical symptoms. I mention all these newly discovered general characteristics of the dream in order to warn you against them or at least in order not to leave you in doubt as to how I judge them.

4. At one time the objective value of dream research was called into question by the observation that patients undergoing analysis accommodate the content of their dreams to the favorite theories of their physicians, so that some dream predominantly of sexual impulses, others of the desire for power and still others even of rebirth (W. Stekel). The weight of this observation is diminished by the consideration that people dreamed before there was such a thing as a psychoanalytic treatment to influence their dreams, and that those who are now undergoing treatment were also in the habit of dreaming before the treatment was commenced. The meaning of this novel discovery can soon be recognized as a matter of course and as of no consequence for the theory of the dream. Those day-remnants which give rise to the dream are the overflow from the strong interest of the waking life. If the remarks of the physician and the stimuli which he gives have become significant to the patient under analysis, then they become a part of the day's remnants, can serve as psychic stimuli for the formation of a dream along with other, emotionally-charged, unsolved interests of the day, and operate much as do the somatic stimuli which act upon the sleeper during his sleep. Just like these other incitors of t' dream, the sequence of ideas which the physician sets in mc may appear in the manifest content, or may be traced in latent content of the dream. Indeed, we know that one produce dreams experimentally, or to speak more accura

one can insert into the dream a part of the dream material.
Thus the analyst in influencing his patients, merely plays the
role of an experimenter in the manner of Mourly Vold, who
places the limbs of his subjects in certain positions.

One can often influence the dreamer as to the *subject-matter*
of his dream, but one can never influence *what he will dream*
about it. The mechanism of the dream-work and the unconscious
wish that is hidden in the dream are beyond the reach of all
foreign influences. We already realized, when we evaluated the
dreams caused by bodily stimuli, that the peculiarity and self-
sufficiency of the dream life shows itself in the reaction with
which the dream retorts to the bodily or physical stimuli which
are presented. The statement here discussed, which aims to
throw doubt upon the objectivity of dream research, is again
based on a confusion—this time of the whole dream with the
dream material.

This much, ladies and gentlemen, I wanted to tell you concerning the problems of the dream. You will suspect that I have
omitted a great deal, and have yourselves discovered that I had
to be inconclusive on almost all points. But that is due to the
relation which the phenomena of the dream have to those of the
neuroses. We studied the dream by way of introduction to the
study of the neuroses, and that was surely more correct than
the reverse would have been. But just as the dream prepares us
for the understanding of the neuroses, so in turn the correct
evaluation of the dream can only be gained after a knowledge
of neurotic phenomena has been won.

I do not know what you will think about this, but I must assure
you that I do not regret having taken so much of your interest
and of your available time for the problems of the dream. There
is no other field in which one can so quickly become convinced
of the correctness of the assertions by which psychoanalysis
stands or falls. It will take the strenuous labor of many months,
even years, to show that the symptoms in a case of neurotic
break-down have their meaning, serve a purpose, and result
from the fortunes of the patient. On the other hand, the efforts
of a few hours suffice in proving the same content in a dream
product which at first seems incomprehensibly confused, and
thereby to confirm all the hypotheses of psychoanalysis, the unconsciousness of psychic processes, the special mechanism which

they follow, and the motive forces which manifest themselves in them. And if we associate the thorough analogy in the construction of the dream and the neurotic symptom with the rapidity of transformation which makes of the dreamer an alert and reasonable individual, we gain the certainty that the neurosis also is based only on a change in the balance of the forces of psychic life.

III

GENERAL THEORY OF THE NEUROSES

SIXTEENTH LECTURE

GENERAL THEORY OF THE NEUROSES

Psychoanalysis and Psychiatry

I AM very glad to welcome you back to continue our discussions. I last lectured to you on the psychoanalytic treatment of errors and of the dream. To-day I should like to introduce you to an understanding of neurotic phenomena, which, as you soon will discover, have much in common with both of those topics. But I shall tell you in advance that I cannot leave you to take the same attitude toward me that you had before. At that time I was anxious to take no step without complete reference to your judgment. I discussed much with you, I listened to your objections, in short, I deferred to you and to your "normal common sense." That is no longer possible, and for a very simple reason. As phenomena, the dream and errors were not strange to you. One might say that you had as much experience as I, or that you could easily acquire as much. But neuroses are foreign to you; since you are not doctors yourselves you have had access to them only through what I have told you. Of what use is the best judgment if it is not supported by familiarity with the material in question?

Do not, however, understand this as an announcement of dogmatic lectures which demand your unconditional belief. That would be a gross misunderstanding. I do not wish to convince you. I am out to stimulate your interest and shake your prejudices. If, in consequence of not knowing the facts, you are not in a position to judge, neither should you believe nor condemn. Listen and allow yourselves to be influenced by what I tell you. One cannot be so easily convinced; at least if he comes by convictions without effort, they soon prove to be valueless and unable to hold their own. He only has a right to conviction who has handled the same material for many years and who in so doing has gone through the same new and surprising experiences again and again. Why, in matters of intellect, these

209

lightning conversions, these momentary repulsions? Do you not feel that a *coup de foudre,* that love at first sight, originates in quite a different field, namely, in that of the emotions? We do not even demand that our patients should become convinced of and predisposed to psychoanalysis. When they do, they seem suspicious to us. The attitude we prefer in them is one of benevolent scepticism. Will you not also try to let the psychoanalytic conception develop in your mind beside the popular or "psychiatric"? They will influence each other, mutually measure their strength, and some day work themselves into a decision on your part.

On the other hand, you must not think for a moment that what I present to you as the psychoanalytic conception is a purely speculative system. Indeed, it is a sum total of experiences and observations, either their direct expression or their elaboration. Whether this elaboration is done adequately and whether the method is justifiable will be tested in the further progress of the science. After two and a half decades, now that I am fairly advanced in years, I may say that it was particularly difficult, intensive and all-absorbing work which yielded these observations. I have often had the impression that our opponents were unwilling to take into consideration this objective origin of our statements, as if they thought it were only a question of subjective ideas arising haphazard, ideas to which another may oppose his every passing whim. This antagonistic behavior is not entirely comprehensible to me. Perhaps the physician's habit of steering clear of his neurotic patients and listening so very casually to what they have to say allows him to lose sight of the possibility of deriving anything valuable from his patients' communications, and therefore, of making penetrating observations on them. I take this opportunity of promising you that I shall carry on little controversy in the course of my lectures, least of all with individual controversialists. I have never been able to convince myself of the truth of the saying that controversy is the father of all things. I believe that it comes down to us from the Greek sophist philosophy and errs as does the latter through the overvaluation of dialectics. To me, on the contrary, it seems as if the so-called scientific criticism were on the whole unfruitful, quite apart from the fact that it is almost always carried on in a most personal spirit. For my part, up to a few years ago, I could even boast that I had entered into a regular scientific dispute with only one scholar (Lowenfeld, of Munich). The end of this was that we became friends and have remained friends to this day. But I did not repeat this attempt for a long time, because I was not certain that the outcome would be the same.

Now you will surely judge that so to reject the discussion of literature must evidence stubborness, a very special obtuseness against objections, or, as the kindly colloquialisms of science have it, "a complete personal bias." In answer, I would say that should you attain to a conviction by such hard labor, you would thereby derive a certain right to sustain it with some tenacity. Furthermore, I should like to emphasize the fact that I have modified my views on certain important points in the course of my researches, changed them and replaced them by new ones, and that I naturally made a public statement of that fact each time. What has been the result of this frankness? Some paid no attention at all to my self-corrections and even to-day criticize me for assertions which have long since ceased to have the same meaning for me. Others reproach me for just this deviation, and on account of it declare me unreliable. For is anyone who has changed his opinions several times still trustworthy; is not his latest assertion, as well, open to error? At the same time he who holds unswervingly to what he has once said, or cannot be made to give it up quickly enough, is called stubborn and biased. In the face of these contradictory criticisms, what else can one do but be himself and act according to his own dictates? That is what I have decided to do, and I will not allow myself to be restrained from modifying and adapting my theories as the progress of my experience demands. In the basic ideas I have hitherto found nothing to change, and I hope that such will continue to be the case.

Now I shall present to you the psychoanalytic conception of neurotic manifestations. The natural thing for me to do is to connect them to the phenomena we have previously treated, for the sake of their analogy as well as their contrast. I will select as symptomatic an act of frequent occurrence in my office hour. Of course, the analyst cannot do much for those who seek him in his medical capacity, and lay the woes of a lifetime before him in fifteen minutes. His deeper knowledge makes it difficult for him to deliver a snap decision as do other physicians—"There is nothing wrong with you"—and to give the advice, "Go to a watering-place for a while." One of our colleagues, in answer to the question as to what he did with his office patients, said, shrugging his shoulders, that he simply "fines them so many kronen for their mischief-making." So it will not surprise you to hear that even in the case of very busy analysts, the hours for consultation are not very crowded. I have had the ordinary door between my waiting room and my office doubled and strengthened by a covering of felt. The purpose of this little arrangement cannot be doubted. Now it happens over and over again that people who are admitted from my waiting room omit to close the door behind them; in fact, they almost always leave both doors open. As soon as I have noticed this I insist rather gruffly that he or she go back in order to rectify the omission, even though it be an elegant gentleman or a lady in all her finery. This gives an impression of misapplied pedantry. I have, in fact, occasionally discredited myself by such a demand, since the individual concerned was one of those who cannot touch even a door knob, and prefer as well to have their attendants spared this contact. But most frequently I was right, for he who conducts himself in this way, and leaves the door from the waiting room into the physician's consultation room open, belongs to the rabble and deserves to be received inhospitably. Do not, I beg you, defend him until you have heard what follows. For the fact is that this negligence of the patient's only occurs when he has been alone in the waiting room and so leaves an empty room behind him, never when others, strangers, have been waiting with him. If that latter is the case, he knows very well that it is in his interest not to be listened to while he is talking to the physician, and never omits to close both the doors with care.

This omission of the patient's is so predetermined that it becomes neither accidental nor meaningless, indeed, not even unimportant, for, as we shall see, it throws light upon the relation of this patient to the physician. He is one of the great number of those who seek authority, who want to be dazzled, intimidated. Perhaps he had inquired by telephone as to what time he had best call, he had prepared himself to come on a crowd of suppliants somewhat like those in front of a branch milk station. He now enters an empty waiting room which is, moreover, most modestly furnished, and he is disappointed. He must demand reparation from the physician for the wasted respect that he had tendered him, and so he omits to close the door between the reception room and the office. By this, he means to say to the physician: "Oh, well, there is no one here anyway, and probably no one will come as long as I am here." He would also be quite unmannerly and supercilious during the consultation if his presumption were not at once restrained by a sharp reminder.

You will find nothing in the analysis of this little symptomatic act which was not previously known to you. That is to say, it asserts that this act is not accidental, but has a motive, a meaning, a purpose, that it has its assignable connections psychologically, and that it serves as a small indication of a more important psychological process. But above all it implies that the process thus intimated is not known to the consciousness of the individual in whom it takes place, for none of the patients who left the two doors open would have admitted that they meant by this omission to show me their contempt. Some could probably recall a slight sense of disappointment at entering an empty waiting room, but the connection between this impression and the symptomatic act which followed—of these, his consciousness was surely not aware.

Now let us place, side by side with this small analysis of a symptomatic act, an observation on a pathological case. I choose one which is fresh in my mind and which can also be described with relative brevity. A certain measure of minuteness of detail is unavoidable in any such account.

A young officer, home on a short leave of absence, asked me to see his mother-in-law who, in spite of the happiest circumstances, was embittering her own and her people's existence by a senseless idea. I am introduced to a well preserved lady of fifty-three with pleasant, simple manners, who gives the following account without any hesitation: She is most happily married and lives in the country with her husband, who operates a large factory. She cannot say enough for the kind thoughtfulness of her husband. They had married for love thirty years ago, and since then there had never been a shadow, a quarrel or cause for jealousy. Now, even though her two children are well married, the husband and father does not yet want to retire, from a feeling of duty. A year ago there happened the incredible thing, incomprehensible to herself as well. She gave complete credence to an anonymous letter which accused her excellent husband of having an affair with a young girl—and since then her happiness is destroyed. The more detailed circumstances were somewhat as follows: She had a chambermaid with whom she had perhaps too often discussed intimate matters. This girl pursued another young woman with positively malicious enmity because the latter had progressed so much further in life, despite the fact that she was of no better origin. Instead of going into domestic service, the girl had obtained a business training, had entered the factory and in consequence of the shorthandedness due to the drafting of the clerks into the army had advanced to a good position. She now lives in the factory itself, meets all the gentlemen socially, and is even addressed as "Miss." The girl who had remained behind in life was of course ready to speak all possible evil of her one-time schoolmate. One day our patient and her chambermaid were talking of an old gentleman who had been visiting at the house, and of whom it was known that he did not live with his wife, but kept another woman as his mistress. She does not know how it happened that she suddenly remarked, "That would be the most awful thing that could happen to me, if I should ever hear that my good husband also had a mistress." The next day she received an anonymous letter through the mail which, in a disguised handwriting, carried this very communication which she had conjured up. She concluded—it seems justifiably—that the letter was the handiwork of her malignant chambermaid, for the letter named as the husband's mistress the self-same woman whom the maid persecuted with her hatred. Our patient, in spite of the fact that she immediately saw through the intrigue and had seen enough in her town to know how little credence such cowardly denunciations deserve, was nevertheless at once prostrated by the letter. She became dreadfully excited and promptly sent for her husband in order to heap the bitterest reproaches upon him. Her husband laughingly denied the accusation and did the best that could be done. He called in the family physician, who was as well the doctor in attendance at the factory, and the latter added his efforts to quiet the unhappy woman. Their further procedure was also entirely reasonable. The chambermaid was dismissed, but the pretended rival was not. Since then, the patient claims she has repeatedly so far calmed herself as no longer to believe the contents of the anonymous letter, but this relief was neither thoroughgoing nor lasting. It was enough to hear the name of the young lady spoken or to meet her on the street in order to precipitate a new attack of suspicion, pain and reproach.

This, now, is the case history of this good woman. It does not need much psychiatric experience to understand that her portrayal of her own case was, if anything, rather too mild in contrast to other nervous patients. The picture, we say, was dissimulated; in reality she had never overcome her belief in the accusation of the anonymous letter.

Now what position does a psychiatrist take toward such a case? We already know what he would do in the case of the symptomatic act of the patient who does not close the doors to the waiting room. He declares it an accident without psychological interest, with which he need not concern himself. But this attitude cannot be maintained toward the pathological case of the jealous woman. The symptomatic act seems no great matter, but the symptom itself claims attention by reason of its gravity. It is bound up with intense subjective suffering while objectively it threatens to break up a home; therefore its claim to psychiatric interest cannot be put aside. The first endeavor of the psychiatrist is to characterize the symptom by some distinctive feature. The idea with which this woman torments herself cannot in itself be called nonsensical, for it does happen that elderly married men have affairs with young girls. But there is something else about it that is nonsensical and incredible. The patient has no reason beyond the declaration in the anonymous letter to believe that her tender and faithful husband belongs to this sort of married men, otherwise not uncommon. She knows that this letter in itself carries no proof; she can satisfactorily explain its origin; therefore she ought to be able to persuade herself that she has no reason to be jealous. Indeed she does this, but in spite of it she suffers every bit as much as she would if she acknowledged this jealousy as fully justified. We are agreed to call ideas of this sort, which are inaccessible to arguments based on logic or on facts.

"obsessions." Thus the good lady suffers from an *"obsession of jealousy"* that is surely a distinctive characterization for this pathological case.

Having reached this first certainty, our psychiatric interest will have become aroused. If we cannot do away with a delusion by taking reality into account, it can hardly have arisen from reality. But the delusion, what is its origin? There are delusions of the most widely varied content. Why is it that in our case the content should be jealousy? In what types of persons are obsessions liable to occur, and, in particular, obsessions of jealousy? We would like to turn to the psychiatrist with such questions, but here he leaves us in the lurch. There is only one of our queries which he heeds. He will examine the family history of this woman and *perhaps* will give us the answer: "The people who develop obsessions are those in whose families similar and other psychic disturbances have repeatedly occurred." In other words, if this lady develops an obsession she does so because she was predisposed to it by reason of her heredity. That is certainly something, but is it all that we want to know? Is it all that was effective in causing this break-down? Shall we be content to assume that it is immaterial, accidental and inexplicable why the obsession of jealousy develops rather than any other? And may we also accept this sentence about the dominance of the influence of heredity in its negative meaning, that is, that no matter what experiences came to this human being she was predestined to develop some kind of obsession? You will want to know why scientific psychiatry will give no further explanation. And I reply, "He is a rascal who gives more than he owns." The psychiatrist does not know of any path that leads him further in the explanation of such a case. He must content himself with the diagnosis and a prognosis which, despite a wealth of experience, is uncertain.

Yet, can psychoanalysis do more at this point? Indeed yes! I hope to show you that even in so inaccessible a case as this it can discover something which makes the further understanding possible. May I ask you first to note the apparently insignificant fact that the patient actually provoked the anonymous letter which now supports her delusion. The day before, she announces to the intriguing chambermaid that if her husband were to have an affair with a young girl it would be the worst

misfortune that could befall her. By so doing she re&
the maid the idea of sending her the anonymous lett
obsession thus attains a certain independence from th   ...... ,
it existed in the patient beforehand—perhaps as a dread; or was
it a wish! Consider, moreover, these additional details yielded
by an analysis of only two hours. The patient was indeed most
helpful when, after telling her story, she was urged to communicate her further thoughts, ideas and recollections. She declared
that nothing came to her mind, that she had already told everything. After two hours the undertaking had really to be given
up because she announced that she already felt cured and was
sure that the morbid idea would not return. Of course, she said
this because of this resistance and her fear of continuing the
analysis. In these two hours, however, she had let fall certain
remarks which made possible definite interpretation, indeed
made it incontestable; and this interpretation throws a clear
light on the origin of her obsession of jealousy. Namely, she
herself was very much infatuated with a certain young man, the
very same son-in-law upon whose urging she had come to consult me professionally. She knew nothing of this infatuation,
or at least only a very little. Because of the existing relationship, it was very easy for this infatuation to masquerade under
the guise of harmless tenderness. With all our further experience it is not difficult to feel our way toward an understanding
of the psychic life of this honest woman and good mother. Such
an infatuation, a monstrous, impossible thing, could not be
allowed to become conscious. But it continued to exist and
unconsciously exerted a heavy pressure. Something had to
happen, some sort of relief had to be found and the mechanism
of displacement which so constantly takes part in the origin of
obsessional jealousy offered the most immediate mitigation. If
not only she, old woman that she was, was in love with a young
man but if also her old husband had an affair with a young
girl, then she would be freed from the voice of her conscience
which accused her of infidelity. The phantasy of her husband's
infidelity was thus like a cooling salve on her burning wound.
Of her own love she never became conscious, but the reflection
of it, which would bring her such advantages, now became compulsive, obsessional and conscious. Naturally all arguments directed against the obsession were of no avail since they were

directed only to the reflection, and not to the original force to which it owed its strength and which, unimpeachable, lay buried in the unconscious.

Let us now piece together these fragments to see what a short and impeded psychoanalysis can nevertheless contribute to the understanding of this case. It is assumed of course that our inquiries were carefully conducted, a point which I cannot at this place submit to your judgment. In the first place, the obsession becomes no longer nonsensical nor incomprehensible, it is full of meaning, well motivated and an integral part of the patient's emotional experience. Secondly, it is a necessary reaction toward an unconscious psychological process, revealed in other ways, and it is to this very circumstance that it owes its obsessional nature, that is, its resistance to arguments based on logic or fact. In itself the obsession is something wished for, a kind of consolation. Finally, the experiences underlying the condition are such as unmistakably determine an obsession of jealousy and no other. You will also recognize the part played by the two important analogies in the analysis of the symptomatic act with reference to its meaning and intent and also to its relation to an unconscious factor in the situation.

Naturally, we have not yet answered all the questions which may be put on the basis of this case. Rather the case bristles with further problems of a kind which we have not yet been able to solve in any way, and of others which could not be solved because of the disadvantage of the circumstances under which we were working. For example: why is this happily married woman open to an infatuation for her son-in-law, and why does the relief which could have been obtained in other ways come to her by way of this mirror-image, this projection of her own condition upon her husband? I trust you will not think that it is idle and wanton to open such problems. Already we have much material at our disposal for their possible solution. This woman is in that critical age when her sexual needs undergo a sudden and unwelcome exaggeration. This might in itself be sufficient. In addition, her good and faithful mate may for many years have been lacking in that sufficient sexual capacity which the well-preserved woman needs for her satisfaction. We have learned by experience to know that those very men whose faithfulness is thus placed beyond a doubt are most gentle in

their treatment of their wives and unusually forbearing toward
their nervous complaints.   Furthermore, the fact that it was
just the young husband of a daughter who became the object of
her abnormal infatuation is by no means insignificant. A strong
erotic attachment to the daughter, which in the last analysis
leads back to the mother's sexual constitution, will often find
a way to live on under such a disguise. May I perhaps remind
you in this connection that the relationship between mother and
son-in-law has seemed particularly delicate since all time and is
one which among primitive peoples gave rise to very powerful
taboos and avoidances.[1] It often transgresses our cultural
standards positively as well as negatively. I cannot tell you
of course which of these three factors were at work in our case;
whether two of them only, or whether all of them coöperated,
for as you know I did not have the opportunity to continue the
analysis beyond two hours.

I realize at this point, ladies and gentlemen, that I have been
speaking entirely of things for which your understanding was
not prepared. I did this in order to carry through the comparison of psychiatry and psychoanalysis. May I now ask one
thing of you? Have you noticed any contradiction between
them? Psychiatry does not apply the technical methods of
psychoanalysis, and neglects to look for any significance in the
content of the obsession. Instead of first seeking out more
specific and immediate causes, psychiatry refers us to the very
general and remote source—heredity. But does this imply a
contradiction, a conflict between them? Do they not rather
supplement one another? For does the hereditary factor deny
the significance of the experience, is it not rather true that both
operate together in the most effective way? You must admit that
there is nothing in the nature of psychiatric work which must
repudiate psychoanalytic research. Therefore, it is the psychiatrists who oppose psychoanalysis, not psychiatry itself. Psychoanalysis stands in about the same relation to psychiatry as does
histology to anatomy. The one studies the outer forms of organs,
the other the closer structure of tissues and cells. A contradiction between two types of study, where one simplifies the other,
is not easily conceivable. You know that anatomy to-day forms
the basis of scientific medicine, but there was a time when the

[1] Compare S. Freud, *Totem and Taboo*, 1913.

dissection of human corpses to learn the inner structure of the body was as much frowned upon as the practice of psychoanalysis, which seeks to ascertain the inner workings of the human soul, seems proscribed to-day. And presumably a not too distant time will bring us to the realization that a psychiatry which aspires to scientific depth is not possible without a real knowledge of the deeper unconscious processes in the psychic life.

Perhaps this much-attacked psychoanalysis has now found some friends among you who are anxious to see it justify itself as well from another aspect, namely, the therapeutic side. You know that the therapy of psychiatry has hitherto not been able to influence obsessions. Can psychoanalysis perhaps do so, thanks to its insight into the mechanism of these symptoms? No, ladies and gentlemen, it cannot; for the present at least it is just as powerless in the face of these maladies as every other therapy. We can understand what it was that happened within the patient, but we have no means of making the patient himself understand this. In fact, I told you that I could not extend the analysis of the obsession beyond the first steps. Would you therefore assert that analysis is objectionable in such cases because it remains without result? I think not. We have the right, indeed we have the duty to pursue scientific research without regard to an immediate practical effect. Some day, though we do not know when or where, every little scrap of knowledge will have been translated into skill, even into therapeutic skill. If psychoanalysis were as unsuccessful in all other forms of nervous and psychological disease as it is in the case of the obsession, it would nevertheless remain fully justified as an irreplaceable method of scientific research. It is true that we would then not be in a position to practice it, for the human subjects from which we must learn, live and will in their own right; they must have motives of their own in order to assist in the work, but they would deny themselves to us. Therefore let me conclude this session by telling you that there are comprehensive groups of nervous diseases concerning which our better understanding has actually been translated into therapeutic power; moreover, that in disturbances which are most difficult to reach we can under certain conditions secure results which are second to none in the field of internal therapeutics.

The Meaning of the Symptoms

IN the last lecture I explained to you that clinical psychiatry concerns itself very little with the form under which the symptoms appear or with the burden they carry, but that it is precisely here that psychoanalysis steps in and shows that the symptom carries a meaning and is connected with the experience of the patient. The meaning of neurotic symptoms was first discovered by J. Breuer in the study and felicitous cure of a case of hysteria which has since become famous (1880-82). It is true that P. Janet independently reached the same result; literary priority must in fact be accorded to the French scholar, since Breuer published his observations more than a decade later (1893-95) during his period of collaboration with me. On the whole it may be of small importance to us who is responsible for this discovery, for you know that every discovery is made more than once, that none is made all at once, and that success is not meted out according to deserts. America is not named after Columbus. Before Breuer and Janet, the great psychiatrist Leuret expressed the opinion that even for the deliria of the insane, if we only understood how to interpret them, a meaning could be found. I confess that for a considerable period of time I was willing to estimate very highly the credit due to P. Janet in the explanation of neurotic symptoms, because he saw in them the expression of subconscious ideas (*idées incon scientes*) with which the patients were obsessed. But since then Janet has expressed himself most conservatively, as though he wanted to confess that the term "subconscious" had been for him nothing more than a mode of speech, a shift, "*une façon de parler*," by the use of which he had nothing definite in mind. I now no longer understand Janet's discussions, but I believe that he has needlessly deprived himself of high credit.

The neurotic symptoms then have their meaning just like errors and the dream, and like these they are related to the lives of the persons in whom they appear. The importance of this insight into the nature of the symptom can best be brought home to you by way of examples. That it is borne out always and in all cases, I can only assert, not prove. He who gathers his own experience will be convinced of it. For certain reasons, however, I shall draw my instances not from hysteria, but from another fundamentally related and very curious neurosis concerning which I wish to say a few introductory words to you. This so-called compulsion neurosis is not so popular as the widely known hysteria; it is, if I may use the expression, not so noisily ostentatious, behaves more as a private concern of the patient, renounces bodily manifestations almost entirely and creates all its symptoms psychologically. Compulsion neurosis and hysteria are those forms of neurotic disease by the study of which psychoanalysis has been built up, and in whose treatment as well the therapy celebrates its triumphs. Of these the compulsion neurosis, which does not take that mysterious leap from the psychic to the physical, has through psychoanalytic research become more intimately comprehensible and transparent to us than hysteria, and we have come to understand that it reveals far more vividly certain extreme characteristics of the neuroses.

The chief manifestations of compulsion neurosis are these: the patient is occupied by thoughts that in reality do not interest him, is moved by impulses that appear alien to him, and is impelled to actions which, to be sure, afford him no pleasure, but the performance of which he cannot possibly resist. The thoughts may be absurd in themselves or thoroughly indifferent to the individual, often they are absolutely childish and in all cases they are the result of strained thinking, which exhausts the patient, who surrenders himself to them most unwillingly. Against his will he is forced to brood and speculate as though it were a matter of life or death to him. The impulses, which the patient feels within himself, may also give a childish or ridiculous impression, but for the most part they bear the terrifying aspect of temptations to fearful crimes, so that the patient not only denies them, but flees from them in horror and protects himself from actual execution of his desires through inhibitory renunciations and restrictions upon his personal liberty. As a matter of fact he never, not a single time, carries any of these impulses into effect; the result is always that his

evasion and precaution triumph. The patient really carries out
only very harmless trivial acts, so-called compulsive acts, for
the most part repetitions and ceremonious additions to the occupations of every-day life, through which its necessary performances—going to bed, washing, dressing, walking—become long-
winded problems of almost insuperable difficulty. The abnormal
ideas, impulses and actions are in nowise equally potent in
individual forms and cases of compulsion neurosis; it is the rule,
rather, that one or the other of these manifestations is the
dominating factor and gives the name to the disease; that all
these forms, however, have a great deal in common is quite
undeniable.

Surely this means violent suffering. I believe that the wildest
psychiatric phantasy could not have succeeded in deriving anything comparable, and if one did not actually see it every day,
one could hardly bring oneself to believe it. Do not think, however, that you give the patient any help when you coax him to
divert himself, to put aside these stupid ideas and to set himself
to something useful in the place of his whimsical occupations.
This is just what he would like of his own accord, for he possesses all his senses, shares your opinion of his compulsion symptoms, in fact volunteers it quite readily. But he cannot do
otherwise; whatever activities actually are released under compulsion neurosis are carried along by a driving energy, such as
is probably never met with in normal psychic life. He has only
one remedy—to transfer and change. In place of one stupid
idea he can think of a somewhat milder absurdity, he can proceed from one precaution and prohibition to another, or carry
through another ceremonial. He may shift, but he cannot
annul the compulsion. One of the chief characteristics of the
sickness is the instability of the symptoms; they can be shifted
very far from their original form. It is moreover striking that
the contrasts present in all psychological experience are so very
sharply drawn in this condition. In addition to the compulsion
of positive and negative content, an intellectual doubt makes
itself felt that gradually attacks the most ordinary and assured
certainties. All these things merge into steadily increasing uncertainty, lack of energy, curtailment of personal liberty, despite
the fact that the patient suffering from compulsion neurosis is
originally a most energetic character, often of extraordinary ob-

stinacy, as a rule intellectually gifted above the average. For the most part he has attained a desirable stage of ethical development, is overconscientious and more than usually correct. You can imagine that it takes no inconsiderable piece of work to find one's way through this maze of contradictory characteristics and symptoms. Indeed, for the present our only object is to understand and to interpret some symptoms of this disease.

Perhaps in reference to our previous discussions, you would like to know the position of present-day psychiatry to the problems of the compulsion neurosis. This is covered in a very slim chapter. Psychiatry gives names to the various forms of compulsion, but says nothing further concerning them. Instead it emphasizes the fact that those who show these symptoms are degenerates. That yields slight satisfaction, it is an ethical judgment, a condemnation rather than an explanation. We are led to suppose that it is in the unsound that all these peculiarities may be found. Now we do believe that persons who develop such symptoms must differ fundamentally from other people. But we would like to ask, are they more "degenerate" than other nervous patients, those suffering, for instance, from hysteria or other diseases of the mind? The characterization is obviously too general. One may even doubt whether it is at all justified, when one learns that such symptoms occur in excellent men and women of especially great and universally recognized ability. In general we glean very little intimate knowledge of the great men who serve us as models. This is due both to their own discretion and to the lying propensities of their biographers. Sometimes, however, a man is a fanatic disciple of truth, such as Emile Zola, and then we hear from him the strange compulsion habits from which he suffered all his life.[1]

Psychiatry has resorted to the expedient of speaking of "superior degenerates." Very well—but through psychoanalysis we have learned that these peculiar compulsion symptoms may be permanently removed just like any other disease of normal persons. I myself have frequently succeeded in doing this.

I will give you two examples only of the analysis of compulsion symptoms, one, an old observation, which cannot be replaced by anything more complete, and one a recent study. I am limiting myself to such a small number because in an account of this

[1] E. Toulouse, Emile Zola—*Enquête medico—psychologique*, Paris, 1896.

nature it is necessary to be very explicit and to enter into every detail.

A lady about thirty years old suffered from the most severe compulsions. I might indeed have helped her if caprice of fortune had not destroyed my work—perhaps I will yet have occasion to tell you about it. In the course of each day the patient often executed, among others, the following strange compulsive act. She ran from her room into an adjoining one, placed herself in a definite spot beside a table which stood in the middle of the room, rang for her maid, gave her a trivial errand to do, or dismissed her without more ado, and then ran back again. This was certainly not a severe symptom of disease, but it still deserved to arouse curiosity. Its explanation was found, absolutely without any assistance on the part of the physician, in the very simplest way, a way to which no one can take exception. I hardly know how I alone could have guessed the meaning of this compulsive act, or have found any suggestion toward its interpretation. As often as I had asked the patient: "Why do you do this? Of what use is it?" she had answered, "I don't know." But one day after I had succeeded in surmounting a grave ethical doubt of hers she suddenly saw the light and related the history of the compulsive act. More than ten years prior she had married a man far older than herself, who had proved impotent on the bridal night. Countless times during the night he had run from his room to hers to repeat the attempt, but each time without success. In the morning he said angrily: "It is enough to make one ashamed before the maid who does the beds," and took a bottle of red ink that happened to be in the room, and poured its contents on the sheet, but not on the place where such a stain would have been justifiable. At first I did not understand the connection between this reminiscence and the compulsive act in question, for the only agreement I could find between them was in the running from one room into another,—possibly also in the appearance of the maid. Then the patient led me to the table in the second room and let me discover a large spot on the cover. She explained also that she placed herself at the table in such a way that the maid could not miss seeing the stain. Now it was no longer possible to doubt the intimate relation of the scene after her bridal night and her present compulsive act, but there were still a number of things to be learned about it.

In the first place, it is obvious that the patient identifies herself with her husband, she is acting his part in her imitation of his running from one room into the other. We must then admit—if she holds to this role—that she replaces the bed and sheet by table and cover. This may seem arbitrary, but we have not studied dream symbolism in vain. In dreams also a table which must be interpreted as a bed, is frequently seen. "Bed and board" together represent married life, one may therefore easily be used to represent the other.

The evidence that the compulsive act carries meaning would thus be plain; it appears as a representation, a repetition of the original significant scene. However, we are not forced to stop at this semblance of a solution; when we examine more closely the relation between these two people, we shall probably be enlightened concerning something of wider importance, namely, the purpose of the compulsive act. The nucleus of this purpose is evidently the summoning of the maid; to her she wishes to show the stain and refute her husband's remark: "It is enough to shame one before the maid." He—whose part she is playing—therefore feels no shame before the maid, hence the stain must be in the right place. So we see that she has not merely repeated the scene, rather she has amplified it, corrected it and "turned it to the good." Thereby, however, she also corrects something else,—the thing which was so embarrassing that night and necessitated the use of the red ink—impotence. The compulsive act then says: "No, it is not true, he did not have to be ashamed before the maid, he was not impotent." After the manner of a dream she represents the fulfillment of this wish in an overt action, she is ruled by the desire to help her husband over that unfortunate incident.

Everything else that I could tell you about this case supports this clue more specifically; all that we otherwise know about her tends to strengthen this interpretation of a compulsive act incomprehensible in itself. For years the woman has lived separated from her husband and is struggling with the intention to obtain a legal divorce. But she is by no means free from him; she forces herself to remain faithful to him, she retires from the world to avoid temptation; in her imagination she

excuses and idealizes him. The deepest secret of her malady is
that by means of it she shields her husband from malicious
gossip, justifies her separation from him, and renders possible
for him a comfortable separate life. Thus the analysis of a
harmless compulsive act leads to the very heart of this case and
at the same time reveals no inconsiderable portion of the secret
of the compulsion neurosis in general. I shall be glad to have
you dwell upon this instance, as it combines conditions that one
can scarcely demand in other cases. The interpretation of the
symptoms was discovered by the patient herself in one flash,
without the suggestion or interference of the analyst. It came
about by the reference to an experience, which did not, as is
usually the case, belong to the half-forgotten period of childhood,
but to the mature life of the patient, in whose memory it had
remained unobliterated. All the objections which critics ordinarily offer to our interpretation of symptoms fail in this case
Of course, we are not always so fortunate.

And one thing more! Have you not observed how this insignificant compulsive act initiated us into the intimate life of the
invalid? A woman can scarcely relate anything more intimate
than the story of her bridal night, and is it without further
significance that we just happened to come on the intimacies of
her sexual life? It might of course be the result of the selection
I have made in this instance. Let us not judge too quickly and
turn our attention to the second instance, one of an entirely
different kind, a sample of a frequently occurring variety,
namely, the sleep ritual.

A nineteen-year old, well-developed, gifted girl, an only child,
who was superior to her parents in education and intellectual
activity, had been wild and mischievous in her childhood, but
has become very nervous during the last years without any
apparent outward cause. She is especially irritable with her
mother, always discontented, depressed, has a tendency toward
indecision and doubt, and is finally forced to confess that she
can no longer walk alone on public squares or wide thorough-
fares. We shall not consider at length her complicated condition, which requires at least two diagnoses—agoraphobia and
compulsion neurosis. We will dwell only upon the fact that this
girl has also developed a sleep ritual, under which she allows
her parents to suffer much discomfort. In a certain sense, we

may say that every normal person has a sleep ritual, in other
words that he insists on certain conditions, the absence of which
hinders him from falling asleep; he has created certain observances by which he bridges the transition from waking to
sleeping and these he repeats every evening in the same manner.
But everything that the healthy person demands in order to
obtain sleep is easily understandable and, above all, when external conditions necessitate a change, he adapts himself easily
and without loss of time. But the pathological ritual is rigid,
it persists by virtue of the greatest sacrifices, it also masks itself
with a reasonable justification and seems, in the light of superficial observation, to differ from the normal only by exaggerated
pedantry. But under closer observation we notice that the mask
is transparent, for the ritual covers intentions that go far beyond
this reasonable justification, and other intentions as well that
are in direct contradiction to this reasonable justification. Our
patient cites as the motive of her nightly precautions that she
must have quiet in order to sleep; therefore she excludes all
sources of noise. To accomplish this, she does two things: the
large clock in her room is stopped, all other clocks are removed;
not even the wrist watch on her night-table is suffered to remain.
Flowerpots and vases are placed on her desk so that they cannot
fall down during the night, and in breaking disturb her sleep.
She knows that these precautions are scarcely justifiable for the
sake of quiet; the ticking of the small watch could not be heard
even if it should remain on the night-table, and moreover we
all know that the regular ticking of a clock is conducive to
sleep rather than disturbing. She does admit that there is not
the least probability that flowerpots and vases left in place
might of their own accord fall and break during the night. She
drops the pretense of quiet for the other practice of this sleep
ritual. She seems on the contrary to release a source of disturbing noises by the demand that the door between her own
room and that of her parents remain half open, and she insures
this condition by placing various objects in front of the open
door. The most important observances concern the bed itself.
The large pillow at the head of the bed may not touch the
wooden back of the bed. The small pillow for her head must
lie on the large pillow to form a rhomb; she then places her
head exactly upon the diagonal of the rhomb. Before covering

herself, the featherbed must be shaken so that its foot end becomes quite flat, but she never omits to press this down and redistribute the thickness.

Allow me to pass over the other trivial incidents of this ritual; they would teach us nothing new and cause too great digression from our purpose. Do not overlook, however, the fact that all this does not run its course quite smoothly. Everything is pervaded by the anxiety that things have not been done properly; they must be examined, repeated. Her doubts seize first on one, then on another precaution, and the result is that one or two hours elapse during which the girl cannot and the intimidated parents dare not sleep.

These torments were not so easily analyzed as the compulsive act of our former patient. In the working out of the interpretations I had to hint and suggest to the girl, and was met on her part either by positive denial or mocking doubt. This first reaction of denial, however, was followed by a time when she occupied herself of her own accord with the possibilities that had been suggested, noted the associations they called out, produced reminiscences, and established connections, until through her own efforts she had reached and accepted all interpretations. In so far as she did this, she desisted as well from the performance of her compulsive rules, and even before the treatment had ended she had given up the entire ritual. You must also know that the nature of present-day analysis by no means enables us to follow out each individual symptom until its meaning becomes clear. Rather it is necessary to abandon a given theme again and again, yet with the certainty that we will be led back to it in some other connection. The interpretation of the symptoms in this case, which I am about to give you, is a synthesis of results, which, with the interruptions of other work, needed weeks and months for their compilation.

Our patient gradually learns to understand that she has banished clocks and watches from her room during the night because the clock is the symbol of the female genital. The clock, which we have learned to interpret as a symbol for other things also, receives this role of the genital organ through its relation to periodic occurrences at equal intervals. A woman may for instance be found to boast that her menstruation is as ˮ ˮ as clockwork The special fear of our patient, howe that the ticking of the clock would disturb her in her sleep. The ticking of the clock may be compared to the throbbing of the clitoris during sexual excitement. Frequently she had actually been awakened by this painful sensation and now this fear of an erection of the clitoris caused her to remove all ticking clocks during the night. Flowerpots and vases are, as are all vessels, also female symbols. The precaution, therefore, that they should not fall and break at night, was not without meaning. We know the widespread custom of breaking a plate or dish when an ˙engagement is celebrated. The fragment of which each guest possesses himself symbolizes his renunciation of his claim to the bride, a renunciation which we may assume as based on the monogamous marriage law. Furthermore, to this part of her ceremonial our patient adds a reminiscence and several associations. As a child she had slipped once and fallen with a bowl of glass or clay, had cut her finger, and bled violently. As she grew up and learned the facts of sexual intercourse, she developed the fear that she might not bleed during her bridal night and so not prove to be a virgin. Her precaution against the breaking of vases was a rejection of the entire virginity complex, including the bleeding connected with the first cohabitation. She rejected both the fear to bleed and the contradictory fear not to bleed. Indeed her precautions had very little to do with a prevention of noise.

One day she guessed the central idea of her ceremonial, when she suddenly understood her rule not to let the pillow come in contact with the bed. The pillows always had seemed a woman to her, the erect back of the bed a man. By means of magic, we may say, she wished to keep apart man and wife; it was her parents she wished to separate, so to prevent their marital intercourse. She had sought to attain the same end by more direct methods in earlier years, before the institution of her ceremonial. She had simulated fear or exploited a genuine timidity in order to keep open the door between the parents' bedroom and the nursery. This demand had been retained in her present ceremonial. Thus she had gained the opportunity of overhearing her parents, a proceeding which at one time subjected her to months of sleeplessness. Not content with this disturbance to her parents, she was at that time occasionally able to gain her point and sleep between father and mother in their very bed. Then "pillow" and "wooden wall" could really not come in contact. Finally when she became so big that her presence between the parents could not longer be borne comfortably, she consciously simulated fear and actually succeeded in changing places with her mother and taking her place at her father's side. This situation was undoubtedly the starting point for the phantasies, whose after-effects made themselves felt in her ritual.

If a pillow represented a woman, then the shaking of the featherbed till all the feathers were lumped at one end, rounding it into a prominence, must have its meaning also. It meant the impregnation of the wife; the ceremonial, however, never failed to provide for the annulment of this pregnancy by the flattening down of the feathers. Indeed, for years our patient had feared that the intercourse between her parents might result in another child which would be her rival. Now, where the large pillow represents a woman, the mother, then the small pillow could be nothing but the daughter. Why did this pillow have to be placed so as to form a rhomb; and why did the girl's head have to rest exactly upon the diagonal? It was easy to remind the patient that the rhomb on all walls is the rune used to represent the open female genital. She herself then played the part of the man, the father, and her head took the place of the male organ. (Cf. the symbol of beheading to represent castration.)

Wild ideas, you will say, to run riot in the head of a virgin girl. I admit it, but do not forget that I have not created these ideas but merely interpreted them. A sleep ritual of this kind is itself very strange, and you cannot deny the correspondence between the ritual and the phantasies that yielded us the interpretation. For my part I am most anxious that you observe in this connection that no single phantasy was projected in the ceremonial, but a number of them had to be integrated,—they must have their nodal points somewhere in space. Observe also that the observance of the ritual reproduce the sexual desire now positively, now negatively, and serve in part as their rejection, again as their representation.

It would be possible to make a better analysis of this ritual by relating it to other symptoms of the patient. But we cannot digress in that direction. Let the suggestion suffice that girl is subject to an erotic attachment to her father, the be

ning of which goes back to her earliest childhood. That perhaps
is the reason for her unfriendly attitude toward her mother.
Also we cannot escape the fact that the analysis of this symptom again points to the sexual life of the patient. The more
we penetrate to the meaning and purpose of neurotic symptoms,
the less surprising will this seem to us.

By means of two selected illlustrations I have demonstrated
to you that neurotic symptoms carry just as much meaning as
do errors and the dream, and that they are intimately connected
with the experience of the patient. Can I expect you to believe
this vitally significant statement on the strength of two examples? No. But can you expect me to cite further illustrations
until you declare yourself convinced? That too is impossible,
since considering the explicitness with which I treat each individual case, I would require a five-hour full semester course for
the explanation of this one point in the theory of the neuroses.
I must content myself then with having given you one proof
for my assertion and refer you for the rest to the literature
of the subject, above all to the classical interpretation of symptoms in Breuer's first case (hysteria) as well as to the striking
clarification of obscure symptoms in the so-called dementia
praecox by C. G. Jung, dating from the time when this scholar
was still content to be a mere psychoanalyst—and did not yet
want to a prophet; and to all the articles that have subsequently
appeared in our periodicals. It is precisely investigations of this
sort which are plentiful. Psychoanalysts have felt themselves
so much attracted by the analysis, interpretation and translation
of neurotic symptoms, that by contrast they seem temporarily
to have neglected other problems of neurosis.

Whoever among you takes the trouble to look into the matter
will undoubtedly be deeply impressed by the wealth of evidential
material. But he will also encounter difficulties. We have
learned that the meaning of a symptom is found in its relation
to the experience of the patient. The more highly individualized
the symptom is, the sooner we may hope to establish these relations. Therefore the task resolves itself specifically into the
discovery for every nonsensical idea and useless action of a past
situation wherein the idea had been justified and the action
purposeful. A perfect example for this kind of symptom is the
compulsive act of our patient who ran to the table and rang

for the maid. But there are symptoms of a very different nature which are by no means rare. They must be called typical symptoms of the disease, for they are approximately alike in all cases, in which the individual differences disappear or shrivel to such an extent that it is difficult to connect them with the specific experiences of the patient and to relate them to the particular situations of his past. Let us again direct our attention to the compulsion neurosis. The sleep ritual of our second patient is already quite typical, but bears enough individual features to render possible what may be called an *historic* interpretation. But all compulsive patients tend to repeat, to isolate their actions from others and to subject them to a rhythmic sequence. Most of them wash too much. Agoraphobia (topophobia, fear of spaces), a malady which is no longer grouped with the compulsion neurosis, but is now called anxiety hysteria, invariably shows the same pathological picture; it repeats with exhausting monotony the same feature, the patient's fear of closed spaces, of large open squares, of long stretched streets and parkways, and their feeling of safety when acquaintances accompany them, when a carriage drives after them, etc. On this identical groundwork, however, the individual differences between the patients are superimposed—moods one might almost call them, which are sharply contrasted in the various cases. The one fears only narrow streets, the other only wide ones, the one can go out walking only when there are few people abroad, the other when there are many. Hysteria also, aside from its wealth of individual features, has a superfluity of common typical symptoms that appear to resist any facile historical methods of tracing them. But do not let us forget that it is by these typical symptoms that we get our bearings in reaching a diagnosis. When, in one case of hysteria we have finally traced back a typical symptom to an experience or a series of similar experiences, for instance followed back an hysterical vomiting to its origin in a succession of disgust impressions, another case of vomiting will confuse us by revealing an entirely different chain of experiences, seemingly just as effective. It seems almost as though hysterical patients must vomit for some reason as yet unknown, and that the historic factors, revealed by analysis, are chance pretexts, seized on opportunity best offered to serve the purposes of a deeper need.

Thus we soon reach the discouraging conclusion that although we can satisfactorily explain the individual neurotic symptom by relating it to an experience, our science fails us when it comes to the typical symptoms that occur far more frequently. In addition, remember that I am not going into all the detailed difficulties which come up in the course of resolutely hunting down an historic interpretation of the symptom. I have no intention of doing this, for though I want to keep nothing from you, and so paint everything in its true colors, I still do not wish to confuse and discourage you at the very outset of our studies. It is true that we have only begun to understand the interpretation of symptoms, but we wish to hold fast to the results we have achieved, and struggle forward step by step toward the mastery of the still unintelligible data. I therefore try to cheer you with the thought that a fundamenal difference between the two kinds of symptoms can scarcely be assumed. Since the individual symptoms are so obviously dependent upon the experience of the patient, there is a possibility that the typical symptoms revert to an experience that is in itself typical and common to all humanity. Other regularly recurring features of neurosis, such as the repetition and doubt of the compulsion neurosis, may be universal reactions which are forced upon the patient by the very nature of the abnormal change. In short, we have no reason to be prematurely discouraged; we shall see what our further results will yield.

We meet a very similar difficulty in the theory of dreams, which in our previous discussion of the dream I could not go into. The manifest content of dreams is most profuse and individually varied, and I have shown very explicitly what analysis may glean from this content. But side by side with these dreams there are others which may also be termed "typical" and which occur similarly in all people. These are dreams of identical content which offer the same difficulties for their interpretation as the typical symptom. They are the dreams of falling, flying, floating, swimming, of being hemmed in, of nakedness, and various other anxiety dreams that yield first one and then another interpretation for the different patients, without resulting in an explanation of their monotonous and typical

recurrence. In the matter of these dreams also, we see a fundamental groundwork enriched by individual additions. Probably
they as well can be fitted into the theory of dream life, built
up on the basis of other dreams,—not however by straining the
point, but by the gradual broadening of our views.

EIGHTEENTH LECTURE

GENERAL THEORY OF THE NEUROSES

Traumatic Fixation—The Unconscious

I SAID last time that we would not continue our work from the standpoint of our doubts, but on the basis of our results. We have not even touched upon two of the most interesting conclusions, derived equally from the same two sample analyses.

In the first place, both patients give us the impression of being *fixated* upon some very definite part of their past; they are unable to free themselves therefrom, and have therefore come to be completely estranged both from the present and the future. They are now isolated in their ailment, just as in earlier days people withdrew into monasteries there to carry along the burden of their unhappy fates. In the case of the first patient, it is her marriage with her husband, really abandoned, that has determined her lot. By means of her symptoms she continues to deal with her husband; we have learned to understand those voices which plead his case, which excuse him, exalt him, lament his loss. Although she is young and might be coveted by other men, she has seized upon all manner of real and imaginary (magic) precautions to safeguard her virtue for him. She will not appear before strangers, she neglects her personal appearance; furthermore, she cannot bring herself to get up readily from any chair on which she has been seated. She refuses to give her signature, and finally, since she is motivated by her desire not to let anyone have anything of hers, she is unable to give presents.

In the case of the second patient, the young girl, it is an erotic attachment for her father that had established itself in the years prior to puberty, which plays the same role in her life. She also has arrived at the conclusion that she may not marry so long as she is sick. We may suspect she became ill in order that she need not marry, and that she might stay with her father.

236

It is impossible to evade the question of how, in what manner, and driven by what motives, an individual may come by such a remarkable and unprofitable attitude toward life. Granted of course that this bearing is a general characteristic of neurosis, and not a special peculiarity of these two cases, it is nevertheless a general trait in every neurosis of very great importance in practice. Breuer's first hysterical patient was fixated in the same manner upon the time when she nursed her very sick father. In spite of her recuperation she has, in certain respects, since that time, been done with life; although she remained healthy and able, she did not enter on the normal life of women. In every one of our patients we may see, by the use of analysis, that in his disease-symptoms and their results he has gone back again into a definite period of his past. In the majority of cases he even chooses a very early phase of his life, sometime a childhood phase, indeed, laughable as it may appear, a phase of his very suckling existence.

The closest analogies to these conditions of our neurotics are furnished by the types of sickness which the war has just now made so frequent—the so-called traumatic neuroses. Even before the war there were such cases after railroad collisions and other frightful occurrences which endangered life. The traumatic neuroses are, fundamentally, not the same as the spontaneous neuroses which we have been analysing and treating; moreover, we have not yet succeeded in bringing them within our hypotheses, and I hope to be able to make clear to you wherein this limitation lies. Yet on one point we may emphasize the existence of a complete agreement between the two forms. The traumatic neuroses show clear indications that they are grounded in a fixation upon the moment of the traumatic disaster. In their dreams these patients regularly live over the traumatic situation; where there are attacks of an hysterical type, which permit of an analysis, we learn that the attack approximates a complete transposition into this situation. It is as if these patients had not yet gotten through with the traumatic situation, as if it were actually before them as a task which was not yet mastered. We take this view of the matter in all seriousness; it shows the way to an *economic* view of psychic occurrences. For the expression "traumatic" has no other than an economic meaning, and the disturbance permanently attacks the ma·

ment of available energy. The traumatic experience is one
which, in a very short space of time, is able to increase the
strength of a given stimulus so enormously that its assimilation,
or rather its elaboration, can no longer be effected by normal
means.

This analogy tempts us to classify as traumatic those experiences as well upon which our neurotics appear to be fixated.
Thus the possibility is held out to us of having found a simple
determining factor for the neurosis. It would then be comparable to a traumatic disease, and would arise from the inability
to meet an overpowering emotional experience. As a matter
of fact this reads like the first formula, by which Breuer and I,
in 1893–1895, accounted theoretically for our new observations.
A case such as that of our first patient, the young woman separated from her husband, is very well explained by this conception. She was not able to get over the unfeasibility of her
marriage, and has not been able to extricate herself from this
trauma. But our very next, that of the girl attached to her
father, shows us that the formula is not sufficiently comprehensive. On the one hand, such baby love of a little girl for her
father is so usual, and so often outlived that the designation
"traumatic" would carry no significance; on the other hand,
the history of the patient teaches us that this first erotic fixation
apparently passed by harmlessly at the time, and did not again
appear until many years later in the symptoms of the compulsion
neurosis. We see complications before us, the existence of a
greater wealth of determining factors in the disease, but we also
suspect that the traumatic viewpoint will not have to be given
up as wrong; rather it will have to subordinate itself when it is
fitted into a different context.

Here again we must leave the road we have been traveling.
For the time being, it leads us no further and we have many
other things to find out before we can go on again. But before
we leave this subject let us note that the fixation on some particular phase of the past has bearings which extend far beyond
the neurosis. Every neurosis contains such a fixation, but every
fixation does not lead to a neurosis, nor fall into the same class
with neuroses, nor even set the conditions for the development
of a neurosis. Mourning is a type of emotional fixation on a
theory of the past, which also brings with it the most complete

alienation from the present and the future. But mourning is
sharply distinguished from neuroses that may be designated as
pathological forms of mourning.

It also happens that men are brought to complete deadlock by
a traumatic experience that has so completely shaken the foundations on which they have built their lives that they give up all
interest in the present and future, and become completely ab-
sorbed in their retrospections; but these unhappy persons are
not necessarily neurotic. We must not overestimate this one
feature as a diagnostic for a neurosis, no matter how invariable
and potent it may be.

Now let us turn to the second conclusion of our analysis, which
however we will hardly need to limit subsequently. We have
spoken of the senseless compulsive activities of our first patient,
and what intimate memories she disclosed as belonging to them;
later we also investigated the connection between experience
and symptom and thus discovered the purpose hidden behind
the compulsive activity. But we have entirely omitted one factor that deserves our whole attention. As long as the patient
kept repeating the compulsive activity she did not know that
it was in any way related with the experience in question.
The connection between the two was hidden from her, she truthfully answered that she did not know what compelled her to do
this. Once, suddenly, under the influence of the cure, she hit
upon the connection and was able to tell it to us. But still she
did not know of the end in the service of which she performed
the compulsive activities, the purpose to correct a painful part
of the past and to place the husband, still loved by her, upon
a higher level. It took quite a long time and a great deal of
trouble for her to grasp and admit to me that such a motive
alone could have been the motive force of the compulsive
activity.

The relation between the scene after the unhappy bridal night
and the tender motive of the patient yield what we have called
the meaning of the compulsive activity. But both the
"whence" and the "why" remained hidden from her as long
as she continued to carry out the compulsive act. Psychological processes had been going on within her for which the
compulsive act found an expression. She could, in a normal
frame of mind, observe their effect, but none of the psych·

logical antecedents of her action had come to the knowledge of her consciousness. She had acted in just the same manner as a hypnotized person to whom Bernheim had given the injunction that five minutes after his awakening in the ward he was to open an umbrella, and he had carried out this order on awakening, but could give no motive for his so doing. We have exactly such facts in mind when we speak of the existence of *unconscious psychological processes.* Let anyone in the world account for these facts in a more correct scientific manner, and we will gladly withdraw completely our assumption of unconscious psychological processes. Until then, however, we shall continue to use this assumption, and when anyone wants to bring forward the objection that the unconscious can have no reality for science and is a mere makeshift, (*une façon de parler*), we must simply shrug our shoulders and reject his incomprehensible statement resignedly. A strange unreality which can call out such real and palpable effects as a compulsion symptom!

In our second patient we meet with fundamentally the same thing. She had created a decree which she must follow: the pillow must not touch the head of the bed; yet she does not know how it originated, what its meaning is, nor to what motive it owes the source of its power. It is immaterial whether she looks upon it with indifference or struggles against it, storms against it, determines to overcome it. She must nevertheless follow it and carry out its ordinance, though she asks herself, in vain, why. One must admit that these symptoms of compulsion neurosis offer the clearest evidence for a special sphere of psychological activity, cut off from the rest. What else could be back of these images and impulses, which appear from one knows not where, which have such great resistance to all the influences of an otherwise normal psychic life; which give the patient himself the impression that here are super-powerful guests from another world, immortals mixing in the affairs of mortals. Neurotic symptoms lead unmistakably to a conviction of the existence of an unconscious psychology, and for that very reason clinical psychiatry, which recognizes only a conscious psychology, has no explanation other than that they are present as indications of a particular kind of degeneration. To be sure, the compulsive images and impulses are not themselves unconscious—no more so than the carrying out of the compulsive-acts escapes conscious observation. They would not have been symptoms had they not penetrated through into consciousness. But their psychological antecedents as disclosed by the analysis, the associations into which we place them by our interpretations, are unconscious, at least until we have made them known to the patient during the course of the analysis.

Consider now, in addition, that the facts established in our two cases are confirmed in all the symptoms of all neurotic diseases, that always and everywhere the meaning of the symptoms is unknown to the sufferer, that analysis shows without fail that these symptoms are derivatives of unconscious experiences which can, under various favorable conditions, become conscious. You will understand then that in psychoanalysis we cannot do without this unconscious psyche, and are accustomed to deal with it as with something tangible. Perhaps you will also be able to understand how those who know the unconscious only as an idea, who have never analyzed, never interpreted dreams, or never translated neurotic symptoms into meaning and purpose, are most ill-suited to pass an opinion on this subject. Let us express our point of view once more. Our ability to give meaning to neurotic symptoms by means of analytic interpretation is an irrefutable indication of the existence of unconscious psychological processes—or, if you prefer, an irrefutable proof of the necessity for their assumption.

But that is not all. Thanks to a second discovery of Breuer's, for which he alone deserves credit and which appears to me to be even more far-reaching, we are able to learn still more concerning the relationship between the unconscious and the neurotic symptom. Not alone is the meaning of the symptoms invariably hidden in the unconscious; but the very existence of the symptom is conditioned by its relation to this unconscious. You will soon understand me. With Breuer I maintain the following: Every time we hit upon a symptom we may conclude that the patient cherishes definite unconscious experiences which withhold the meaning of the symptoms. Vice versa, in order that the symptoms may come into being, it is also essential that this meaning be unconscious. Symptoms are not built up out of conscious experiences; as soon as the unconscious processes in question become conscious, the symptom disappears. Yor will at once recognize here the approach to our therapy, a wɩ

to make symptoms disappear. It was by these means that
Breuer actually achieved the recovery of his patient, that is,
freed her of her symptoms; he found a technique for bringing
into her consciousness the unconscious experiences that carried
the meaning of her symptoms, and the symptoms disappeared.

This discovery of Breuer's was not the result of a speculation,
but of a felicitous observation made possible by the coöperation
of the patient. You should therefore not trouble yourself to
find things you already know to which you can compare these
occurrences, rather you should recognize herein a new fundamental fact which in itself is capable of much wider application.
Toward this further end permit me to go over this ground
again in a different way.

The symptom develops as a substitution for something else
that has remained suppressed. Certain psychological experiences should normally have become so far elaborated that consciousness would have attained knowledge of them. This did
not take place, however, but out of these interrupted and disturbed processes, imprisoned in the unconscious, the symptom
arose. That is to say, something in the nature of an interchange
had been effected; as often as therapeutic measures are successful in again reversing this transposition, psychoanalytic
therapy solves the problem of the neurotic symptom.

Accordingly, Breuer's discovery still remains the foundation
of psychoanalytic therapy. The assertion that the symptoms
disappear when one has made their unconscious connections
conscious, has been borne out by all subsequent research, although the most extraordinary and unexpected complications
have been met with in its practical execution. Our therapy
does its work by means of changing the unconscious into the
conscious, and is effective only in so far as it has the opportunity
of bringing about this transformation.

Now we shall make a hasty digression so that you do not by
any chance imagine that this therapeutic work is too easy.
From all we have learned so far, the neurosis would appear as
the result of a sort of ignorance, the incognizance of psychological processes that we should know of. We would thus very
closely approximate the well-known Socratic teachings, according to which evil itself is the result of ignorance. Now the
experienced physician will, as a rule, discover fairly readily

what psychic impulses in his several patients have remained
unconscious. Accordingly it would seem easy for him to cure
the patient by imparting this knowledge to him and freeing him
of his ignorance. At least the part played by the unconscious
meaning of the symptoms could easily be discovered in this
manner, and it would only be in dealing with the relationship
of the symptoms to the experiences of the patient that the physician would be handicapped. In the face of these experiences,
of course, he is the ignorant one of the two, for he did not go
through these experiences, and must wait until the patient remembers them and tells them to him. But in many cases this
difficulty could be readily overcome. One can question the
relatives of the patient concerning these experiences, and they
will often be in a position to point out those that carry any
traumatic significance; they may even be able to inform the
analyst of experiences of which the patient knows nothing because they occurred in the very early years of his life. By a
combination of such means it would seem that the pathogenic
ignorance of the patient could be cleared up in a short time and
without much trouble.

If only that were all! We have made discoveries for which
we were at first unprepared. Knowing and knowing is not
always the same thing; there are various kinds of knowing that
are psychologically by no means comparable. *"Il y a fagots et
fagots,"*[1] as Molière says. The knowledge of the physician is not
the same as that of the patient and cannot bring about the same
results. The physician can gain no results by transferring
his knowledge to the patient in so many words. This is perhaps
putting it incorrectly, for though the transference does not result in dissolving the symptoms, it does set the analysis in
motion, and calls out an energetic denial, the first sign usually
that this has taken place. The patient has learned something
that he did not know up to that time, the meaning of his symptoms, and yet he knows it as little as before. So we discover
there is more than one kind of ignorance. It will require a
deepening of our psychological insight to make clear to us
wherein the difference lies. But our assertion nevertheless remains true that the symptoms disappear with the knowledge
of their meaning. For there is only one limiting condition;

[1] There are fagots and fagots.

the knowledge must be founded on an inner change in the patient which can be attained only through psychic labors directed toward a definite end. We have here been confronted by problems which will soon lead us to the elaboration of a dynamics of symptom formation.

I must stop to ask you whether this is not all too vague and too complicated? Do I not confuse you by so often retracting my words and restricting them, spinning out trains of thought and then rejecting them? I should be sorry if this were the case. However, I strongly dislike simplification at the expense of truth, and am not averse to having you receive the full impression of how many-sided and complicated the subject is. I also think that there is no harm done if I say more on every point than you can at the moment make use of. I know that every hearer and reader arranges what is offered him in his own thoughts, shortens it, simplifies it and extracts what he wishes to retain. Within a given measure it is true that the more we begin with the more we have left. Let me hope that, despite all the by-play, you have clearly grasped the essential parts of my remarks, those about the meaning of symptoms, about the unconscious, and the relation between the two. You probably have also understood that our further efforts are to take two directions: first, the clinical problem — to discover how persons become sick, how they later on accomplish a neurotic adaptation toward life; secondly, a problem of psychic dynamics, the evolution of the neurotic symptoms themselves from the prerequisites of the neuroses. We will undoubtedly somewhere come on a point of contact for these two problems.

I do not wish to go any further to-day, but since our time is not yet up I intend to call your attention to another characteristic of our two analyses, namely, the memory gaps or amnesias, whose full appreciation will be possible later. You have heard that it is possible to express the object of psychoanalytic treatment in a formula: all pathogenic unconscious experience must be transposed into consciousness. You will perhaps be surprised to learn that this formula can be replaced by another: all the memory gaps of the patient must be filled out, his amnesias must be abolished. Practically this amounts to the same thing. Therefore an important role in the development of his symptoms must be accredited to the amnesias of the neurotic. The analysis of our first case, however, will hardly justify this valuation of the amnesia. The patient has not forgotten the scene from which the compulsion act derives—on the contrary, she remembers it vividly, nor is there any other forgotten factor which comes into play in the development of these symptoms. Less clear, but entirely analogous, is the situation in the case of our second patient, the girl with the compulsive ritual. She, too, has not really forgotten the behavior of her early years, the fact that she insisted that the door between her bedroom and that of her parents be kept open, and that she banished her mother out of her place in her parents' bed. She recalls all this very clearly, although hesitatingly and unwillingly. Only one factor stands out strikingly in our first case, that though the patient carries out her compulsive act innumerable times, she is not once reminded of its similarity with the experience after the bridal-night; nor was this memory even suggested when by direct questions she was asked to search for its motivation. The same is true of the girl, for in her case not only her ritual, but the situation which provoked it, is repeated identically night after night. In neither case is there any actual amnesia, no lapse of memory, but an association is broken off which should have called out a reproduction, a revival in the memory. Such a disturbance is enough to bring on a compulsion neurosis. Hysteria, however, shows a different picture, for it is usually characterized by most grandiose amnesias. As a rule, in the analysis of each hysterical symptom, one is led back to a whole chain of impressions which, upon their recovery, are expressly designated as forgotten up to the moment. On the one hand this chain extends back to the earliest years of life, so that the hysterical amnesias may be regarded as the direct continuation of the infantile amnesias, which hides the beginnings of our psychic life from those of us who are normal. On the other hand, we discover with surprise that the most recent experiences of the patient are blurred by these losses of memory—that especially the provocations which favored or brought on the illness are, if not entirely wiped out by the amnesia, at least partially obliterated. Without fail important details have disappeared from the general picture of such a recent memo— or are placed by false memories. Indeed it happens a' regularly that just before the completion of an analysis, c memories of recent experiences suddenly come to light. They had been held back all this time, and had left noticeable gaps in the context.

We have pointed out that such a crippling of the ability to recall is characteristic of hysteria. In hysteria symptomatic conditions also arise (hysterical attacks) which need leave no trace in the memory. If these things do not occur in compulsion-neuroses, you are justified in concluding that these amnesias exhibit psychological characteristics of the hysterical change, and not a general trait of the neuroses. The significance of this difference will be more closely limited by the following observations. We have combined two things as the meaning of a symptom, its "whence," on the one hand, and its "whither" or "why," on the other. By these we mean to indicate the impressions and experiences whence the symptom arises, and the purpose the symptom serves. The "whence" of a symptom is traced back to impressions which have come from without, which have therefore necessarily been conscious at some time, but which may have sunk into the unconscious—that is, have been forgotten. The "why" of the symptom, its tendency, is in every case an endopsychic process, developed from within, which may or may not have become conscious at first, but could just as readily never have entered consciousness at all and have been unconscious from its inception. It is, after all, not so very significant that, as happens in the hysterias, amnesia has covered over the "whence" of the symptom, the experience upon which it is based; for it is the "why," the tendency of the symptom, which establishes its dependence on the unconscious, and indeed no less so in the compulsion neuroses than in hysteria. In both cases the "why" may have been unconscious from the very first.

By thus bringing into prominence the unconscious in psychic life, we have raised the most evil spirits of criticism against psychoanalysis. Do not be surprised at this, and do not believe that the opposition is directed only against the difficulties offered by the conception of the unconscious or against the relative inaccessibility of the experiences which represent it. I believe it comes from another source. Humanity, in the course of time, has had to endure from the hands of science two great outrages against its naive self-love. The first was when humanity discovered that our earth was not the center of the universe, but only a tiny speck in a world-system hardly conceivable in its magnitude.   This is associated in our minds with the name "Copernicus," although Alexandrian science had taught much the same thing.   The second occurred when biological research robbed man of his apparent superiority under special creation, and rebuked him with his descent from the animal kingdom, and his ineradicable animal nature.   This re-valuation, under the influence of Charles Darwin, Wallace and their predecessors, was not accomplished without the most violent opposition of their contemporaries.   But the third and most irritating insult is flung at the human mania of greatness by present-day psychological research, which wants to prove to the "I" that it is not even master in its own home, but is dependent upon the most scanty information concerning all that goes on unconsciously in its psychic life.   We psychoanalysts were neither the first, nor the only ones to announce this admonition to look within ourselves.   It appears that we are fated to represent it most insistently and to confirm it by means of empirical data which are of importance to every single person.   This is the reason for the widespread revolt against our science, the omission of all considerations of academic urbanity, and emancipation of the opposition from all restraints of impartial logic.   We were compelled to disturb the peace of the world, in addition, in another manner, of which you will soon come to know.

NINETEENTH LECTURE

Resistance and Suppression

IN order to progress in our understanding of the neuroses, we need new experiences and we are about to obtain two. Both are very remarkable and were at the time of their discovery, very surprising. You are, of course, prepared for both from our discussions of the past semester.

In the first place: When we undertake to cure a patient, to free him from the symptoms of his malady, he confronts us with a vigorous, tenacious resistance that lasts during the whole time of the treatment. That is so peculiar a fact that we cannot expect much credence for it. The best thing is not to mention this fact to the patient's relatives, for they never think of it otherwise than as a subterfuge on our part in order to excuse the length or the failure of our treatment. The patient, moreover, produces all the phenomena of this resistance without even recognizing it as such; it is always a great advance to have brought him to the point of understanding this conception and reckoning with it. Just consider, this patient suffers from his symptoms and causes those about him to suffer with him. He is willing, moreover, to take upon himself so many sacrifices of time, money, effort and self-denial in order to be freed. And yet he struggles, in the very interests of his malady, against one who would help him. How improbable this assertion must sound! And yet it is so, and if we are reproached with its improbability, we need only answer that this fact is not without its analogies. Whoever goes to a dentist with an unbearable toothache may very well find himself thrusting away the dentist's arm when the man makes for his sick tooth with a pair of pincers.

The resistance which the patient shows is highly varied, exceedingly subtle, often difficult to recognize, Protean-like in its manifold changes of form. It means that the doctor must become suspicious and be constantly on his guard against the patient. In psychoanalytic therapy we make use, as you know, of that technique which is already familiar to you from the interpretation of dreams. We tell the patient that without further reflection he should put himself into a condition of calm self-observation and that he must then communicate whatever results this introspection gives him—feelings, thoughts, reminiscences, in the order in which they appear to his mind. At the same time, we warn him expressly against yielding to any motive which would induce him to choose or exclude any of his thoughts as they arise, in whatever way the motive may be couched and however it may excuse him from telling us the thought: "that is too unpleasant," or "too indiscreet" for him to tell; or "it is too unimportant," or "it does not belong here," "it is nonsensical." We impress upon him the fact that he must skim only across the surface of his consciousness and must drop the last vestige of a critical attitude toward that which he finds. We finally inform him that the result of the treatment and above all its length is dependent on the conscientiousness with which he follows this basic rule of the analytic technique. We know, in fact, from the technique of interpreting dreams, that of all the random notions which may occur, those against which such doubts are raised are invariably the ones to yield the material which leads to the uncovering of the unconscious.

The first reaction we call out by laying down this basic technical rule is that the patient directs his entire resistance against it. The patient tries in every way to escape its requirements. First he will declare that he cannot think of anything, then, that so much comes to his mind that it is impossible to seize on anything definite. Then we discover with no slight displeasure that he has yielded to this or that critical objection, for he betrays himself by the long pauses which he allows to occur in his speaking. He then confesses that he really cannot bring himself to this, that he is ashamed to; he prefers to let this motive get the upper hand over his promise. He may say that he did think of something but that it concerns someone else and is for that reason exempt. Or he says that what he just thought of is really too trivial, too stupid and too foolish. I surely could not have meant that he should take such thoughts into accou͠ᵗ Thus it goes on, with untold variations, in the face of whiᵣ continually reiterate that "telling everything" really means telling everything.

One can scarcely find a patient who does not make the attempt to reserve some province for himself against the intrusion of the analysis. One patient, whom I must reckon among the most highly intelligent, thus concealed an intimate love relation for weeks; and when he was asked to explain this infringement of our inviolable rule, he defended his action with the argument that he considered this one thing was his private affair. Naturally, analytic treatment cannot countenance such right of sanctuary. One might as well try in a city like Vienna to allow an exception to be made of great public squares like the Hohe Markt or the Stephans Platz and say that no one should be arrested in those places—and then attempt to round up some particular wrong-doer. He will be found nowhere but in those sanctuaries. I once brought myself around to permit such an exception in the case of a man on whose capacity for work a great deal depended, and who was bound by his oath of service, which forbade him to tell anyone of certain things. To be sure, he was satisfied with the results—but not I; I resolved never to repeat such an attempt under these conditions.

Compulsion neurotics are exceedingly adept at making this technical rule almost useless by bringing to bear all their over-conscientiousness and their doubts upon it. Patients suffering from anxiety-hysteria sometimes succeed in reducing it to absurdity by producing only notions so remote from the thing sought for that analysis is quite unprofitable. But it is not my intention to go into the way in which these technical difficulties may be met. It is enough to know that finally, by means of resolution and perseverance, we do succeed in wresting a certain amount of obedience from the patient toward this basic rule of the technique; the resistance then makes itself felt in other ways. It appears in the form of an intellectual resistance, battles by means of arguments, and makes use of all difficulties and improbabilities which a normal yet uninstructed thinking is bound to find in the theory of analysis. Then we hear from one voice alone the same criticisms and objections which thunder about us in mighty chorus in the scientific literature. Therefore the critics who shout to us from outside cannot tell us anything new. It is a veritable tempest in a teapot. Still the patient can be argued with, he is anxious to persuade us to instruct him, to teach him, to lead him to the literature, so that he may continue working things out for himself. He is very ready to become an adherent of psychoanalysis on condition that analysis spare him personally. But we recognize this curiosity as a resistance, as a diversion from our special objects, and we meet it accordingly. In those patients who suffer from compulsion neuroses, we must expect the resistance to display special tactics. They frequently allow the analysis to take its way, so that it may succeed in throwing more and more light on the problems of the case, but we finally begin to wonder how it is that this clearing up brings with it no practical progress, no diminution of the symptom. Then we may discover that the resistance has entrenched itself in the doubts of the compulsion neurosis itself and in this position is able successfully to resist our efforts. The patient has said something like this to himself: "This is all very nice and interesting. And I would be glad to continue it. It would affect my malady considerably if it were true. But I don't believe that it is true and as long as I don't believe it, it has nothing to do with my sickness." And so it may go on for a long time until one finally has shaken this position itself; it is then that the decisive battle takes place.

The intellectual resistances are not the worst, one can always get ahead of them. But the patient can also put up resistances, within the limits of the analysis, whose conquest belongs to the most difficult tasks of our technique. Instead of recalling, he actually goes again through the attitudes and emotions of his previous life which, by means of the so-called "transference," can be utilized as resistances to the physician and the treatment. If the patient is a man, he takes this material as a rule from his relations to his father, in whose place he now puts the physician, and in so doing constructs a resistance out of his struggle for independence of person and opinion; out of his ambition to equal or to excel his father; out of his unwillingness to assume the burden of gratitude a second time in his life. For long times at a stretch one receives the impression that the patient desires to put the physician in the wrong and to let him feel his helplessness by triumphing over him, and that this desire has completely replaced his better intention of making an end to his sickness. Women are adepts at exploiting, for purposes of the resistance, a tender, erotically tinged transference to the physician. When this leaning attains a certain intensity, all interest for the actual situation of the treatment is lost, together with every sense of the responsibility which was assumed by undertaking it. The never-failing jealousy as well as the embitterment over the inevitable repudiation, however gently effected, all must serve to spoil the personal understanding between patient and physician and thus to throw out one of the most powerful propelling forces of the analysis.

Resistances of this sort must not be narrow-mindedly condemned. They contain so much of the most important material of the patient's past and reproduce it in such a convincing manner, that they become of the greatest aid to the analysis, if a skillful technique is able to turn them in the right direction. It is only remarkable that this material is at first always in the service of the resistance, for which it serves as a barrier against the treatment. One can also say that here are traits of character, adjustments of the ego which were mobilized in order to defeat the attempted change. We are thus able to learn how these traits arose under the conditions of the neurosis, as a reaction to its demands, and to see features more clearly in this character which could otherwise not have shown up so clearly or at least not to this extent, and which one may therefore designate as latent. You must also not get the impression that we see an unforeseen endangering of the analytic influence in the appearance of these resistances. On the contrary, we know that these resistances must come to light; we are dissatisfied only when we do not provoke them in their full strength and so make them plain to the patient. Indeed, we at last understand that overcoming these resistances is the essential achievement of analysis and is that portion of the work which alone assures us that we have accomplished something with the patient.

You must also take into account the fact that any accidental occurrences which arise during the treatment will be made use of by the patient as a disturbance—every diverting incident, every statement about analysis from an inimical authority in his circle, any chance illness or any organic affection which complicates the neurosis; indeed, he even uses every improvement of his condition as a motive for abating his efforts. You will then have gained an approximate, though still an incomplete picture

of the forms and devices of the resistance which must be met and
overcome in the course of every analysis. I have given this
point such detailed consideration because I am about to inform
you that our dynamic conception of the neurosis is based on
this experience with the resistance of neurotic patients against
the banishment of their symptoms. Breuer and I both originally
practiced psycho-therapy by means of hypnosis. Breuer's first
patient was treated throughout under a condition of hypnotic
suggestibility, and I at first followed his example. I admit that
my work at that time progressed easily and agreeably and also
took much less time. But the results were capricious and not
permanent; therefore I finally gave up hypnotism. Then only
did I realize that no insight into the forces which produce these
diseases was possible as long as one used hypnotism. The condition of hypnosis could prevent the physician from realizing the
existence of a resistance. Hypnosis drives back the resistance
and frees a certain field for the work of analysis, but similarly
to the doubt in the compulsion neurosis, in so doing it clogs the
boundaries of this field till they become impenetrable. That is
why I can say that true psychoanalysis began when the help
of hypnotism was renounced.

But if the establishment of the resistance thus becomes a
matter of such importance, then surely we must give our caution
full rein, and follow up any doubts as to whether we are not
all too ready in our assumption of their existence. Perhaps
there really are neurotic cases in which associations appear
for other reasons, perhaps the arguments against our hypothesis
really deserve more consideration and we are unjustified in
conveniently rejecting all intellectual criticisms of analysis as a
resistance. Indeed, ladies and gentlemen, but our judgment was
by no means readily arrived at. We had opportunity to observe
every critical patient from the first sign of the resistance till
after its disappearance. In the course of the treatment, the
resistance is moreover constantly changing in intensity. It is
always on the increase as we approach a new theme, is strongest
at the height of its elaboration, and dies down again when this
theme has been abandoned. Furthermore, unless we have made
some unusual and awkward technical error, we never have to
deal with the full measure of resistance of which the patie
is capable. We could therefore convince ourselves that

same man took up and discarded his critical attitude innumerable times in the course of the analysis. Whenever we are on the
point of bringing before his consciousness some piece of unconscious material which is especially painful to him, then
he is critical in the extreme. Even though he had previously
understood and accepted a great deal, nevertheless all record
of these gains seems now to have been wiped out. He may,
in his desire to resist at any cost, present a picture of veritable
emotional feeblemindedness. If one succeeds in helping him
to overcome this new resistance, then he regains his insight and
his understanding. Thus his criticism is not an independent
function to be respected as such; it plays the role of handy-man
to his emotional attitude and is guided by his resistance. If
something displeases him, he can defend himself against it very
ingeniously and appear most critical. But if something strikes
his fancy, then he may show himself easily convinced. Perhaps
none of us are very different, and the patient under analysis
shows this dependence of the intellect on the emotional life so
plainly only because, under the analysis, he is so hard pressed.

In what way shall we now account for the observation that
the patient so energetically resists our attempts to rid him
of his symptoms and to make his psychic processes function in
a normal way? We tell ourselves that we have here come up
against strong forces which oppose any change in the condition;
furthermore, that these forces must be identical with those
which originally brought about the condition. Some process
must have been functional in the building up of these symptoms,
a process which we can now reconstruct by means of our experiences in solving the meaning of the symptoms. We already
know from Breuer's observations that the existence of a symptom presupposes that some psychic process was not carried to its
normal conclusion, so that it could not become conscious. The
symptom is the substitute for that which did not take place.
Now we know where the forces whose existence we suspect must
operate. Some violent antagonism must have been aroused to
prevent the psychic process in question from reaching consciousness, and it therefore remained unconscious. As an unconscious
thought it had the power to create a symptom. The same struggle during the analytic treatment opposes anew the efforts to
carry this unconscious thought over into consciousness. This

process we felt as a resistance. That pathogenic process which is made evident to us through the resistance, we will name *repression*.

We are now ready to obtain a more definite idea of this process of repression. It is the preliminary condition for the formation of symptoms; it is also a thing for which we have no parallel. If we take as prototype an impulse, a psychological process which is striving to convert itself into action, we know that it may succumb before a rejection, which we call "repudiation" or "condemnation." In the course of this struggle, the energy which the impulse had at its disposal was withdrawn from it, it becomes powerless; yet it may subsist in the form of a memory. The whole process of decision occurs with the full knowledge of the ego. The state of affairs is very different if we imagine that this same impulse has been subjected to repression. In that case, it would retain its energy and there would be no memory of it left; in addition, the process of repression would be carried out without the knowledge of the ego. Through this comparison, however, we have come no nearer understanding the nature of repression.

I now go into the theoretical ideas which alone have shown themselves useful in making the conception of repression more definite. It is above all necessary that we progress from a purely descriptive meaning of the word "unconscious" to its more systematic meaning; that is, we come to a point where we must call the consciousness or unconsciousness of a psychic process only one of its attributes, an attribute which is, moreover, not necessarily unequivocal. If such a process remained unconscious, then this separation from consciousness is perhaps only an indication of the fate to which it has submitted and not this fate itself. To bring this home to us more vividly, let us assume that every psychological process—with one exception, which I will go into later—first exists in an unconscious state or phase and only goes over from this into a conscious phase, much as a photographic picture is first a negative and then becomes a picture by being printed. But not every negative need become a positive, and just as little is it necessary that every unconscious psychological process should be changed into a conscious one. We find it advantageous to express ourselves as follows: Any particular process belongs in the first place the psychological system of the unconscious; from this system it can under certain conditions go over into the system of the conscious. The crudest conception of these systems is the one which is most convenient for us, namely, a representation in space. We will compare the system of the unconscious to a large ante-chamber, in which the psychic impulses rub elbows with one another, as separate beings. There opens out of this ante-chamber another, a smaller room, a sort of parlor, which consciousness occupies. But on the threshold between the two rooms there stands a watchman; he passes on the individual psychic impulses, censors them, and will not let them into the parlor if they do not meet with his approval. You see at once that it makes little difference whether the watchman brushes a single impulse away from the threshold, or whether he drives it out again after it has already entered the parlor. It is a question here only of the extent of his watchfulness, and the timeliness of his judgment. Still working with this simile, we proceed to a further elaboration of our nomenclature. The impulses in the ante-chamber of the unconscious cannot be seen by the conscious, which is in the other room; therefore for the time being they must remain unconscious. When they have succeeded in pressing forward to the threshold, and have been sent back by the watchman, then they are unsuitable for consciousness and we call them *suppressed*. Those impulses, however, which the watchman has permitted to cross the threshold have not necessarily become conscious; for this can happen only if they have been successful in attracting to themselves the glance of the conscious. We therefore justifiably call this second room the system of the *fore-conscious*. In this way the process of becoming conscious retains its purely descriptive sense. Suppression then, for any individual impulse, consists in not being able to get past the watchman from the system of the unconscious to that of the fore-conscious. The watchman himself is long since known to us; we have met him as the resistance which opposed us when we attempted to release the suppression through analytic treatment.

Now I know you will say that these conceptions are as crude as they are fantastic, and not at all permissible in a scientific discussion. I know they are crude—indeed, we even know that they are incorrect, and if we are not very much mistaken we have a better substitute for them in readiness. Whether they will continue then to appear so fantastic to you I do not know. For the time being, they are useful conceptions, similar to the manikin *Ampère* who swims in the stream of the electric current. In so far as they are helpful in the understanding of our observation, they are by no means to be despised. I should like to assure you that these crude assumptions go far in approximating the actual situation—the two rooms, the watchman on the threshold between the two, and consciousness at the end of the second room in the role of an onlooker. I should also like to hear you admit that our designations—*unconscious, foreconscious,* and *conscious* are much less likely to arouse prejudice, and are easier to justify than others that have been used or suggested—such as *sub-conscious, inter-conscious, between-conscious,* etc.

This becomes all the more important to me if you should warn me that this arrangement of the psychic apparatus, such as I have assumed in the explanation of neurotic symptoms, must be generally applicable and must hold for normal functioning as well. In that, of course, you are right. We cannot follow this up at present, but our interest in the psychology of the development of the symptom must be enormously increased if through the study of pathological conditions we have the prospect of finding a key to the normal psychic occurrences which have been so well concealed.

You will probably recognize what it is that supports our assumptions concerning these two systems and their relation to consciousness. The watchman between the unconscious and the fore-conscious is none other than the censor under whose control we found the manifest dream to obtain its form. The residue of the day's experiences, which we found were the stimuli which set off the dream, are fore-conscious materials which at night, during sleep, had come under the influence of unconscious and suppressed wishes. Borne along by the energy of the wish, these stimuli were able to build the latent dream. Under the control of the unconscious system this material was worked over, went through an elaboration and displacement such as the normal psychic life or, better said, the fore-conscious system, either does not know at all or tolerates only exceptionally. In our eyes the characteristics of each of the two are

were betrayed by this difference in their functioning. The dependent relation between the fore-conscious and the conscious was to us only an indication that it must belong to one of the two systems. The dream is by no means a pathological phenomenon; it may appear in every healthy person under the conditions of sleep. Any assumption as to the structure of the psychic apparatus which covers the development of both the dream and the neurotic symptom has also an undeniable claim to be taken into consideration in any theory of normal psychic life.

So much, then, for suppression. It is, however, only a prerequisite for the evolution of the symptom. We know that the symptom serves as a substitute for a process kept back by suppression. Yet it is no simple matter to bridge this gap between the suppression and the evolution of the substitute. We have first to answer several questions on other aspects of the problem concerning the suppression and its substantiation: What kind of psychological stimuli are at the basis of the suppression; by what forces is it achieved; for what motives? On these matters we have only one insight that we can go by. We learned in the investigation of resistance that it grows out of the forces of the "I," in other words from obvious and latent traits of character. It must be from the same traits also that suppression derived support; at least they played a part in its development. All further knowledge is still withheld from us.

A second observation, for which I have already prepared, will help us further at this point. By means of analysis we can assign one very general purpose to the neurotic symptom. This is of course nothing new to you. I have already shown it to you in the two cases of neuroses. But, to be sure, what is the significance of two cases! You have the right to demand that it be shown to you innumerable times. But I am unable to do this. Here again your own experience must step in, or your belief, which may in this matter rely upon the unanimous account of all psychoanalysts.

You will remember that in these two cases, whose symptoms we subjected to searching investigation, the analysis introduced us to the most intimate sexual life of these patients. In the first case, moreover, we could identify with unusual clearness the purpose or tendency of the symptoms under investigation. Perhaps in the second case it was slightly covered by another factor—one we will consider later. Now, the same thing that we saw in these two examples we would see in all other cases that we subjected to analysis. Each time, through analysis, we would be introduced to the sexual wishes and experiences of the patient, and every time we would have to conclude that their symptoms served the same purpose. This purpose shows itself to be the satisfaction of sexual wishes; the symptoms serve as a sexual satisfaction for the patient, they are a substitute for such satisfactions as they miss in reality.

Recall the compulsive act of our first patient. The woman longs for her intensely beloved husband, with whom she cannot share her life because of his shortcoming and weaknesses. She feels she must remain true to him, she can give his place to no one else. Her compulsive symptom affords her that for which she pines, ennobles her husband, denies and corrects his weaknesses,—above all, his impotence. This symptom is fundamentally a wish-fulfillment, exactly as is a dream; moreover, it is what a dream not always is, an erotic wish-fulfillment. In the case of our second patient you can see that one of the component purposes of her ceremonial was the prevention of the intercourse of her parents or the hindrance of the creation of a new child thereby. You have perhaps also guessed that essentially she strove to put herself in the place of her mother. Here again we find the removal of disturbances to sexual satisfaction and the fulfillment of personal sexual wishes. We shall soon turn to the complications of whose existence we have given you several indications.

I do not want to make reservations as to the universal applicability of these declarations later on, and therefore I wish to call to your attention the fact that everything that I say here about suppression, symptom-development and symptom-interpretation has been learned from three types of neuroses—anxiety-hysteria, conversion-hysteria, and compulsion-neuroses—and for the time being is relevant to these forms only. These three conditions, which we are in the habit of combining into one group under the name of *"transference neuroses,"* also limit the field open to psychoanalytic therapy. The other neuroses have not been nearly so well studied by psychoanalysis,—in one group, in fact, the impossibility of therapeutic influence has been the

reason for the neglect. But you must not forget that psychoanalysis is still a very young science, that it demands much time
and care in preparation for it, that not long ago it was still in
the cradle, so to speak. Yet at all points we are about to penetrate into the understanding of those other conditions which are
not transference neuroses. I hope I shall still be able to speak
to you of the developments that our assumptions and results
have undergone by being correlated with this new material, and
to show you that these further studies have not led to contradictions but rather to the production of still greater uniformity.
Granted that everything, then, that has been said here, holds
good for the three transference neuroses, allow me to add a
new bit of information to the evaluation of its symptoms. A
comparative investigation into the causes of the disease discloses
a result that may be confined into the formula: in some way
or other these patients fell ill through *self-denial* when reality
withheld from them the satisfaction of their sexual wishes.
You recognize how excellently well these two results are found
to agree. The symptoms must be understood, then, as a substitute satisfaction for that which is missed in life.

To be sure, there are all kinds of objections possible to the
declaration that neurotic symptoms are substitutes for sexual
satisfaction. I shall still go into two of them today. If you
yourself have analytically examined a fairly large number of
neurotics you will perhaps gravely inform me that in one class
of cases this is not at all applicable, the symptoms appear rather
to have the opposite purpose, to exclude sexual satisfaction, or
discontinue it. I shall not deny the correctness of your interpretation. The psychoanalytic content has a habit of being more
complicated than we should like to have it. Had it been so
simple, perhaps we should have had no need for psychoanalysis
to bring it to light. As a matter of fact, some of the traits of
the ceremonial of our second patient may be recognized as of
this ascetic nature, inimical to sexual satisfaction; for example,
the fact that she removes the clocks, which have the magic qualities of preventing nightly erections, or that she tries to prevent
the falling and breaking of vessels, which symbolizes a protection
of her virginity. In other cases of bed-ceremonials which I was
able to analyze, this negative character was far more evident;
the ceremonial might consist throughout of protective regula-

tions against sexual recollections and temptations. On the other hand, we have often discovered in psychoanalysis that opposites do not mean contradictions. We might extend our assertion and say the symptoms purpose either a sexual satisfaction or a guard against it; that in hysteria the positive wish-fulfillment takes precedence, while in the compulsion neuroses the negative, ascetic characteristics have the ascendancy. We have not yet been able to speak of that aspect of the mechanism of the symptoms, their two-sidedness, or polarity, which enables them to serve this double purpose, both the sexual satisfaction and its opposite. The symptoms are, as we shall see, compromise results, arising from the integration of two opposed tendencies; they represent not only the suppressed force but also the suppressing factor, which was originally potent in bringing about the negation. The result may then favor either one side or the other, but seldom is one of the influences entirely lacking. In cases of hysteria, the meeting of the two purposes in the same symptom is most often achieved. In compulsion-neuroses, the two parts often become distinct; the symptom then has a double meaning, it consists of two actions, one following the other, one releasing the other. It will not be so easy to put aside a further misgiving. If you should look over a large number of symptom-interpretations, you would probably judge offhand that the conception of a sexual substitute-satisfaction has been stretched to its utmost limits in these cases. You will not hesitate to emphasize that these symptoms offer nothing in the way of actual satisfaction, that often enough they are limited to giving fresh life to sensations or phantasies from some sexual complex. Further, you will declare that the apparent sexual satisfaction so often shows a childish and unworthy character, perhaps approximates an act of onanism, or is reminiscent of filthy naughtiness, habits that are already forbidden and broken in childhood. Finally, you will express your surprise that one should designate as a sexual satisfaction appetites which can only be described as horrible or ghastly, even unnatural. As to these last points, we shall come to no agreement until we have submitted man's sexual life to a thorough investigation, and thus ascertained what one is justified in calling sexual.

The Sexual Life of Man

ONE might think we could take for granted what we are to understand by the term "sexual." Of course, the sexual is the indecent, which we must not talk about. I have been told that the pupils of a famous psychiatrist once took the trouble to convince their teacher that the symptoms of hysteria very frequently represent sexual matters. With this intention they took him to the bedside of a woman suffering from hysteria, whose attacks were unmistakable imitations of the act of delivery. He, however, threw aside their suggestion with the remark, "a delivery is nothing sexual." Assuredly, a delivery need not under all circumstances be indecent.

I see that you take it amiss that I jest about such serious matters. But this is not altogether a jest. In all seriousness, it is not altogether easy to define the concept "sexual." Perhaps the only accurate definition would be everything that is connected with the difference between the two sexes; but this you may find too general and too colorless. If you emphasize the sexual act as the central factor, you might say that everything is sexual which seeks to obtain sensual excitement from the body and especially from the sexual organs of the opposite sex, and which aims toward the union of the genitals and the performance of the sexual act. But then you are really very close to the comparison of sexual and indecent, and the act of delivery is not sexual. But if you think of the function of reproduction as the nucleus of sexuality you are in danger of excluding a number of things that do not aim at reproduction but are certainly sexual, such as onanism or even kissing. But we are prepared to realize that attempts at definition always lead to difficulties; let us give up the attempt to achieve the unusual in our particular case. We may suspect that in the development of the concept "sexual" something occurred which resulted in a false disguise. On the whole, we are quite well oriented as to what people call sexual.

The inclusion of the following factors in our concept "sexual" amply suffices for all practical purposes in ordinary life: the contrast between the sexes, the attainment of sexual excitement, the function of reproduction, the characteristic of an indecency that must be kept concealed. But this is no longer satisfactory to science. For through careful examinations, rendered possible only by the sacrifices and the unselfishness of the subjects, we have come in contact with groups of human beings whose sexual life deviates strikingly from the average. One group among them, the "perverse," have, as it were, crossed off the difference between the sexes from their program. Only the same sex can arouse their sexual desires; the other sex, even the sexual parts, no longer serve as objects for their sexual desires, and in extreme cases, become a subject for disgust. They have to that extent, of course, foregone any participation in reproduction. We call such persons homosexual or inverted. Often, though not always, they are men and women of high physical, intellectual and ethical development, who are affected only with this one portentous abnormality. Through their scientific leaders they proclaim themselves to be a special species of mankind, "a third sex," which shares equal rights with the two other sexes. Perhaps we shall have occasion to examine their claims critically. Of course they are not, as they would like to claim, the "elect" of humanity, but comprise just as many worthless second-rate individuals as those who possess a different sexual organization.

At any rate, this type among the perverse seek to achieve the same ends with the object of their desires as do normal people. But in the same group there exists a long succession of abnormal individuals whose sexual activities are more and more alien to what seems desirable to the sensible person. In their manifold strangeness they seem comparable only to the grotesque freaks that P. Breughel painted as the temptation of Saint Anthony, or the forgotten gods and believers that G. Flaubert pictures in the long procession that passes before his pious penitent. This ill-assorted array fairly clamors for orderly classification if it is not to bewilder our senses. We first divide them, on the one hand, into those whose sexual object has changed, as is the case with homosexualists, and, on the other, those whose sexual aim has changed. Those of the first group have dispensed with the mutual union of the genital organs, and have, as one of the partners of the act, replaced the genitals by another organ or part of the body; they have thus overcome both the shortcomings of organic structure and the usual disgust involved. There are others of this group who still retain the genitals as their object, but not by virtue of their sexual function; they participate for anatomic reasons or rather by reason of their proximity. By means of these individuals we realize that the functions of excretion, which in the education of the child are hushed away as indecent, still remain capable of drawing complete sexual interest on themselves. There are still others who have relinquished the genitals entirely as an objective, have raised another part of the body to serve as the goal of their desire; the woman's breast, the foot, the tress of hair. There are also the fetishists, to whom the body part means nothing, who are gratified by a garment, a piece of white linen, a shoe. And finally there are persons who seek the whole object but with certain peculiar or horrible demands: even those who covet a defenseless corpse for instance, which they themselves must criminally compel to satisfy their desire. But enough of these horrors.

Foremost in the second grouping are those perverted ones who have placed as the end of their sexual desire performances normally introductory or preparatory to it. They satisfy their desire by their eyes and hands. They watch or attempt to watch the other individual in his most intimate doings, or uncover those portions of their own bodies which they should conceal in the vague expectation of being rewarded by a similar procedure on the other person's part. Here also belong the enigmatic sadists, whose affectionate strivings know no other goal than to cause their object pain and agony, varying all the way from humiliating suggestions to the harshest physical ill-treatment. As if to balance the scale, we have on the other hand the masochists, whose sole satisfaction consists in suffering every variety of humiliation and torture, symbolic and real, at the hands of the beloved one. There are still others who combine and confuse a number of these abnormal conditions. Moreover, in both these groups there are those who seek sexual satisfaction in reality, and others who are content merely to imagine such gratification, who need no actual object at all, but can supplant it by their own fantastic creations.

There can be not the least doubt that the sexual activities of these individuals are actually found in the absurdities, caprices and horrors that we have examined. Not only do they themselves conceive them as adequate substitutes, but we must recognize that they take the same place in their lives that normal sex gratification occupies in ours, and for which they bring the same sacrifices, often incommensurate with their ends. It is perfectly possible to trace along broad lines as well as in detail in what way these abnormalities follow the normal procedure and how they diverge from it. You will also find the characteristic of indecency which belongs to the sexual act in these vagaries, only that it is therein magnified to the disreputable.

Ladies and gentlemen, what attitude are we to assume to these unusual varieties of sex gratification? Nothing at all is achieved by the mere expression of indignation and personal disgust and by the assurance that we do not share these lusts. That is not our concern. We have here a field of observation like any other. Moreover, the evasion that these persons are merely rarities, curiosities, is easily refuted. On the contrary, we are dealing with very frequent and widespread phenomena. If, however, we are told that we must not permit them to influence our views on sexual life, since they are all aberrations of the sexual instinct, we must meet this with a serious answer. If we fail to understand these abnormal manifestations of sexuality and are unable to relate them to the normal sexual life, then we cannot understand normal sexuality. It is, in short, our unavoidable task to account theoretically for all the potentialities of the perversions we have gone over and to explain their relation to the so-called normal sexuality.

A penetrating insight due to Ivan Bloch and two new experimental results will help us in this task. Bloch takes exception to the point of view which sees in a perversion a "sign of degeneration"; he proves that such deviations from the aim of the sexual instinct, such loose relations to the object of sexuality, have occurred at all times, among the most primitive and the most highly civilized peoples, and have occasionally achieved toleration and general recognition. The two experimental results were obtained in the course of psychoanalytic investigations of neurotics; they will undoubtedly exert a decided influence on our conceptions of sexual perversion.

We have stated that the neurotic symptoms are substitutions for sexual satisfactions, and I have given you to understand that the proof of this assertion by means of the analysis of symptoms encounters many difficulties. For this statement is only justifiable if, under the term "sexual satisfactions," we include the so-called perverse sexual ends, since with surprising frequency we find symptoms which can be interpreted only in the light of their activity. The claim of rareness made by the homosexualists or the inverted immediately collapses when we learn that in the case of no single neurotic do we fail to obtain evidence of homosexual tendencies, and that in a considerable number of symptoms we find the expression of this latent inversion. Those who call themselves homosexualists are the conscious and manifest inverts, but their number is as nothing before the latent homosexualists. We are forced to regard the desire for an object of one's own sex as a universal aberration of erotic life and to cede increasing importance to it. . Of course the differences between manifest homosexuality and the normal attitude are not thus erased; their practical importance persists, but their theoretic value is greatly decreased. Paranoia, a disturbance which cannot be counted among the transference-neuroses, must in fact be assumed as arising regularly from the attempt to ward off powerful homosexual tendencies. Perhaps you will recall that one of our patients under her compulsive symptoms acted the part of a man, namely that of her own estranged husband; the production of such symptoms, impersonating the actions of men, is very common to neurotic women. Though this cannot be ascribed directly to homosexuality, it is certainly concerned with its prerequisites.

You are probably acquainted with the fact that the neurosis of hysteria may manifest its symptoms in all organic systems and may therefore disturb all functions. Analysis shows that in these symptoms there are expressed all those tendencies termed perverse, which seek to represent the genitals through other organs. These organs behave as substitute genitals; through the study of hysteric symptoms we have come to the conclusion that aside from their functional activities, the organs of the body have a sexual significance, and that the performance of their functions is disturbed if the sexual factor claims too much attention. Countless sensations and innervations, which appear as symptoms of hysteria, in organs apparently not concerned with sexuality, are thus discovered as bound up with the fulfillment of perverse sexual desires through the transference of sex instincts to other organs. These symptoms bring home to us the extent to which the organs used in the consumption of food and in excretion may become the bearers of sexual excitement. We see repeated here the same picture which the perversions have openly and unmistakably lain before us; in hysteria, however, we must make the detour of interpreting symptoms, and in this case the perverse sexual tendencies must be ascribed not to the conscious but to the unconscious life of the individual.

Among the many symptoms manifested in compulsion neurosis, the most important are those produced by too powerful saddistic tendencies, i.e., sexual tendencies with perverted aim. These symptoms, in accordance with the structure of compulsion neurosis, serve primarily as a rejection of these desires, or they express a struggle between satisfaction and rejection. In this struggle, the satisfaction is never excessively curtailed; it achieves its results in the patient's behavior in a roundabout way, by preference turning against his own person in self-inflicted torture. Other forms of neurosis, characterized by intensive worry, are the expression of an exaggerated sexualization of acts that are ordinarily only preparatory to sexual satisfactions; such are the desires to see, to touch, to investigate. Here is thus explained the great importance of the fear of contact and also of the compulsion to wash. An unbelievably large portion of compulsion acts may, in the form of disguised repetitions and modifications, be traced back to onanism, admittedly the only uniform action which accompanies the most varied flights of the sexual imagination.

It would cost me very little effort to interweave far more closely the relation between perversion and neurosis, but I believe that what I have said is sufficient for our purposes. We must avoid the error of overestimating the frequency and intensity of perverse inclinations in the light of these interpretations of symptoms. You have heard that a neurosis may develop from the denial of normal sexual satisfactions. Throug this actual denial the need is forced into the abnormal paths of sex excitement. You will later obtain a better insight into the way this happens. You certainly understand that through such *"collateral"* hindrance, the perverse tendencies must become more powerful than they would have been if no actual obstacle had been put in the way of a normal sexual satisfaction. As a matter of fact, a similar influence may be recognized in manifest perversions. In many cases, they are provoked or motivated by the fact that too great difficulties stand in the way of normal sexual satisfactions, owing to temporary circumstances or to the permanent institutions of society. In other cases, to be sure, the perverse tendencies are entirely independent of such conditions; they are, as it were, the normal kind of sexual life for the individual in question.

Perhaps you are momentarily under the impression that we have confused rather than clarified the relation between normal and perverse sexuality. But keep in mind this consideration. If it is true that a hindrance or withholding of normal sexual satisfaction will bring out perverse tendencies in persons who have not previously shown them, we must assume that these persons must have harbored tendencies akin to perversities—or, if you will, perversities in latent form. This brings us to the second experimental conclusion of which I spoke, namely, that psychoanalytic investigation found it necessary to concern itself with the sexual life of the child, since, in the analysis of symptoms, reminiscences and ideas reverted to the early years of childhood. Whatever we revealed in this manner was corroborated point by point through the direct observation of children. The result was the recognition that all inclinations to perversion have their origin in childhood, that children have tendencies toward them all and practice them in a measure corresponding to their immaturity. Perverse sexuality, in brief, is nothing more than magnified infantile sexuality divided into its separate tendencies.

Now you will certainly see these perversions in another light and no longer ignore their relation to the sexual life of man, at the cost, I do not doubt, of surprises and incongruities painful to your emotions. At first you will undoubtedly be disposed to deny everything—the fact that children have something which may be termed sexual life, the truth of our observations and the justification of our claim to see in the behavior of children any relation to what is condemned in later years as perversity. Permit me first to explain to you the cause of your reluctance and then to present to you the sum of our observations. It is biologically improbable, even absurd, to assume that children have no sexual life—sexual excitements, desires, and some sort of satisfaction—but that they develop it suddenly between the ages of twelve and fourteen. This would be just as improbable from the viewpoint of biology as to say that they were not born with genitals but developed them only in the period of puberty. The new factor which becomes active in them at the time is the function of reproduction, which avails itself for its own purposes of all the physical and psychic material already present. You commit the error of confusing sexuality with reproduction and thereby block the road to the understanding of sexuality, and of perversions and neuroses as well. This error is a prejudice. Oddly enough its source is the fact that you yourselves were children, and as children succumbed to the influence of education. One of the most important educational tasks which society must assume is the control, the restriction of the sexual instinct when it breaks forth as an impulse toward reproduction; it must be subdued to an individual will that is identical with the mandates of society. In its own interests, accordingly, society would postpone full development until the child has reached a certain stage of intellectual maturity, for education practically ceases with the complete emergence of the sexual impulse. Otherwise the instinct would burst all bounds and the work of culture, achieved with such difficulty, would be shattered. The task of restraining this sexuality is never easy; it succeeds here too poorly and there too well. The motivating force of human society is fundamentally economic; since there is not sufficient nourishment to support its members without work on their part, the number of these members must be limited and their energies diverted from sexual activity to labor. Here, again, we have the eternal struggle for life that has persisted from prehistoric times to the present.

Experience must have shown educators that the task of guiding the sexual will of the new generation can be solved only by influencing the early sexual life of the child, the period preparatory to puberty, not by awaiting the storm of puberty. With this intention almost all infantile sex activities are forbidden to the child or made distasteful to him; the ideal goal has been to render the life of the child asexual. In the course of time it has really come to be considered asexual, and this point of view has actually been proclaimed by science. In order not to contradict our belief and intentions, we ignore the sexual activity of the child—no slight thing, at that—or are content to interpret it differently. The child is supposed to be pure and innocent, and whoever says otherwise may be condemned as a shameless blasphemer of the tender and sacred feelings of humanity.

The children are the only ones who do not join in carrying out these conventions, who assert their animal rights, who prove again and again that the road to purity is still before them. It is strange that those who deny the sexuality of children, do not therefore slacken in their educational efforts but rather punish severely the manifestations of the very thing they maintain does not exist, and call it "childish naughtiness." Theoretically it is highly interesting to observe that the period of life which offers most striking evidence against the biased conception of asexual childhood, is the time up to five or six years of age; after that everything is enveloped by a veil of amnesia, which is rent apart only by thorough scientific investigation; it may previously have given way partially in certain forms of dreams.

Now I shall present to you what is most easily recognizable in the sexual life of the child. At first, for the sake of convenience let me explain to you the conception of the libido. Libido, analogous to hunger, is the force through which the instinct, here the sex instinct (as in the case of hunger it is the instinct to eat) expresses itself. Other conceptions, such as sexual excitement and satisfaction, require no elucidation. You will easily see that interpretation plays the greatest part in disclosing the sexuality of the suckling; in fact you will probably cite this as an objection. These interpretations proceed from a foundation of analytic investigation that trace backwards from a given symptom. The suckling reveals the first sexual impulses in connection with other functions necessary for life. His chief interest, as you know, is directed toward the taking in of food; when it has fallen asleep at its mother's breast, fully satisfied, it bears the expression of blissful content that will come back again in later life after the experience of the sexual orgasm. That of course would be too slight evidence to form the basis of a conclusion. But we observe that the suckling wishes to repeat the act of taking in food without actually demanding more food; he is therefore no longer urged by hunger. We say he is sucking, and the fact that after this he again falls asleep with a blissful expression shows us that the act of sucking in itself has yielded him satisfaction. As you know, he speedily arranges matters so that he cannot fall asleep without sucking. Dr. Lindner, an old pediatrist in Budapest, was the first one to ascertain the sexual nature of this procedure. Persons attending to the child, who surely make no pretensions to a theoretic attitude, seem to judge sucking in a similar manner. They do not doubt that it serves a pleasurable satisfaction, term it naughty, and force the child to relinquish it against his will, and if he will not do so of his own accord, through painful measures. And so we learn that the suckling performs actions that have no object save the obtaining of a sensual gratification. We believe that this gratification is first experienced during the taking in of food, but that he speedily learns to separate it from this condition. The gratification can only be attributed to the excitation of the mouth and lips, hence we call these parts of the body *erogenous zones* and the pleasure derived from sucking, *sexual*. Probably we shall have to discuss the justification of this name.

If the suckling could express himself, he would probably recognize the act of sucking at his mother's breast as the most important thing in life. He is not so far wrong, for in this one act he satisfies two great needs of life. With no small degree of surprise we learn through psychoanalysis how much of the physical significance of this act is retained through life. The sucking at the mother's breast becomes the term of departure for all of sexual life, the unattained ideal of later sex gratification, to which the imagination often reverts in times of need. The mother's breast is the first object for the sexual instinct; I can scarcely bring home to you how significant this object is for centering on the sexual object in later life, what profound influence it exerts upon the most remote domains of psychic life through evolution and substitution. The suckling, however, soon relinquishes it and fills its place by a part of his own body. The child sucks his thumb or his own tongue. Thereby he renders himself independent of the consent of the outer world in obtaining his sensual satisfactions, and moreover increases the excitement by including a second zone of his body. The erogenous zones are not equally satisfactory; it is therefore an important experience when, as Dr. Lindner puts it, the child while touching his own body discovers the especially excitable genitals, and so finds the way from sucking to onanism.

Through the evaluation of sucking we become acquainted with two decisive characteristics of infantile sexuality. It arises in connection with the satisfaction of great organic needs and behaves *auto-erotically*, that is to say, it seeks and finds it objects on its own body. What is most clearly discernible during the taking in of food is partially repeated during excretion. We conclude that the nursling experiences pleasure during the excretion of urine and the contents of the intestine and that he soon strives to arrange these acts in a way to secure the greatest possible amount of satisfaction by the corresponding excitement of the erogenous membrane zones. Lou Andreas, with her delicate perceptions, has shown how at this point the outer world first intervenes as a hindrance, hostile to the child's desire for satisfaction—the first vague suggestion of outer and inner conflicts. He may not let his excretions pass from him at a moment agreeable to him, but only when other persons set the time. To induce him to renounce these sources of satisfaction, everything relating to these functions is declared indecent and must be concealed. Here, for the first time, he is to exchange pleasure for social dignity. His own relation to his excretions is originally quite different. He experiences no disgust toward his faeces, values them as a part of his body from which he does not part lightly, for he uses them as the first "present" he can give to persons he esteems particularly. Even after education has succeeded in alienating him from these tendencies, he transfers the evaluation of the faeces to the "present" and to "money." On the other hand, he appears to regard his achievements in urination with especial pride.

I know that you have been wanting to interrupt me for a long time and to cry: "Enough of these monstrosities! Excretion a source of sexual gratification that even the suckling exploits! Faeces a valuable substance! The anus a sort of genital! We do not believe it, but we understand why children's physicians and pedagogues have decidedly rejected psychoanalysis and its results." No, you have merely forgotten that it was my intention to present to you infantile sexuality in connection with the facts of sexual perversion. Why should you not know that in the case of many grown-ups, homosexuals as well as heterosexuals, the locus of intercourse is transferred from the normal to a more remote portion of the body. And that there are many individuals who confess to a pleasurable sensation of no slight degree in the emptying of the bowels during their entire lives? Children themselves will confirm their interest in the act of defecation and the pleasure in watching the defecation of another, when they are a few years older and capable of giving expression to their feelings. Of course, if these children have previously been systematically intimidated, they will understand all too well the wisdom of preserving silence on the subject. As for the other things that you do not wish to believe, let me refer you to the results of analysis and the direct observation of children, and you will realize that it is difficult not to see these things or to see them in a different light. I do not even object to making the relation between child-sexuality and sexual perversion quite obvious to you. It is really only natural; if the child has sexual life at all, it must necessarily be perverse, because aside from a few hazy illusions, the child does not know how sexuality gives rise to reproduction. The common characteristic of all perversions, on the other hand, is that they have abandoned reproduction as their aim. We term sexual activity perverse when it has renounced the aim of reproduction and follows the pursuit of pleasure as an independent goal. And so you realize that the turning point in the development of sexual life lies in its subjugation to the purpose of reproduction. Everything this side of the turning point, everything that has given up this purpose and serves the pursuit of pleasure alone, must carry the term "perverse" and as such be regarded with contempt.

Permit me, therefore, to continue with my brief presentation of infantile sexuality. What I have told you about two organic systems I could supplement by a discussion of all the others. The sexual life of the child exhausts itself in the exercise of a series of partial instincts which seek, independently of one another, to gain satisfaction from his own body or from an external object. Among these organs the genitals speedily pre-

dominate. There are persons who continue the pursuit of satisfaction by means of their own genitals, without the aid of
another genital or object, uninterruptedly from the onanism of
the suckling to the onanism of necessity which arises in puberty,
and even indefinitely beyond that. The theme of onanism alone
would occupy us for a long period of time; it offers material
for diverse observations.

In spite of my inclination to shorten the theme, I must tell
you something about the sexual curiosity of children. It is
most characteristic for child sexuality and significant for the
study of neurotic symptoms. The sexual curiosity of children
begins very early, sometimes before the third year. It is not
connected with the differences of sexes, which means nothing
to the child, since the boy, at any rate, ascribes the same male
genital to both sexes. When the boy first discovers the primary
sexual structure of the female, he tries at first to deny the
evidence of his senses, for he cannot conceive a human being
who lacks the part of his body that is of such importance to
him. Later he is terrified at the possibility revealed to him and
he feels the influence of all the former threats, occasioned by
his intensive preoccupation with his little organ. He becomes
subject to the domination of the castration complex, the formation of which plays an important part in the development of
his character, provided he remains healthy; of his neurosis, if
he becomes diseased; of his resistance, if he is treated analytically. We know that the little girl feels injured on account of
her lack of a large, visible penis, envies the boy his possession,
and primarily from this motive desires to be a man. This wish
manifests itself subsequently in neurosis, arising from some
failure in her role as a woman. During childhood, the clitoris
of the girl is the equivalent of the penis; it is especially excitable,
the zone where auto-erotic satisfaction is achieved. In the transition to womanhood it is most important that the sensations of
the clitoris are completely transferred at the right time to the
entrance of the vagina. In cases of so-called sexual anesthesia
of women the clitoris has obstinately retained its excitability.

The sexual interest of children generally turns first to the
mystery of birth—the same problem that is the basis of the
questions asked by the sphinx of Thebes. This curiosity is for
the most part aroused by the selfish fear of the arrival of a

new child. The answer which the nursery has ready for the child, that the stork brings children, is doubted far more frequently than we imagine, even by very young children. The feeling that he has been cheated out of the truth by grown-ups, contributes greatly to the child's sense of solitude and to his independent development. But the child is not capable of solving this problem unaided. His undeveloped sexual constitution restricts his ability to understand. At first he assumes that children are produced by a special substance in one's food and does not know that only women can bear children. Later he learns of this limitation and relinquishes the derivation of children from food—a supposition retained in the fairy-tale. The growing child soon notices that the father plays some part in reproduction, but what it is he cannot guess. If, by chance, he is witness of a sexual act, he sees in it an attempt to subjugate, a scuffle, the saddistic miscomprehension of coitus; he does not however relate this act immediately to the evolution of the child. When he discovers traces of blood on the bedsheets or on the clothing of his mother, he considers them the proof of an injury inflicted by the father. During the latter part of childhood, he imagines that the sexual organ of the man plays an important part in the evolution of children, but can ascribe only the function of urination to that part of his body.

From the very outset children unite in believing that the birth of the child takes place through the anus; that the child therefore appears as a ball of faeces. After anal interests have been proven valueless, he abandons this theory and assumes that the navel opens or that the region between the two breasts is the birthplace of the child. In this way the curious child approaches the knowledge of sexual facts, which, clouded by his ignorance, he often fails to see. In the years prior to puberty he generally receives an incomplete, disparaging explanation which often causes traumatic consequences.

You have probably heard that the conception "sexual" is unduly expanded by psychoanalysis in order that it may maintain the hypothesis that all neuroses are due to sexual causes and that the meaning of the symptoms is sexual. You are now in a position to judge whether or not this expansion is unjustifiable. We have expanded the conception sexual only to include the sexual life of children and of perverse persons. That is to say, we have reëstablished its proper boundaries. Outside of psychoanalysis sexuality means only a very limited thing: normal sexual life in the service of reproduction.

GENERAL THEORY OF THE NEUROSES

Development of the Libido and Sexual Organizations

I AM under the impression that I did not succeed in convincing you of the significance of perversions for our conception of sexuality. I should therefore like to clarify and add as much as I can.

It was not only perversions that necessitated an alteration of our conception of sexuality, which aroused such vehement contradiction. The study of infantile sexuality did a great deal more along that line, and its close correspondence to the perversions became decisive for us. But the origin of the expressions of infantile sexuality, unmistakable as they are in later years of childhood, seem to be lost in obscurity. Those who disregard the history of evolution and analytic coherence, will dispute the potency of the sexual factor and will infer the agency of generalized forces. Do not forget that as yet we have no generally acknowledged criterion for identifying the sexual nature of an occurrence, unless we assume that we can find it in a relation to the functions of reproduction, and this we must reject as too narrow. The biological criteria, such as the periodicities of twenty-three and twenty-eight days, suggested by W. Fliess, are by no means established; the specific chemical nature which we can possibly assume for sexual occurrences is still to be discovered. The sexual perversions of adults, on the other hand, are tangible and unambiguous. As their generally accepted nomenclature shows, they are undoubtedly sexual in character; whether we designate them as signs of degeneration, or otherwise, no one has yet had the courage to place them outside the phenomena of sex. They alone justify the assertion that sexuality and reproduction are not coincident, for it is clear that all of them disavow the goal of reproduction.

This brings me to an interesting parallel. While "conscious" and "psychic" were generally considered to be identical, we had to make an essay to widen our conception of the "psychic" to recognize as psychic something that was not conscious. Analogously, when "sexual" and "related to reproduction" (or, in shorter form, "genital") has been generally considered identical, psychoanalysis must admit as "sexual" such things as are not "genital," things which have nothing to do with reproduction. It is only a formal analogy, but it does not lack a deeper basis.

But if the existence of sexual perversions is such a compelling argument, why has it not long ago had its effect, and settled the question? I really am unable to say. It appears to be because the sexual perversions are subject to a peculiar ban that extends even into theory, and stands in the way of their scientific appreciation. It seems as if no one could forget that they are not only revolting, but even unnatural, dangerous; as if they had a seductive influence and that at bottom one had to stifle a secret envy of those who enjoyed them. As the count who passes judgment in the famous Tannhauser parody admits:

"And in the mount of Venus, his honor slipped his mind,
It's odd that never happens to people of our kind."

Truthfully speaking, the perverts are rather poor devils who atone most bitterly for the satisfaction they attain with such difficulty.

What makes the perverse activity unmistakably sexual, despite all the strangeness of its object, is that the act in perverse satisfaction most frequently is accompanied by a complete orgasm, and by an ejaculation of the genital product. Of course, this is only true in the case of adults; with children orgasms and genital excretions are hardly possible; they are replaced by rudiments which, again, are not recognized as truly sexual.

In order to complete the appreciation of sexual perversions, I have something to add. Condemned as they are, sharply as they are contrasted with the normal sexual activity, simple observation shows that rarely is normal sex-life entirely free from one or another of the perverse traits. Even the kiss can be claimed to be perverse, for it consists in the union of two erogenous mouth zones in place of the respective genitals. But no one outlaws it as perverse, it is, on the contrary, admitted in theatrical performances as a modified suggestion of the sexual act. This very kissing may easily become a complete perversion if it results in such intensity that it is immediately followed by an emission and orgasm—a thing that is not at all unusual. Further, we can learn that handling and gazing upon the object becomes an essential prerequisite to sexual pleasure; that some, in the height of sexual excitation, pinch and bite, that the greatest excitation is not always called forth in lovers by the genitals, but rather by other parts of the body, and so forth. There is no sense in considering persons with single traits of this kind abnormal, and counting them among the perverts. Rather, we recognize more and more clearly that the essential nature of perversion does not consist in overstepping the sexual aim, nor in a substitution for the genitals, not even in the variety of objects, but simply in the exclusiveness with which these deviations are carried out and by means of which the sexual act that serves reproduction is pushed aside. When the perverse activities serve to prepare or heighten the normal sexual act, they are really no longer perversions. To be sure, the chasm between normal and perverse sexuality is practically bridged by such facts. The natural result is that normal sexuality takes its origin from something existing prior to it, since certain components of this material are thrown out and others are combined in order to make them subject to a new aim—that of reproduction.

Before we make use of our knowledge of perversions to concentrate anew and with clearer perspective on the study of infantile sexuality, I must call your attention to an important difference between the two. Perverse sexuality is as a rule extraordinarily centralized, its whole action is directed toward one, usually an isolated, goal. A partial instinct has the upper hand. It is either the only one that can be demonstrated or it has subjected the others to its purposes. In this respect there is no difference between normal and perverse sexuality other than that the ruling partial instincts, and with them the sexual goals, are different. In the one case as well as in the other there is, so to say, a well organized tyranny, excepting that here one family and there another has appropriated all the power to itself. Infantile sexuality, on the other hand, is on the whole devoid of such centralization and organization, its individual component impulses are of equal power, and each independently goes in search of the acquisition of pleasurable excitement. The lack as well as the presence of centralization fit in well with the fact that both the perverse and the normal sexuality originated from the infantile. There are also cases of perverse sexuality that have much more similarity with the infantile, where, independently of one another, numerous partial instincts have forced their way, insisted on their aims, or rather perpetuated them. In these cases it is more correct to speak of infantilism of sexual life than of perversions.

Thus prepared we can consider a question which we certainly shall not be spared. People will say to us: "Why are you so set on including within sexuality those manifestations of childhood, out of which the sexual later develops, but which, according to your own admission, are of uncertain origin? Why are you not satisfied rather with the physiological description, and simply say that even in the suckling one may notice activities, such as sucking objects or holding back excrements, which show us that he strives towards an *organic pleasure?* In that way you would have avoided the estranging conception of sexual life in the tiniest child." I have nothing to say against organic pleasure; I know that the most extreme excitement of the sexual union is only an organic pleasure derived from the activity of the genitals. But can you tell me when this organic pleasure, originally not differentiated, acquires the sexual character that it undoubtedly does possess in the later phases of development? Do you know more about the "organic pleasure" than about sexuality? You will answer, the sexual character is acquired when the genitals begin to play their role; sexual means genital. You will even reject the contrary evidence of the perversions by confronting me with the statement that in most perversions it is a matter of achieving the genital orgasm, although by other means than a union of the genitals. You would really command a much better position if you did not regard as characteristic of the sexual that untenable relation to reproduction seen in the perversions, if you replaced it by activity of the genitals. Then we no longer differ very widely; the genital organs merely replace other organs. What do you make of the numerous practices which show you that the genitals may be represented by other organs in the attainment of gratification, as is the case in the normal kiss, or the perverse practices of "fast life," or the symptoms of hysteria? In these neuroses it is quite usual for stimulations, sensations and innervations, even the process of erection, which is localized in the genitals, to be transferred to other distant parts of the body, so that you have nothing to which you can hold as characteristics of the sexual. You will have to decide to follow my example and expand the designation "sexual" to include the strivings of early childhood toward organic pleasure.

Now, for my justification, I should like you to give me the time for two more considerations. As you know, we call the doubtful and indefinable pleasure activities of earliest childhood sexual because our analysis of the symptoms leads us to them by way of material that is undeniably sexual. We admit that it need not for that reason in itself be sexual. But take an analogous case. Suppose there were no way to observe the development of two dicotyledonous plants from their seeds—the apple tree and the bean. In both cases, however, imagine it possible to follow their evolution from the fully developed plant backwards to the first seedling with two leaf-divisions. The two little leaves are indistinguishable, in both cases they look exactly alike. Shall I conclude from this that they really are the same and that the specific differences between an apple tree and bean plant do not appear until later in the history of the plant? Or is it biologically more correct to believe that this difference is already present in the seedling, although the two little leaves show no differences? We do the same thing when we term as sexual the pleasure derived from the activities of the suckling. Whether each and every organic enjoyment may be called sexual, or if besides the sexual there is another that does not deserve this name, is a matter I cannot discuss here. I know too little about organic pleasure and its conditions, and will not be at all surprised if the retrogressive character of the analysis leads us back finally to a generalized factor.

One thing more. You have on the whole gained very little for what you are so anxious to maintain, the sexual purity of the child, even when you can convince me that the activities of the suckling had better not be called sexual. For from the third year on, there is no longer any doubt concerning the presence of a sexual life in the child. At this time the genitals already begin to become active; there is perhaps regularly a period of infantile masturbation, in other words, a gratification by means of the genitals. The psychic and social expressions of the sexual life are no longer absent; choice of an object, affectionate preference for certain persons, indeed, a leaning toward one of the two sexes, jealousy—all these have been established independently by unprejudiced observation, prior to the advent of psychoanalysis, and confirmed by every careful observer. You will say that you had no doubt as to the early awakening of affection, you will take issue only with its sexual nature. Children between the ages of three and eight have already learned to hide these things, but if you look sharply you can always gather sufficient evidence of the "sexual" purpose of this affection. What escapes you will be amply supplied by investigation. The sexual goals of this period of life are most intimately connected with the contemporaneous sexual theories, of which I have given you some examples. The perverse nature of some of these goals is the result of the constitutional immaturity of the child, who has not yet discovered the goal of the act of copulation.

From about the sixth or the eighth year on a pause in, and reversion of, sexual development is noticeable, which in the cases that reach the highest cultural standard deserves the name of a latent period. The latent period may also fail to appear and there need not be an interruption of sexual activity and sexual interests at any period. Most of the experiences and impulses prior to the latent period then fall victim to the infantile amnesia, the forgetting we have already discussed, which cloaks our earliest childhood and makes us strangers to it. | In every psychoanalysis we are confronted with the task of leading this forgotten period of life back into memory; one cannot resist the supposition that the beginning of sexual life it contains furnishes the motive for this forgetting, namely, that this forgetting is a result of suppression.

The sexual life of the child shows from the third year that it has much in common with that of the adult; it is distinguished from the latter, as we already know, by the lack of stable organization under the primacy of the genitals, by the unavoidable traits of perversion, and, naturally, by the far lesser intensity of the whole impulse. Theoretically the most interesting phases of the sexual development or, as we would rather say, the libido-development, so far as theory is concerned, lie back of this period. This development is so rapidly gone through that perhaps it would never have been possible for direct observation to grasp its fleeting pictures. Psychoanalytic investigation of the neuroses has for the first time made it possible to discover more remote phases of the libido-development. These are, to be sure, nothing but constructions, but if you wish to carry on psychonalaysis in a practical way you will find that they are necessary and valuable constructions. You will soon understand why pathology may disclose conditions which we would have overlooked in the normal object.

We can now declare what form the sexual life of the child takes before the primacy of the genitals is established. This primacy is prepared in the first infantile epoch prior to the latent period, and is continuously organized from puberty on. There is in this early period a sort of loose organization, which we shall call *pre-genital*. In the foreground of this phase, however, the partial instincts of the genitals are not prominent, rather the *sadistic* and *anal*. The contrast between *masculine* and *feminine* plays no part as yet, its place is taken by the contrast between *active* and *passive*, which we may designate as the forerunner of sexual polarity, with which it is later fused. That which appears masculine to us in the activity of this phase, observed from the standpoint of the later genital stage, is the expression of an instinct to mastery, which may border on cruelty. Impulses with passive goals attach themselves to the erogenous zone of the rectal opening. Most important at this time, curiosity and the instinct to watch are powerful. The genital really takes part in the sexual life only in its role as excretory organ for the bladder. Objects are not lacking to the partial impulses of this period, but they do not necessarily combine into a single object. The sadistico-anal organization is the step antecedent to the phase of genital primacy. A more penetrating study furnishes proof how much of this is retained for the later and final form, and in what ways its partial instincts are forced into line under the new genital organization. Back of the sadistico-anal phase of libido-development, we get a view of an earlier, even more primitive phase of organization, in which the erogenous mouth-zone plays the chief role. You may surmise that the sexual activity of sucking belongs to it, and may wonder at the intuition of the ancient Egyptians, whose art characterized the child, as well as the god Horus, with the finger in his mouth. Abraham only recently published material concerning the traces which this primitive oral phase has left upon the sexual life of later years.

I can surmise that these details about sexual organization have burdened your mind more than they have informed you. Perhaps I have again gone into detail too much. But be patient; what you have heard will become more valuable through the uses to which it is later put. Keep well in mind the impression that sexual life, as we call it, the function of the libido, does not make its appearance as a completed whole, nor does it develop in its own image, but goes through a series of successive phases which are not similar to each other. In fact, it is a developmental sequence, like that from the grub to the butterfly. The turning point of the development is the subordination of all sexual partial-instincts to the primacy of the genitals, and thereby the subjection of sexuality to the function of reproduction. Originally it is a diffused sexual life, one which consists of independent activities of single partial instincts which strive towards organic gratification. This anarchy is modified by approaches to pre-genital organization, first of all the sadistico-anal phase, prior to this the oral phase, which is perhaps the most primitive. Added to this there are the various processes, as yet not well known, which carry over one organization level to the later and more advanced phase. The significance, for the understanding of the neuroses, of the long evolutionary path of the libido which carries it over so many grades we shall discuss on another occasion.

Today we shall look at another angle of the development, namely the relation of the partial instinct to the object. We shall make a hurried survey of this development in order to spend more time upon a relatively later product. Some of the components of the sex instincts have had an object from the very beginning and hold fast to it; such are the instinct to mastery (sadism), curiosity, and the impulse to watch. Other impulses which are more clearly attached to specific erogenous zones of the body have this object only in the beginning, as long as they adhere to the functions which are not sexual; they release this object when they free themselves from these non-sexual functions. The first object of the oral component of the sexual impulse is the mother's breast, which satisfies the hunger of the infant. By the act of sucking, the erotic component which is also satisfied by the sucking becoming independent, it gives up the foreign object and replaces it by some part of its own body. The oral impulse becomes *auto-erotic*, just as the anal and other erogenous impulses are from the very beginning. Further development, to express it most briefly, has two goals—first, to give up auto-eroticism, and, again, to substitute for the object of one's own body a foreign object; second, to unify the different objects into a single impulse, replace them by a single object. To be sure, that can happen only if this single object is itself complete, a body similar to one's own. Nor can it be consummated without leaving behind as useless a large number of the auto-erotic instinctive impulses.

The processes of finding the object are rather involved, and have as yet had no comprehensive exposition. For our purpose, let us emphasize the fact that when the process has come to a temporary cessation in the childhood years, before the latent period, the object it has found is seen to be practically identical with the first object derived from its relation to the object of the oral pleasure impulse. It is, if not the mother's breast, the mother herself. We call the mother the first *object of love*. For we speak of love when we emphasize the psychic side of sex-impulses, and disregard or for a moment wish to forget the fundamental physical or "sensual" demands of the instincts. At the time when the mother becomes the object of love, the psychic work of suppression which withdraws the knowledge of a part of his sexual goal from his consciousness has already begun in the child. The selection of the mother as the object of love involves everything we understand by the Oedipus complex which has come to have such great significance in the psychoanalytic explanation of neuroses, and which has had no small part in arousing opposition to psychoanalysis.

Here is a little experience which took place during the present war: A brave young disciple of psychoanalysis is a doctor at the German front somewhere in Poland, and attracts the attention of his colleagues by the fact that he occasionally exercises an unexpected influence in the case of a patient. Upon being questioned he admits that he works by means of psychoan and is finally induced to impart his knowledge to his coll

Every evening the physicians of the corps, colleagues and superiors, gather in order to listen to the inmost secrets of analysis. For a while this goes on nicely, but after he has told his audience of the Oedipus-complex, a superior rises and says he does not believe it, that it is shameful for the lecturer to tell such things to them, brave men who are fighting for their fatherland, and who are the fathers of families, and he forbade the continuation of the lectures. This was the end.

Now you will be impatient to discover what this frightful Oedipus-complex consists of. The name tells you. You all know the Greek myth of King Oedipus, who is destined by the fates to kill his father, and take his mother to wife, who does everything to escape the oracle and then does penance by blinding himself when he discovers that he has, unknowingly, committed these two sins. I trust many of you have yourselves experienced the profound effect of the tragedy in which Sophocles handles this material. The work of the Attic poet presents the manner in which the deed of Oedipus, long since accomplished, is finally brought to light by an artistically prolonged investigation, continuously fed with new evidence; thus far it has a certain similarity to the process of psychoanalysis. In the course of the dialogue it happens that the infatuated mother-wife, Jocasta, opposes the continuation of the investigation. She recalls that many men have dreamed that they have cohabited with their mothers, but one should lay little stress on dreams. We do not lay little stress on dreams, least of all typical dreams such as occur to many men, and we do not doubt that this dream mentioned by Jocasta is intimately connected with the strange and frightful content of the myth.

It is surprising that Sophocles' tragedy does not call forth much greater indignation and opposition on the part of the audience, a reaction similar to, and far more justified, than the reaction to our simple military physician. For it is a fundamentally immoral play, it dispenses with the moral responsibility of men, it portrays godlike powers as instigators of guilt, and shows the helplessness of the moral impulses of men which contend against sin. One might easily suppose that the burden of the myth purposed accusation against the gods and Fate, and in the hands of the critical Euripides, always at odds with the gods, it would probably have become such an accusation.

But there is no trace of this in the work of the believer Sophocles. A pious sophistry which asserts that the highest morality is to bow to the will of the gods, even if they command a crime, helps him over the difficulty. I do not think that this moral constitutes the power of the drama, but so far as the effect goes, that is unimportant; the listener does not react to it, but to the secret meaning and content of the myth. He reacts as though through self-analysis he had recognized in himself the Oedipus-complex, and had unmasked the will of the gods, as well as the oracle, as sublime disguises of his own unconsciousness. It is as though he remembered the wish to remove his father, and in his place to take his mother to wife, and must be horrified at his own desires. He also understands the voice of the poet as if it were telling him: "You revolt in vain against your responsibility, and proclaim in vain the efforts you have made to resist these criminal purposes. In spite of these efforts, you are guilty, for you have not been able to destroy the criminal purposes, they will persist unconsciously in you." And in that there is psychological truth. Even if man has relegated his evil impulses to the unconscious, and would tell himself that he is no longer answerable for them, he will still be compelled to experience this responsibility as a feeling of guilt which he cannot trace to its source.

It is not to be doubted for a moment that one may recognize in the Oedipus-complex one of the most important sources for the consciousness of guilt with which neurotics are so often harassed. But furthermore, in a study of the origins of religion and morality of mankind which I published in 1913, under the title of *Totem and Taboo*, the idea was brought home to me that perhaps mankind as a whole has, at the beginning of its history, come by its consciousness of guilt, the final source of religion and morality, through the Oedipus-complex. I should like to say more on this subject, but perhaps I had better not. It is difficult to turn away from this subject now that I have begun speaking of it, but we must return to individual psychology.

What does direct observation of the child at the time of the selection of its object, before the latent period, show us concerning the Oedipus-complex? One may easily see that the man would like to have the mother all to himself. that h the presence of his father disturbing, he becomes irritated when the latter permits himself to show tenderness towards the mother, and expresses his satisfaction when the father is away or on a journey. Frequently he expresses his feelings directly in words, promises the mother he will marry her. One may think this is very little in comparison with the deeds of Oedipus, but it is actually enough, for it is essentially the same thing. The observation is frequently clouded by the circumstance that the same child at the same time, on other occasions, gives evidence of great tenderness towards its father; it is only that such contradictory, or rather, *ambivalent* emotional attitudes as would lead to a conflict in the case of an adult readily take their place side by side in a child, just as later on they permanently exist in the unconscious. You might wish to interpose that the behavior of the child springs from egoistic motives and does not justify the setting up of an erotic complex. The mother provides for all the necessities of the child, and it is therefore to the child's advantage that she troubles herself for no one else. This, too, is correct, but it will soon be clear that in this, as in similar situations, the egoistic interest offers only the opportunity upon which the erotic impulse seizes. If the little one shows the most undisguised sexual curiosity about his mother, if he wants to sleep with her at night, insists upon being present while she is dressing, or attempts to caress her, as the mother can so often ascertain and laughingly relates, it is undoubtedly due to the erotic nature of the attachment to his mother. We must not forget that the mother shows the same care for her little daughter without achieving the same effect, and that the father often vies with her in caring for the boy without being able to win the same importance in his eyes as the mother. In short, it is clear that the factor of sex-preference cannot be eliminated from the situation by any kind of criticism. From the standpoint of egoistic interest it would merely be stupid of the little fellow not to tolerate two persons in his services rather than only one.

I have, as you will have noticed, described only the relation of the boy to his father and mother. As far as the little girl is concerned, the process is the same with the necessary modifications. The affectionate devotion to the father, the desire to set aside the mother as superfluous and to take her place, a coquetry which already works with all the arts of later womanhood, give such a charming picture, especially in the baby girl, that we are apt to forget its seriousness, and the grave consequences which may result from this infantile situation. Let us not fail to add that frequently the parents themselves exert a decisive influence over the child in the wakening of the Oedipus attitude, in that they themselves follow a sex preference when there are a number of children. The father in the most unmistakable manner shows preference for the daughter, while the mother is most affectionate toward the son. But even this factor cannot seriously undermine the spontaneous character of the childish Oedipus-complex. The Oedipus-complex expands and becomes a family-complex when other children appear. It becomes the motive force, revived by the sense of personal injury, which causes the child to receive its brothers and sisters with aversion and to wish to remove them without more ado. It is much more frequent for the children to express these feelings of hatred than those arising from the parent-complex. If such a wish is fulfilled, and death takes away the undesired increase in the family, after a short while we may discover through analysis what an important experience this death was for the child, even though he had not remembered it. The child forced into second place by the birth of a little brother or sister, and for the first time practically isolated from his mother, is loathe to forgive her for this; feelings which we would call extreme bitterness in an adult are aroused in him and often become the basis of a lasting estrangement. We have already mentioned that sexual curiosity with all its consequences usually grows out of these experiences of the child. With the growing up of these brothers and sisters the relation to them undergoes the most significant changes. The boy may take his sister as the object for his love, to replace his faithless mother; situations of dangerous rivalry, which are of vast importance for later life, arise even in the nursery among numerous brothers who court the affection of a younger sister. A little girl finds in her older brother a substitute for her father, who no longer acts towards her with the same affection as in former years, or she takes a younger sister as a substitute for the child that she vainly wished of her father.

Such things, and many more of a similar character, are show by the direct observation of children and the consideratio their vivid childish recollections, which are not influenced by the analysis. You will conclude, among other things, that the position of a child in the sequence of his brothers and sisters is of utmost importance for the entire course of his later life, a factor which should be considered in every biography. In the face of these explanations that are found with so little effort, you will hardly recall without smiling the scientific explanations for the prohibition of incest. What inventions! By living together from early childhood the sexual attraction must have been diverted from these members of the family who are of opposite sex, or a biological tendency against in-breeding finds its psychic equivalent in an innate dread of incest! In this no account is taken of the fact that there would be no need of so unrelenting a prohibition by law and morality if there were any natural reliable guards against the temptation of incest. Just the opposite is true. The first choice of an object among human beings is regularly an incestuous one, in the man directed toward the mother and sister, and the most stringent laws are necessary to prevent this persisting infantile tendency from becoming active. Among the primitive races the prohibitions against incest are much more stringent than ours, and recently Th. Reik showed in a brilliant paper that the puberty-rites of the savages, which represent a rebirth, have the significance of loosing the incestuous bonds of the boy to his mother, and of establishing the reconciliation with the father.

Mythology teaches that incest, apparently so abhorred by men, is permitted to the gods without further thought, and you may learn from ancient history that incestuous marriage with his sister was holy prescript for the person of the ruler (among the ancient Pharaohs and the Incas of Peru). We have here a privilege denied the common herd.

Incest with his mother is one of the sins of Oedipus, patricide the other. It might also be mentioned that these are the two great sins which the first social-religious institution of mankind, totemism, abhors. Let us turn from the direct observation of the child to analytic investigation of the adult neurotic. What does analysis yield to the further knowledge of the Oedipus-complex? This is easily told. It shows the patient up in the light of the myth; it shows that each of these neurotics was himself an Oedipus or, what amounts to the same thing, became a Hamlet in the reaction to the complex. To be sure, the analytic representation of the Oedipus-complex enlarges upon and is a coarser edition of the infantile sketch. The hatred of the father, the death-wish with regard to him, are no longer timidly suggested, the affection for the mother recognizes the goal of possessing her for a wife. Dare we really accredit these horrible and extreme feelings to those tender childhood years, or does analysis deceive us by bringing in some new element? It is not difficult to discover this. Whenever an account of past events is given, be it written even by a historian, we must take into account the fact that inadvertently something has been interpolated from the present and from intervening times into the past; so that the entire picture is falsified. In the case of the neurotic it is questionable whether this interpolation is entirely unintentional or not; we shall later come to learn its motives and must justify the fact of "imagining back" into the remote past. We also easily discover that hatred of the father is fortified by numerous motives which originate in later times and circumstances, since the sexual wishes for the mother are cast in forms which are necessarily foreign to the child. But it would be a vain endeavor to explain the whole of the Oedipus-complex by "imagining back," and as related to later times. The infantile nucleus and more or less of what has been added to it continues to exist and may be verified by the direct observation of the child.

The clinical fact which we meet with in penetrating the form of the Oedipus-complex as established by analysis, is of the greatest practical importance. We learn that at the period of puberty, when the sexual instinct first asserts its demands in full strength, the old incestuous and familiar objects are again taken up and seized anew by the libido. The infant's choice of an object was feeble, but it nevertheless set the direction for the choice of an object in puberty. At that time very intense emotional experiences are brought into play and directed towards the Oedipus-complex, or utilized in the reaction to it. However, since their presuppositions have become unsupportable, they must in large part remain outside of consciousness. From this time on the human individual must devote himself to the great task of freeing himself from his parents, and only after he h' freed himself can he cease to be a child, and become a memb

of the social community. The task confronting the son consists
of freeing himself from his libidinous wishes towards his mother
and utilizing them in the quest for a really foreign object for
his love. He must also effect a reconciliation with his father,
if he has stayed hostile to him, or if in the reaction to his
infantile opposition he has become subject to his domination, he
must now free himself from this pressure. These tasks are set
for every man; it is noteworthy how seldom their solution is
ideally achieved, i.e., how seldom the solution is psychologically
as well as socially correct. Neurotics, however, find no solution
whatever; the son remains during his whole life subject to the
authority of his father, and is not able to transfer his libido
to a foreign sexual object. Barring the difference in the specific
relation, the same fate may befall the daughter. In this sense
the Oedipus-complex is correctly designated as the nucleus of
the neurosis.

You can imagine how rapidly I am reviewing a great number
of conditions which are associated with the Oedipus-complex, of
practical as well as of theoretical importance. I cannot enter
upon their variations or possible inversions. Of its less immediate relations I only wish to indicate the influence which the
Oedipus-complex has been found to exert on literary production.
In a valuable book, Otto Rank has shown that the dramatists
of all times have taken their materials principally from the
Oedipus- and incest-complexes, with their variations and disguises. Moreover, we will not forget to mention that the two
guilty wishes of Oedipus were recognized long before the time of
psychoanalysis as the true representatives of the unrestrained life
of impulses. Among the writings of the encyclopedist Diderot
we find a famous dialogue, *The Nephew of Ramau,* which no
less a person than Goethe has translated into German. In this
you may read the remarkable sentence: *"If the little savage
were left to himself he would preserve all his imbecility, he
would unite the passions of a man of thirty to the unreasonableness of the child in the cradle; he would twist his father's neck
and bed with his mother."*

There is also one other thing of which I must needs speak.
The mother-wife of Oedipus shall not have reminded us of the
dream in vain. Do you still remember the result of our dream
analysis, that the wishes out of which the dream is constructed

so frequently are of a perverse, incestuous nature, or disclose an enmity toward near and beloved relatives the existence of which had never been suspected? At the time we did not trace the sources of these evil impulses. Now you may see them for yourselves. They represent the disposition made in early infancy of the libidinous energy, with the objects, long since given up in conscious life, to which it had once clung, which are now shown at night to be still present and in a certain sense capable of activity. But since all people have such perverse, incestuous and murderous dreams, and not the neurotics alone, we may conclude that even those who are normal have passed through the same evolutionary development, through the perversions and the direction of the libidio toward the objects of the Oedipus-complex. This, then, is the way of normal development, upon which the neurotics merely enlarge. They show in cruder form what dream analysis exposes in the healthy dreamer as well. Accordingly here is one of the motives which led us to deal with the study of the dream before we considered the neurotic symptom.

GENERAL THEORY OF THE NEUROSES

Theories of Development and Regression—Etiology

WE have learned that the libidio goes through an extensive development before it can enter the service of reproduction in a way which may be regarded as normal. Now I wish to present to you what importance this fact possesses for the causation of neuroses.

I believe we are in harmony with the teachings of general pathology in assuming that this development involves two dangers, inhibition and regression. In other words, with the universal tendency of biological processes toward variation, it must necessarily happen that not all preparatory phases of a given function are equally well passed through or accomplished with comparable thoroughness. Certain components of a function may be permanently held back in an early stage of development and the complete development is therefore retarded to a certain extent.

Let us seek analogies for these processes from other fields. If a whole people leaves its dwellings to seek a new home, as frequently happened in the early periods of the history of mankind, their entire number will certainly not reach the new destination. Setting aside other losses, small groups or associations of these wandering peoples would stop on the way, and, while the majority passes on, they would settle down at these way-stations. Or, to seek a more appropriate comparison: You know that in the most highly evolved mammals, the male seminal glands, which originally are located in the far depths of the abdominal cavity, begin to wander during a certain period of intra-uterine life until they reach a position almost immediately under the skin of the pelvic extremity. In the case of a number of male individuals, one of the paired glands may as a result of this wandering remain in the pelvic cavity, or may be permanently located in the canal through which both glands must pass in their journey, or finally the canal itself may stay open permanently instead of growing together with the seminal glands after the change of position has taken place normally. When, as a young student, I was doing my first piece of scientific research under the direction of von Brücke, I was working on the dorsal nerve-roots in the spinal cord of a small fish very archaic in form. I discovered that the nerve ganglia of these roots grow out from large cells which lie in the grey matter of the dorsal column, a condition no longer true of other vertebrates. But I soon discovered that such nerve cells are found outside the grey matter all the way to the so-called spinal ganglion of the dorsal root. From this I concluded that the cells of this group of ganglia had traveled from the spinal cord to the roots of the nerves. This same result is attested by embryology. In this little fish, however, the entire path of the journey was traceable by the cells that had remained behind. Closer observation will easily reveal to you the weak points of these comparisons. Therefore let me simply say that with reference to every single sexual impulse, I consider it possible for several of its components to be held back in the earlier stages of development while other components have worked themselves out to completion. You will realize that we think of every such impulse as a current continuously driving on from the very beginning of life, and that our resolving it into individual movements which follow separately one upon the other is to a certain extent artificial. Your impression that these concepts require further clarification is correct, but an attempt would lead to too great digression. Before we pass on, however, let us agree to call this arrest of a partial impulse in an early stage of development, a *fixation* of the instinct.

Regression is the second danger of this development by stages. Even those components which have achieved a degree of progress may readily turn backward to these earlier stages. Having attained to this later and more highly developed form, the impulse is forced to a regression when it encounters great external difficulties in the exercise of its function, and accordingly cannot reach the goal which will satisfy its strivings. We can obviously assume that fixation and regression are not independent of each other. The stronger the fixations in the process of develop prove to be, the more readily will the function evade ext difficulties by a regression back to those fixations, and th

capable will the fully developed function be to withstand the
hindrances that stand in the way of its exercise. Remember
that if a people in its wandering has left large groups at certain
way-stations, it is natural for those who have gone on to return
to these stations if they are beaten or encounter a mighty foe.
The more they have left on the way, however, the greater is
their chance of defeat.

For your comprehension of the neuroses it is necessary to
keep in mind this connection between fixation and regression.
This will give you a secure hold upon the question of the cause
of neuroses—of the etiology of neuroses—which we shall soon
consider.

For the present we have still to discuss various aspects of
regression. With the knowledge you have gained concerning
the development of the function of libido, you must expect two
kinds of regression: incestuous return to the first libidinous
objects and return of the entire sexual organization to an earlier
stage of development. Both occur in the transference neuroses
and play an important part in its mechanism. Especially is
the return to the first incestuous objects of libido a feature that
the neurotic exhibits with positively tiresome regularity. We
could say far more about regression of libido if we took into
consideration another group of neuroses: neurotic narcism
But we cannot do this now. These conditions give us a clue to
other stages of development of the function of libido, which have
not been mentioned previously, and correspondingly show new
kinds of regression. But I think the most important task
before me at this point is to warn you not to confuse *regression*
and *suppression*, and aid you to see clearly the connection between the two processes. Suppression, as you know, is the process by which an act capable of becoming conscious, in other
words, an act that belongs to the fore-conscious system, is
rendered unconscious and accordingly is thrust back into the
unconscious system. Similarly we speak of suppression when the
unconscious psychic act never has been admitted into the adjoining fore-conscious system but is arrested by the censor at the
threshold. Kindly observe that the conception of suppression
has nothing to do with sexuality. It describes a purely psychological process, which could better be characterized by terming
it *lecalized*. By that we mean that it is concerned with the

spatial relationships within the psyche, or if we drop this crude
metaphor, with building up the psychological apparatus out of
separate, psychic systems.

Through these comparisons we observe that up to this point
we have not used the word regression in its general, but in a
very special sense. If you accord it the general meaning of
return from a higher to a lower stage of development you must
include suppression as a form of regression, for suppression may
also be described as the reversion to an earlier and lower stage
in the development of a psychic act. Only in regard to suppression, this tendency to revert is not necessarily involved, for
when a psychic act is held back in the early unconscious stage
we also term it suppression in a dynamic sense. Suppression is
a localized and dynamic conception, regression purely descriptive. What up this point we have called regression and considered in its relation to fixation, was only the return of libido
to former stages of its development. The nature of this latter
conception is entirely distinct and independent of suppression.
We cannot call the libido regressions purely psychical processes
and do not know what localization in the psychological apparatus
we should assign to them. Even though the libido exerts a
most powerful influence on psychic life, its organic significance
is still the most conspicuous.

Discussions of this sort, gentlemen, are bound to be somewhat
dry. To render them more vivid and impressive, let us return
to clinical illustrations. You know that hysteria and compulsion-
neurosis are the two chief factors in the group of transference
neuroses. In hysteria, libidinous return to primary, incestuous
sexual objects is quite regular, but regression to a former stage
of sexual organization very rare. In the mechanism of hysteria
suppression plays the chief part. If you will permit me to supplement our previous positive knowledge of this neurosis by a
constructive suggestion, I could describe the state of affairs
in this manner: the union of the partial instincts under the
domination of the genitals is accomplished, but its results encounter the opposition of the fore-conscious system which, of
course, is bound up with consciousness. Genital organization,
therefore, may stand for the unconscious but not for th—
conscious. Through this rejection on the part of the
scious, a situation arises which in certain aspects is si

the condition existing before the genitals had attained their primacy. Of the two libido regressions, the regression to a former stage of sexual organization is by far the more conspicuous. Since it is lacking in hysteria and our entire conception of the neuroses is still too much dominated by the study of hysteria which preceded it in point of time, the meaning of libido regression became clearer to us much later than that of repression. Let us be prepared to widen and change our attitude still more when we consider other narcistic neuroses besides compulsion-neurosis and hysteria in our discussion.

In contrast to this, regression of libido in compulsion-neurosis turns back most conspicuously to the earlier sadistico-anal organization, which accordingly becomes the most significant factor expressed by the symptoms. Under these conditions the love impulse must mask itself as a sadistic impulse. The compulsion idea must therefore be reinterpreted. Isolated from other superimposed factors, which though they are not accidental are also indispensable, it no longer reads: "I want to murder you "; rather it says " I want to enjoy you in love." Add to this, that simultaneously regression of the object has also set in, so that this impulse is invariably directed toward the nearest and dearest persons, and you can imagine with what horror the patient thinks of these compulsion ideas and how alien they appear to his conscious perception. In the mechanism of these neuroses, suppression, too, assumes an important part, which it is not easy to explain in a superficial discussion of this sort. Regression of the libido without suppression would never result in neurosis but would finally end in perversion. This makes it obvious that suppression is the process most characteristic of neurosis, and typifies it most perfectly. Perhaps I shall at some future time have the opportunity of presenting to you our knowledge of the mechanism of perversions and then you will see that here also things do not work themselves out as simply as we should best like to construe them.

You will most readily reconcile yourself with these elucidations of fixation and regression, when you consider them as a preface to the investigation of the etiology of neuroses. Towards this I have only advanced a single fact: that people become neurotically ill when the possibility of satisfying their libido is removed, ill with "denial," as I expressed myself, and that their symptoms are the substitutes for the denied gratification. Of course, that does not mean that every denial of libidinous satisfaction makes every person neurotic, but merely that in all cases known of neurosis, the factor of denial was traceable. The syllogism therefore cannot be reversed. You also understand, I trust, that this statement is not supposed to reveal the entire secret of the etiology of neurosis, but only emphasizes an important and indispensable condition.

Now, we do not know, in the further discussion of this statement, whether to emphasize the nature of denial or the individuality of the person affected by it. Denial is very rarely complete and absolute; to cause a pathological condition, the specific gratification desired by the particular person in question must be withheld, the certain satisfaction of which he alone is capable. On the whole there are many ways of enduring abstinence from libidinous gratification without succumbing to a neurosis by reason thereof. Above all we know of people who are able to endure abstinence without doing themselves injury; they are not happy under the circumstances, they are filled with yearning, but they do not become ill. Furthermore, we must take into consideration that the impulses of the sex instinct are extraordinarily *plastic*, if I may use that term in this connection. One thing may take the place of the other; one may assume the other's intensity; if reality refuses the one gratification, the satisfaction of another may offer full compensation. The sexual impulses are like a network of communicating channels filled with fluids; they are this in spite of their subjugation to the primacy of the genitals, though I realize it is difficult to unite these two ideas in one conception. The component impulses of sexuality as well as the total sexual desire, which represents their aggregate, show a marked ability to change their object, to exchange it, for instance, for one more easily attainable. This displacement and the readiness to accept substitutes must exert powerful influences in opposition to the pathological effect of abstinence. Among these processes which resist the ill effects of abstinence, one in particular has won cultural significance. Sexual desire relinquishes either its goal of partial gratification of desire, or the goal of desire ' reproduction, and adopts another aim, genetically related abandoned one, save that it is no longer sexual but n

termed social. This process is called "sublimation," and in
adopting this process we subscribe to the general standard which
places social aims above selfish sexual desires. Sublimation is,
as a matter of fact, only a special case of the relation of sexual
to non-sexual desires. We shall have occasion to talk more about
this later in another connection.

Now your impression will be that abstinence has become an
insignificant factor, since there are so many methods of enduring
it. Yet this is not the case, for its pathological power is unim-
paired. The remedies are generally not sufficient. The measure
of unsatisfied libido which the average human being can stand is
limited. The plasticity and freedom of movement of libido is
by no means retained to the same extent by all individuals;
sublimation can, moreover, never account for more than a certain small fraction of the libido, and finally most people possess
the capacity for sublimation only to a very slight degree. The
most important of these limitations clearly lies in the adaptability of the libido, as it renders the gratification of the individual dependent upon the attainment of only a very few aims
and objects. Kindly recall that incomplete development of the
libido leaves extensive and possibly even numerous libido fixations in earlier developmental phases of the processes of sexual
organization and object-finding, and that these phases are
usually not capable of affording a real gratification. You will
then recognize libido fixation as the second powerful factor which
together with abstinence constitutes the causative factors of the
illness. We may abbreviate schematically and say that libido
fixation represents the internal disposing factor, abstinence the
accidental external factor of the etiology of neurosis.

I seize the opportunity to warn you of taking sides in a most
unnecessary conflict. In scientific affairs it is a popular proceeding to emphasize a part of the truth in place of the whole
truth and to combat all the rest, which has lost none of its verity,
in the name of that fraction. In this way various factions
have already separated out from the movement of psychoanalysis; one faction recognizes only the egoistic impulses and denies
the sexual, another appreciates the influence of objective tasks
in life, but ignores the part played by the individual past, and
so on. Here is occasion for a similar antithesis and subject
for dispute: are neuroses *exogenous* or *endogenous* diseases, are

they the inevitable results of a special constitution or the product of certain harmful (traumatic) impressions; in particular, are they called forth by libido fixation (and the sexual constitution which goes with this) or through the pressure of forbearance? This dilemma seems to me no whit wiser than another I could present to you: is the child created through the generation of the father or the conception of the mother? Both factors are equally essential, you will answer very properly. The conditions which cause neuroses are very similar if not precisely the same. For the consideration of the causes of neuroses, we may arrange neurotic diseases in a series, in which two factors, sexual constitution and experience, or, if you wish, libido-fixation and self-denial, are represented in such a way that one increases as the other decreases. At one end of the series are the extreme cases, of which you can say with full conviction: These persons would have become ill because of the peculiar development of their libido, no matter what they might have experienced, no matter how gently life might have treated them. At the other end are cases which would call forth the reversed judgment, that the patients would undoubtedly have escaped illness if life had not thrust certain conditions upon them. But in the intermediate cases of the series, predisposing sexual constitution and subversive demands of life combine. Their sexual constitution would not have given rise to neurosis if the victims had not had such experiences, and their experiences would not have acted upon them traumatically if the conditions of the libido had been otherwise. Within this series I may grant a certain preponderance to the weight carried by the predisposing factors, but this admission, too, depends upon the boundaries within which you wish to delimit nervousness.

Allow me to suggest that you call such series *complementary series*. We shall have occasion to establish other series of this sort.

The tenacity with which the libido clings to certain tendencies and objects, the so-called *adhesiveness* of the libido, appears to us as an independent factor, individually variable, the determining conditions of which are completely unknown to us, but the importance of which for the etiology of the neuroses we can no longer underestimate. At the same time we must not overestimate the closeness of this interrelation. A similar a⸱

ness of the libido occurs—for unknown reasons—in normal persons under various conditions, and is a determining factor in the perverse, who are in a certain sense the opposite of nervous. Before the period of psychoanalysis, it was known (Binet) that the anamnesia of the perverse is often traced back to an early impression—an abnormality in the tendency of the instinct or its choice of object—and it is to this that the libido of the individual has clung for life. Frequently it is hard to say how such an impression becomes capable of attracting the libido so intensively. I shall give you a case of this kind which I observed myself. A man, to whom the genital and all other sex stimuli of woman now mean nothing, who in fact can only be thrown into an irresistible sexual excitation by the sight of a shoe on a foot of a certain form, is able to recall an experience he had in his sixth year, which proved decisive for the fixation of his libido. One day he sat on a stool beside his governess, who was to give him an English lesson. She was an old, shriveled, unbeautiful girl with washed-out blue eyes and a pug nose, who on this day, because of some injury, had put a velvet slipper on her foot and stretched it out on a footstool; the leg itself she had most decorously covered. After a diffident attempt at normal sexual activity, undertaken during puberty, such a thin sinewy foot as his governess' had become the sole object of his sexuality; and the man was irresistibly carried away if other features, reminiscent of the English governess, appeared in conjunction with the foot. Through this fixation of the libido the man did not become neurotic but perverse, a foot fetishist, as we say. So you see that, although exaggerated and premature fixation of the libido is indispensable for the causation of neuroses, its sphere of action exceeds the limits of neuroses immeasurably. This condition also, taken by itself, is no more decisive than abstinence.

And so the problem of the cause of neuroses seems to become more complicated. Psychoanalytic investigation does, in fact, acquaint us with a new factor, not considered in our etiological series, which is recognized most easily in those cases where permanent well-being is suddenly disturbed by an attack of neurosis. These individuals regularly show signs of contradiction between their wishes, or, as we are wont to say, indication of psychic *conflict*. A part of their personality represents certain wishes, another rebels against them and resists them. A neurosis cannot come into existence without such conflict. This may seem to be of small significance. You know that our psychic life is con. tinually agitated by conflicts for which we must find a solution. Certain conditions, therefore, must exist to make such a conflict pathological. We want to know what these conditions are, what psychic powers form the background for these pathological conflicts, what relation the conflict bears to the causative factors.

I hope I shall be able to give you satisfactory answers to these questions even if I must make them schematically brief. Self-denial gives rise to conflict, for libido deprived of its gratification is forced to seek other means and ends. A pathogenic conflict arises when these other means and ends arouse the disfavor of one part of the personality, and a veto ensues which makes the new mode of gratification impossible for the time being. This is the point of departure for the development of the symptoms, a process which we shall consider later. The rejected libidinous desires manage to have their own way, through circuitous byways, but not without catering to the objections through the observance of certain symptom-formation; the symptoms are the new or substitute satisfaction which the condition of self-denial has made necessary.

We can express the significance of the psychic conflict in another way, by saying: the *outer* self-denial, in order to become pathological, must be supplemented by an *inner* self-denial. Outer denial removes one possibility of gratification, inner denial would like to exclude another possibility, and it is this second possibility which becomes the center of the ensuing conflict. I prefer this form of presentation because it possesses secret content. It implies the probability that the inner impediment found its origin in the prehistoric stage of human development in real external hindrances.

What powers are these which interpose objections to libidinous desire, who are the other parties to the pathological conflict? They are, in the widest sense, the non-sexual impulses. We call them comprehensively the "ego impulses"; psychoanalysis of transference neuroses does not grant us ready access to their further investigation, but we learn to know them, in a measure, through the resistance they offer to analysis. The pathological struggle is waged between ego-impulses and sexual impulses.

a series of cases it appears as though conflict could exist between various purely sexual desires; but that is really the same thing, for of the two sexual desires involved in the conflict, one is always considerate of the ego, while the other demands that the ego be denied, and so it remains a conflict between the ego and sexuality.

Again and again when psychoanalysis claimed that psychological event was the result of sexual impulses, indignant protest was raised that in psychic life there were other impulses and interests besides the sexual, that everything could not be derived from sexuality, etc. Well, it is a great pleasure to share for once the opinion of one's opponents. Psychoanalysis never forgot that non-sexual impulses exist. It insisted on the decided distinction between sexual and ego-impulses and maintained in the face of every objection not that neuroses arise from sexuality, but that they owe their origin to the conflict between sexuality and the ego. Psychoanalysis can have no reasonable motive for denying the existence or significance of ego-impulses, even though it investigates the influence sexual impulses play in illness and in life. Only it has been destined to deal primarily with sexual impulses, because transference neuroses have furnished the readiest access to their investigation, and because it had become obligatory to study what others had neglected.

It does not follow, either, that psychoanalysis has never occupied itself at all with the non-sexual side of personality. The very distinction of the ego from sexuality has shown most clearly that the ego-impulses also pass through a significant development, which is by no means entirely independent of the development of the libido, nor does it fail to exert a reaction upon it. To be sure, we know much less about the evolution of the ego than about libido development, for so far only the study of narcistic neuroses has promised to throw light on the structure of the ego. There is extant the notable attempt of Ferenczi to construct theoretically the stages of ego development, and furthermore we already possess two fixed points from which to proceed in our evolution of this development. We do not dream of asserting that the libidinous interests of a person are from the outset opposed to the interests of self-preservation; in every stage, rather, the ego will strive to remain in harmony with its sexual organization at that time, and accommodate itself thereto.

The succession of the separate phases of development of libido probably follows a prescribed program; but we cannot deny that this sequence can be influenced by the ego, and that a certain parallelism of the phases of development of the ego and the libido may also be assumed. Indeed, the disturbance of this parallelism could become a pathological factor. One of the most important insights we have to gain is the nature of the attitude which the ego exhibits when an intensive fixation of its libido is left behind in one stage of its development. It may countenance the fixation and accordingly become perverse or, what amounts to the same thing, become infantile. Or it may be averse to this attachment of the libido, the result of which is that wherever the libido is subject to *fixation*, there the ego undergoes *suppression*.

In this way we reach the conclusion that the third factor of the etiology of neuroses is the tendency to *conflict*, upon which the development both of the ego and libido are dependent. Our insight into the causation of the neuroses has therefore been amplified. First, the most generalized factor, self-denial, then the fixation of the libido, by which it is forced into certain directions, and thirdly, the tendency to conflict in the development of the ego, which has rejected libidinous impulses of this kind. The state of affairs is therefore not so confused and difficult to see through, as you may have imagined it to be in the course of my explanation. But of course we are to discover that we have not, as yet, reached the end. We must add still a new factor and further analyze one we already know.

To show you the influence of ego development in the formation of a conflict, and so to give an illustration of the causation of neuroses, I should like to cite an example which, although it is entirely imaginary, is not far removed from probability in any respect. Drawing upon the title of a farce by Nestroy, I shall label this example "On the ground floor and in the first story." The janitor lives on the ground floor, while the owner of the house, a rich, distinguished man, occupies the first story. Both have children, and we shall assume that the owner permits his little daughter to play unwatched with the child of the people. Then it may easily happen that the games of the children become "naughty," that is, they assume a sexual character; they play "father and mother," watch each other in the performance of

intimate performances and mutually stimulate their genitak
The janitor's daughter, who, in spite of her five or six years of
age, has had occasion to make observations on the sexuality of
adults, probably played the part of the seducer. These experiences, even though they be of short duration, are sufficient to
set in motion certain sexual impulses in both children, which
continue in the form of onanism for several years after the
common games have ceased. So far the consequences are similar;
the final result will be very different. The janitor's daughter
will continue onanism possibly to the commencement of her
periods, abandon it then without difficulty, not many years later
find a lover, perhaps bear a child, choose this or that path of life,
which may likely enough make of her a popular artist who ends
as an aristocrat. Perhaps the outcome will be less brilliant, but
at any rate she will work out her life, free from neurosis, un-
harmed by her premature sexual activity. Very different is the
effect on the other child. Even while she is very young she
will realize vaguely that she has done wrong. In a short while,
perhaps only after a violent struggle, she will renounce the
gratification of onanism, yet still retain an undercurrent of
depression in her attitude. If, during her early childhood, she
chances to learn something about sexual intercourse, she will
turn away in explicable disgust and seek to remain innocent.
Probably she is at the time subjected anew to an irresistible impulse to onanism, of which she does not dare to complain. When
the time arrives for her to find favor in the eyes of a man,
a neurosis will suddenly develop and cheat her out of marriage
and the joy of life. When analysis succeeds in gaining insight
into this neurosis, it will reveal that this well-bred, intelligent
girl of high ideals, has completely suppressed her sexual desires,
but that unconsciously they cling to the meager experiences she
had with the friend of her childhood.

The difference of these two destinies, arising from the same
experience, is due to the fact that one ego has experienced development while the other has not. The janitor's daughter in
later years looks upon sexual intercourse as the same natural
and harmless thing it had seemed in her childhood. The owner's
daughter had experienced the influence of education and had
recognized its claims. Thus stimulated, her ego had forged its
ideals of womanly purity and lack of desire which, however,

could not agree with any sexual activity; her intellectual development had made unworthy her interest in the woman's part she was to play. This higher moral and intellectual evolution of her ego was in conflict with the claims of her sexuality.

I should like to consider today one more point in the development of the ego, partly because it opens wide vistas, partly because it will justify the sharp, perhaps unnatural line of division we are wont to draw between sexual and ego impulses. In estimating the several developments of ego and of libido, we must emphasize an aspect which has not frequently been appreciated heretofore. Both the ego and the libido are fundamentally heritages, abbreviated repetitions of an evolution which mankind has, in the course of long periods of time, traversed from primeval ages. The libido shows its phylogenetic origin most readily, I should say. Recall, if you please, that in one class of animals the genital apparatus is closely connected with the mouth, that in another it cannot be separated from the excretory apparatus, and in others it is attached to organs of locomotion. Of all these things you will find a most fascinating description in the valuable book of W. Bölsche. Animals portray, so to speak, all kinds of perversions which have become set as their permanent sexual organizations. In man this phylogenetic aspect is partly clouded by the circumstance that these activities, although fundamentally inherited, are achieved anew in individual development, presumably because the same conditions still prevail and still continue to exert their influence on each personality. I should say that originally they served to call forth an activity, where they now serve only as a stimulus for recollection. There is no doubt that in addition the course of development in each individual, which has been innately determined, may be disturbed or altered from without by recent influences. That power which has forced this development upon mankind, and which today maintains the identical pressure, is indeed known to us: it is the same self-denial enforced by the realities— or, given its big and actual name, *Necessity*, the struggle for existence, the 'Ανάγχη. This has been a severe teacher, but under him we have become potent. The neurotics are those children upon whom this severity has had a bad effect—but there is ris¹ in all education This appreciation of the struggle of life

the moving force of development need not prejudice us against
the importance of "innate tendencies in evolution" if their
existence can be proved.

It is worth noting that sexual instincts and instincts of self-
preservation do not behave similarly when they are confronted
with the necessities of actuality. It is easier to educate the
instincts of self-preservation and everything that is connected
with them; they speedily learn to adapt themselves to necessity
and to arrange their development in accordance with the mandates of fact. That is easy to understand, for they cannot procure the objects they require in any other way; without these
objects the individual must perish. The sex instincts are more
difficult to educate because at the outset they do not suffer
from the need of an object. As they are related almost para-
sitically to the other functions of the body and gratify themselves auto-erotically by way of their own body, they are at
first withdrawn from the educational influence of real necessity.
In most people, they maintain themselves in some way or other
during the entire course of life as those characteristics of obstinacy and inaccessibility to influence which are generally col-
lectively called unreasonableness. The education of youth generally comes to an end when the sexual demands are aroused
to their full strength. Educators know this and act accordingly;
but perhaps the results of psychoanalysis will influence them to
transfer the greatest emphasis to the education of the early years
of childhood, beginning with the suckling. The little human
being is frequently a finished product in his fourth or fifth year,
and only reveals gradually in later years what has long been
ready within him.

To appreciate the full significance of the aforementioned difference between the two groups of instincts, we must digress
considerably and introduce a consideration which we must needs
call *economic*. Thereby we enter upon one of the most important
but unfortunately one of the most obscure domains of psychoanalysis. We ask ourselves whether a fundamental purpose is
recognizable in the workings of our psychological apparatus,
and answer immediately that this purpose is the pursuit of
pleasurable excitement. It seems as if our entire psychological
activity were directed toward gaining pleasurable stimulation,

toward avoiding painful ones; that it is regulated automatically by the *principle of pleasure*. Now we should like to know, above all, what conditions cause the creation of pleasure and pain, but here we fall short. We may only venture to say that pleasurable excitation *in some way* involves lessening, lowering or obliterating the amount of stimuli present in the psychic apparatus. This amount, on the other hand, is increased by pain. Examination of the most intense pleasurable excitement accessible to man, the pleasure which accompanies the performance of the sexual act, leaves small doubt on this point. Since such processes of pleasure are concerned with the destinies of quantities of psychic excitation or energy, we call considerations of this sort economic. It thus appears that we can describe the tasks and performances of the psychic apparatus in different and more generalized terms than by the emphasis of the pursuit of pleasure. We may say that the psychic apparatus serves the purpose of mastering and bringing to rest the mass of stimuli and the stimulating forces which approach it. The sexual instincts obviously show their aim of pleasurable excitement from the beginning to the end of their development; they retain this original function without much change. The ego instincts strive at first for the same thing. But through the influence of their teacher, necessity, the ego instincts soon learn to adduce some qualification to the principle of pleasure. The task of avoiding pain becomes an objective almost comparable to the gain of pleasure; the ego learns that its direct gratification is unavoidably withheld, the gain of pleasurable excitement postponed, that always a certain amount of pain must be borne and certain sources of pleasure entirely relinquished. This educated ego has become "reasonable." It is no longer controlled by the principle of pleasure, but by the *principle of fact,* which at bottom also aims at pleasure, but pleasure which is postponed and lessened by considerations of fact.

The transition from the pleasure principle to that of fact is the most important advance in the development of the ego. We already know that the sexual instincts pass through this stage unwillingly and late. We shall presently learn the consequence to man of the fact that his sexuality admits of such a loose relation to the external realities of his life. Yet or

observation belongs here. Since the ego of man has, like the
libido, its history of evolution, you will not be surprised to hear
that there are "ego-regressions," and you will want to know what
role this return of the ego to former phases of development plays
in neurotic disease.

The Development of the Symptoms

IN the layman's eyes the symptom shows the nature of the disease, and cure means removal of symptoms. The physician, however, finds it important to distinguish the symptoms from the disease and recognizes that doing away with the symptoms is not necessarily curing the disease. Of course, the only tangible thing left over after the removal of the symptoms is the capacity to build new symptoms. Accordingly, for the time being, let us accept the layman's viewpoint and consider the understanding of the symptoms as equivalent to the understanding of the sickness.

The symptoms,—of course, we are dealing here with psychic (or psychogenic) symptoms, and psychic illness—are acts which are detrimental to life as a whole, or which are at least useless; frequently they are obnoxious to the individual who performs them and are accompanied by distaste and suffering. The principal injury lies in the psychic exertion which they cost, and in the further exertion needed to combat them. The price these efforts exact may, when there is an extensive development of the symptoms, bring about an extraordinary impoverishment of the personality of the patient with respect to his available psychic energy, and consequently cripple him in all the important tasks of life. Since such an outcome is dependent on the amount of energy so utilized, you will readily understand that "being sick" is essentially a practical concept. But if you take a theoretical standpoint and disregard these quantitative relations, you can readily say that we are all sick, or rather neurotic, since the conditions favorable to the development of symptoms are demonstrable also among normal persons.

As to the neurotic symptoms, we already know that they are the result of a conflict aroused by a new form of gratifying the libido. The two forces that have contended against each other meet once more in the symptom; they become reconciled through

311

the compromise of a symptom development. That is why the symptom is capable of such resistance; it is sustained from both sides. We also know that one of the two partners to the conflict is the unsatisfied libido, frustrated by reality, which must now seek other means for its satisfaction. If reality remains inflexible even where the libido is prepared to take another object in place of the one denied it, the libido will then finally be compelled to resort to regression and to seek gratification in one of the earlier stages in its organizations already out-lived, or by means of one of the objects given up in the past. Along the path of regression the libido is enticed by fixations which it has left behind at these stages in its development.

Here the development toward perversion branches off sharply from that of the neuroses. If the regressions do not awaken the resistance of the ego, then a neurosis does not follow and the libido arrives at some actual, even if abnormal, satisfaction. The ego, however, controls not alone consciousness, but also the approaches to motor innervation, and hence the realization of psychic impulses. If the ego then does not approve this regression, the conflict takes place. The libido is locked out, as it were, and must seek refuge in some place where it can find an outlet for its fund of energy, in accordance with the controlling demands for pleasurable gratification. It must withdraw from the ego. Such an evasion is offered by the fixations established in the course of its evolution and now traversed regressively, against which the ego had, at the time, protected itself by suppressions. The libido, streaming back, occupies these suppressed positions and thus withdraws from before the ego and its laws. At the same time, however, it throws off all the influences acquired under its tutelage. The libido could be guided so long as there was a possibility of its being satisfied; under the double pressure of external and internal denial it becomes unruly and harks back to former and more happy times. Such is its character, fundamentally unchangeable. The ideas which the libido now takes over in order to hold its energy belong to the system of the unconscious, and are therefore subject to its peculiar processes, especially elaboration and displacement. Conditions are set up here which are entirely comparable to those of dream formation. Just as the latent dream, the fulfillment of a wish-phantasy, is first built up in the unconsciousness, but must then pass through conscious processes before, censored and approved, it can enter into the compromise construction of the manifest dream, so the ideas representing the libido in the unconscious must still contend against the power of the fore-conscious ego. The opposition that has arisen against it in the ego follows it down by a "counter-siege" and forces it to choose such an expression as will serve at the same time to express itself. Thus, then, the symptom comes into being as a much distorted offshoot from the unconscious libidinous wish-fulfillment, an artificially selected ambiguity—with two entirely contradictory meanings. In this last point alone do we realize a difference between dream and symptom development, for the only fore-conscious purpose in dream formation is the maintenance of sleep, the exclusion from consciousness of anything which may disturb sleep; but it does not necessarily oppose the unconscious wish impulse with an insistent "No." Quite the contrary; the purpose of the dream may be more tolerant, because the situation of the sleeper is a less dangerous one. The exit to reality is closed only through the condition of sleep.

You see, this evasion which the libido finds under the conditions of the conflict is possible only by virtue of the existing fixations. When these fixations are taken in hand by the regression, the suppression is side-tracked and the libido, which must maintain itself under the conditions of the compromise, is led off or gratified. By means of such a detour by way of the unconscious and the old fixations, the libido has at last succeeded in breaking its way through to some sort of gratification, however extraordinarily limited this may seem and however unrecognizable any longer as a genuine satisfaction. Now allow me to add two further remarks concerning this final result. In the first place, I should like you to take note of the intimate connection between the libido and the unconscious on the one hand, and on the other of the ego, consciousness, and reality. The connection that is evidenced here, however, does not indicate that originally they in any way belong together. I should like you to bear continually in mind that everything I have said here, and all that will follow, pertains only to the symptom development of hysterical neurosis.

Where, now, can the libido find the fixations which it have in order to force its way through the suppressions?]

activities and experiences of infantile sexuality, in its abandoned component-impulses, its childish objects which have been given up. The libido again returns to them. The significance of this period of childhood is a double one; on the one hand, the instinctive tendencies which were congenital in the child first showed themselves at this time; secondly, at the same time, environmental influences and chance experiences were first awakening his other instincts. I believe our right to establish this bipartite division cannot be questioned. The assertion that the innate disposition plays a part is hardly open to criticism, but analytic experience actually makes it necessary for us to assume that purely accidental experiences of childhood are capable of leaving fixations of the libido. I do not see any theoretical difficulties here. Congenital tendencies undoubtedly represent the after-effects of the experiences of an earlier ancestry; they must also have once been acquired; without such acquired characters there could be no heredity. And is it conceivable that the inheritance of such acquired characters comes to a standstill in the very generation that we have under observation? The significance of infantile experience, however, should not, as is so often done, be completely ignored as compared with ancestral experiences or those of our adult years; on the contrary, they should meet with an especial appreciation. They have such important results because they occur in the period of uncompleted development, and because of this very fact are in a position to cause a traumatic effect. The researches on the mechanics of development by Roux and others have shown us that a needle prick into an embryonic cell mass which is undergoing division results in most serious developmental disturbances. The same injury to a larva or a completed animal can be borne without injury.

The libido fixation of adults, which we have referred to as representative of the constitutional factor in the etiological comparison of the neuroses, can be thought of, so far as we are concerned, as divisible into two separate factors, the inherited disposition and the tendency acquired in early childhood. We know that a schematic representation is most acceptable to the student. Let us combine these relations as follows:

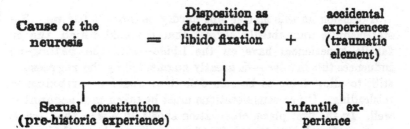

The hereditary sexual constitution provides us with manifold tendencies, varying with the special emphasis given one or the other component of the instinct, either individually or in combination. With the factor of infantile experience, there is again built up a complementary series within the sexual constitution which is perfectly comparable with our first series, namely, the gradations between disposition and the chance experiences of the adult. Here again we find the same extreme cases and similar relations in the matter of substitution. At this point the question becomes pertinent as to whether the most striking regressions of the libido, those which hark back to very early stages in sexual organization, are not essentially conditioned by the hereditary constitutional factor. The answer to this question, however, may best be put off until we are in a position to consider a wider range in the forms of neurotic disease.

Let us devote a little time to the consideration of the fact that analytic investigation of neurotics shows the libido to be bound up with the infantile sexual experiences of these persons. In this light they seem of enormous importance for both the life and health of mankind. With respect to therapeutic work their importance remains undiminished. But when we do not take this into account we can herein readily recognize the danger of being misled by the situation as it exists in neurotics into adopting a mistaken and one-sided orientation toward life. In figuring the importance of the infantile experiences we must also subtract the influences arising from the fact that the libido has returned to them by regression, after having been forced out of its later positions. Thus we approach the opposite conclusion, that experiences of the libido had no importance whatever in their own time, but rather acquired it at the time of regression. You will remember that we were led to a similar alternative in the discussion of the Oedipus-complex.

A decision on this matter will hardly be difficult for us. The statement is undoubtedly correct that the hold which the infantile experiences have on the libido—with the pathogenic influences this involves—is greatly augmented by the regression; still, to allow them to become definitive would nevertheless be misleading. Other considerations must be taken into account as well. In the first place, observation shows, in a way that leaves no room for doubt, that infantile experiences have their particular significance which is evidenced already during childhood. There are, furthermore, neuroses in children in which the factor of displacement in time is necessarily greatly minimized or is entirely lacking, since the illness follows as an immediate consequence of the traumatic experience. The study of these infantile neuroses keeps us from many dangerous misunderstandings of adult neuroses, just as the dreams of children similarly serve as the key to the understanding of the dreams of adults. As a matter of fact, the neuroses of children are very frequent, far more frequent than is generally believed. They are often overlooked, dismissed as signs of badness or naughtiness, and often suppressed by the authority of the nursery; in retrospect, however, they may be easily recognized later. They occur most frequently in the form of *anxiety hysteria*. What this implies we shall learn upon another occasion. When a neurosis breaks out in later life, analysis regularly shows that it is a direct continuation of that infantile malady which had perhaps developed only obscurely and incipiently. However, there are cases, as already stated, in which this childish nervousness continues, without any interruption, as a lifelong affliction. We have been able to analyze a very few examples of such neuroses during childhood, while they were actually going on; much more often we had to be satisfied with obtaining our insight into the childhood neurosis subsequently, when the patient is already well along in life, under conditions in which we are forced to work with certain corrections and under definite precautions.

Secondly, we must admit that the universal regression of the libido to the period of childhood would be inexplicable if there were nothing there which could exert an attraction for it. The fixation which we assume to exist towards specific developmental phases, conveys a meaning only if we think of it as stabilizing a definite amount of libidinous energy. Finally, I am able to remind you that here there exists a complementary relationship between the intensity and the pathogenic significance of the infantile experiences to the later ones which is similar to that studied in previous series. There are cases in which the entire causal emphasis falls upon the sexual experiences of childhood, in which these impressions take on an effect which is unmistakably traumatic and in which no other basis exists for them beyond what the average sexual constitution and its immaturity can offer. Side by side with these there are others in which the whole stress is brought to bear by the later conflicts, and the emphasis the analysis places on childhood impressions appears entirely as the work of regression. There are also extremes of "retarded development" and "regression," and between them every combination in the interaction of the two factors.

These relations have a certain interest for that pedagogy which assumes as its object the prevention of neuroses by an early interference in the sexual development of the child. So long as we keep our attention fixed essentially on the infantile sexual experiences, we readily come to believe we have done everything for the prophylaxis of nervous afflictions when we have seen to it that this development is retarded, and that the child is spared this type of experience. Yet we already know that the conditions for the causation of neuroses are more complicated and cannot in general be influenced through one single factor. The strict protection in childhood loses its value because it is powerless against the constitutional factor; furthermore, it is more difficult to carry out than the educators imagine, and it brings with it two new dangers that cannot be lightly dismissed. It accomplishes too much, for it favors a degree of sexual suppression which is harmful for later years, and it sends the child into life without the power to resist the violent onset of sexual demands that must be expected during puberty. The profit, therefore, which childhood prophylaxis can yield is most dubious; it seems, indeed, that better success in the prevention of neuroses can be gained by attacking the problem through a changed attitude toward facts.

Let us return to the consideration of the symptoms. They serve as substitutes for the gratification which has been forborne, by a regression of the libido to earlier days, with a return to former development phases in their choice of object and in their organization. We learned some time ago that the neurotic is held fast somewhere in his past; we now know that it is a period of his past in which his libido did not miss the satisfaction which made him happy. He looks for such a time in his life until he has found it, even though he must hark back to his suckling days as he retains them in his memory or as he reconstructs them in the light of later influences. The symptom in some way again yields the old infantile form of satisfaction, distorted by the censoring work of the conflict. As a rule it is converted into a sensation of suffering and fused with other causal elements of the disease. The form of gratification which the symptom yields has much about it that alienates one's sympathy. In this we omit to take into account, however, the fact that the patients do not recognize the gratification as such and experience the apparent satisfaction rather as suffering, and complain of it. This transformation is part of the psychic conflict under the pressure of which the symptom must be developed. What was at one time a satisfaction for the individual must now awaken his antipathy or disgust. We know a simple but instructive example for such a change of feeling. The same child that sucked the milk with such voracity from its mother's breast is apt to show a strong antipathy for milk a few years later, which is often difficult to overcome. This antipathy increases to the point of disgust when the milk, or any substituted drink, has a little skin over it. It is rather hard to throw out the suggestion that this skin calls up the memory of the mother's breast, which was once so intensely coveted. In the meantime, to be sure, the traumatic experience of weaning has intervened.

There is something else that makes the symptoms appear remarkable and inexplicable as a means of libidinous satisfaction. They in no way recall anything from which we normally are in the habit of expecting satisfaction. They usually require no object, and thereby give up all connection with external reality. We understand this to be a result of turning away from fact and of returning to the predominance of pleasurable gratification. But it is also a return to a sort of amplified autoeroticism, such as was yielded the sex impulse in its earliest satisfactions. In the place of a modification in the outside world, we have a physical change, in other words, an internal reaction in place of an external one, an adjustment instead of an activity. Viewed from a phylogenetic standpoint, this expresses a very significant regression. We will grasp this better when we consider it in connection with a new factor which we are still to discover from the analytic investigation of symptom development. Further, we recall that in symptom formation the same processes of the unconscious have been at work as in dream formation—elaboration and displacement. Similarly to the dream, the symptom represents a fulfillment, a satisfaction after the manner of the infantile; by the utmost elaboration this satisfaction can be compressed into a single sensation or innervation, or by extreme displacement it may be restricted to a tiny element of the entire libidinous complex. It is no wonder that we often have difficulties in recognizing in the symptom the libidinous satisfaction which we anticipate and always find verified.

I have indicated that we must still become familiar with a new factor. It is something really surprising and confusing. You know that by analysis of the symptoms we arrive at a knowledge of the infantile experiences upon which the libido is fixated and out of which the symptoms are formed. Well, the surprising thing is this, that these infantile scenes are not always true. Indeed, in the majority of cases they are untrue, and in some instances they are directly contrary to historical truth. You see that this discovery, as no other, serves either to discredit the analysis which has led to such a result, or to discredit the patients upon whose testimony the analysis, as well as the whole understanding of neuroses, is built up. In addition there is something else utterly confusing about it. If the infantile experiences, revealed by analysis, were in every case real, we should have the feeling of walking on sure ground; if they were regularly falsified, disclosed themselves as inventions or phantasies of the patients, we should have to leave this uncertain ground and find a surer footing elsewhere. But it is neither the one nor the other, for when we look into the matter we find that the childhood experiences which are recalled or reconstructed in the course of the analysis may in some instances be false, in others undeniably true, and in the majority a mixture of truth and fiction. The symptoms then are the representation of actual experiences to which we may

an influence in the fixation of the libido, or the representation
of phantasies of the patient which, of course, can be of no etiological significance. It is hard to find one's way here. The first
foothold is given perhaps by an analogous discovery, namely,
that the same scattered childhood memories that individuals
always have had and have been conscious of prior to an analysis
may be falsified as well, or at least may contain a generous
mixture of true and false. Evidence of error very seldom offers
difficulties, and we at least gain the satisfaction of knowing
that the blame for this unexpected disappointment is not to be
laid at the door of analysis, but in some way upon the patients.

After reflecting a bit we can easily understand what is so
confusing in this matter. It is the slight regard for reality,
the neglect to keep fact distinct from phantasy. We are apt to
feel insulted that the patient has wasted our time with invented
tales. There is an enormous gap in our thinking between reality
and invention and we accord an entirely different valuation to
reality. The patient, too, takes this same viewpoint in his
normal thinking. When he offers the material which, by way of
the symptom, leads back to the wish situations which are
modeled upon the childhood experiences, we are at first, to be
sure, in doubt whether we are dealing with reality or with
phantasy. Later certain traits determine this decision; we are
confronted with the task of acquainting the patient with them.
This can never be accomplished without difficulty. If at the
outset we tell him that he is going to reveal phantasies with which
he has veiled his childhood history, just as every people weaves
myths around its antiquity, we notice (to our comfort) that his
interest in the further pursuit of the subject suddenly di-
minishes. He, too, wants to discover realities, and despises all
"notions." But if until this is accomplished we allow him
to believe that we are investigating the actual occurrences of
his childhood, we run the risk of later being charged with error
and with our apparent gullibility. For a long time he is unable to reconcile himself to the idea of considering phantasy and
reality on equal terms and he tends, with reference to the
childish experiences to be explained, to neglect for the time
being the difference between the real and the imaginary. And
yet this is obviously the only correct attitude toward these
psychological products because they are, in a sense, real. It is

a fact that the patient is able to create such phantasies for him-self, and this is of scarcely less importance for his neurosis than if he had really undergone the experience which he imagines. These phantasies possess *psychological* reality in contrast to *physical* reality, and so we gradually come to understand that *in the realm of neuroses the psychological reality is the deter-mining factor.*

Among the experiences which recur continually in the early history of neurotics and, in fact, are never lacking, some are of particular significance and accordingly I consider them worthy of special treatment. I shall enumerate a few examples of this species: observation of the parental intercourse, seduction by an adult, and the threat of castration. It would be a grievous error to assume that physical reality can never be accorded them; this may often be proved beyond doubt by the testimony of adult relatives. So, for example, it is not at all unusual if the little boy who begins to play with his penis, and does not yet know that one must conceal this, is threatened by his parents or nurse with the cutting off of the organ or the guilty hand. Parents often admit upon questioning that they thought they had done the right thing by this intimidation; many individuals retain a correct, conscious memory of these threats, especially if it has occurred in later childhood. When the mother or some other woman makes the threat she usually delegates the responsibility of executing it to the father or to the doctor. In the famous *Struwwelpeter* by the pediatrist Hoffman, of Frankfort, rhymes which owe their popularity to his very fine understanding of the sexual and other complexes of childhood, you find a milder substitute for castration in the cutting off of the thumbs as a punishment for insistent sucking. But it is highly improbable that the threat of castration is actually made as often as it occurs in the analyses of neurotics. We are content to understand that the child imaginatively con-structs this threat for himself from suggestions, from the knowl-edge that auto-erotic satisfaction is forbidden, and from the impression of castration he has received in discovering the fe-male genital. It is, moreover, in no way impossible tha' little child, so long as he is not credited with any understa or memory, will, even in families outside the proletariat, b a witness to the sexual act between his parents or some group-ups, and it cannot be disproved that the child *subsequently* understands this impression, and may react upon it. But when this intercourse is described with minute details which could hardly have been observed, or if it turns out to be, as it so frequently does, an intercourse which was not face to face, *more ferarum*, there is no longer any doubt that this phantasy is derived from the observation of the intercourse of animals (dogs) and the unsatisfied curiosity of the child in his period of puberty. The greatest feat of the imagination is the phantasy of having witnessed the coitus of the parents while still unborn in the mother's womb. Of especial interest is the phantasy of having been seduced, because so often it is not a phantasy at all, but a real memory. But luckily it is not real so often as first appears from the results of analysis. Seduction by older children, or children of the same age, is much more frequent than seduction by adults, and if, in the case of little girls, the father quite regularly appears as the seducer in the occurrences which they relate, neither the fantastic nature of this accusation nor its motive can be doubted. The child as a rule covers the auto-erotic period of his sexual activity, where there has been no actual seduction, with the seduction-phantasy. He spares himself the shame of onanism by imagining the presence of an object for his desires in that early period. As a matter of fact, you must not be misled in attributing sexual misuse of the child by its nearest male relatives solely and always to phantasy. Most analysts have probably treated cases in which such relations were real and could be proved beyond doubt, with the qualification that in such cases they belong to the later years of childhood and were transposed to an earlier time.

We cannot avoid the impression that such experiences of childhood are in some way necessary to the neurosis, that they are claimed by its iron rule. If they exist in reality, then well and good, but if reality has withheld them they are constructed from suggestions and supplemented by the imagination. The result is the same, and to this day we have been unable to trace any difference in the results, whether fancy or fact played the larger part in these childish occurrences. Here again we encounter one of the complementary relationships so frequently met with; it is, to be sure, the most estranging of all those we have become acquainted with. Whence comes the need for these phantasies, and the material for them? There can be no doubt as to the sources of the impulse, but we must explain why the same phantasies are always created with the same content. I have an answer in readiness which I know you will think very far-fetched. I am of the opinion that these *primal phantasies*— so I should like to term these, and certainly some others also— are a phylogenetic possession. In them the individual reaches out beyond his own life, into the experiences of antiquity, where his own experience has become all too rudimentary. It seems very possible to me that everything which is obtained during an analysis in the guise of phantasy, the seduction of children, the release of sexual excitement by watching parental intercourse, the threat of castration—or rather castration itself— were once realities in the primeval existence of mankind and that the imaginative child is merely filling in the gaps of individual truth with prehistoric truth. We have again and again suspected that the psychology of neuroses stores up more of the antiquities of human development than all other sources.

What we have just discussed makes it necessary for us to enter further into the origin and significance of that mental activity that is called imagination. As you well know, it enjoys universal esteem, although we have never clearly understood its place in the psychic life. I have this much to say about it. As you know, the ego of man is slowly educated by the influence of external necessity to an appreciation of reality and a pursuit of the principle of reality, and must therefore renounce temporarily or permanently various objects and goals of its strivings for satisfaction, sexual and otherwise. But renunciation of gratification has always been difficult for man. He cannot accomplish it without something in the nature of compensation. Accordingly he has reserved for himself a psychological activity wherein all these abandoned sources of pleasures and means of pleasurable gratification are granted a further existence, a form of existence in which they are freed from the requirements of reality and what we like to call the test of reality. Every impulse is soon transformed into the form of its own fulfillment. There is no doubt that dwelling on the imagined fulfillment of a given wish affords some satisfaction, although the realization that it is unreal is unobscured. In the activity of the imagination, man enjoys that freedom from external compulsion that he has long since renounced. He has made it possible to be alternately a pleasure-seeking animal and a reasoning human being. He finds that the scant satisfaction that he can force out of reality is not enough. "There is no getting along without auxiliary-constructions," Th. Fontaine once said. The creation of the psychic realm of fancy has its complete counterpart in the establishment of "preserves" and "conservation projects" in those places where the demands of husbandry, traffic and industry threaten quickly to change the original face of the earth into something unrecognizable. The national reserves maintain this old condition of things, which otherwise has everywhere been regretfully sacrificed to necessity. Everything may grow and spread there as it will, even that which is useless and harmful. The psychic realm of phantasy is such a reservation withdrawn from the principles of reality.

The best known productions of phantasy are the so-called "day dreams," which we already know, pictured satisfactions of ambitious, of covetous and erotic wishes, which flourish the more grandly the more reality admonishes them to modesty and patience. There is unmistakably shown in them the nature of imaginative happiness, the restoration of the independence of pleasurable gratification from the acquiescence of reality. We know such day dreams are nuclei and models for the dreams of night. The night dream is essentially nothing but a day dream, distorted by the nocturnal forms of psychological activity, and made available by the freedom which the night gives to instinctive impulses. We have already become acquainted with the idea that a day dream is not necessarily conscious, that there are also unconscious day dreams. Such unconscious day dreams are as much the source of night dreams as of neurotic symptoms.

The significance of phantasy for the development of symptoms will become clear to you by the following: We have said that in a case of renunciation, the libido occupies regressively the positions once abandoned by it, to which, nevertheless, it has clung in certain ways. We shall neither retract this statement nor correct it, but we shall insert a missing link. How does the libido find its way to these points of fixation? Well, every object and tendency of the libido that has been abandoned, is not abandoned in every sense of the word. They, or their derivatives, are still held in presentations of the phantasy, with a certain degree of intensity. The libido need only retire to the imagination in order to find from them the open road to all suppressed fixations. These phantasies were happy under a sort of tolerance, there was no conflict between them and the ego, no matter how acute the contrast, so long as a certain condition was observed—a condition *quantitative* in nature that is now disturbed by the flowing back of the libido to the phantasies. By this addition the accumulation of energy in the phantasies is heightened to such a degree that they become assertive and develop a pressure in the direction of realization. But that makes a conflict between them and the ego inevitable. Whether formerly conscious or unconscious, they now are subject to suppression by the ego and are victims to the attraction of the unconscious. The libido wanders from phantasies now unconscious to their sources in unconsciousness, and back to its own points of fixation.

The return of the libido to phantasy is an intermediate step on the road to symptom development and well deserves a special designation. C. G. Jung coined for it the very appropriate name of *introversion*, but inappropriately he also lets it stand for other things. Let us therefore retain the idea that introversion signifies the turning aside of the libido from the possibilities of actual satisfaction and the excessive accumulation of the phantasies hitherto tolerated as harmless. An introvert is not yet a neurotic, but he finds himself in a labile situation; he must develop symptoms at the next dislocation of forces, if he does not find other outlets for his pent-up libido. The intangible, nature of neurotic satisfaction and the neglect of the difference between imagination and reality are already determined by arrest in the phase of introversion.

You have certainly noticed that in the last discussions I have introduced a new factor into the structure of the etiological chain, namely, the quantity, the amount of energy that comes under consideration. We must always take this factor into account. Purely qualitative analysis of the etiological conditions is not sufficient. Or, to put it in another way, a *dynamic* conception alone of these psychic processes is not enough; there is need of an *economic* viewpoint. We must say to ourselves that the conflict between two impulses is not released before occupation-intensities have been reached, even though tl

tative conditions have long been potent. Similarly, the pathogenic significance of the constitutional factors is guided by
how much *more* of a given component impulse is present in the
predisposition over and above that of another; one can even
conceive the predispositions of all men to be qualitatively the
same and to be differentiated only by these quantitative conditions. The quantitative factor is no less important for the power
of resistance against neurotic ailments. It depends upon *what
amount* of unused libido a person can hold freely suspended,
and upon *how large a fraction* of the libido he is able to direct
from the sexual path to the goal of sublimation. The final goal
of psychological activity, which may be described qualitatively
as striving towards pleasure-acquisition and avoidance of unpleasantness, presents itself in the light of economic considerations as the task of overcoming the gigantic stimuli at work in
the psychological apparatus, and to prevent those obstructions
which cause unpleasantness.

So much I wanted to tell you about symptom development
in the neuroses. Yes, but do not let me neglect to emphasize this
especially: everything I have said here relates to the symptom
development in hysteria. Even in compulsion neuroses, which
retain the same fundamentals, much is found that is different.
The counter-siege directed against the claims of the instincts,
of which we have spoken in connection with hysteria, press to
the fore in compulsion neuroses, and control the clinical picture
by means of so-called "reaction-formations." The same kind
and more far-reaching variations are discoverable among the
other neuroses, where the investigations as to the mechanism of
symptom development have in no way been completed.

Before I leave you today I should like to have your attention
for a while for an aspect of imaginative life which is worthy
of the most general interest. For there is a way back from
imagination to reality and that is—art. The artist is an incipient
introvert who is not far from being a neurotic. He is impelled
by too powerful instinctive needs. He wants to achieve honor,
power, riches, fame and the love of women. But he lacks the
means of achieving these satisfactions. So like any other unsatisfied person, he turns away from reality, and transfers all
his interests, his libido, too, to the elaboration of his imaginary
wishes, all of which might easily point the way to neurosis. A

great many factors must combine to present this termination of his development; it is well known how often artists especially suffer from a partial inhibition of their capacities through neurosis. Apparently their constitutions are strongly endowed with an ability to sublimize and to shift the suppression determining their conflicts. The artist finds the way back to reality in this way. He is not the only one who has a life of imagination. The twilight-realm of phantasy is upheld by the sanction of humanity and every hungry soul looks here for help and sympathy. But for those who are not artists, the ability to obtain satisfaction from imaginative sources is very restricted. Their relentless suppressions force them to be satisfied with the sparse day dreams which may become conscious. If one is a real artist he has more at his disposal. In the first place, he understands how to elaborate his day dreams so that they lose their essentially personal element, which would repel strangers, and yield satisfaction to others as well. He also knows how to disguise them so that they do not easily disclose their origin in their despised sources. He further possesses the puzzling ability of molding a specific material into a faithful image of the creatures of his imagination, and then he is able to attach to this representation of his unconscious phantasies so much pleasurable gratification that, for a time at least, it is able to outweigh and release the suppressions. If he is able to accomplish all this, he makes it possible for others, in their return, to obtain solace and consolation from their own unconscious sources of gratification which had become inaccessible. He wins gratitude and admiration for himself and so, by means of his imagination, achieves the very things which had at first only an imaginary existence for him: honor, power, and the love of women.

TWENTY-FOURTH LECTURE

GENERAL THEORY OF THE NEUROSES

Ordinary Nervousness

IN our last discussion we accomplish a difficult task. Now I shall temporarily leave our subject and address myself to you.

For I know quite well that you are dissatisfied. You thought that an introduction to psychoanalysis would be quite a different matter. You expected to hear vivid illustrations instead of theories. You will tell me that when I gave you the illustration of "on the ground floor in the first story," you had grasped something of the causation of neurosis, only of course this should have been a real observation and not an imaginary story. Or, when in the beginning I described two symptoms (not imaginary also, let us hope) whose analysis revealed a close connection with the life of the patient, you first came to grasp the meaning of the symptoms and you hoped that I would proceed in the same way. Instead I have given you theories—lengthy, difficult to see in perspective and incomplete, to which something new was constantly being added. I worked with conceptions that I had not previously presented to you, abandoned descriptive for dynamic conceptions, and these in turn for economic ones. I made it hard for you to understand how many of the artificial terms I made use of still carry the same meaning and are used interchangeably only for the sake of euphony. Finally, I allowed broad conceptions to pass in review before you: the principles of pleasure and of fact and their phylogenetically inherited possession; and then, instead of introducing you to definite facts, I allowed them to become increasingly vague till they seemed to fade into dim distances.

Why did I not begin my introduction to the theory of neurosis with the facts that you yourselves know about nervousness, with something that has always ———— your interest, with the peculiar temperament of nervous people, their incomprehensible reactions to external influences, to human intercourse, their irritability, their uselessness? Why did I not lead you step by step from the understanding of simple, everyday forms to the problems of mysterious and extreme manifestations of nervousness?

I cannot even say that you are wrong. I am not so infatuated with my art of representation as to see some special attraction in every blemish. I myself believe that I could have proceeded differently, to your better advantage, and this indeed had been my intention. But one cannot always carry out one's sensible intentions. The nature of the subject matter issues its own commands, and easily modifies our plans. Even so usual a performance as the organization of well-known material is not entirely subject to the particular purposes of the author. It forms itself as it will and later one wonders why it turned out so and not otherwise.

Probably one of the reasons is that the title, *A General Introduction to Psychoanalysis,* no longer applies to this part, which deals with the neuroses. The introduction to psychoanalysis is found in the study of errors and the dream; the theory of neurosis is psychoanalysis itself. I do not think that in so short a time I could have given you a knowledge of the theory of neurosis other than in concentrated form. It was necessary to present to you connectedly the meaning and interpretation of the symptoms, their external and internal conditions and their bearing on the mechanism of symptom formation. This I have attempted to do; it is practically the nucleus of the material that modern psychoanalysis is able to offer. We had to say quite a good deal concerning the libido and its development, and something as well concerning the development of the ego. The introduction had already prepared you for the presuppositions of our technique, for the large aspects of the unconscious and of suppression (resistance). In a subsequent lecture you will learn from what points psychoanalysis proceeds organically. For the present I have not sought to hide from you the fact that all our results are based on the study of a single group of nervous affections, the so-called transference neuroses. Though you have gained no positive knowledge and have not retained every detail, still I hope that you have a fair picture of the methods, the problems and the results of psychoanalysis.

I have assumed that it was your wish for me to begin my presentation of neuroses with a description of nervous behavior, the nature of neurotic suffering, and the way in which the nervous meet the conditions of their illness and adapt themselves to these. Such subject matter is certainly interesting and well worth knowing. It is moreover not very hard to handle, yet it is not wise to begin with its consideration. There is danger of not discovering the unconscious, of overlooking the great significance of the libido, of judging all conditions as they appear to the ego of the nervous person. It is obvious that this ego is neither a reliable nor an impartial authority. For this very ego is the force that denies and suppresses the unconscious; when the unconscious is concerned, how then could we expect justice to be done? The rejected claims of sexuality stand first in the line of these suppressions; it is natural that from the standpoint of the ego we can never learn their extent and significance. As soon as we attain to the point of view of suppression, we are sufficiently warned not to make one of the contending factions, above all not to make the victor judge of the struggle. We are prepared to find that the testimony of the ego may lead us astray. If one is to believe the evidence of the ego, it would appear to have been active all along, all its symptoms would have been actively willed and formed. Yet we know that it has passively allowed a great deal to occur, a fact which it subsequently seeks to conceal and to palliate. To be sure, it does not always attempt this; in the case of the symptoms of compulsion neurosis it must admit that it is being opposed by something alien, which it can resist only with difficulty.

Whoever does not heed these warnings not to mistake the prevarications of the ego for truth, has clear sailing; he avoids all the resistances which oppose the psychoanalytic emphasis upon the unconscious, on sexuality, and on the passiveness of the ego. He will assert with Alfred Adler that the "nervous character" is the cause instead of the result of the neurosis, but he will not be able to explain a single detail of symptom formation or to interpret a single dream.

You will ask: Is it not possible to do justice to the part the ego plays in nervousness and in symptom formation without crudely neglecting the factors revealed by psychoanalysis? I answer you: Surely it must be possible and at some time or other it will take place; but the methods by which we organize the work of psychoanalysis do not favor our beginning with just this task. We can foresee the time when this task will claim the attention of psychoanalysis. There are forms of neuroses, the so-called narcistic neuroses, in which the ego is far more deeply involved than in anything we have studied heretofore. The analytic investigation of these conditions will enable us to judge reliably and impartially the part that the ego plays in neurotic illness.

One of the relations which the ego bears to its neurosis is so obvious that it must be considered at the very outset. In no case does it seem to be absent, and it is most clearly recognizable in the traumatic neuroses, conditions which we do not as yet clearly understand. You must know that in the causation and mechanisms of all possible forms of neurosis, the same factors are active again and again; it is only the emphasis that is shifted from one to the other of these factors in symptom formation. The members of a company of actors each have certain parts to play—hero, villain, confidant, etc.—yet each will select a different drama for his benefit. Thus the phantasies which undergo conversion into symptoms are especially easy to detect in hysteria; compulsion neuroses are essentially dominated by the reactionary formations, or counter-seizures of the ego; what we designate as *secondary elaboration* in dreams dominates paranoia in the form of delusions, etc.

In traumatic neuroses, particularly if they are caused by the horrors of war, we are especially impressed by a selfish ego-impulse which seeks protection and personal advantage. This in itself is not a sufficient cause for illness, but it can favor its beginning and also feed its needs once it has been established. This motive serves to protect the ego from the dangers whose imminence precipitated the disease, and does not permit convalescence until the recurrence of these dangers seems impossible, or until compensation has been obtained for the danger that has been undergone.

But the ego betrays similar interest in the origin and maintenance of all other neuroses. We have already said that the ego suffers the symptom to exist, because one of its phases gratifies the egoistic tendency toward suppression. Besides, the ending of the conflict by means of symptom development is the path of least resistance, and a most convenient solution for the principle of pleasure. Through symptom formation the ego is undoubtedly spared a severe and unpleasant inner task. There are cases where even the physician must admit that the resolution of the conflict into neurosis is the most harmless outcome and one most easily tolerated by society. Do not be surprised, then, to learn that occasionally even the physician takes the part of the illness he is battling against. He does not have to restrict himself to the role of the fanatic warrior for health in all situations of life. He knows that the world contains not only neurotic misery, but also real, incurable suffering. He knows that necessity may even require a human being to sacrifice his health, and he learns that by this sacrifice on the part of one individual untold wretchedness may be spared for many others. So if we say that the neurotic escapes the conflict *by taking refuge in illness*, we must admit that in some cases this escape is justifiable, and the physician who has diagnosed the state of affairs will retire silently and tactfully.

But let us not consider these special cases in our further discussion. In average cases the ego, by having recourse to neurosis, obtains a certain inner *advantage from the disease*. Under certain conditions of life, there may also be derived a tangible external advantage, more or less valuable in reality. Let me direct your attention to the most frequent occurrences of this sort. Women who are brutally treated and mercilessly exploited by their husbands almost always adopt the evasion of the neurosis, provided that their predisposition permits this. This usually follows when the woman is too cowardly or too virtuous to seek secret solace in the arms of another, or when she dare not separate from her husband in the face of all opposition, when she has no prospect of maintaining herself or of finding a better husband and especially when her sexual emotions still bind her to this brutal man. Her illness becomes a weapon in her struggle with him, one that she can use for self-protection and misuse for purposes of vengeance. She probably dare not complain of her marriage, but she can complain of her illness. The doctor becomes her assistant. She forces her inconsiderate husband to spare her, to attend to her wishes, to permit her absence from the he   · free her from the oppressions of her married li   uch external or accidental gain through illness is considerable and can find no substitute in fact, you can prophesy that the possibility of influencing neurosis through therapy is very slight.

You will tell me that what I have said about the advantage gained from the disease speaks entirely for the hypothesis I have rejected, namely, that the ego itself wills and creates the neurosis. Just a moment! It probably does not mean more than that the ego passively suffers the neurosis to exist, which it is unable to prevent anyway. It makes the most of the neurosis, if anything can be made of it at all. This is only one side of the question, the advantageous side. The ego is willing to endure the advantages of the neurosis, but there are not only advantages. As a rule it soon appears that the ego has made a poor deal in accepting the neurosis. It has paid too high a price for the mitigation of the conflict; and the sensations of suffering which the symptoms bring with them are perhaps every bit as bad as the agonies of conflict, usually they cause even greater discomfort. The ego wants to rid itself of the pain of the symptoms without relinquishing the gain of illness, and that is impossible. Thus the ego is discovered as by no means so active as it had thought itself to be, and this we want to keep in mind.

If you were to come into contact with neurotics as a physician, you would soon cease to expect that those who complain most woefully of their illness are the ones who will oppose its therapy with the least resistance or who will welcome any help. On the contrary, you would readily understand that everything contributing to the advantage derived from the disease will strengthen the resistance to the suppression and heighten the difficulty of the therapy. We must also add another and later advantage to the gain of illness which is born with the symptom. If a psychic organization, such as this illness, has persisted for a long time, it finally behaves as an independent unit, it expresses something like self-preservation, attains a kind of *modus vivendi* between itself and other parts of psychic life, even those that are fundamentally hostile to it. And occasions will probably arise where it can prove again to be both useful and valuable, by which it will attain a *secondary function*, which gives strength to its existence. Instead of an illustration from pathology take a striking example from everyday life.

An efficient workman who earns his living is crippled for his occupation by some disaster; his work is over for him. After a while, however, he receives a small accident insurance, and learns to exploit his injury by begging. His new existence, though most undesirable, is based upon the very thing that robbed him of his former maintenance. If you could cure his defect, he would be without a means of subsistence, he would have no livelihood. The question would arise: Is he capable of resuming his former work? That which corresponds to such secondary exploitation of illness in neurosis we may add to the primary benefit derived therefrom and may term it a *secondary* advantage of disease.

In general I should like to warn you not to underestimate the practical significance of the advantage from illness and yet not to be too much impressed by it theoretically. Aside from the previously recognized exceptions, I am always reminded of Oberländer's pictures on "the intelligence of animals" which appeared in the *Fliegende Blätter*. An Arab is riding a camel on a narrow path cut through a steep mountain side. At a turn of the trail he is suddenly confronted by a lion who makes ready to spring. He sees no way out, on one side the precipice, on the other the abyss; retreat and flight—both are impossible; he gives himself up as lost. Not so the camel. He leaps into the abyss with his rider—and the lion is left in the lurch. The help of neurosis is as a rule no kinder to the rider. It may be due to the fact that the settlement of the conflict through symptom development is nevertheless an automatic process, not able to meet the demands of life, and for whose sake man renounces the use of his best and loftiest powers. If it were possible to choose, it were indeed best to perish in an honorable struggle with destiny.

I still owe you further explanation as to why, in my presentation of the theory of neurosis, I did not proceed from ordinary nervousness as a starting point. You may assume that, had I done this, the proof of the sexual origin of neurosis would have been more difficult for me, and so I refrained. There you are mistaken. In transference neurosis we must work at interpretations of the symptoms to arrive at this conclusion. In the ordinary forms of the so-called true neuroses, however, the etiological significance of sexual life is a crude fact open to observa-

tion. I discovered it twenty years ago when I asked myself
one day why we regularly barred out questions concerning
sexual activity in examining nervous patients. At that time I
sacrificed my popularity among my patients to my investigations, yet after a brief effort I could state that no neurosis, no
true neurosis at least, is present with a normal sexual life. Of
course, this statement passes too lightly over the individual
differences, it is unclear through the vagueness with which it
uses the term "normal," but even to-day it retains its value
for purposes of rough orientation. At that time I reached the
point of drawing comparisons between certain forms of nervousness and sexual abnormalities, and I do not doubt that I could
repeat the same observations now, if similar material were at
my disposal. I frequently noticed that a man who contented
himself with incomplete sexual gratification, with manual anon-
ism, for instance, would suffer from a true neurosis, and that
this neurosis would promptly give way to another form, if another sexual regime no less harmful were substituted. From
the change in the condition of the patient I was able to guess
the change in the mode of his sexual life. At that time I
learned to hold obstinately to my conjectures until I had overcome the patient's prevarications and had forced him to confirm
my suppositions. To be sure, then he preferred to consult other
physicians who did not inquire so insistently into his sexual life.

At that time it did not escape my notice that the origin of
the disease could not always be traced back to sexual life;
sexual abnormality would cause the illness in one person, while
another would fall ill because he had lost his fortune or had
suffered an exhausting organic disease. We gained insight into
this variation by means of the interrelations between the ego
and the libido, and the more profound our insight became, the
more satisfactory were the results. A person begins to suffer
from neurosis when his ego has lost the capacity of accommo-
dating the libido. The stronger the ego, the easier the solution
of the problem; a weakening of the ego from any cause whatsoever has the same effect as a superlative increase of the claims
of the libido. There are other and more intimate relations
between the ego and the libido which I shall not discuss, as we
are not concerned with them here. To us it is of enlightening
significance that in every case, regardless of the way in which

the illness was caused, the symptoms of neurosis were opposed by the libido and thus gave evidence for its abnormal use.

Now, however, I want to draw your attention to the difference between the symptoms of the true neuroses and the psycho-neuroses, the first group of which, the transference neurosis, has occupied us considerably. In both cases the symptoms proceed from the libido. They are accordingly abnormal uses of it, substitutes for gratification. But the symptoms of the true neurosis —such as pressure in the head, sensations of pain, irritability of an organ, weakening or inhibition of a function—these have no meaning, no psychic significance. They are manifested not only in the body, as for instance hysteric symptoms, but are in themselves physical processes whose creation is devoid of all the complicated psychic mechanism with which we have become acquainted. They really embody the character that has so long been attributed to the psychoneurotic symptom. But how can they then correspond to uses of the libido, which we have come to know as a psychological force? That is quite simple. Let me recall one of the very first objections that was made to psychoanalysis. It was stated that psychoanalysis was concerned with a purely psychological theory of neurotic manifestations; that this was a hopeless outlook since psychological theories could never explain illness. The objectors chose to forget that the sexual function is neither purely psychic nor merely somatic. It influences physical as well as psychic life. In the symptoms of the psychoneuroses we have recognized the expression of a disturbance in psychic processes. And so we shall not be surprised to discover that the true neuroses are the direct somatic consequences of sexual disturbances.

The medical clinic gives us a valuable suggestion (observed by many research workers) for the comprehension of the true neuroses. In all the details of their symptomatology, and as well in their characteristic power to influence all organic systems and all functions, the true neuroses reveal a marked similarity to the conditions of those diseases which originate through the chronic influence of foreign poisons and as well through their acute diminution; with conditions prevalent in intoxication and abstinence. The two groups of conditions are brought still closer together by the relation of intermediate conditions, which, following M. Basedowi, we have learned to attribute to the influ-

ence of toxic substances, but of toxins, however, which are not
introduced into the body from without, but arise in its own
metabolism. These analogies, I think, lead us directly to the
consideration of these neuroses as disturbances in sexual metabolism. It may be that more sexual toxins are produced than the
individual can dispose of, or that inner, even psychic conditions,
stand in the way of the proper elaboration of these substances.
The language of the people has always favored such assumptions
as to the nature of sexual desires. It calls love an "intoxication"; it will have love-madness aroused through potions, and
thus sees the motive force removed, as it were, to the outer world.
For the rest, the phrase "sexual metabolism" or "chemism of
sexuality" is a chapter-head without content. We know nothing
about it and cannot even decide whether we are to assume two
sexual substances, the male and the female, or, if there is
only *one* sexual toxin, which to consider the carrier of all the
stimulating power of the libido. The structure of psychoanalysis
that we have erected is really only a superstructure which at
some future time must be placed upon its organic foundation;
but what this is we do not know as yet.

Psychoanalysis is characterized as a science, not by reason of
the subject matter it handles but by the technique it employs.
This can be employed in dealing with the history of civilization,
the science of religion or mythology, as well as with the theory
of neurosis, without altering its character. The revealing of the
unconscious in psychic life is all it aims to accomplish. The
problems of the true neuroses, whose symptoms probably originate in direct toxic damage, yield no point of attack to psychoanalysis. Psychoanalysis can do little for their elucidation, and
must leave the task to biological-medical research. Perhaps you
understand now why I did not choose to organize my material
differently. If I had given to you an *Introduction to the
Theory of the Neuroses* as you wished, it would unquestionably
have been correct to proceed from the simple forms of the true
neuroses to those complex illnesses caused by a disturbance of
the libido. In discussing the true neuroses I would have had to
bring together the facts we have gleaned from various quarters
and present what we think we know of them. Only later, under
the psychoneuroses, would psychoanalysis have been discussed
as the most important technical aid for insight into these con-

ditions. I had, however, intended and announced *A General Introduction to Psychoanalysis,* and it seemed to me more important to give you an idea of psychoanalysis than to present certain positive facts about neuroses; and so I could not place the true neuroses into the foreground, for they prove sterile for the purposes of psychoanalysis. I believe that I have made the wiser choice for you, since psychoanalysis deserves the interest of every educated person because of its profound hypotheses and far-reaching connections. The theory of neurosis, on the other hand, is a chapter of medicine like any other.

You are, however, justified in expecting some interest on our part in the true neuroses. Because of their intimate connection with psychoneuroses we find this decidedly necessary. I shall tell you then that we distinguish three pure forms of true neuroses: *neurasthenia, anxiety neurosis* and *hypochondria.* Even this classification has not remained uncontradicted. The terms are all widely used, but their connotation is vague and uncertain. Besides, there are in this world of confusion physicians who object to any distinctions between manifestations, any emphasis of clinical detail, who do not even recognize the separation of true neuroses and psychoneuroses. I think they have gone too far and have not chosen the road which leads to progress. The types of neuroses we have mentioned occur occasionally in pure form; more often they are blended with one another or with a psychoneurotic condition. This need not discourage us to the extent of abandoning the task of distinction. Think of the difference between the study of minerals and that of ores in mineralogy. Minerals are described as individuals; frequently of course they occur as crystals, separated sharply from their surroundings. Ores consist of an aggregate of minerals which have coalesced not accidentally, but as a result of the conditions of their origin. We understand too little of the process of development of neuroses, to create anything similar to the study of ores. But we are surely working in the right direction when we isolate the known clinical factors, comparable to the separate minerals, from the great mass.

A noteworthy connection between the symptoms of the true neuroses and the psychoneuroses adds a valuable contribution to our knowledge of symptom formation in the latter. The symptom in the true neuroses is frequently the nucleus and incipient stage of development of the psychoneurotic symptom. Such a connection is most easily observed between neurasthenia and the transference neuroses, which are termed conversion hysteria, between anxiety neurosis and anxiety hysteria, but also between hypochondria and paraphrenia (dementia praecox and paranoia), forms of neuroses of which we shall speak subsequently. Let us take as an illustration the hysteric headache or backache. Analysis shows that through elaboration and displacement this pain has become the gratification substitute for a whole series of libidinous phantasies or reminiscences. But once upon a time this pain was real, a direct sexual toxic symptom, the physical expression of libidinous excitation. We do not wish to assert, by any means, that all hysteric symptoms can be traced to such a nucleus, but it is true that this is frequently the case, and that all influences upon the body through libidinous excitation, whether normal or pathological, are especially significant for the symptom development in hysteria. They play the part of the grain of sand which the mollusc has enveloped in mother-of-pearl. In the same way passing signs of sexual excitation, which accompany the sexual act, are used by psychoneurosis as the most convenient and appropriate material for symptom formation.

A similar procedure is of diagnostic and therapeutic interest especially. Persons who are disposed to be neurotic, without suffering from a flourishing neurosis, frequently set in motion the work of symptom development as the result of an abnormal physical change—often an inflammation or an injury. This development rapidly makes the symptom given by reality the representative of the unconscious phantasies that had been lurking for an opportunity to seize upon a means of expression. In such a case the physician will try different ways of therapy. Either he will try to do away with the organic basis without bothering about its noisy neurotic elaboration, or he will struggle with the neurosis brought out by the occasion, and ignore its organic cause. The result will justify now one, now the other method of procedure; no general laws can be laid down for such mixed cases.

TWENTY-FIFTH LECTURE

GENERAL THEORY OF THE NEUROSES

Fear and Anxiety

PROBABLY you will term what I told you about ordinary nervousness in my last lecture most fragmentary and unsatisfactory information. I know this, and I think you were probably most surprised that I did not mention fear, which most nervous people complain of and describe as their greatest source of suffering. It can attain a terrible intensity which may result in the wildest enterprises. But I do not wish to fall short of your expectations in this matter. I intend, on the contrary, to treat the problem of the fear of nervous people with great accuracy and to discuss it with you at some length.

Fear itself needs no introduction; everyone has at some time or other known this sensation or, more precisely, this effect. It seems to me that we never seriously inquired why the nervous suffered so much more and so much more intensely under this condition. Perhaps it was thought a matter of course; it is usual to confuse the words "nervous" and "anxious" as though they meant the same thing. That is unjustifiable; there are anxious people who are not nervous, and nervous people who suffer from many symptoms, but not from the tendency to anxiety.

However that may be, it is certain that the problem of fear is the meeting point of many important questions, an enigma whose complete solution would cast a flood of light upon psychic life. I do not claim that I can furnish you with this complete solution, but you will certainly expect psychoanalysis to deal with this theme in a manner different from that of the schools of medicine. These schools seem to be interested primarily in the anatomical cause of the condition of fear. They say the medulla oblongata is irritated, and the patient learns that he is suffering from neurosis of the nervus vague. The medulla oblongata is a very serious and beautiful object. I remember exactly how much time and trouble I devoted to the study of it, years ago. But today I must say that I know of nothing more indifferent to me for the psychological comprehension of fear, than knowledge of the nerve passage through which these sensations must pass.

One can talk about fear for a long time without even touching upon nervousness. You will understand me without more ado, when I term this fear *real* fear in contrast to *neurotic* fear. Real fear seems quite rational and comprehensible to us. We may testify that it is a reaction to the perception of external danger, viz., harm that is expected and foreseen. It is related to the flight reflex and may be regarded as an expression of the instinct of self-preservation. And so the occasions, viz., the objects and situations which arouse fear, will depend largely on our knowledge of and our feeling of power over the outer world. We deem it quite a matter of course that the savage fears a cannon or an eclipse of the sun, while the white man, who can handle the instrument and prophesy the phenomenon, does not fear these things. At other times superior knowledge promulgates fear, because it recognizes the danger earlier. The savage, for instance, will recoil before a footprint in the woods, meaningless to the uninstructed, which reveals to him the proximity of an animal of prey; the experienced sailor will notice a little cloud, which tells him of a coming hurricane, with terror, while to the passenger it seems insignificant.

After further consideration, we must say to ourselves that the verdict on real fear, whether it be rational or purposeful, must be thoroughly revised. For the only purposeful behavior in the face of imminent danger would be the cool appraisal of one's own strength in comparison with the extent of the threatening danger, and then decide which would presage a happier ending: flight, defense, or possibly even attack. Under such a proceeding fear has absolutely no place; everything that happens would be consummated just as well and better without the development of fear. You know that if fear is too strong, it proves absolutely useless and paralyzes every action, even flight. Generally the reaction against danger consists in a mixture of fear and resistance. The frightened animal is afraid and flees.

But the purposeful factor in such a case is not fear but flight.

We are therefore tempted to claim that the development of fear is never purposeful. Perhaps closer examination will give us greater insight into the fear situation. The first factor is the expectancy of danger which expresses itself in heightened sensory attention and in motor tension. This expectancy is undoubtedly advantageous; its absence may be responsible for serious consequences. On the one hand, it gives rise to motor activity, primarily to flight, and on a higher plane to active defense; on the other hand, it gives rise to something which we consider the condition of fear. In so far as the development is still incipient, and is restricted to a mere signal, the more undisturbed the conversion of the readiness to be afraid into action the more purposeful the entire proceeding. The readiness to be afraid seems to be the purposeful aspect; evolution of fear itself, the element that defeats its own object.

I avoid entering upon a discussion as to whether our language means the same or distinct things by the words anxiety, fear or fright. I think that anxiety is used in connection with a condition regardless of any objective, while fear is essentially directed toward an object. Fright, on the other hand, seems really to possess a special meaning, which emphasizes the effects of a danger which is precipitated without any expectance or readiness of fear. Thus we might say that anxiety protects man from fright.

You have probably noticed the ambiguity and vagueness in the use of the word "anxiety." Generally one means a subjective condition, caused by the perception that an "evolution of fear" has been consummated. Such a condition may be called an emotion. What is an emotion in the dynamic sense? Certainly something very complex. An emotion, in the first place, includes indefinite motor innervations or discharges; secondly, definite sensations which moreover are of two kinds, the perception of motor activities that have already taken place, and the direct sensations of pleasure and pain, which give the effect of what we call its feeling tone. But I do not think that the true nature of the emotion has been fathomed by these enumerations. We have gained deeper insight into some emotions and realize that the thread which binds together such a complex as we have described is the repetition of a c   nt experience.

This experience might be an early impression of a very general sort, which belongs to the antecedent history of the species rather than to that of the individual. To be more clear: the emotional condition has a structure similar to that of an hysterical attack; it is the upshot of a reminiscence. The hysteric attack, then, is comparable to a newly formed individual emotion, the normal emotion to an hysteria which has become a universal heritage.

Do not assume that what I have said here about emotions is derived from normal psychology. On the contrary, these are conceptions that have grown up with and are at home only in psychoanalysis. What psychology has to say about emotions—the James-Lange theory, for instance—is absolutely incomprehensible for us psychoanalysts, and cannot be discussed. Of course, we do not consider our knowledge about emotions very certain; it is a preliminary attempt to become oriented in this obscure region. To continue: We believe we know the early impression which the emotion of fear repeats. We think it is birth itself which combines that complex of painful feelings, of a discharge of impulses, of physical sensations, which has become the prototype for the effect of danger to life, and is ever after repeated within us as a condition of fear. The tremendous heightening of irritability through the interruption of the circulation (internal respiration) was at the time the cause of the experience of fear; the first fear was therefore toxic. The name anxiety—angustial—narrowness, emphasizes the characteristic tightening of the breath, which was at the time a consequence of an actual situation and is henceforth repeated almost regularly in the emotion. We shall also recognize how significant it is that this first condition of fear appeared during the separation from the mother. Of course, we are convinced that the tendency to repetition of the first condition of fear has been so deeply ingrained in the organism through countless generations, that not a single individual can escape the emotion of fear; not even the mythical Macduff who was "cut out of his mother's womb," and therefore did not experience birth itself. We do not know the prototype of the condition of fear in the case of other mammals, and so we do not know the complex of emotions that in them is the equivalent of our fear.

Perhaps it will interest you to hear how the idea that birth is the source and prototype of the emotion of fear, happened to occur to me. Speculation plays the smallest part in it; I borrowed it from the native train of thought of the people. Many years ago we were sitting around the dinner table—a number of young physicians—when an assistant in the obstetrical clinic told a jolly story of what had happened in the last examination for midwives. A candidate was asked what it implied if during delivery the foeces of the newborn was present in the discharge of waters, and she answered promptly "the child is afraid." She was laughed at and "flunked." But I silently took her part and began to suspect that the poor woman of the people had, with sound perception, revealed an important connection.

Proceeding now to neurotic fear, what are its manifestations and conditions? There is much to be described. In the first place we find a general condition of anxiety, a condition of free-floating fear as it were, which is ready to attach itself to any appropriate idea, to influence judgment, to give rise to expectations, in fact to seize any opportunity to make itself felt. We call this condition "expectant fear" or "anxious expectation." Persons who suffer from this sort of fear always prophesy the most terrible of all possibilities, interpret every coincidence as an evil omen, and ascribe a dreadful meaning to all uncertainty. Many persons who cannot be termed ill show this tendency to anticipate disaster. We blame them for being over-anxious or pessimistic. A striking amount of expectant fear is characteristic of a nervous condition which I have named "anxiety neurosis," and which I group with the true neuroses.

A second form of fear in contrast to the one we have just described is psychologically more circumscribed and bound up with certain objects or situations. It is the fear of the manifold and frequently very peculiar phobias. Stanley Hall, the distinguished American psychologist, has recently taken the trouble to present a whole series of these phobias in gorgeous Greek terminology. They sound like the enumeration of the ten Egyptian plagues, except that their number exceeds ten, by far. Just listen to all the things which may become the objects of contents of a phobia: Darkness, open air, open squares, cats, spiders, caterpillars, snakes, mice, thunder-storms, sharp points, blood, enclosed spaces, crowds, solitude, passing over a bridge, travel on land and sea, etc. A first attempt at orientation in this chaos leads readily to a division into three groups. Some of the fearful objects and situations have something gruesome for normal people too, a relation to danger, and so, though they are exaggerated in intensity, they do not seem incomprehensible to us. Most of us, for instance, experience a feeling of repulsion in the presence of a snake. One may say that snakephobia is common to all human beings, and Charles Darwin has described most impressively how he was unable to control his fear of a snake pointing for him, though he knew he was separated from it by a thick pane of glass. The second group consists of cases which still bear a relation to danger, but this is of a kind which we are disposed to belittle rather than to overestimate. Most of the situation-phobia belong here. We know that by taking a railroad journey we entail greater chance of disaster than by staying at home. A collision, for instance, may occur, or a ship sink, when as a rule we must drown; yet we do not think of these dangers, and free from fear we travel on train and boat. We cannot deny that if a bridge should collapse at the moment we are crossing it, we would fall into the river, but that is such a rare occurrence that we do not take the danger into account. Solitude too has its dangers and we avoid it under certain conditions; but it is by no means a matter of being unable to suffer it for a single moment. The same is true for the crowd, the enclosed space, the thunder-storm, etc. It is not at all the content but the intensity of these neurotic phobias that appears strange to us. The fear of the phobia cannot even be described. Sometimes we almost receive the impression that the neurotic is not really afraid of the same things and situations that can arouse fear in us, and which he calls by the same name.

There remains a third group of phobias which is entirely unintelligible to us. When a strong, adult man is afraid to cross a street or a square of his own home town, when a healthy, well-developed woman becomes almost senseless with fear because a cat has brushed the hem of her dress or a mouse has scurried through the room—how are we to establish the relation to danger that obviously exists under the phobia? In these animal phobias it cannot possibly be a question of the heightening of common human antipathies. For, as an illustration of the antithesis, there are numerous persons who cannot pass a cat without calling and petting it. The mouse of which women are so much afraid, is at the same time a first class pet name. Many a girl who has been gratified to have her lover call her so, screams when she sees the cunning little creature itself. The behavior of the man who is afraid to cross the street or the square can only be explained by saying that he acts like a little child. A child is really taught to avoid a situation of this sort as dangerous, and our agoraphobist is actually relieved of his fear if some one goes with him across the square or street.

The two forms of fear that have been described, free-floating fear and the fear which is bound up with phobias, are independent of one another. The one is by no means a higher development of the other; only in exceptional cases, almost by accident, do they occur simultaneously. The strongest condition of general anxiety need not manifest itself in phobias; and persons whose entire life is hemmed in by agoraphobia can be entirely free of pessimistic expectant fear. Some phobias, such as the fear of squares or of trains, are acquired only in later life, while others, the fear of darkness, storms and animals, exist from the very beginning. The former signify serious illness, the latter appear rather as peculiarities, moods. Yet whoever is burdened with fear of this second kind may be expected to harbor other and similar phobias. I must add that we group all these phobias under *anxiety hysteria*, and therefore regard it as a condition closely related to the well-known conversion hysteria.

The third form of neurotic fear confronts us with an enigma; we loose sight entirely of the connection between fear and threatening danger. This anxiety occurs in hysteria, for instance, as the accompaniment of hysteric symptoms, or under certain conditions of excitement, where we would expect an emotional manifestation, but least of all of fear, or without reference to any known circumstance, unintelligible to us and to the patient. Neither far nor near can we discover a danger or a cause which might have been exaggerated to such significance. Through these spontaneous attacks we learn that the complex which we call the condition of anxiety can be resolved into its components. The whole attack may be represented by a single intensively developed symptom, such as a trembling, dizziness, palpitation of the heart, or tightening of breath; the general undertone by which we usually recognize fear may be utterly lacking or vague. And yet these conditions, which we describe as "anxiety equivalents," are comparable to anxiety in all its clinical and etiological relations.

Two questions arise. Can we relate neurotic fear, in which danger plays so small a part or none at all, to real fear, which is always a reaction to danger? And what can we understand as the basis of neurotic fear? For the present we want to hold to our expectations: "Wherever there is fear, there must be a cause for it."

Clinical observation yields several suggestions for the comprehension of neurotic fear, the significance of which I shall discuss with you.

1. It is not difficult to determine that expectant fear or general anxiety is closely connected with certain processes in sexual life, let us say with certain types of libido. Utilization, the simplest and most instructive case of this kind, results when persons expose themselves to frustrated excitation, viz., if their sexual excitation does not meet with sufficient relief and is not brought to a satisfactory conclusion, in men, during the time of their engagement to marry, for instance, or in women whose husbands are not sufficiently potent or who, from caution, execute the sexual act in a shortened or mutilated form. Under these circumstances libidinous excitement disappears and anxiety takes its place, both in the form of expectant fear and in attacks and anxiety equivalents. The cautious interruption of the sexual act, when practiced as the customary sexual regime, so frequently causes the anxiety neurosis in men, and especially in women, that physicians are wise in such cases to examine primarily this etiology. On innumerable occasions we have learned that anxiety neurosis vanishes when the sexual misuse is abandoned.

So far as I know, the connection between sexual restraint and conditions of anxiety is no longer questioned even by physicians who have nothing to do with psychoanalysis. But I can well imagine that they do not desist from reversing the connection and saying that these persons have exhibited a tendency to anxiety from the outset and therefore practice reserve in sexual matters. The behavior of women whose sexual conduct is passive, viz., is determined by the treatment of the husband, contradicts this supposition. The more temperamental, that is, the more disposed toward sexual intercourse and capable of gratification is the woman, the more will she react to the impotence of the man, or to the *coitus interruptus*, by anxiety manifestations. In anaesthetic or only slightly libidinous women, such misuse will not carry such consequences.

Sexual abstinence, recommended so warmly by the physicians of to-day, has the same significance in the development of conditions of anxiety only when the libido, to which satisfactory relief is denied, is sufficiently strong and not for the most part accounted for by sublimation. The decision whether illness is to result always depends upon the quantitative factors. Even where character formation and not disease is concerned, we easily recognize that sexual constraint goes hand in hand with a certain anxiety, a certain caution, while fearlessness and bold daring arise from free gratification of sexual desires. However much these relations are altered by various influences of civilization, for the average human being it is true that anxiety and sexual constraint belong together.

I have by no means mentioned all the observations that speak for the genetic relation of the libido to fear. The influence on the development of neurotic fear of certain phases of life, such as puberty and the period of menopause, when the production of libido is materially heightened, belongs here too. In some conditions of excitement we may observe the mixture of anxiety and libido and the final substitution of anxiety for libido. These facts give us a twofold impression, first that we are concerned with an accumulation of libido, which is diverted from its normal channel, second that we are working with somatic processes. Just how anxiety originates from the libido we do not know; we can only ascertain that the libido is in abeyance, and that we observe anxiety in its place.

2. We glean a second hint from the analysis of the psychoneuroses, especially of hysteria. We have heard that in addition to the symptoms, fear frequently accompanies this condition; this, however, is free floating fear, which is manifested either as an attack or becomes a permanent condition. The patients cannot tell what they are afraid of and connect their fear, through an unmistakable secondary elaboration, with phobias nearest at hand; death, insanity, paralysis. When we analyze the situation which gave rise to the anxiety or to symptoms accompanied by it, we can generally tell which normal psycho-

logic process has been omitted and has been replaced by the phenomenon of fear. Let me express it differently: we reconstruct the unconscious process as though it had not experienced suppression and had continued its way into consciousness uninterruptedly. Under these conditions as well this process would have been accompanied by an emotion, and we now learn with surprise that when suppression has occurred the emotion accompanying the normal process has been replaced by fear, regardless of its original quality. In hysteric conditions of fear, its unconscious correlative may be either an impulse of similar character, such as fear, shame, embarrassment or positive libidinous excitation, or hostile and aggressive emotion such as fury or rage. Fear then is the common currency for which all emotional impulses can be exchanged, provided that the idea with which it has been associated has been subject to suppression.

3. Patients suffering from compulsive acts are remarkably devoid of fear. They yield us the data for our third point. If we try to hinder them in the performance of their compulsive acts, of their washing or their ceremonials, or if they themselves dare to give up one of their compulsions, they are seized with terrible fear that again exacts obedience to the compulsion. We understand that the compulsive act had veiled fear and had been performed only to avoid it. In compulsion neurosis then, fear, which would otherwise be present, is replaced by symptom development. Similar results are yielded by hysteria. Following the process of suppression we find the development, either of anxiety alone or of anxiety and symptom development, or finally a more complete symptom development and no anxiety. In an abstract sense, then, it would be correct to say that symptoms are formed only to evade development of fear, which otherwise could not be escaped. According to this conception, fear is seen to occupy the center of the stage in the problems of neurosis.

Our observations on anxiety neuroses led to the conclusion that when the libido was diverted from its normal use and anxiety thus released, it occurred on the basis of somatic processes. The analyses of hysteria and compulsion neuroses furnish the correlative observations that similar diversion with similar results may also be the consequence of a constraint of psychic forces. Such then is our knowledge of the origin of

neurotic fear; it still sounds rather vague. But as yet I know
no path that would lead us further. The second task we have
set ourselves is still more difficult to accomplish. It is the establishment of a connection between neurotic fear, which is misused libido, and real fear, which is a reaction to danger. You
may believe that these things are quite distinct and yet we have
no criterion for distinguishing the sensations of real and neurotic
fear.

The desired connection is brought about by presupposing the
antithesis of the ego to libido that is so frequently claimed. We
know that the development of fear is the ego's reaction to
danger, the signal for preparation for flight, and from this we
are led to believe that in neurotic fear the ego attempts to escape
the claims of its libido, and treats this inner danger as though
it came from without. Accordingly our expectation that where
there is fear there must be something to be afraid of, is fulfilled.
But the analogy admits of further application. Just as the
attempt to flee external danger is relieved by standing one's
ground, and by appropriate steps toward defense, so the development of neurotic fear is arrested as fast as the symptom develops, for by means of it the fear is held in check.

Our difficulties in understanding now lie elsewhere. The
fear, which represents flight of the ego before the libido, is
supposed to have sprung from the libido itself. That is obscure
and warns us not to forget that the libido of a person belongs
fundamentally to him and cannot confront him as an external
force. The localized dynamics of fear development are still
unintelligible; we do not know what psychic energies are released or from what psychic systems they are derived. I cannot
promise to solve this problem, but we still have two trails to
follow which lead us to direct observations and analytic investigation which can aid our speculations. We turn to the origin
of fear in the child, and to the source of neurotic fear which
attaches itself to phobias.

Fear in children is quite common and it is very hard to tell
whether it is neurotic or real fear. Indeed, the value of this
distinction is rendered questionable by the behavior of children.
On the one hand we are not surprised that the child fears all
strange persons, new situations and objects, and we explain this
———'— very easily by his weakness and ignorance. We ascribe

to the child a strong disposition to real fear and would consider it purposeful if this fear were in fact a heritage. Herein the child would only repeat the behavior of prehistoric man and of the primitive man of today who, on account of his ignorance and helplessness, fears everything that is new, and much that is familiar, all of which can no longer inspire us with fear. If the phobias of the child were at least partially such as might be attributed to that primeval period of human development, this would tally entirely with our expectations.

On the other hand, we cannot overlook the fact that not all children are equally afraid, and that those very children who express particular timidity toward all possible objects and situations subsequently prove to be nervous. Thus the neurotic disposition reveals itself by a decided tendency to real fear; anxiety rather than nervousness appears to be primary. We therefore arrive at the conclusion that the child (and later the adult) fears the power of his libido because he is anxious in the face of everything. The derivation of anxiety from the libido is hence put aside. Any investigation of the conditions of real fear consistently leads to the conclusion that consciousness of one's own weakness and helplessness—inferiority, in the terminology of A. Adler—when it is able to persist from childhood to maturity, is the cause underlying the neuroses.

This sounds so simple and convincing that it has a claim upon our attention. To be sure, it would result in our shifting the basis of nervousness. The persistence of the feeling of inferiority, and its prerequisite condition of anxiety and its subsequent development of symptoms, is so firmly established that it is rather the exceptional case, when health is the outcome, which requires an explanation. What can be learned from careful observation of the fear of children? The little child is primarily afraid of strange people; situations wax important only because they involve people, and objects become influential much later. But the child does not fear these strange persons because he attributes evil intentions to them, because he compares his weakness with their strength or recognizes them as dangerous to his existence, his safety and freedom from pain. Such a child, suspicious, afraid of the aggressive impulse which dominates the world, would prove a sad theoretic construction. The child is afraid of a stranger because he is adjusted to a dear, beloved person, his mother. His disappointment and longing are transformed into fear, his unemployed libido, which cannot yet be held suspended, is diverted by fear. It cannot be termed a coincidence that this situation, which is a typical example of all childish fear, is a repetition of the first condition of fear during birth, viz., separation from the mother.

The first situation phobias of children are darkness and solitude; the former often persists throughout life; common to both is the absence of the dear nurse, the mother. I once heard a child, who was afraid of the dark, call into an adjoining room, "Auntie, talk to me, I am afraid." "But what good will that do you? You cannot see me!" Whereupon the child answered, "If someone speaks, it is brighter." The yearning felt in darkness is converted into the fear of darkness. Far from saying that neurotic fear is only a secondary, a special case of real fear, we observe in little children something that resembles the behavior of real fear and has in common with neurotic fear, this characteristic feature: origin from unemployed libido. The child seems to bring very little real fear into the world. In all situations which may later become the conditions of phobias, on elevations, narrow bridges across water, on railroad and boat trips, the child exhibits no fear. And the more ignorant he is, the less fear he feels. It would be most desirable to have a greater heritage of such life-preservative instincts; the task of supervision, which is to hinder him from exposing himself to one danger after another, would be lessened. In reality the child at first overestimates his powers and behaves fearlessly because he does not recognize dangers. He will run to the water's edge, mount the window sill, play with fire or with sharp utensils, in short, he will do everything that would harm him and alarm his guardians. The awakening of real fear is the result of education, since we may not permit him to pass through the instructive experience himself.

If there are children who meet this education to fear half way, and who discover dangers of which they have not been warned, the explanation suffices that their constitution contains a greater measure of libidinous need or that they have been spoiled early through libidinous gratification. No wonder that those persons who are nervous in later life are recruited from the ranks of these childr⸺ ⸺ know that the creation of neurosis is made easy by the inability to endure a considerable amount of pent-up libido for any length of time. You see that here too we must do justice to the constitutional factor, whose rights we never wish to question. We fight shy of it only when others neglect all other claims for this, and introduce the constitutional factor where it does not belong according to the combined results of observation and analysis, or where it must be the last consideration.

Let us extract the sum of our observations on the anxiety of children: Infantile fear has very little to do with real fear, but is closely related to the neurotic fear of adults. It originates in unemployed libido and replaces the object of love that is lacking by an external object or situation.

Now you will be glad to hear that the analysis of phobias cannot teach much more that is new. The same thing occurs in them as in the fear of children; unemployed libido is constantly being converted into real fear and so a tiny external danger takes the place of the demands of the libido. This coincidence is not strange, for infantile phobias are not only the prototypes but the direct prerequisite and prelude to later phobias, which are grouped with the anxiety hysterias. Every hysteria phobia can be traced to childish fear of which it is a continuation, even if it has another content and must therefore receive a different name. The difference between the two conditions lies in their mechanism. In the adult the fact that the libido has momentarily become useless in the form of longing, is not sufficient to effect the transformation of fear into libido. He has long since learned to maintain such libido in a suspended state or to use it differently. But when the libido is part of a psychic impulse which has experienced suppression, similar conditions to those of the child, who cannot distinguish the conscious from the unconscious, are reëstablished. The regression to infantile phobia is the bridge where the transformation of libido into fear is conveniently effected. We have, as you know, spoken a great deal about suppression, but we have always followed the fate of the conception that was to be suppressed, because this was easier to recognize and to present. We have always omitted from our consideration what happened to the emotion that clung to the suppressed idea; and only now we learn that whatever quality this emotion might have manifested under normal conditions, its fate is a transformation into fear. This transformation of emotion is by far the more important part of the suppression process. It is not so easy to discuss, because we cannot assert the existence of unconscious emotions in the same sense as unconscious ideas. With one difference, an idea remains the same whether it is conscious or unconscious; we can give an account of what corresponds to an unconscious idea. But an emotion is a release and must be judged differently from an idea. Without a deeper reflection and clarification of our hypotheses of psychic processes, we cannot tell what corresponds to its unconscious stage. We cannot undertake this here. But we want to retain the impression we have gained, that the development of anxiety is closely connected with the unconscious system.

I said that the transformation into fear, rather a discharge in the form of fear, is the immediate fate of suppressed libido. Not the only or final fate, I must add. These neuroses are accompanied by processes that strive to restrain the development of fear, and succeed in various ways. In phobias, for instance, two phases of the neurotic process can be clearly distinguished. The first effects the suppression of libido and its transition to fear, which is joined to an external danger. The second consists in building up all those precautions and safety devices which are to prevent contact with this danger which is dealt with as an external fact. Suppression corresponds to the ego's flight from the libido, which it regards dangerous. The phobia is comparable to a fortification against outer danger, which is represented by the much feared libido. The weakness of the phobias' system of defense lies in the fact that the fort has been strengthened from without and has remained vulnerable within. The projection of peril from the libido into the environment is never very successful. In other neuroses, therefore, other systems of defense are used against the possibility of fear development. That is an interesting aspect of the psychology of neurosis. Unfortunately its study would lead us to digress too far, and presupposes a more thorough and special knowledge of the subject. I shall add only one thing more. I have already spoken to you of the counter siege by which the ego imprisons the suppression and which it must maintain permanently for the suppression to subsist. The task of this counter siege is to carry out diverse forms of defense against the fear development which follows the suppression.

To return to the phobias, I may now say that you realize how insufficient it would be to explain only their content, to be interested only in knowing that this or that object or situation is made the subject of a phobia. The content of the phobia has about the same importance for it as the manifest dream facade has for the dream. With some necessary restrictions, we admit that among the contents of the phobias are some that are especially qualified to be objects of fear through phylogenetic inheritance, as Stanley Hall has emphasized. In harmony with this is the fact that many of these objects of fear can establish connections with danger only by symbolic relations.

And so we are convinced of the central position that the problem of fear assumes in the questions of the neurotic psychology. We are deeply impressed with how closely the development of fear is interwoven with the fate of the libido and the unconscious system. There is only one disconnected point, one inconsistency in our hypothesis: the indisputable fact that real fear must be considered an expression of the ego's instincts of self-preservation.

The Libido Theory and Narcism

REPEATEDLY in the past and more recently we have dealt with the distinction between the ego instincts and the sexual instincts. At first, suppression taught us that the two may be flatly opposed to each other, that in the struggle the sexual instincts suffer apparent defeat and are forced to obtain satisfaction by other regressive methods, and so find the compensation for defeat in their invulnerability. After that we learned that at the outset both have a different relation to the educator, Nesessity, so that they do not develop in the same manner and do not enter into the same relationship with the principle of reality. We come to realize that the sexual instincts are much more closely allied to the emotional condition of fear than the ego instincts. This result appears incomplete only in one respect, which, however, is most important. For further evidence we shall mention the significant fact that non-satisfaction of hunger and thirst, the two most elementary instincts of self-preservation, never result in their reversal into anxiety, while the transformation of unsatisfied libido into fear is, as we have heard, one of the best known and most frequently observed phenomena.

No one can contest our perfect justification in separating the ego from sexual instincts. It is affirmed by the existence of sexual desire, which is a very special activity of the individual. The only question is, what significance shall we give to this distinction, how decisive is it? The answer will depend upon the results of our observations; on how far the sexual instincts, in their psychological and somatic manifestations, behave differently from the others that are opposed to them; on how important are the consequences which result from these differences. We have, of course, no motive whatever for insisting upon

a certain intangible difference in the character of the two
groups of instincts. Both are only designations of the sources
of energy of the individual. The discussion as to whether they
are fundamentally of the same or of a different character, and
if the same, when it was that they separated from one another,
cannot profit by the conceptions, but must deal rather with the
underlying biological facts. At present we know very little about
this, and even if we knew more it would not be relevant to our
analytic task.

Obviously, we should gain slight profit if, following the example of Jung, we were to emphasize the original unity of all
instincts, and were to call the energy expressed in all of them
"libido." Since the sexual function cannot be eliminated from
psychic life by any device, we are forced to speak of sexual and
asexual libido. As in the past, we rightly retain the name libido
for the instincts of sexual life.

I believe, therefore, that the question, how far the justifiable
distinction of the instincts of sex and of self-preservation may
be carried, is of little importance for psychoanalysis; and psychoanalysis is moreover not competent to deal with it. From a
biological standpoint there are, to be sure, various reasons for
believing that this distinction is significant. Sexuality is the
only function of the living organism which extends beyond the
individual and sees to his kinship with the species. It is undeniable that its practice does not always benefit the individual
as do his other performances. For the price of ecstatic pleasures
it involves him in dangers which threaten his life and frequently
cause death. Probably peculiar metabolic processes, different
from all others, are required to maintain a part of the individual
life for its progeny. The individual who places himself in the
foreground and regards his sexuality as a means to his gratification is, from a biological point of view, only an episode in a
series of generations, a transient appendage to a germ-plasm
which is virtually endowed with immortality, just as though he
were the temporary partner in a corporation which continues
to persist after his death.

For psychoanalytic explanation of neuroses, however, there
is no need to enter upon these far-reaching implications. By
separate observation of the sexual and the ego instincts, we have
gained the key to the understanding of transference-neuroses

We were able to trace them back to the fundamental situation where the sexual instinct and the instinct of self-preservation had come in conflict with one another, or biologically although not so accurately, expressed where the part played by the ego, that of independent individuality, was opposed to the other, that of a link in a series of generations. Only human beings are capable of such conflict, and therefore, taken all in all, neurosis is the prerogative of man, and not of animals. The excessive development of his libido and the elaboration of a varied and complicated psychic life thus made possible, appear to have created the conditions prerequisite for conflict. It is clear that these conditions are also responsible for the great progress that man has made beyond his kinship with animals. The capacity for neurosis is really only the reverse side of his talents and gifts. But these are only speculations, which divert us from our task.

Until now we worked with the impulse that we can distinguish the ego and the sexual instincts from one another by their manifestations. We could do this without difficulty in the transference neuroses. We called the accumulation of energy which the ego directed towards the object of its sexual striving libido and all others, which proceeded from the instincts of self-preservation, interest. We were able to achieve our first insight into the workings of psychic forces by observing the accumulation of the libido, its transformations and its final destiny. The transference neuroses furnished the best material for this. But the ego, composed from various organizations, their construction and functioning, remained hidden and we were led to believe that only the analysis of other neurotic disturbances would raise the veil.

Very soon we began to extend these psychoanalytic conceptions to other conditions. As early as 1908, K. Abraham asserted, after a discussion with me, that the principal characteristic of dementia praecox (which may be considered one of the psychoses) is *that there is no libidinous occupation of objects* (*The Psycho-sexual Differences between Hysteria and Dementia Praecox*). But then the question arose, what happens to the libido of the demented, which is diverted from its objects? Abraham did not hesitate to give the answer, "It is turned back upon the ego, and *this reflected turning back is the source of the*

megalomania in dementia praecox." This hallucination of
greatness is exactly comparable to the well-known over-estimation
of the objects habitual to lovers. So, for the first time, we gained
an understanding of psychotic condition by comparing it with
the normal course of love.

These first interpretations of Abraham's have been maintained
in psychoanalysis, and have become the basis of our attitude
towards the psychoses. Slowly we familiarized ourselves with
the idea that the libido, which we find attached to certain objects,
which expresses a striving to attain gratification from these
objects, may also forsake them and put in their place the person's own ego. Gradually these ideas were developed more and
more consistently. The name for this placing of the libido—
narcism—was borrowed from one of the perversions described
by P. Naecke. In it the grown individual lavishes upon his own
body all the affection usually devoted to some foreign sex object.

We reflected that if such a fixation of libido on one's own
body and person instead of on some external object exists, this
cannot be an exceptional or trivial occurrence. It is much more
probable that this narcism is the general and original condition,
out of which the love for an object later develops, without however necessarily causing narcism to disappear. From the evolutionary history of object-libido we remembered that in the beginning many sex instincts seek auto-erotic gratification, and
that this capacity for auto-eroticism forms the basis for the
retardation of sexuality in its education to conformity with fact.
And so, auto-eroticism was the sexual activity of the narcistic
stage in the placing of the libido.

To be brief: We represented the relation of the ego-libido
to the object-libido in a way which I can explain by an analogy
from zoology. Think of the simplest forms of life, which consist of a little lump of protoplasmic substance which is only
slightly differentiated. They stretch out protrusions, known as
pseudopia, into which the protoplasm flows. But they can withdraw these protrusions and assume their original shape. Now
we compare the stretching out of these processes with the radia-
tion of libido to the objects, while the central mass of libido can
remain in the ego, and we assume that under normal conditions
ego-libido can be changed into object-libido, and this can again
be taken up into the ego, without any trouble.

With the help of this representation we can now explain a great number of psychic conditions, or to express it more modestly, describe them, in the language of the libido theory; conditions that we must accredit to normal life, such as the psychic attitude during love, during organic sickness, during sleep. We assumed that the conditions of sleep rest upon withdrawal from the outer world and concentration upon the wish to sleep. The nocturnal psychic activity expressed in the dream we found in the service of a wish to sleep and, moreover, governed by wholly egoistic motives. Continuing in the sense of libido theory: sleep is a condition in which all occupations of objects, the libidinous as well as the egoistic, are given up, and are withdrawn into the ego. Does this not throw a new light upon recovery during sleep, and upon the nature of exhaustion in general? The picture of blissful isolation in the intra-uterine life, which the sleeper conjures up night after night, thus also completes the picture from the psychic side. In the sleeper the original condition of libido division is again restored, a condition of complete narcism in which libido and ego-interest are still united and live indistinguishably in the self-sufficient ego.

We must observe two things: First, how can the conceptions of narcism and egoism be distinguished? I believe narcism is the libidinous complement of egoism. When we speak of egoism we mean only the benefits to the individual; if we speak of narcism we also take into account his libidinous satisfaction. As practical motives the two can be followed up separately to a considerable degree. One can be absolutely egoistic, and still have strong libidinous occupation of objects, in so far as the libidinous gratification by way of the object serves the needs of the ego. Egoism will then take care that the striving for the object results in no harm to the ego. One can be egoistic and at the same time excessively narcistic, i.e., have very slight need of an object. This need may be for direct sexual satisfaction or even for those higher desires, derived from need, which we are in the habit of calling love as opposed to sensuality. In all of these aspects, egoism is the self-evident, the constant, and narcism the variable element. The antithesis of egoism, *altruism*, is not the same as the conception of libidinous occupation of objects. Altruism differs from it in the absence of desire for sexual satisfaction. But in the state of being completely in love, altruism and libidinous occupation with an object clash. The sex object as a rule draws upon itself a part of the narcism of the ego. This is generally called "sexual over-estimation" of the object. If the altruistic transformation from egoism to the sex object is added, the sex object becomes all powerful; it has virtually sucked up the ego.

I think you will find it a pleasant change if after the dry phantasy of science I present to you a poetic representation of the economic contrast between narcism and being in love. I take it from the *Westostliche Divans* of Goethe:

SULEIKA:

Conqueror and serf and nation;
    They proclaim it joyously;
Mankind's loftiest elation,
    Shines in personality.
Life's enchantment lures and lingers,
    Of yourself is not afar,
All may slip through passive fingers,
    If you tarry as you are.

HATEM:

Never could I be thus ravished,
    Other thoughts are in my mind,
All the gladness earth has lavished
    In Suleika's charms I find.
When I cherish her, then only
    Dearer to myself I grow,
If she turned to leave me lonely
    I should lose the self I know.
Hatem's happiness were over,—
    But his changeling soul would glide
Into any favored lover
    Whom she fondles at her side.

The second observation is supplementary to the dream theory. We cannot explain the origin of the dream unless we assume that the suppressed unconscious has achieved a certain independence of the ego. It does not conform to the wish for sleep and retains its hold on the energies that have seized it, even when all the occupations with objects dependent upon the ego have been released for the benefit of sleep. Not until then can we understand how this unconscious can take advantage of the nocturnal discontinuance or deposition of the censor, and can seize control of fragments left over from the day to fashion a forbidden dream wish from them. On the other hand, it is to the already existing connections with these supposed elements that these fragments owe a part of the resistance directed against the withdrawal of the libido, and controlled by the wish for sleep. We also wish to supplement our conception of dream formation with this trait of dynamic importance.

Organic diseases, painful irritations, inflammation of the organs create a condition which clearly results in freeing the libido of its objects. The withdrawn libido again finds itself in the ego and occupies the diseased part of the part. We may even venture to assert that under these conditions the withdrawal of the libido from its objects is more conspicuous than the withdrawal of egoistic interest from the outside world. This seems to open the way to an understanding of hypochondria, where an organ occupies the ego in a similar way without being diseased, according to our conception. I shall resist the temptation of continuing along this line, or of discussing other situations which we can understand or represent through the assumption that the object libido travels to the ego. For I am eager to meet two objections, which I know are absorbing your attention. In the first place, you want to call me to account for my insistence upon distinguishing in sleep, in sickness and in similar situations between libido and interest, sexual instincts and ego instincts, since throughout the observations can be explained by assuming a single and uniform energy, which, freely mobile, occupies now the object, now the ego, and enters into the services of one or the other of these impulses. And, secondly, how can I venture to treat the freeing of libido from its object as the source of a pathological condition, since such transformation of object-libido into ego-libido—or more generally, ego-energy—belongs to the normal, daily and nightly repeated occurrences of psychic dynamics?

The answer is: Your first objection sounds good. The discussion of the conditions of sleep, of sickness and of being in love would in themselves probably never have led to a distinction between ego-libido and object-libido, or between libido and interest. But you do not take ˙   ˙ the investigations from

which we have set out, in the light of which we now regard the
psychic situations under discussion. The necessity of distinguishing between libido and interest, that is, between sexual
instincts and those of self-preservation, is forced upon us by our
insight into the conflict out of which the transference neuroses
emerge. We can no longer reckon without it. The assumption
that object-libido can change into the ego-libido, in other words,
that we must reckon with an ego-libido, appeared to us the only
possible one wherewith to solve the riddle of the so-called narcistic neuroses—for instance, dementia praecox—or to justify
the similarities and differences in a comparison of hysteria and
compulsion. We now apply to sickness, sleep and love that
which we found undeniably affirmed elsewhere. We may proceed with such applications as far as they will go. The only
assertion that is not a direct refutation of our analytic experience is that libido remains libido whether it is directed towards
objects or toward the ego itself, and is never transferred into
egoistic interest, and vice-versa. But this assertion is of equal
weight with the distinction of sex and ego instincts which we
have already critically appraised, and which we will maintain
from methodological motives until it may possibly be disproved.

Your second objection, too, raises a justified question, but it
points in a wrong direction. To be sure the retreat of object-
libido into the ego is not purely pathogenic; we see that it occurs
each time before going to sleep, only to be released again upon
awaking. The little protoplasmic animal draws in its protrusions, only to send them out again on a later occasion. But it is
quite another matter when a specific, very energetic process com-
pels the withdrawal of libido from the object. The libido has
become narcistic and cannot find its way back to the object, and
this hindrance to the mobility of the libido certainly becomes
pathogenic. It appears that an accumulation of narcistic libido
cannot be borne beyond a certain point. We can imagine that
the reason for occupation with the object is that the ego found
it necessary to send out its libido in order not to become diseased
because it was pent up. If it were our plan to go further into
the subject of dementia praecox, I would show you that this
process which frees the libido from the objects and bars the
way back to them, is closely related to the process of suppres-

sion, and must be considered as its counterpart. But above all you would recognize familiar ground, for the conditions of these processes are practically identical, as far as we can now see, with those of suppression. The conflict appears to be the same, and to take place between the same forces. The reason for a result as different as, for instance, the result in hysteria, can be found only in a difference of dispositions. The vulnerable point in the libido development of these patients lies in another phase; the controlling fixation, which, as you will remember, permits the breach resulting in the formation of symptoms, is in another place probably in the stage of primitive narcism, to which dementia praecox returns in its final stage. It is noteworthy that for all the narcistic neuroses, we must assume fixation points of the libido which reach back into far earlier phases of development than in cases of hysteria or compulsion neuroses. But you have heard that the conceptions obtained in our study of transference neuroses are sufficient to orient us in the narcistic neuroses, which present far greater practical difficulties. The similarities are considerable; it is fundamentally the same field of observation. But you can easily imagine how hopeless the explanations of these conditions, which belong to psychiatry, appear to him who is not equipped for this task with an analytic knowledge of transference neuroses.

The picture given by the symptoms of dementia praecox, which, moreover, is highly variable, is not exclusively determined by the symptoms. These result from forcing the libido away from the objects and accumulating it in the ego in the form of narcistic libido. A large space is occupied by other phenomena, which result from the impulses of the libido to regain the objects, and so show an attempt toward restitution and healing. These symptoms are in fact the more conspicuous, the more clamorous; they show an unquestionable similarity to those of hysteria, or less often to those of compulsion neurosis, and yet they are different in every respect. It appears that in dementia praecox the libido in its endeavor to return to the objects, i.e., to the images of the objects, really captures something, but only their shadows—I mean, the verbal images belonging to them. This is not the place to discuss this matter, but I believe that these revers̶ ̶ ̶ ̶ of the libido have permitted us an insight into what really determines the difference between a conscious and an unconscious representation.

I have now brought you into the field where we may expect the further progress of analytic work. Since we can now employ the conception of ego-libido, the narcistic neuroses have become accessible to us. We are confronted with the problem of finding a dynamic explanation of these conditions and at the same time of enlarging our knowledge of psychic life by an understanding of the ego. The ego psychology, which we strive to understand, must not be founded upon introspective data, but rather, as in the libido, upon analysis of the disturbances and decompositions of the ego. When this greater task is accomplished we shall probably disparage our previous knowledge of the fate of the libido which we gained from our study of the transference neuroses. But there is still much to be said in this matter. Narcistic neuroses can scarcely be approached by the same technique which served us in the transference neuroses. Soon you will hear why. After forging ahead a little in the study of narcistic neuroses we always seem to come to a wall which impedes progress. You know that in the transference neuroses we also encountered such barriers of resistance, but we were able to break them down piece by piece. In narcistic neuroses the resistance is insuperable; at best we are permitted to cast a curious glance over the wall to spy out what is taking place on the other side. Our technical methods must be replaced by others; we do not yet know whether or not we shall be able to find such a substitute. To be sure, even these patients furnish us with ample material. They do say many things, though not in answer to our questions, and for the time being we are forced to interpret these utterances through the understanding we have gained from the symptoms of transference neuroses. The coincidence is sufficiently great to assure us a good beginning. How far this technique will go, remains to be seen.

There are additional difficulties that impede our progress. The narcistic conditions and the psychoses related to them can only be solved by observers who have schooled themselves in analytic study of transference neuroses. But our psychiatrists do not study psychoanalysis and we psychoanalysts see too few psychiatric cases. A race of psychiatrists that has gone through the school of psychoanalysis as a preparatory science must first grow up. The beginnings of this are now being made in America, where many leading psychiatrists explain the teachings of psychoanalysis to their students, and where many owners of sanatoriums and directors of institutes for the insane take pains to observe their patients in the light of these teachings. But even here we have occasionally been successful in casting a glance over the narcistic wall and I shall tell you a few things that we think we have discovered.

The disease of paranoia, chronic systematic insanity, is given a very uncertain position by the attempts at classification of present-day psychiatry. There is no doubt of its close relationship to dementia praecox. I once was so bold as to propose that paranoia and dementia praecox could be classed together under the common name of paraphrenia. The types of paranoia are described according to their content as: megalomania, the mania of persecution, eroto mania, mania of jealousy, etc. From psychiatry we do not expect attempts at explanation. As an example of such an attempt, to be sure an antiquated and not entirely valid example, I might mention the attempt to develop one symptom directly out of another by means of an intellectual rationalization, as: the patient who primarily believes he is being persecuted draws the conclusion from this persecution that he must be an extraordinarily important personality and thus develops megalomania. In our analytical conception megalomania is the immediate outcome of exaggeration of the ego, which results from the drawing-in of libidinous occupation with objects, a secondary narcism as a recurrence of the originally early infantile form. In cases of the mania of persecution we have noticed a few things that lead us to follow a definite track. In the first place, we observed that in the great majority of cases the persecutor was of the same sex as the persecuted. This could still be explained in a harmless way, but in a few carefully studied cases it was clearly shown that the person of the same sex, who was most loved in normal times, became the persecutor after the malady set in. A further development is made possible by the fact that one loved person is replaced by another, according to familiar affinities, e.g., the father by the teacher or the superior. We concluded from such ever-increasing experiences, that paranoia persecutoria is the form in which the individual guards himself against a homosexual tendency that has become too powerful. The change from affection to hate, which notoriously may take the form of serious threats against the life of the loved and hated person, expresses the transformation of libidinous impulse into fear, which is a regularly recurring result of the process of suppression. As an illustration I shall cite the last case in which I made observations on this subject. A young physician had to be sent away from his home town because he had threatened the life of the son of a university professor, who up to that time had been his best friend. He ascribed truly devilish intentions to his erstwhile friend and credited him with power of a demon. He was to blame for all the misfortunes that had in recent years befallen the family of the patient, for all his personal and social ill-luck. But this was not enough. The wicked friend, and his father the professor, had been the cause of the war and had called the Russians into the land. He had forfeited his life a thousand times and our patient was convinced that with the death of the culprit all misfortune would come to an end. And yet his old affection for his friend was so great that it had paralyzed his hand when he had had the opportunity of shooting down the enemy at close quarters. In my short consultations with the patient, I discovered that the friendship between the two dated back to early school-life. Once at least the bonds of friendship had been over-stepped; a night spent together had been the occasion for complete sexual intercourse. Our patient never felt attracted to women, as would have been natural to his age or his charming personality. At one time he was engaged to a beautiful and distinguished young girl, but she broke off the engagement because she found so little affection in her fiancé. Years later his malady broke out just at that moment when for the first time he had succeeded in giving complete gratification to a woman. When this woman embraced him, full of gratitude and devotion, he suddenly felt a strange pain which cut around his skull like a sharp incision. His later interpretation of this sensation was that an incision such as is used to expose a part of the brain had been performed upon him, and since his friend had become a pathological anatomist, he gradually came to the conclusion that he alone could have sent him this last woman as a temptation. From that time on his eyes were also opened to the other persecutions in which he was to be the victim of the intrigues of his former friend.

But how about those cases where the persecutor is not of the same sex as the persecuted, where our explanation of a guard against homosexual libido is apparently contradicted? A short time ago I had occasion to investigate such a case and was able to glean corroboration from this apparent contradiction. A young girl thought she was followed by a man, with whom she had twice had intimate relations. She had, as a matter of fact, first laid these maniacal imputations at the door of a woman, whom we may consider as having played the part of a mother-substitute in her psychic life. Only after the second meeting did she progress to the point of diverting this maniacal idea from the woman and of transferring it to the man. The condition that the persecutor must be of the same sex was also originally maintained in this instance. In her claim before the lawyer and the physician, this patient did not mention this first stage of her mania, and this caused the appearance of a contradiction to our theory of paranoia.

Homosexual choice of object is originally more natural to narcism than the heterosexual. If it is a matter of thwarting a strong and undesirable homosexual impulse, the way back to narcism is made especially easy. Until now I have had very little opportunity of speaking to you about the fundamental conditions of love-life, so far as we know them, and now I cannot make up for lost time. I only want to point out that the choice of an object, that progress in the development of the libido which comes after the narcistic stage, can proceed according to two different types—either according to the *narcistic* type, which puts a very similar personality in the place of the personal ego, or according to the *dependent* type, which chooses those persons who have become valuable by satisfying needs of life other than as objects of the libido. We also accredit a strong fixation of the libido to the narcistic type of object-choice when there is a disposition toward manifest homosexuality.

You will recall that in our first meeting of this semester I told you about the case of a woman who suffered from the mania of jealousy. Since we are so near the end you certainly will be glad to hear the psychoanalytic explanation of a maniacal idea. But I have less to say about it than you expect. The maniacal idea as well as the compulsion idea cannot be assailed by logical arg   al experience. This is explained by their relation to the unconscious, which is represented by the maniacal idea or the compulsion idea, and held down by whichever is effective. The difference between the two is based upon respective localization and dynamic relations of the two conditions.

As in paranoia, so also in melancholia, of which, moreover, very different clinical forms are described. We have discovered a point of vantage which will yield us an insight into the inner structure of the condition. We realize that the self-accusations with which these melancholic patients torture themselves in the most pitiless way, really apply to another person, namely, the sex object which they have lost, or which through some fault has lost value for them. From this we may conclude that the melancholic has withdrawn his libido from the object. Through a process which we designate as "narcistic identification" the object is built up within the ego itself, is, so to say, projected upon the ego. Here I can give you only a descriptive representation, as yet without reference to the topical and dynamic relations. The personal ego is now treated in the same manner as the abandoned object, and suffers all the aggression and expressions of revenge which were planned for the object. Even the suicidal tendencies of melancholia are more comprehensible when we consider that this bitterness of the patient falls alike on the ego itself and on the object of its love and hate. In melancholia as well as in other narcistic conditions a feature of emotional life is strikingly shown which, since the time of Bleuler, we have been accustomed to designate as *ambivalence*. By this we mean that hostile and affectionate feelings are directed against one and the same person. I have, in the course of these discussions, unfortunately not been in a position to tell you more about this emotional ambivalence.

We have, in addition to narcistic identification, an hysterical identification as well, which moreover has been known to us for a much longer time. I wish it were possible to determine clearly the difference between the two. Of the periodic and cyclic forms of melancholia I can tell you something that you will certainly be glad to hear, for it is possible, under favorable circumstances—I have twice had the experience—to prevent these emotional conditions (or their antitheses) by means of analytic treatment in the free intervals between the attacks. We learn that in melancholia as well as in mania, it is a matter of finding a special way for solving the conflict, the prerequisites for which entirely coincide with those of other neuroses. You can imagine how much there still is for psychoanalysis to learn in this field.

I told you, too, that we hoped to gain a knowledge of the structure of the ego, and of the separate factors out of which it is built by means of the analysis of narcistic conditions. In one place we have already made a beginning. From the analysis of the maniacal delusion of being watched we concluded that in the ego there is really an agent which continually watches, criticizes and compares the other part of the ego and thus opposes it. We believe that the patient imparts to us a truth that is not yet sufficiently appreciated, when he complains that all his actions are spied upon and watched, all his thoughts recorded and criticized. He errs only in transferring this distressing force to something alien, outside of himself. He feels the dominance of a factor in his ego, which compares his actual ego and all of its activities to an *ideal ego* that he has created in the course of his development. We also believe that the creation of this ideal ego took place with the purpose of again establishing that self-satisfaction which is bound up with the original infantile narcism, but which since then has experienced so many disturbances and disparagements. In this self-observing agent we recognize the ego-censor, the conscience; it is the same factor which at night exercises dream-censorship, and which creates the suppressions against inadmissible wish-impulses. Under analysis in the maniacal delusion of being watched it reveals its origin in the influence of parents, tutors and social environment and in the identification of the ego with certain of these model individuals.

These are some of the conclusions which the application of psychoanalysis to narcistic conditions has yielded us. They are certainly all too few, and they often lack that accuracy which can only be acquired in a new field with the attainment of absolute familiarity. We owe them all to the exploitation of the conception of ego-libido or narcistic libido, by the aid of which we have extended to narcistic neuroses those observations which were confirmed in the transference neuroses. But now you will ask, is it possible for us to succeed in subordinating all the disturbances of narcistic conditions and the psychoses to the libido

theory in such a way that in every case we recognize the libidinous factor of psychic life as the cause of the malady, and never
make an abnormality in the functioning of the instincts of self-
preservation answerable? Ladies and gentlemen, this conclusion
does not seem urgent to me, and above all not ripe for decision.
We can best leave it calmly to the progress of the science. I
should not be surprised to find that the power to exert a pathogenic influence is really an exclusive prerogative of the libidinous
impulses, and that the libido theory will celebrate its triumphs
along the whole line from the simplest true neurosis to the most
difficult psychotic derangement of the individual. For we know
it to be a characteristic of the libido that it is continually struggling against subordinating itself to the realities of the world.
But I consider it most probable that the ego instincts are
indirectly swept along by the pathogenic excitations of the libido
and forced into a functional disturbance. Moreover, I cannot
see any defeat for our trend of investigation when we are confronted with the admission that in difficult psychoses the ego
impulses themselves are fundamentally led astray; the future
will teach us—or at least it will teach you. Let me return for
one moment more to fear, in order to eliminate one last ambiguity that we have left. We have said that the relation between fear and the libido, which in other respects seems clearly
defined, does not fit in with the assumption that in the face of
danger real fear should become the expression of the instinct of
self-preservation. This, however, can hardly be doubted. But
suppose the emotion of fear is not contested by the egoistic ego
impulse, but rather by the ego-libido? The condition of fear is
in all cases purposeless and its lack of purpose is obvious when
it reaches a higher level. It then disturbs the action, be it flight
or defense, which alone is purposeful, and which serves the ends
of self-preservation. If we accredit the emotional component
of actual fear to the ego-libido, and the accompanying activity
to the egoistic instinct to self-preservation, we have overcome
every theoretical difficulty. Furthermore, you do not really believe that we flee *because* we experience fear? On the contrary,
we first are afraid *and then* take to flight from the same motive
that is awakened by the realization of danger. Men who have
survived the endangering of their lives tell us that they were
not at all afraid, they only acted. They turned the weapon
against the wild animal, and that was in fact the most purposeful

Transference

WE ARE nearing the close of our discussions, and you probably cherish certain expectations, which shall not be disappointed. You think, I suppose, that I have not guided you through thick and thin of psychoanalytic subject matter to dismiss you without a word about therapy, which furnishes the only possibility of carrying on psychoanalysis. I cannot possibly omit this subject, for the observation of some of its aspects will teach you a new fact, without which the understanding of the diseases we have examined would be most incomplete.

I know that you do not expect any guidance in the technique of practising analysis for therapeutic purposes. You wish to know only along what general lines psychoanalytic therapy works and approximately what it accomplishes. And you have an undeniable right to know this. I shall not actually tell you, however, but shall insist that you guess it yourselves.

Only think! You know everything essential, from the conditions which precipitate the illness to all the factors at work within. Where is there room for therapeutic influence? In the first place, there is hereditary disposition; we do not speak of it often because it is strongly emphasized from another quarter, and we have nothing new to say about it. But do not think that we underestimate it. Just because we are therapeutists, we feel its power distinctly. At any rate, we cannot change it; it is a given fact which erects a barrier to our efforts. In the second place, there is the influence of the early experiences of childhood, which are in the habit of becoming sharply emphasized under analysis; they belong to the past and we cannot undo them. And then everything that we include in the term "actual forbearance"—misfortunes ·   ·f which privations of love arise, poverty, family discord, unfortunate choice in marriage, unfavorable social conditions and the severity of moral claims. These would certainly offer a foothold for very effectual therapy. But it would have to be the kind of therapy which, according to the Viennese folk-tale, Emperor Joseph practiced: the beneficial interference of a potentate, before whose will men bow and difficulties vanish. But who are we, to include such charity in the methods of our therapy? Poor as we are, powerless in society, forced to earn our living by practicing medicine, we are not even in a position to treat free of charge those patients who are unable to pay, as physicians who employ other methods of treatment can do. Our therapy is too long drawn-out, too extended for that. But perhaps you are still holding to one of the factors already mentioned, and think that you have found a factor through which our influence may be effective. If the restrictions of morality which are imposed by society have a share in the privation forced upon the patient, treatment might give him the courage, or possibly even the prescription itself, to cross these barriers, might tell him how gratification and health can be secured in the renunciation of that ideal which society has held up to us but often disregards. One grows healthy then, by giving one's sexuality full reign. Such analytic treatment, however, would be darkened by a shadow; it does not serve our recognized morality. The gain to the individual is a loss to society.

But, ladies and gentlemen, who has misinformed you to this degree? It is inconceivable that the advice to give one's sexuality full reign can play a part in analytic therapy, if only from the circumstance we have ourselves described, that there is going on within the patient a bitter conflict between libidinous impulse and sexual suppression, between sensual and ascetic tendencies. This conflict is not abolished by giving one of these tendencies the victory over its opponent. We see that in the case of the nervous, asceticism has retained the upper hand. The consequence of this is that the suppressed sexual desire gains breathing space by the development of symptoms. If, on the other hand, we were to give the victory to sexuality, symptoms would have to replace the sexual suppression, which has been pushed aside. Neither of the two decisions can end the inner conflict, one part always remains unsatisfied. There are only a

few cases wherein the conflict is so labile, that a factor such a
the intervention of the physician could be decisive, and thes
cases really require no analytic treatment. Persons who can b:
so much influenced by a physician would have found some solu
tion without him. You know that when an abstinent young ma:
decides upon illegitimate sex-intercourse, or when an unsatisfied
woman seeks compensation from another man, they have generally not waited for the permission of a physician, far less c'
an analyst, to do this.

In studying the situation, one essential point is generally overlooked, that the pathogenic conflict of the neurotic must not be
confused with normal struggles between psychic impulses c'
which all have their root in the same psychological soil. The
neurotic struggle is a strife of forces, one of which has attained
the level of the fore-conscious and the conscious, while the other
has been held back in the unconscious stage. That is why the
conflict can have no outcome; the struggling parties approach
each other as little as in the well-known instance of the polar-
bear and the whale. A real decision can be reached only if both
meet on the same ground. To accomplish this is, I believe, the
sole task of therapy.

Moreover, I assure you that you are misinformed if you assume that advice and guidance in the affairs of life is an integral
part of the analytic influence. On the contrary, we reject this
role of the mentor as far as possible. Above all, we wish to
attain independent decisions on the part of the patient. With
this intention in mind, we require him to postpone all vital
resolutions such as choice of a career, marriage or divorce, until
the close of the treatment. You must confess that this is not
what you had imagined. It is only in the case of certain very
young or entirely helpless persons that we cannot insist upon
the desired limitation. Here we must combine the function of
physician and educator; we are well aware of the responsibility
and behave with the necessary precaution.

Judging from the zeal with which I defend myself against
the accusation that analytic treatment urges the nervous person
to give his sexuality full reign, you must not gather that we
influence him for the benefit of conventional morality. We are
just as far removed from that. We are no reformers, it is true,
only observers, but we cannot help observing with critical eyes,

and we have found it impossible to take the part of conventional sex morality, or to estimate highly the way in which society has tried to regulate the problems of sexual life in practice. We can prove to society mathematically that its code of ethics has exacted more sacrifices than is its worth, and that its procedure rests neither on veracity nor wisdom. We cannot spare our patients the task of listening to this criticism. We accustom them to weigh sexual matters, as well as others, without prejudice; and when, after the completion of the cure, they have become independent and choose some intermediate course between unrestrained sexuality and asceticism, our conscience is not burdened by the consequences. We tell ourselves: whoever has been successfully educated in being true to himself is permanently protected against the danger of immorality, even if his moral standard diverges from that of society. Let us, moreover, be careful not to overestimate the significance of the problem of abstinence with respect to its influence on neuroses. Only the minority of pathogenic situations of forbearance, with a subsequent condition of pent-up libido, can be resolved without more ado by such sexual intercourse as can be procured with little trouble.

And so you cannot explain the therapeutic influence of psychoanalysis by saying that it simply recommends giving full sway to sexuality. You must seek another solution. I think that while I was refuting this supposition of yours, one of my remarks put you on the right track. Our usefulness consists in replacing the unconscious by the conscious, in translating the unconscious into the conscious. You are right; that is exactly it. By projecting the unconscious into the conscious, we do away with suppressions, we remove conditions of symptom formation and transform a pathogenic into a normal conflict which can be decided in some way or other. This is the only psychic change we produce in our patients; its extent is the extent of our helpfulness. Wherever no suppression and no analogous psychic process can be undone, there is no place for our therapy.

We can express the aim of our efforts by various formulae of rendering the unconscious conscious, removing suppressions, filling out amnestic gaps—it all amounts to the same thing. But perhaps this admission does not satisfy you. You imagined that when a nervous person became cured something very different happened, that after having been subjected to the laborious process of psychoanalysis, he was transformed into a different human being. And now I tell you that the entire result is only that he has a little less of the unconscious, a little more of the conscious within him. Well, you probably underestimate the significance of such an inner change. The person cured of neurosis has really become another human being. Fundamentally, of course, he has remained the same. That is to say, he has only become what he might have been under the most favorable conditions. But that is saying a great deal. When you learn all that has to be done, the effort required to effect apparently so slight a change in psychic life, the significance of such a difference in the psychic realm will be credible to you.

I shall digress for a moment to ask whether you know what is meant by a causal therapy? This name is given to the procedure which does not take the manifestations of disease for its point of departure, but seeks to remove the causes of disease. Is our psychoanalytical therapy causal or not? The answer is not simple, but perhaps it will give us the opportunity of convincing ourselves that this point of departure is comparatively fruitless. In so far as analytical therapy does not concern itself immediately with the removal of symptoms, it may be termed causal. Yet in another respect, you might say this would hardly follow. For we have followed the causal chain back far beyond the suppressions to the instinctive tendencies and their relative intensity as given by the constitution of the patient, and finally the nature of the digression in the abnormal process of its development. Assume for a moment that it were possible to influence these functions chemically, to increase or to decrease the quantity of the libido that happens to be present, to strengthen one impulse at the expense of another. This would be causal therapy in its true sense and our analysis would have furnished the indispensable preparatory work of reconnaissance. You know that there is as yet no possibility of so influencing the processes of the libido. Our psychic therapy interposes elsewhere, not exactly at those sources of the phenomena which have been disclosed to us, but sufficiently far beyond the symptoms, at an opening in the structure of the disease which has become accessible to us by means of peculiar conditions.

What must we do in order to replace the unconscious by the conscious in our patient? At one time we thought this was quite simple, that all we had to do was to reconstruct the unconscious and then tell the patient about it. But we already know this was a shortsighted error. Our knowledge of the unconscious has not the same value as his; if we communicate our knowledge to him it will not stand *in place of* the unconscious within him, but will exist *beside* it, and only a very small change will have been effected. We must rather think of the unconscious as *localized*, and must seek it in memory at the point where it came into existence by means of a suppression. This suppression must be removed before the substitution of the conscious for the unconscious can be successfully effected. How can such a suppression be removed? Here our task enters a second phase. First to find the suppression, then to remove the resistance by which this suppression is maintained.

How can we do away with resistance? In the same way—by reconstructing it and confronting the patient with it. For resistance arises from suppression, from the very suppression which we are trying to break up, or from an earlier one. It has been established by the counter-attack that was instigated to suppress the offensive impulse. And so now we do the very thing we intended at the outset: interpret, reconstruct, communicate—but now we do it in the right place. The counter-seizure of the idea or resistance is not part of the unconscious but of the ego, which is our fellow-worker. This holds true even if resistance is not conscious. We know that the difficulty arises from the ambiguity of the word "unconscious," which may connote either a phenomenon or a system. That seems very difficult, but it is only a repetition, isn't it? We were prepared for it a long time ago. We expect resistance to be relinquished, the counter-siege to collapse, when our interpretation has enabled the ego to recognize it. With what impulses are we able to work in such a case? In the first place, the patient's desire to become well, which has led him to accommodate himself to co-operate with us in the task of the cure; in the second place, the help of his intelligence, which is supported by the interpretation we offer him. There is no doubt that after we have made clear to him what he may expect, the patient's intelligence can identify resistances, and find their translation into the suppressions more readily. If I say to you, "Look up into the sky, you can see a balloon there," you will find it more readily than if I had just asked you to look up to see whether you could discover anything. And unless the student who for the first time works with a microscope is told by his teacher what he may look for, he will not see anything, even if it is present and quite visible.

And now for the fact! In a large number of forms of nervous illness, in hysteria, conditions of anxiety and compulsion neuroses, one hypothesis is correct. By finding the suppression, revealing resistance, interpreting the thing suppressed, we really succeed in solving the problem, in overcoming resistance, in removing suppression, in transforming the unconscious into the conscious. While doing this we gain the clearest impression of the violent struggle that takes place in the patient's soul for the subjugation of resistance—a normal psychological struggle, in one psychic sphere between the motives that wish to maintain the counter-siege and those which are willing to give it up. The former are the old motives that at one time effected suppression; among the latter are those that have recently entered the conflict, to decide it, we trust, in the sense we favor. We have succeeded in reviving the old conflict of the suppression, in reopening the case that had already been decided. The new material we contribute consists in the first place of the warning, that the former solution of the conflict had led to illness, and the promise that another will pave the way to health; secondly, the powerful change of all conditions since the time of that first rejection. At that time the ego had been weak, infantile and may have had reason to denounce the claims of the libido as if they were dangerous. Today it is strong, experienced and is supported by the assistance of the physician. And so we may expect to guide the revived conflict to a better issue than a suppression, and in hysteria, fear and compulsion neuroses, as I have said before, success justifies our claims.

There are other forms of illness, however, in which our therapeutic procedure never is successful, even though the causal conditions are similar. Though this may be characterized topically in a different way, in them there was also an original conflict between the ego and libido, which led to supression. Here, too, it is possible to discover the occasions when suppressions occurred in the life of the patient. We employ the same procedure, are prepared to furnish the same promises, give the same kind of help. We again present to the patient the connections we expect him to discover, and we have in our favor the same interval in time between the treatment and these suppressions favoring a solution of the conflict; yet in spite of these conditions, we are not able to overcome the resistance, or to remove the suppression. These patients, suffering from paranoia, melancholia, and dementia praecox, remain untouched on the whole, and proof against psychoanalytic therapy. What is the reason for this? It is not lack of intelligence; we require, of course, a certain amount of intellectual ability in our patients; but those suffering from paranoia, for instance, who effect such subtle combinations of facts, certainly are not in want of it. Nor can we say that other motive forces are lacking. Patients suffering from melancholia, in contrast to those afflicted with paranoia, are profoundly conscious of being ill, of suffering greatly, but they are not more accessible. Here we are confronted with a fact we do not understand, which bids us doubt if we have really understood all the conditions of success in other neuroses.

In the further consideration of our dealings with hysterical and compulsion neurotics we soon meet with a second fact, for which we were not at all prepared. After a while we notice that these patients behave toward us in a very peculiar way. We thought that we had accounted for all the motive forces that could come into play, that we had rationalized the relation between the patient and ourselves until it could be as readily surveyed as an example in arithmetic, and yet some force begins to make itself felt that we had not considered in our calculations. This unexpected something is highly variable. I shall first describe those of its manifestations which occur frequently and are easy to understand.

We see our patient, who should be occupying himself only with finding a way out of his painful conflicts, become especially interested in the person of the physician. Everything connected with this person is more important to him than his own affairs and diverts him from his illness. Dealings with him are very pleasant for the time being. He is especially cordial, seeks to show his gratitude wherever he can, and manifests refinements and merits of character that we hardly had expected to find

The physician forms a very favorable opinon of the patient and praises the happy chance that permitted him to render assistance to so admirable a personality. If the physician has the opportunity of speaking to the relatives of the patient he hears with pleasure that this esteem is returned. At home the patient never tires of praising the physician, of prizing advantages which he constantly discovers. "He adores you, he trusts you blindly, everything you say is a revelation to him," the relatives say. Here and there one of the chorus observes more keenly and remarks, "It is a positive bore to hear him talk, he speaks only of you; you are his only subject of conversation."

Let us hope that the physician is modest enough to ascribe the patient's estimation of his personality to the encouragement that has been offered him and to the widening of his intellectual horizon through the astounding and liberating revelations which the cure entails. Under these conditions analysis progresses splendidly. The patient understands every suggestion, he concentrates on the problems that the treatment requires him to solve, reminiscences and ideas flood his mind. The physician is surprised by the certainty and depth of these interpretations and notices with satisfaction how willingly the sick man receives the new psychological facts which are so hotly contested by the healthy persons in the world outside. An objective improvement in the condition of the patient, universally admitted, goes hand in hand with this harmonious relation of the physician to the patient under analysis.

But we cannot always expect to have fair weather. There comes a day when the storm breaks. Difficulties turn up in the treatment. The patient asserts that he can think of nothing more. We are under the impression that he is no longer interested in the work, that he lightly passes over the injunction that, heedless of any critical impulse, he must say everything that comes to his mind. He behaves as though he were not under treatment, as though he had closed no agreement with the physician; he is clearly obsessed by something he does not wish to divulge. This is a situation which endangers the success of the treatment. We are distinctly confronted with a tremendous resistance. What can have happened?

Provided we are able once more to clarify the situation, we recognize the cause of the disturbance to have been intens-

affctionate emotions, which the patient has transferred to the physician. This is certainly not justified either by the behavior of the physician or by the relations the treatment has created. The way in which this affection is manifested and the goals it strives for will depend on the personal affiliations of the two parties involved. When we have here a young girl and a man who is still young we receive the impression of normal love. We find it quite natural that a girl should fall in love with a man with whom she is alone a great deal, with whom she discusses intimate matters, who appears to her in the advantageous light of a beneficent adviser. In this we probably overlook the fact that in a neurotic girl we should rather presuppose a derangement in her capacity to love. The more the personal relations of physician and patient diverge from this hypothetical case, the more are we puzzled to find the same emotional relation over and over again. We can understand that a young woman, unhappy in her marriage, develops a serious passion for her physician, who is still free; that she is ready to seek divorce in order to belong to him, or even does not hesitate to enter into a secret love affair, in case the conventional obstacles loom too large. Similar things are known to occur outside of psychoanalysis. Under these circumstances, however, we are surprised to hear women and girls make remarks that reveal a certain attitude toward the problems of the cure. They always knew that love alone could cure them, and from the very beginning of their treatment they anticipated that this relationship would yield them what life had denied. This hope alone has spurred them on to exert themselves during the treatments, to overcome all the difficulties in communicating their disclosures. We add on our own account—"and to understand so easily everything that is generally most difficult to believe." But we are amazed by such a confession; it upsets our calculations completely. Can it be that we have omitted the most important factor from our hypothesis?

And really, the more experience we gain, the less we can deny this correction, which shames our knowledge. The first few times we could still believe that the analytic cure had met with an accidental interruption, not inherent to its purpose. But when this affectionate relation between physician and patient occurs regularly in every new case, under the most unfavorab conditions and even under grotesque circumstances; when it occurs in the case of the elderly woman, and is directed toward the grey-beard, or to one in whom, according to our judgment, no seductive attractions exist, we must abandon the idea of an accidental interruption, and realize that we are dealing with a phenomenon which is closely interwoven with the nature of the illness.

The new fact which we recognize unwillingly is termed *transference*. We mean a transference of emotions to the person of the physician, because we do not believe that the situation of the cure justifies the genesis of such feelings. We rather surmise that this readiness toward emotion originated elsewhere, that it was prepared within the patient, and that the opportunity given by analytic treatment caused it to be transferred to the person of the physician. Transference may occur as a stormy demand for love or in a more moderate form; in place of the desire to be his mistress, the young girl may wish to be adopted as the favored daughter of the old man, the libidinous desire may be toned down to a proposal of inseparable but ideal and platonic friendship. Some women understand how to sublimate the transference, how to modify it until it attains a kind of fitness for existence; others manifest it in its original, crude and generally impossible form. But fundamentally it is always the same and can never conceal that its origin is derived from the same source.

Before we ask ourselves how we can accommodate this new fact, we must first complete its description. What happens in the case of male patients? Here we might hope to escape the troublesome infusion of sex difference and sex attraction. But the answer is pretty much the same as with women patients. The same relation to the physician, the same over-estimation of his qualities, the same abandon of interest toward his affairs, the same jealousy toward all those who are close to him. The sublimated forms of transference are more frequent in men, the direct sexual demand is rarer to the extent to which manifest homosexuality retreats before the methods by which these instinct components may be utilized. In his male patients more often than in his women patients, the physician observes a manifestation of transference which at first sight seems to contradict everything previously described: a hostile or *negative* transference.

In the first place, let us realize that the transference occurs in the patient at the very outset of the treatment and is, for a time, the strongest impetus to work. We do not feel it and need not heed it as long as it acts to the advantage of the analysis we are working out together. When it turns into resistance, however, we must pay attention to it. Then we discover that two contrasting conditions have changed their relation to the treatment. In the first place there is the development of an affectionate inclination, clearly revealing the signs of its origin in sexual desire which becomes so strong as to awaken an inner resistance against it. Secondly, there are the hostile instead of the tender impulses. The hostile feelings generally appear later than the affectionate impulses or succeed them. When they occur simultaneously they exemplify the ambivalence of emotions which exists in most of the intimate relations between all persons. The hostile feelings connote an emotional attachment just as do the affectionate impulses, just as defiance signifies dependence as well as does obedience, although the activities they call out are opposed. We cannot doubt but that the hostile feelings toward the physician deserve the name of transference, since the situation which the treatment creates certainly could not give sufficient cause for their origin. This necessary interpretation of negative transference assures us that we have not mistaken the positive or affectionate emotions that we have similarly named.

The origin of this transference, the difficulties it causes us, the means of overcoming it, the use we finally extract from it—these matters must be dealt with in the technical instruction of psychoanalysis, and can only be touched upon here. It is out of the question to yield to those demands of the patient which take root from the transference, while it would be unkind to reject them brusquely or even indignantly. We overcome transference by proving to the patient that his feelings do not originate in the present situation, and are not intended for the person of the physician, but merely repeat what happened to him at some former time. In this way we force him to transform his repetition into a recollection. And so transference, which whether it be hostile or affectionate, seems in every case to be the gre———

menace of the cure, really becomes its most effectual tool, which aids in opening the locked compartments of the psychic life. But I should like to tell you something which will help you to overcome the astonishment you must feel at this unexpected phenomenon. We must not forget that this illness of the patient which we have undertaken to analyze is not consummated or, as it were, congealed; rather it is something that continues its development like a living being. The beginning of the treatment does not end this development. When the cure, however, first has taken possession of the patient, the productivity of the illness in this new phase is concentrated entirely on one aspect: the relation of the patient to the physician. And so transference may be compared to the cambrium layer between the wood and the bark of a tree, from which the formation of new tissues and the growth of the trunk proceed at the same time. When the transference has once attained this significance the work upon the recollections of the patient recedes into the background. At that point it is correct to say that we are no longer concerned with the patient's former illness, but with a newly created, transformed neurosis, in place of the former. We followed up this new edition of an old condition from the very beginning, we saw it originate and grow; hence we understand it especially well, because we ourselves are the center of it, its object. All the symptoms of the patient have lost their original meaning and have adapted themselves to a new meaning, which is determined by its relation to transference. Or, only such symptoms as are capable of this transformation have persisted. The control of this new, artificial neurosis coincides with the removal of the illness for which treatment was sought in the first place, namely, with the solution of our therapeutic problem. The human being who, by means of his relations to the physician, has freed himself from the influences of suppressed impulses, becomes and stays free in his individual life, when the influence of the physician is subsequently removed.

Transference has attained extraordinary significance, has become the centre of the cure, in the conditions of hysteria, anxiety and compulsion neuroses. Their conditions therefore are properly included under the term transference neuroses. Whoever in his analytic experience has come into contact with the existence of transference can no longer doubt the character of those suppressed impulses that express themselves in the symptoms of these neuroses and requires no stronger proof of their libidinous character. We may say that our conviction that the meaning of the symptoms is substituted libidinous gratification was finally confirmed by this explanation of transference.

Now we have every reason to correct our former dynamic conception of the healing process, and to bring it into harmony with our new discernment. If the patient is to fight the normal conflict that our analysis has revealed against the suppressions, he requires a tremendous impetus to influence the desirable decision which will lead him back to health. Otherwise he might decide for a repetition of the former issue and allow those factors which have been admitted to consciousness to slip back again into suppression. The deciding vote in this conflict is not given by his intellectual penetration—which is neither strong nor free enough for such an achievement—but only by his relation to the physician. Inasmuch as his transference carries a positive sign, it invests the physician with authority and is converted into faith for his communications and conceptions. Without transference of this sort, or without a negative transfer, he would not even listen to the physician and to his arguments. Faith repeats the history of its own origin; it is a derivative of love and at first requires no arguments. When they are offered by a beloved person, arguments may later be admitted and subjected to critical reflection. Arguments without such support avail nothing, and never mean anything in life to most persons. Man's intellect is accessible only in so far as he is capable of libidinous occupation with an object, and accordingly we have good ground to recognize and to fear the limit of the patient's capacity for being influenced by even the best analytical technique, namely, the extent of his narcism.

The capacity for directing libidinous occupation with objects towards persons as well must also be accorded to all normal persons. The inclination to transference on the part of the neurotic we have mentioned, is only an extraordinary heightening of this common characteristic. It would be strange indeed if a human trait so wide-spread and significant had never been noticed and turned to account. But that has been done. Bernheim, with unerring perspicacity, based his theory of hypnotic manifestations on the statement that all persons are open to

suggestion in some way or other.   Suggestibility in his sense is
nothing more than an inclination to transference, bounded so
narrowly that there is no room for any negative transfer.   But
Bernheim could never define suggestion or its origin.   For him
it was a fundamental fact, and he could never tell us anything
regarding its origin.   He did not recognize the dependence of
suggestibility upon sexuality and the activity of the libido.   We,
on the other hand, must realize that we have excluded hypnosis
from our technique of neurosis only to rediscover suggestion in
the shape of transference.

But now I shall pause and let you put in a word.   I see that
an objection is looming so large within you that if it were not
voiced you would be unable to listen to me.   "So at last you
confess that like the hypnotists, you work with the aid of suggestion.   That is what we have been thinking for a long time.
But why choose the detour over reminiscences of the past, revealing of the unconscious, interpretation and retranslation of distortions, the tremendous expenditure of time and money, if the
only efficacious thing is suggestion?   Why do you not use suggestion directly against symptoms, as the others do, the honest
hypnotists?   And if, furthermore, you offer the excuse that by
going your way you have made numerous psychological discoveries which are not revealed by direct suggestion, who shall
vouch for their accuracy?   Are not they, too, a result of suggestion, that is to say, of unintentional suggestion?   Can you
not, in this realm also, thrust upon the patient whatever you
wish and whatever you think is so?"

Your objections are uncommonly interesting, and must be
answered.   But I cannot do it now for lack of time.   Till the
next time, then.   You shall see, I shall be accountable to you.
Today I shall only end what I have begun.   I promised to explain, with the aid of the factor of transference, why our therapeutic efforts have not met with success in narcistic neuroses.

This I can do in a few words and you will see how simply
the riddle can be solved, how well everything harmonizes.   Observation shows that persons suffering from narcistic neuroses
have no capacity for transference, or only insufficient remains
of it.   They reject the physician not with hostility, but with
indifference.   That is why he cannot influence them.   His words
leave them cold, make no impression, and so the mechanism of

the healing process, which we are able to set in motion elsewhere, the renewal of the pathogenic conflict and the overcoming of the resistance to the suppression, cannot be reproduced in them. They remain as they are. Frequently they are known to attempt a cure on their own account, and pathological results have ensued. We are powerless before them.

On the basis of our clinical impressions of these patients, we asserted that in their case libidinous occupation with objects must have been abandoned, and object-libido must have been transformed into ego-libido. On the strength of this characteristic we had separated it from the first group of neurotics (hysteria, anxiety and compulsion neuroses). Their behavior under attempts at therapy confirms this supposition. They show no neurosis. They, therefore, are inaccessible to our efforts and we cannot cure them.

TWENTY-EIGHTH LECTURE

GENERAL THEORY OF THE NEUROSES

Analytical Therapy

YOU know our subject for today. You asked me why we do not make use of direct suggestion in psycho-analytic therapy, when we admit that our influence depends substantially upon transference, i.e., suggestion, for you have come to doubt whether or not we can answer for the objectivity of our psychological discoveries in the face of such a predominance of suggestion. I promised to give you a comprehensive answer.

Direct suggestion is suggestion directed against the expression of the symptoms, a struggle between your authority and the motives of the disease. You pay no attention during this process to the motives, but only demand of the patient that he suppress their expression in symptoms. So it makes no difference in principle whether you hypnotize the patient or not. Bernheim, with his usual perspicacity, asserted that suggestion is the essential phenomenon underlying hypnotism, that hypnotism itself is already a result of suggestion, is a suggested condition. Bernheim was especially fond of practising suggestion upon a person in the waking state, and could achieve the same results as with suggestion under hypnosis.

What shall I deal with first, the evidence of experience or theoretic considerations?

Let us begin with our experiences. I was a pupil of Bernheim's, whom I sought out in Nancy in 1889, and whose book on suggestion I translated into German. For years I practised hypnotic treatment, at first by means of prohibitory suggestions alone, and later by this method in combination with investigation of the patient after the manner of Breuer. So I can speak from experience about the results of hypnotic or suggestive therapy. If we judge Bernheim's method according to the old doctor's password that an ideal therapy must be rapid, reliable and not unpleasant for the patient, we find it fulfills at least two of these requirements. It can be carried out much more rapidly, indescribably more rapidly than the analytic method, and it brings the patient neither trouble nor discomfort. In the long run it becomes monotonous for the physician, since each case is exactly the same; continually forbidding the existence of the most diverse symptoms under the same ceremonial, without being able to grasp anything of their meaning or their significance. It is second-rate work, not scientific activity, and reminiscent of magic, conjuring and hocus-pocus; yet in the face of the interest of the patient this cannot be considered. The third requisite, however, was lacking. The procedure was in no way reliable. It might succeed in one case, and fail with the next; sometimes much was accomplished, at other times little, one knew not why. Worse than this capriciousness of the technique was the lack of permanency of the results. After a short time, when the patient was again heard from, the old malady had reappeared, or it had been replaced by a new malady. We could start in again to hypnotize. At the same time we had been warned by those who were experienced that by frequent repetitions of hypnotism we would deprive the patient of his self-reliance and accustom him to this therapy as though it were a narcotic. Granted that we did occasionally succeed as well as one could wish; with slight trouble we achieved complete and permanent results. But the conditions for such a favorable outcome remained unknown. I have had it happen that an aggravated condition which I had succeeded in clearing up completely by a short hypnotic treatment returned unchanged when the patient became angry and arbitrarily developed ill feeling against me. After a reconciliation I was able to remove the malady anew and with even greater thoroughness, yet when she became hostile to me a second time it returned again. Another time a patient whom I had repeatedly helped through nervous conditions by hypnosis, during the treatment of an especially stubborn attack, suddenly threw her arms around my neck. This made it necessary to consider the question, whether one wanted to or not, of the nature and source of the suggestive authority.

So much for experience. It shows us that in renouncing direct suggestion we have given up nothing that is not replaceable

Now let us add a few further considerations. The practice of hypnotic therapy demands only a slight amount of work of the patient as well as of the physician. This therapy fits in perfectly with the estimation of neuroses to which the majority of physicians subscribe. The physician says to the neurotic, "There is nothing the matter with you; you are only nervous, and so I can blow away all your difficulties with a few words in a few minutes." But it is contrary to our dynamic conceptions that we should be able to move a great weight by an inconsiderable force, by attacking it directly and without the aid of appropriate preparations. So far as conditions are comparable, experience shows us that this performance does not succeed with the neurotic. But I know this argument is not unassailable; there are also "redeeming features."

In the light of the knowledge we have gained from psychoanalysis we can describe the difference between hypnotic and psychoanalytic suggestion as follows: Hypnotic therapy seeks to hide something in psychic life, and to gloss it over; analytic therapy seeks to lay it bare and to remove it. The first method works cosmetically, the other surgically. The first uses suggestion in order to prevent the appearance of the symptoms, it strengthens suppression, but leaves unchanged all other processes that have led to symptom development. Analytic therapy attacks the illness closer to its sources, namely in the conflicts out of which the symptoms have emerged, it makes use of suggestion to change the solution of these conflicts. Hypnotic therapy leaves the patient inactive and unchanged, and therefore without resistance to every new occasion for disease. Analytic treatment places upon the physician, as well as upon the patient, a difficult responsibility; the inner resistance of the patient must be abolished. The psychic life of the patient is permanently changed by overcoming these resistances, it is lifted upon a higher plane of development and remains protected against new possibilities of disease. The work of overcoming resistance is the fundamental task of the analytic cure. The patient, however, must take it on himself to accomplish this, while the physician, with the aid of suggestion, makes it possible for him to do so. The suggestion works in the nature of an *education*. We are therefore justified in saying that analytic treatment is a sort of *after-education*.

I hope I have made it clear to you wherein our technique of using suggestion differs therapeutically from the only use possible in hypnotic therapy. With your knowledge of the relation between suggestion and transference you will readily understand the capriciousness of hypnotic therapy which attracted our attention, and you will see why, on the other hand, analytic suggestion can be relied upon to its limits. In hypnosis we depend on the condition of the patient's capacity for transference, yet we are unable to exert any influence on this capacity. The transference of the subject may be negative, or, as is most frequent, ambivalent; the patient may have protected himself against suggestion by very special adjustments, yet we are unable to learn anything concerning them. In psychoanalysis we work with the transference itself, we do away with the forces opposing it, prepare the instrument with which we are to work. So it becomes possible to derive entirely new uses from the power of suggestion; we are able to control it, the patient does not work himself into any state of mind he pleases, but in so far as we are able to influence him at all, we can guide the suggestion.

Now you will say, regardless of whether we call the driving force of our analysis transference or suggestion, there is still the danger that through our influence on the patient the objective certainty of our discoveries becomes doubtful. That which becomes a benefit to therapy works harm to the investigation. This objection is most often raised against psychoanalysis, and it must be admitted that even if it does not hit the mark, it cannot be waved aside as stupid. But if it were justified, psychoanalysis would be nothing more than an extraordinarily well disguised and especially workable kind of treatment by suggestion, and we may lay little weight upon all its assertions concerning the influences of life, psychic dynamics, and the unconscious. This is in fact the opinion held by our opponents; we are supposed especially to have "balked into" the patients everything that supports the importance of sexual experiences, and often the experiences themselves, after the combinations themselves have grown up in our degenerate imaginations. We can refute these attacks most easily by calling on the evidence of experience rather than by resorting to theory. Anyone who has himself performed a psychoanalysis has been able to convince himself innumerable times that it is impossible thus to sugge-

anything to the patient. There is no difficulty, of course, in making the patient a disciple of any one theory, and thus causing him to share the possible error of the physician. With respect to this he behaves just like any other person, like a student, but he has influenced only his intelligence, not his disease. The solving of his conflicts and the overcoming of his resistances succeeds only if we have aroused in him representations of such expectations as can agree with reality. What was inapplicable in the assumptions of the physician falls away during the course of the analysis; it must be withdrawn and replaced by something more nearly correct. By employing a careful technique we seek to prevent the occurrence of temporary results arising out of suggestion, yet there is no harm if such temporary results occur, for we are never satisfied with early successes. We do not consider the analysis finished until all the obscurities of the case are cleared up, all amnestic gaps filled out and the occasions which originally called out the suppressions discovered. We see in results that are achieved too quickly a hindrance rather than a furtherance of analytic work and repeatedly we undo these results again by purposely breaking up the transference upon which they rest. Fundamentally it is this feature which distinguishes analytical treatment from the purely suggestive technique and frees analytic results from the suspicion of having been suggested. Under every other suggestive treatment the transference itself is most carefully upheld and the influence left unquestioned; in analytic treatment, however, the transference becomes the subject of treatment and is subject to criticism in whatever form it may appear. At the end of an analytic cure the transference itself must be abolished; therefore the effect of the treatment, whether positive or negative, must be founded not upon suggestion but upon the overcoming of inner resistances, upon the inner change achieved in the patient, which the aid of suggestion has made possible.

Presumably the creation of the separate suggestions is counteracted, in the course of the cure, by our being continually forced to attack resistances which have the ability to change themselves into negative (hostile) transferences. Furthermore, let me call your attention to the fact that a large number of results of analysis, otherwise perhaps subject to the suspicion that they are products of suggestion, can be confirmed from other unquestionable sources. As authoritative witnesses in this case we refer to the testimony of dements and paranoiacs, who are, naturally far removed from any suspicion of suggestive influence. Whatever these patients can tell us about symbolic translations and phantasies which have forced their way into their consciousness agrees faithfully with the results of our investigations upon the unconscious of transference-neurotics, and this gives added weight to the objective correctness of our interpretations which are so often doubted. I believe you will not go wrong if you give your confidence to analysis with reference to these factors.

We now want to complete our statement concerning the mechanism of healing, by including it within the formulae of the libido theory. The neurotic is incapable both of enjoyment and work; first, because his libido is not directed toward any real object, and second because he must use up a great deal of his former energy to keep his libido suppressed and to arm himself against its attacks. He would become well if there could be an end to the conflict between his ego and his libido, and if his ego could again have the libido at its disposal. The task of therapy, therefore, consists of freeing the libido from its present bonds, which have estranged it from the ego, and furthermore to bring it once more into the service of the ego. Where is the libido of the neurotics? It is easy to find; it is bound to the symptoms which at that time furnish it with the only available substitute satisfaction. We have to become master of the symptoms, and abolish them, which is of course exactly what the patient asks us to do. To abolish the symptoms it becomes necessary to go back to their origin, to renew the conflict out of which they emerged, but this time with the help of motive forces that were originally not available, to guide it toward a new solution. This revision of the process of suppression can be accomplished only in part by following the traces in memory of the occurrences which led to the suppression. The decisive part of the cure is accomplished by means of the relationship to the physician, the transference, by means of which new editions of the old conflict are created. Under this situation the patient would like to behave as he had behaved originally, but by summoning all his available psychic power we compel him to reach a different decision. Transference, then, becomes the battlefield on which all the contending forces are to meet.

The full strength of the libido, as well as the entire resistance against it, is concentrated in this relationship to the physician; so it is inevitable that the symptoms of the libido should be laid bare. In place of his original disturbance the patient manifests the artificially constructed disturbance of transference; in place of heterogeneous unreal objects for the libido you now have only the person of the physician, a single object, which, however, is also fantastic. The new struggle over this object is, however, raised to the highest psychic level with the aid of the physician's suggestions, and proceeds as a normal psychic conflict. By avoiding a new suppression the estrangement between the ego and the libido comes to an end, the psychic unity of the personality is restored. When the libido again becomes detached from the temporary object of the physician it cannot return to its former objects, but is now at the disposal of the ego. The forces we have overcome in the task of therapy are on the one hand the aversion of the ego for certain directions of the libido, which had expressed itself as a tendency to suppression, and on the other hand the tenacity of the libido, which is loathe to leave an object which it has once occupied.

Accordingly the work of therapy falls into two phases: first, all the libido is forced from the symptoms into the transference, and concentrated there; secondly, the struggle over this new object is carried on and the libido set free. The decisive change for the better in this renewed conflict is the throwing out of the suppression, so that the libido cannot this time again escape the ego by fleeing into the unconscious. This is accomplished by the change in the ego under the influence of the physician's suggestion. In the course of the work of interpretation, which translates unconscious into conscious, the ego grows at the expense of the unconscious; it learns forgiveness toward the libido, and becomes inclined to permit some sort of satisfaction for it. The ego's timidity in the face of the demands of the libido is now lessened by the prospect of occupying some of the libido through sublimation. The more the processes of the treatment correspond to this theoretic description the greater will be the success of psychoanalytic therapy. It is limited by the lack of mobility of the libido, which can stand in the way of releasing its objects, and by the obstinate narcism which will not permit the object-transference to effect more than just so much. Perhaps we shall obtain further light on the dynamics of the healing process by the remark that we are able to gather up the entire libido which has become withdrawn from the control of the ego by drawing a part of it to ourselves in the process of transference.

It is to be remembered that we cannot reach a direct conclusion as to the disposition of the libido during the disease from the distributions of the libido which are effected during and because of the treatment. Assuming that we have succeeded in curing the case by means of the creation and destruction of a strong father-transference to the physician, it would be wrong to conclude that the patient had previously suffered from a similar and unconscious attachment of his libido to his father. The father-transference is merely the battlefield upon which we were able to overcome the libido; the patient's libido had been concentrated here from its other positions. The battlefield need not necessarily have coincided with the most important fortresses of the enemy. Defense of the hostile capital need not take place before its very gates. Not until we have again destroyed the transfrence can we begin to reconstruct the distribution of the libido that existed during the illness.

From the standpoint of the libido theory we might say a last word in regard to the dream. The dreams of neurotics, as well as their errors and haphazard thoughts, help us in finding the meaning of the symptoms and in discovering the disposition of the libido. In the form of the wish fulfillment they show us what wish impulses have been suppressed, and to what objects the libido, withdrawn from the ego, has been attached. That is why interpretation of dreams plays a large role in psychoanalytic treatment, and is in many cases, for a long time, the most important means with which we work. We already know that the condition of sleep itself carries with it a certain abatement of suppressions. Because of this lessening of the pressure upon it, it becomes possible for the suppressed impulse to create in the dream a much clearer expression than the symptom can furnish during the day. So dream-study is the easiest approach to a knowledge of the libidinous suppressed unconscious which has been withdrawn from the ego.

Dreams of neurotics differ in no essential point from the dreams of normal persons; you might even say they cannot be distinguished. It would be unreasonable to explain the dreams of the nervous in any way which could not be applied to the dreams of the normal. So we must say the difference between neurosis and health applies only during the day, and does not continue in dream life. We find it necessary to attribute to the healthy numerous assumptions which have grown out of the connections between the dreams and the symptoms of the neurotic. We are not in a position to deny that even a healthy man possesses those factors in his psychic life which alone make possible the development of the dream and of the symptom as well. We must conclude, therefore, that the healthy have also made use of suppressions and are put to a certain amount of trouble to keep those impulses under control; the system of their unconscious, too, conceals impulses which are suppressed, yet are still possessed of energy, and *a part of their libido is also withdrawn from the control of their ego.* So the healthy man is virtually a neurotic, but dreams are apparently the only symptoms which he can manifest. Yet if we subject our waking hours to a more penetrating analysis we discover, of course, that they refute this appearance and that this seemingly healthy life is shot through with a number of trivial, practically unimportant symptom formations.

The difference between nervous health and neurosis is entirely a practical one which is determined by the available capacity for enjoyment and accomplishment retained by the individual. It varies presumably with the relative proportion of the energy totals which have remained free and those which have been bound by suppressions, and is quantitative rather than qualitative. I do not have to remind you that this conception is the theoretical basis for the certainty that neuroses can be cured, despite their foundation in constitutional disposition.

This is accordingly what we may make out of the identity between the dreams of the healthy and those of the neurotic for the definition of health. As regards the dream itself, we must note further that we cannot separate it from its relation to neurotic symptoms. We must recognize that it is not completely defined as a translation of thoughts into an archaic form of expression, that is, we must assume it discloses a disposition of libido and of object-occupations which have actually taken place.

We have about come to the end. Perhaps you are disappointed that I have dealt only with theory in this chapter on psychoanalytic therapy, and have said nothing concerning the conditions under which the cure is undertaken, or of the successes which it achieves. But I shall omit both. I shall omit the first because I had intended no practical training in the practice of psychoanalysis, and I shall neglect the second for numerous reasons. At the beginning of our talks I emphasized the fact that under favorable circumstances we attain results which can be favorably compared with the happiest achievements in the field of internal therapy, and, I may add, these results could not have been otherwise achieved. If I were to say more I might be suspected of wishing to drown the voices of disparagement, which have become so loud, by advertising our claims. We psychoanalysts have repeatedly been threatened by our medical colleagues, even in open congresses, that the eyes of the suf-- fering public must be opened to the worthlessness of this method of treatment by a statistical collection of analytic failures and injuries. But such a collection, aside from the biased, denunciatory character of its purpose, would hardly be able to give a correct picture of the therapeutic values of analysis. Analytic therapy is, as you know, still young; it took a long time to establish the technique, and this could be done only during the course of the work and under the influence of accumulating experience. As a result of the difficulties of instruction the physician who begins the practice of psychoanalysis is more dependent upon his capacity to develop on his own account than is the ordinary specialist, and the results he achieves in his first years can never be taken as indicative of the possibilities of analytic therapy.

Many attempts at treatment failed in the early years of analysis because they were made on cases that were not at all suited to the procedure, and which today we exclude by our classification of symptoms. But this classification could be made only after practice. In the beginning we did not know that paranoia and dementia praecox are, in their fully developed phases, inaccessible, and we were justified in trying out our method on all kinds of conditions. Besides, the greatest number of failures in those first years were not due to the fault of the physician or because of unsuitable choice of subjects, but to the unpropitiousness of external conditions. We have hitherto spoken only of internal resistances, those of the patient, which are necessary and may be overcome. External resistances to psychoanalysis, due to the circumstances of the patient and his environment, have little theoretical interest, but are of great practical importance. Psychoanalytic treatment may be compared to a surgical operation, and has the right to be undertaken under circumstances favorable to its success. You know what precautions the surgeon is accustomed to take: a suitable room, good light, assistance, exclusion of relatives, etc. How many operations would be successful, do you think, if they had to be performed in the presence of all the members of the family, who would put their fingers into the field of operation and cry aloud at every cut of the knife? The interference of relatives in psychoanalytical treatment is a very great danger, a danger one does not know how to meet. We are armed against the internal resistances of the patient which we recognize as necessary, but how are we to protect ourselves against external resistance? It is impossible to approach the relatives of the patient with any sort of explanation, one cannot influence them to hold aloof from the whole affair, and one cannot get into league with them because we then run the danger of losing the confidence of the patient, who rightly demands that we in whom he confides take his part. Besides, those who know the rifts that are often formed in family life will not be surprised as analysts when they discover that the patient's nearest relatives are less interested in seeing him cured than in having him remain as he is. Where, as is so often the case, the neurosis is connected with conflicts with members of the family, the healthy member does not hesitate long in the choice between his own interest and that of the cure of the patient. It is not surprising if a husband looks with disfavor upon a treatment in which, as he may correctly suspect, the register of his sins is unrolled; nor are we surprised, and surely we cannot take the blame, when our efforts remain fruitless and are prematurely broken off because the resistance of the husband is added to that of the sick wife. We had only undertaken something which, under the existing circumstance, it was impossible to carry out.

Instead of many cases, I shall tell you of just one in which, because of professional precautions, I was destined to play a sad role. Many years ago I treated a young girl who for a long time was afraid to go on the street, or to remain at home alone. The patient hesitatingly admitted that her phantasy had been caused by accidentally observing affectionate relations between her mother and a well-to-do friend of the family. But she was so clumsy—or perhaps so sly—as to give her mother a hint of what had been discussed during the analysis, and changed her behavior toward her mother, insisting that no one but her mother should protect her against the fear of being alone, and anxiously barring the way when her mother wished to leave the house. The mother had previously been very nervous herself, but had been cured years before in a hydropathic sanatorium. Let us say, in that institution she made the acquaintance of the man with whom she was to enter upon the relationship which was able to satisfy her in every respect. Becoming suspicious of the stormy demands of the girl, the mother *suddenly* realized the meaning of her daughter's fear. She must have made herself sick to imprison her mother and to rob her of the freedom she needed to maintain relations with her lover. Immediately the mother made an end to the harmful treatment. The girl was put into a sanatorium for the nervous and exhibited for many years as "a poor victim of psychoanalysis." For just as long a period I was pursued by evil slander, due to the unfavorable outcome of this case. I maintained silence because I thought myself bound by the rules of professional discretion. Years later I learned from a colleague who had visited the institution and had seen the agoraphobic girl there, that the relationship between the mother and the wealthy friend of the family was known all over town, and apparently connived at by the husband and father. It was to this "secret" that our treatment had been sacrificed.

In the years before the war, when the influx of patients from all parts made me independent of the favor or disfavor of my native city, I followed the rule of not treating anyone who was not *sui juris,* was not independent of all other persons in his essential relations of life. Every psychoanalyst cannot do this. You may conclude from my warning against the relatives of patients that for purposes of psychoanalysis we should take the patients away from their families, and should limit this therapy to the inmates of sanatoriums. I should not agree you in this; it is much more beneficial for the patients, if they are not in a stage of great exhaustion, to continue in the same circumstances under which they must master the tasks set for them during the treatment. But the relatives ought not to counteract this advantage by their behavior, and above all, they should not antagonize and oppose the endeavors of the physician. But how are we to contend against these influences which are so inaccessible to us! You see how much the prospects of a treatment are determined by the social surroundings and the cultural conditions of a family.

This offers a sad outlook indeed for the effectiveness of psychoanalysis as a therapy, even if we can explain the great majority of our failures by putting the blame on such disturbing external factors! Friends of analysis have advised us to counterbalance such a collection of failures by means of a statistical compilation on our part of our successful cases. Yet I could not try myself to do this. I tried to explain that statistics would be worthless if the collected cases were not comparable, and in fact, the various neuroses which we have undertaken to treat could, as a matter of fact, hardly be compared on the same basis, since they differed in many fundamental respects. Besides, the period of time over which we could report was too short to permit us to judge the permanency of our cures, and concerning certain cases we could not have given any information whatever. They related to persons who had kept their ailments, as well as their treatment, secret, and whose cure must necessarily be kept secret as well. The strongest hindrance, however, lay in the knowledge that men behave most irrationally in matters of therapy, and that we have no prospect of attaining anything by an appeal to reason. A therapeutic novelty is received either with frenzied enthusiasm, as was the case when Koch first made public his tuberculin against tuberculosis, or it is treated with abysmal distrust, as was the really blessed vaccination of Jenner, which even today retains implacable opponents. There was a very obvious prejudice against psychoanalysis. When we had cured a very difficult case we would hear it said: "That is no proof, he would have become well by himself in all this time." Yet when a patient who had already gone through four cycles of depression and mania came into my care during a temporary cessation in the melancholia, and three weeks later found herself in the beginnings of a new attack, all the members of the family as well as the high medical authorities called into consultation, were convinced that the new attack could only be the result of the attempted analysis. Against prejudice we are powerless; you see it again in the prejudices that one group of warring nations has developed against the other. The most sensible thing for us to do is to wait and allow time to wear it away. Some day the same persons think quite differently about the same things than before. Why they formerly thought otherwise remains the dark secret.

It may be possible that the prejudice against psychoanalysis is already on the wane. The continual spread of psychoanalytic doctrine, the increase of the number of physicians in many lands who treat analytically, seems to vouch for it. When I was a young physician I was caught in just such a storm of outraged feeling of the medical profession toward hypnosis, treatment by suggestion, which today is contrasted with psychoanalysis by "sober" men. Hypnotism did not, however, as a therapeutic agent, live up to its promises; we psychoanalysts may call ourselves its rightful heirs, and we have not forgotten the large amount of encouragement and theoretical explanation we owe to it. The injuries blamed upon psychoanalysis are limited essentially to temporary aggravation of the conflict when the analysis is clumsily handled, or when it is broken off unfinished. You have heard our justification for our form of treatment, and you can form your own opinion as to whether or not our endeavors are likely to lead to lasting injury. Misuse of psychoanalysis is possible in various ways; above all, transference is a dangerous remedy in the hands of an unconscientious physician. But no professional method of procedure is protected from misuse; a knife that is not sharp is of no use in effecting a cure.

I have thus reached the end, ladies and gentlemen. It is more than the customary formal speech when I admit that I am myself keenly depressed over the many faults in the lectures I have just delivered. First of all, I am sorry that I have so often promised to return to a subject only slightly touched upon at the time, and then found that the context has not made it possible to keep my word. I have undertaken to inform you concerning an unfinished thing, still in the process of development, and my brief exposition itself was an incomplete thing. Often

I presented the evidence and then did not myself draw the conclusion. But I could not endeavor to make you masters of the subject. I tried only to give you some explanation and stimulation.

END

INDEX

Abel, C., 195
Abel, R., 148
Abraham, K., 284, 358
Abstinence, 299
Accidental and symptomatic acts, 42
Accumulated and combined errors, 37
Adler, A., 208, 380, 351
Agoraphobia, 227, 233
Alexander, dream of, 65
Altruism, 360
Ambivalence, 369
Amnesia, 244; childhood, 168; hysterical, 245; infantile, 245; of the neurotic, 244
Analyses of dreams, 94, 95, 96, 97, 98, 153
Analysis, experimental, dream for. 93
Analytical therapy, 872, 388
Andreas, Lou, 272
Anxiety, 340, 342; dream, 168; equivalents, 347; form of neurotic fear, 346; hysteria, 233, 259, 316, 346; hysteria, resistance in, 250; neurosis, 338, 344, 347
Anxious expectation, 344
Archaic remnants and infantilism in the dream, 167
Art, and the neurosis, 326
Association experiment, 86; free, 84
Auto-eroticism, 359

Back, George, 105
Basedowi, M., 336
Beheading symbol, 231
Bernheim, 81, 240, 885, 388
Binet, 802
Bins, 66
Birth of the hero, myths, 182
Birth, the source of fear, 343; symbols of, 182; theories of children, 274
Bleuler, 86, 369
Bloch, Ivan, 265
Bölsche, W., 307
Breuer, J., 221, 232, 241, 242, 253, 254, 388
Breughel, P., 268

Castration complex, 175
Censor, dream, 110

Charcot, 119
Child, sexual life of, 268, 281
Childhood amnesia, 168; dreams of, 101; egoism in, 171; experiences, phantasy in, 319; loss of memory for, 168; prophylaxis, 317
Children, fear in, 350; sexual curiosity of, 274
Children's dreams, 102; theories of birth, 274
Choice of an object, 368
Clinical problem, 244
Common elements of dreams, 67, 69, 75
Complex, castration, 175; family, 285; Oedipus, 174, 285; parent, 289
Compulsion neurosis, 222, 227, 259, 261, 267, 298, 326; fear in, 349; manifestations of, 222
Compulsion neurotics, resistance in, 250, 251; symptoms, analysis of, 224
Compulsive activity, meaning of, 229; acts, 228; washing as, 233
Condensation, 142
Conflict, role of, in neurosis, 302, 305
Conscious, definition of, 90
Conversion-hysteria, 259, 339
Criticism of dream, 194; of psychoanalysis, reasons for, 246

Darwin, Charles, 247, 345
Day dreams, 76, 105, 324
Death in dreams, 138; wishes, 169
Definition of psychoanalysis, 1
Delusion, 216
Dementia præcox, 339, 358, 363
Development and regression, theories of, 294
Diderot, 292
Difficulties of psychoanalysis, 2, 5
Disease, secondary advantage of, 334
Disguise-memories, 168
Displacement, 114, 144
Dream, the, 63; of Alexander, 65; anxiety, 188; aproaches to study of, 82; archaic remnants and infantilism in the, 167; censor, 110; character of, 69; criticism of,

194; day, 76, 105; definition of, 67, 68; difficulties and preliminary approach to, 68; distortion in, 101, 110, 183; doubtful points concerning, 194; for experimental analysis, 93; hypothesis and technique of interpretation of, 78; infantile, 183; interpretation, rules to be observed in, 91, 92; manifest and latent content of, 90, 96; of a prisoner, 109; the reaction to sleep-disturbing stimuli, 70; stimuli in, 71, 73; symbolism in, 122

Dreams analysed, 94, 95, 96, 97, 98, 153; of childhood, 101; children's, 102; children's, elements of, 101-5; common elements of, 67, 69, 75; death in, 183; elaboration in, 74; examples of, 111; experimentally induced in, 71; of neurotics, 395; typical, 234; visual forms in, 75; wishfulfillment, 107; dream-work, 141; processes of, 142

Du prel, 108

Ego, development of, 304; impulses, 303; instincts, 356; psychology, 365; regressions, 310
Egoism, 360; in childhood, 171
Elements of children's dreams, 101, 102, 103, 104, 105
Erogenous zones, 271
Erotomania, 366
Errors, accumulated and combined, 87; forgetting names, 84; forgetting projects, 34; losing and mislaying objects, 36; misreading, 51; proved by further developments, 39; psychology of, 10, 23; repeated, 37; slips of the pen, 49; of the tongue, 16, 18; expectant fear, 344

Fact, principle of, 309
Family-complex, 289
Fear, 340, 342; in children, 350; in compulsion neurosis, 349; expectant, 344; in hysteria, 348; of the manifold, 344; neurotic, 341; anxiety, form of, 346; clinical observations on, 347; origin of, 350; and real fear, connection between, 350; real, 341; and neurotic fear, connection between, 350
Fechner, G. T., 69
Federn, P., 127
Ferenczi, 304
Fetichism, 302
Fetichists, 264

Fixation of the instinct, 295; traumatic, 296
Flaubert, G., 268
Fliess, W., 277
Fontaine, Th., 324
Fore-conscious, 256
Forgetting, defense against unpleasant recollections, 55; impressions and experiences, 56; names, 34, 55; plans, 52; projects, 34; proper names, 87
Free association, 84; name analysis by, 85
Free-floating fear, 344
Fright, 342

Hall, Stanley, 344, 355
Hildebrand, 71
Hoffman, 321
Homosexualists, 266
Homosexuality, 263
Hypnosis, 253, 886; psycho-therapy by, 253
Hypnotic and psychoanalytic suggestion, difference between, 390
Hypnotism, 81, 388
Hypochondria, 338, 339, 362
Hysteria, 238, 245, 246, 261, 266, 297; anxiety, 283, 316; conversion, 339; fear in, 348
Hysterical amnesias, 245; backache, 339; headache, 339; identification, 369; vomiting, 283
Illness as a defense, 332
Imago, 189
Incest, 176, 290
Infantile amnesias, 245; dream, 183; fear, 353; neurosis, 316; sexuality, 272, 279
Infantilism in the dream, archaic remnants and, 167
Inferiority, 351
Inhibition, 294
Instinct, fixation of, 295
Intellectual resistances, 251
Introversion, 325
Inversions, 149, 263

James-Lange theory of emotion, 348
Janet, P., 221
Jealousy, obsession of, 216
Jenner, 400
Jung, C. J., 86, 282, 325, 357

Koch, 400
Krauss, F. S., 134

Latent dream content, 90, 96
Leuret, 221

Levy, L., 133
Libido, 116, 270; development of, 277, 282; fixation, 300; regressions of, 297; theory, the, 356
Lichtenberg, 27
Lindner, 271
Losing and mislaying objects, 36, 57
Loss of memory for childhood, 168

Maeder, A., 39, 202
Mania of persecution, 366; of jealousy, 366
Manifest dream content, 90, 96
Masochists, 264
Maury, 66, 71
Mayer, 16
Mechanism of the tongue slip, 46
Megalomania, 366
Melancholia, 369
Memory gaps, 244; loss of, for childhood, 168
Meringer, 16
Misreading, 51
Mistakes, general observations on, 57
Myths, birth of the hero, 132

Name analysis by free association, 85
Naecke, P., 359
Narcism, 359, 360
Narcistic identification, 369; neuroses, 298, 365; and transference, 386
Negative transference, 388
Nervousness, fear and, 340; ordinary, 328
Nestroy, 305
Neurasthenia, 338, 339
Neurosis, anxiety, 344; art and, 326; common experiences in history of, 321; compulsion, 222; determining factor in, 321; development of symptoms of, 311; etiology of, 296; general theory of, 294; infantile, 316; narcistic, 298; schematic representation of cause of, 315; spontaneous, 237; symptoms of, 317; traumatic, 237; true, difference between the symptoms of, and the psychoneurosis, 336
Neurotic fear, anxiety form of, 346; clinical observations on, 347; manifestations of, 344; origin of, 350; and real fear, connection between, 350
Neurotic manifestations, psychoanalytic conception of, 211; symptoms, evolution of, 244; meaning

of, 221; objections to interpretations of, 260
Neurotics, dreams of, 395
Nordenskjold, Otto, 107

Oberlander, 334
Object, choice of, 368
Obsession of jealousy, 216
Oedipus complex, 174, 285
Onanism, 272, 274
Organic pleasure, 280

Paranoia, 266, 339, 366
Paraphrenia, 339, 366
Parent-complex, 289
Pathological ritual, 228
Patricide, 290
Perverse, 263; sexuality, 268, 279
Perversions, sex, 175, 278
Pfister, 199
Phantasies, primal, 323
Phantasy in childhood experiences, 319; in children, 322
Phobias, 344; analysis of, 353; situation, in children, 352
Pleasure, principle of, 309
Pleasure-striving, 116
Pre-genital sexual organization, 283
Primal phantasies, 323
Principle of fact, 309; of pleasure, 309
Psychiatry, psychoanalysis and, 209; therapeutics of, 220
Psychic flight from unpleasantness, 55; process, meaning of, 28; definition of, 7; in sleeping and waking, differences between, 69
Psychoanalysis, definition of, 1; difficulties of, 2, 5; and psychiatry, 209; purpose of, 6; reasons for criticism of, 246; therapeutics of, 220
Psychoanalytic conception of neurotic manifestations, 211; suggestion, hypnotic and difference between, 390
Psychology of errors, 10
Psychoneurosis, difference between the symptoms of the true neurosis and, 336; true neurosis and, connection between symptoms of, 338
Psychotherapy by hypnosis, 258
Purpose of psychoanalysis, 6

Rank, O., 21, 108, 132, 139, 154, 175, 292
Reaction-formations, 326
Regression, 295, 296; of Libido, 297; theories of development and, 294
Reik, Th., 290

Repression, 255
Reproduction, 269; sexuality and, 277
Resistance, 92, 248; in anxiety hysteria, 250; in compulsion neurotics, 250, 251; external, 898; forms taken by, 250; internal, 898; intellectual, 251; in narcistic neurosis, 865
Ritual, pathological, 228; sleep, 227
Roux, 814

Sachs, Hanns, 189, 173
Sadistico-anal sexual organization, 283
Sadists, 264
Scherner, K. A., 124
Schirmer, 74
Schwind, 109
Secondary treatment, 151
Sex symbols, 126
Sex, the third, 263
Sexual curiosity of children, 274; defininition of concept, 262; development, 284; instincts, 856; life of the child, 268, 281; life of man, 262; organizations, 277, 283; perversions, 175, 278
Sexuality, perverse, 268; and reproduction, 277
Siebault, 81
Silberer, V., 203
Situation-phobia, 845; phobias in children, 852
Sleep, definition of, 67; ritual, 227
Slips of the tongue, 16; effects of, 18; explanation of, 25, 46; general observations on, 48; of the pen, 49
Sperber, H., 138
Spontaneous neuroses, 287
Stekel, W., 203
Struuelpeter, 821
Sublimation, 8, 800
Substitute names, 87
Suggestibility, 886
Suggestion, 886, 888
Suppression, 46, 248, 256, 259, 296, 298
Symbol, 128; beheading, 281
Symbolism in the dream, 122; in every day life, 180
Symbols, 125, 126; of birth, 182; sex, 126
Symptomatic acts, accidental and, 42

Symptom-development, 259; interpretation, 259; purpose of, 258, 259
Symptoms, individual, 232, 284; meaning of, 221; of neurosis, development of, 811; neurotic, evolution of, 244; objections to interpretations of, 260; significance of phantasy for the development of, 824; typical, 233
System of the unconscious, foreconscious and the conscious, 255–257

Technique in dream interpretation, 82
Therapy, analytical, 872
Therapeutics of psychiatry, 220; of psychoanalysis, 220
Third sex, 263
Tongue slip, mechanism of, 46, 49
Topophobia, 288
Transference, 25, 872, 879; narcistic neuroses and, 886; neuroses, 259, 889, 884
Translation of thoughts into visual images, 145
Traumatic fixation, 286; neuroses, 287
Trenck, 108
True neuroses, 888; and psychoneuroses, connection between symptoms of, 888; symptoms of, 886
Typical symptoms, 284

Unconscious, the, 286, 255; definition of, 90; psychological processes, 240

Vold, J. Mourly, 66, 127
Vomiting, hysterical, 288
von Brücke, 295

Wallace, 247
Washing, a compulsive act, 233
Wishes, death, 169
Wishfulfillment, 180; in dreams, 104, 107; negative, 261; positive, 261
Wundt school, 86

Zola, Emile, 224
Zurich school, 86